Building the New Ashmolean

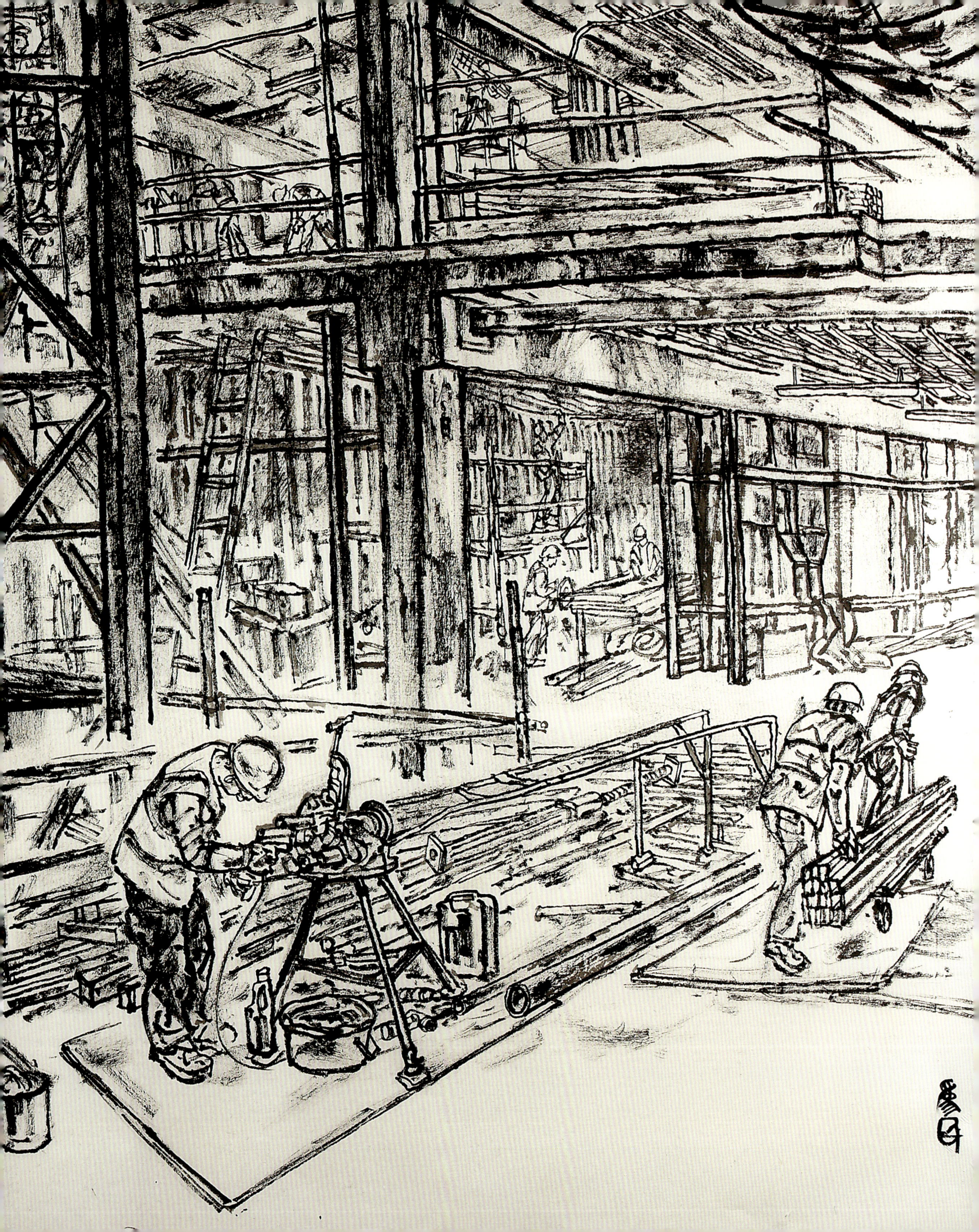

Building the New Ashmolean

Drawings and Prints by Weimin He

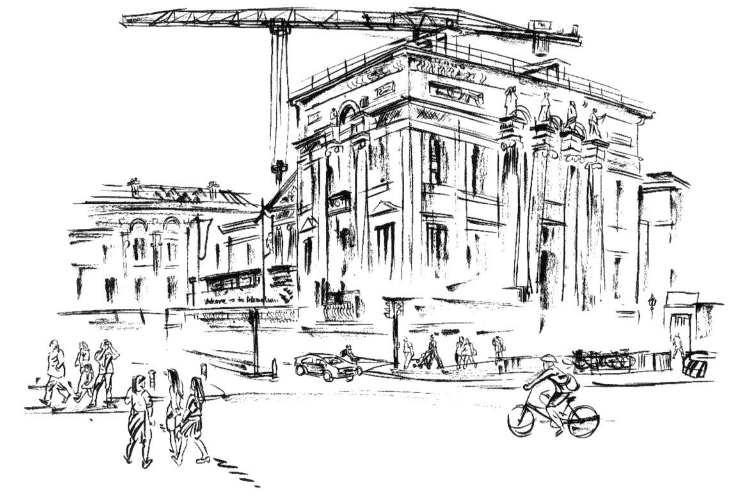

Ashmolean Museum
Oxford

This book is sponsored by BAM Construction Ltd
and Heyan'er Ethical Fashion in Beijing

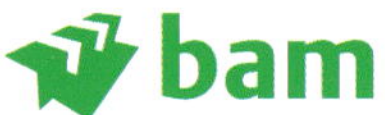

鳴謝：何燕布言布語

Building the New Ashmolean

British Library Cataloguing in Publications Data
A catalogue record for this book is available from the British Library

EAN 13: 978 1 85444 245 1 (paperback) (ISBN: 1 85444 245 7)

Designed and typeset in Monotype Garamond
by James Shurmer

Printed and bound by EPC Direct Ltd.

For further details of these or any of these titles please visit:
www.ashmolean.org/shop

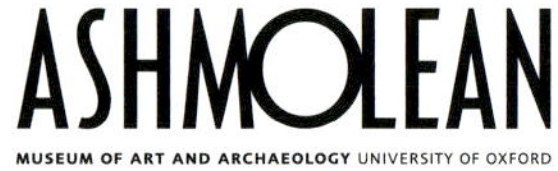

Contents

To my parents He Jixing and Lü Lilian

獻給我的父母：
何吉星、呂麗蓮

Foreword

WEIMIN HE joined the Ashmolean in May 2005 as Christensen Fellow in Chinese Painting. We were particularly pleased to have a practising artist in this position, and when, after three years, the Fellowship came to an end, we asked him to stay on as artist in residence. During the period since Weimin first joined us, the Museum has been undergoing a huge development. We have demolished a building which stood behind Cockerell's great 1845 Museum on Beaumont Street and replaced it with a new 10,000 square metre building. The new construction, designed by the architect Rick Mather, not only doubles the space available on the same footprint for the display of the collection, it also brings environmentally controlled spaces, study rooms, conservation studios, a loading bay, a rooftop restaurant and many other facilities that the Museum was lacking. Weimin has chronicled the transformation of the Ashmolean from the demolition of the old building in the autumn of 2006 to the completion of the new building three years later. He has spent many days on site recording the phases of the demolition and construction as well as the people involved in this long and complex process. He has been a very distinctive figure, standing amid swirling dust and dripping rain with sketch pad in hand to catch moments in the building construction and fleeting expressions of the builders, making many friends and admirers in the process. He has produced a unique account of this development in beautiful ink drawings, pen sketches and woodblock prints. When the new Museum opens in November 2009 visitors will see an exhibition of Weimin's work and I am delighted that this book is being published to accompany the exhibition. It will provide a permanent record of our enterprise seen through Weimin's eyes. For me, this volume will conjure up the stages of the work and, particularly, the individuals who planned, designed and built it. I am very grateful to Weimin for his hard work, dedication, skill and remarkable insight into the characters behind this great project.

In his acknowledgements Weimin has thanked those who have helped him, and I, of course, wish to echo his thanks. I am especially grateful to our builders, BAM, who have supported this publication, and to Weimin's sister, He Yan, and her husband Gao Junfeng for their help with the printing of this book.

Christopher Brown
Director
The Ashmolean Museum of Art and Archaeology, University of Oxford
August 2009

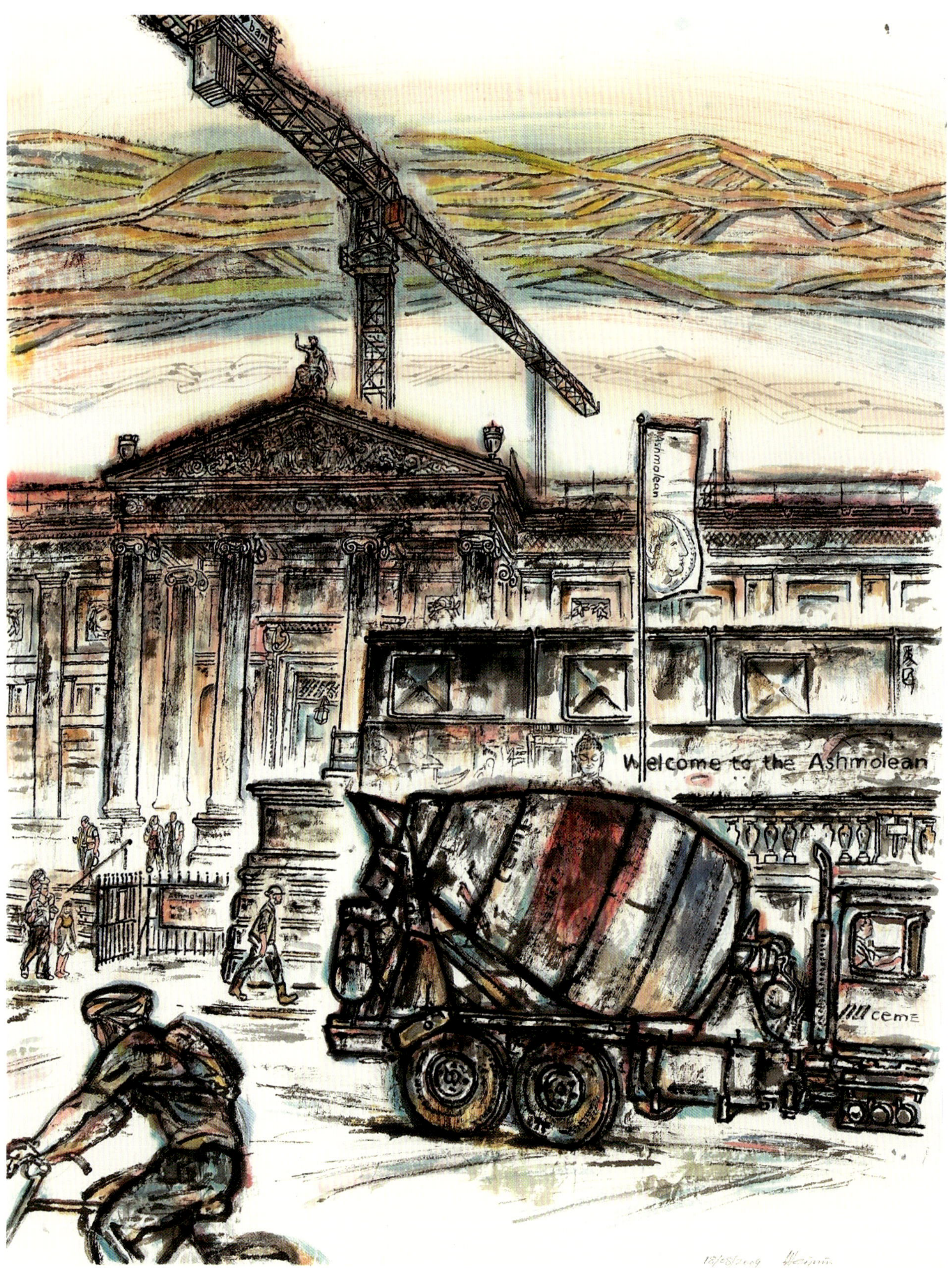

A cement truck passing the Ashmolean
2009. Chinese ink on *xuan* paper. Paper size: 61.1 × 47.2 cm

Introduction

WEIMIN HE is an intriguing paradox: an artist, a scholar and a man of letters in the manner of his pre-modern forebears, yet a modernist in both the content and the technical rendering of his work. The works he draws, designs, cuts and prints clearly follow the traditional concern for linear expression seen in the best of late-Ming printing, yet they are modern in execution and concept. They depict ordinary persons, like ourselves, seen through the eyes of a perceptive observer.

Weimin He was born in 1964 in Mudanjiang in China's north-eastern province of Heilongjiang. He studied printmaking at the Lu Xun Academy of Fine Arts in Shenyang between 1988 and 1991 before establishing himself as a professional printmaker based in the city of Harbin. A scholarship from the Muban Foundation (now The Muban Educational Trust) allowed Weimin to study for a doctoral degree at the University of Ulster, which was awarded in the summer of 2005.

Apart from in a number of one-person exhibitions in Bath, Belfast, Glasgow and Lisburn and at Sotheby's Institute of Art in London, a woodblock print by Weimin was included in 'Chinese Printmaking Today', a major review exhibition held in the British Library during 2003–4. A specially commissioned work contributed to *The Art of Contemporary Chinese Woodcuts*, a portfolio of sixty original woodblock prints by artists from many different parts of China published by the Muban Foundation, London, in 2003.

In the four years since Weimin began his association with the Ashmolean Museum he has played a variety of roles. As Christensen Fellow he contributed to the curatorial work of the Museum, resulting in the exhibition 'Chinese Prints 1950–2006 in the Ashmolean Museum' and joint authorship of the substantial catalogue that accompanied it.

The post of artist in residence that followed in early 2008 has allowed Weimin to return more fully to the development of his creative work. It has been marked by two divergent projects: one has led to numerous acutely observed brush drawings of Museum staff as they prepared for and addressed the complexity of the major rebuilding of the Museum; the other has produced a record of the progress of the rebuilding work itself through a series of on-site drawings of the workers, their machinery and all the rarely seen paraphernalia of building construction.

The drawings of the workers and the building site, although sufficient in themselves, have provided references for a series of woodblock prints that are still in progress. This exhibition therefore shows both work completed and projects still in progress.

Chinese artists have enjoyed a long and creative relationship with the media of drawing and woodblock printmaking, the latter a medium that was first reliably recorded in the very early Tang dynasty and that may even have been used in the late Sui dynasty, early in the seventh century, about 700 years before the first woodblock prints appeared in Europe, in China as in Europe encouraged by religious rather than artistic passions.

By the start of the modern period during the early 1930s, the woodblock printing traditions based on artisanal skills and local technical invention had largely died out as a result of the importation of letterpress and lithographic printing from the West.

However, as these skills died away, new skills and ideas emerged. The socialist writer Lu Xun encouraged a small group of artists in Shanghai to look at the woodblock print anew, as a medium of political and satirical comment in support of the political reforms emerging from the fledgling communist party. Lu Xun had assembled a modest collection of prints by Western artists, which provided a window to Western creative thinking and practice and exerted a profound and lasting influence on the development of Chinese graphic arts well into the 1990s.

The new, modern Chinese prints were drawn, cut, printed and published by the artists themselves, many of them as unfamiliar with these new roles as they were with the medium itself. Their passionate uses of the medium were reactions to the inequalities, injustices and hardships of their world, expressed in technically clumsy, immature, yet direct and powerfully cut and printed works. Weimin is a product of that history. He has modern credentials, yet his work is closely predicated on the tenets of that formative period.

Whereas the traditional craftsmen employed to cut blocks would have followed the lines of another's drawing with the traditional *quan dao* or 'fist knife', its blade ending in a double-pointed concave edge held almost vertically, Weimin displays his modernism in his rejection of the pre-modern *quan dao* in favour of small, straight-edged and slightly concave cutting chisels – not unlike the Japanese *to*. This could be an unspoken homage to Lu Xun's great friend and fellow woodblock-printing enthusiast, the Japanese Uchiyama Kanzo. The chisels are held at a shallow angle to the surface of the wood. In earlier works they were used to reveal a two-dimensional network of soft, worm-like, unmodulated, weighty lines, not unlike the leading of stained-glass windows. Sometimes the preliminary drawing was ignored as the work progressed.

The more recent graphic work has shown a much greater range and weight of lines and descriptive marks. Lines remain predominant but now incorporate changes, variations and textural accents not seen before. As for the cutting chisels, these are now being employed to produce soft, rounded organic forms rather than the hard-edged ones: thick rather than thin; curved rather than angular; active rather than static. It is altogether a wider, more descriptive maturing vocabulary. The stained-glass window is giving way to the scaffolding that man tempered in the structures of his own making.

Weimin's work is clearly in the modern manner, yet it is individual, conceived and drawn by the artist himself. It differs from the traditional both in the nature of its subject matter and in the manner of its gathering. The strident, fist-clenching revolutionaries of the 1950s and 1960s have, in Weimin's work, given way to a gentler dynamic, albeit one that is firmly predicated on acute observation. This is coupled with a great drawing skill, with the brush just as much as with the pencil or felt-tipped pen. Weimin is, above all, a consummate draughtsman, a skilful and inventive craftsman and a dogged researcher.

David Barker

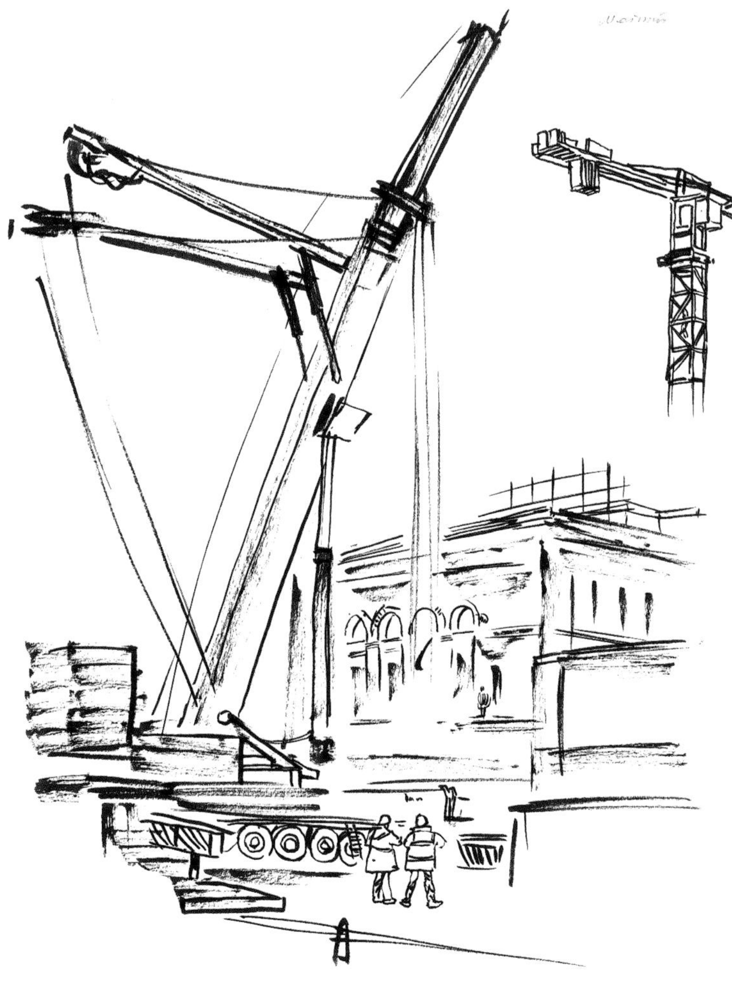

My Artist-in-Residence Project: Building the New Ashmolean

Following the end of my three-year tenure of the Christensen Fellowship in Chinese Painting, I was delighted and felt privileged to be invited to continue working for the Ashmolean as its artist in residence between April and December 2008, to depict the historic redevelopment of the Museum through the media of drawing and printmaking.

My aim in this project has been to depict this transitional moment in the Museum's history through the eyes of an artist. The body of works created consist primarily of ink drawings of individual portrait subjects, sketches of scenes of work on the new building designed by Rick Mather and woodblock prints that were also inspired by the building work.

The portrait drawings of Museum staff with brush and ink started in 2006 with a number of my Eastern Art colleagues. The project expanded from spring 2008, and gradually involved drawing most of the Museum staff. Those who visit a museum are often unaware of the work that goes on behind the scenes. My idea was to record these pillars of the Museum, for it is they, with their knowledge, passion and effort, who help to bring about the less visible transitions in the nature and functions of the Museum behind the façade.

Moreover, with the completion of a new building, those who built it are often forgotten. After witnessing the builders working on the construction site, I had the idea of recording them in the process of using their strength, skills and intelligence to give birth to the magnificent new building. The portrait drawings of BAM staff and individual builders were drawn on album leaves, which quickly received a positive response, particularly from the builders themselves, who seemed proud to have been involved in this Ashmolean project. Many were excited that their portraits would one day be displayed in the building that they had built with their own hands.

The noise, dust and dazzling scene of the building site were a continual inspiration for me in capturing its lively atmosphere. When builders are lifting roof beams, welding metal rods or pouring cement into the mixer, their movements resemble dynamic sculptures. Confronted by these vigorous scenes of work, I often felt overwhelmed, and compositional images occurred to me spontaneously. I often had a feeling that the site was a huge and lively studio with endless subjects to draw. After working, when taking breaks and chatting with the builders over the months, I sometimes felt I was one of them, building not with steel or concrete, but with brushes and inks. I also learnt how sincerely the builders treat their work. All this excitement could never have been experienced in an artist's studio.

On the technical aspect, although pen, marker and pencil were employed for sketching, most portrait drawings were drawn on Chinese *pi*, *xuan* papers or album leaves, with Chinese brushes and inks, which have been used for over a millennium in China. Brush and ink are for me the most expressive tools and media; their flexibility makes their potential limitless. In theory, with no opportunity for revision, a brush stroke has almost zero tolerance of mistakes. However, it is the challenging nature of brush and ink that stimulates and encourages one to master them with full confidence.

For me, drawing is a way of observing, analysing, reassembling and expressing, and is not just a preparation for 'proper' painting or printmaking. Drawing can resemble poetry in literature, and I believe it should be seen as an independent art form in its own right, in parallel with painting or sculpture. Inspirations for my drawing often come from calligraphy, which in China has been regarded as a high art for thousands of years. I try to keep shadows and tones to a minimum in drawing and to allow lines, dots and untouched parts to speak. Drawing with a brush is, I feel, like using the violin bow to play a chord; it is the art of tempo: melody, rhythm, one's personality, emotion and energy will all flow into straight or curved lines, dots, texture or even untouched spaces, through the movement of the brush.

I do not believe there is a short cut in art. For me, a really free style can be achieved only through strict control and persistent practice; sparking inspiration, it should be a natural reward of long-term endeavour. It should come subconsciously out of strict control, like Chinese martial arts, which demand an almost cruel discipline before one can surpass this disciplined stage to reach a realm of freedom. In Daoism, Dao is something that cannot be achieved by pursuing it, and one should always follow one's own nature, not that of the ancients, nor one's contemporaries.

Having worked at the Ashmolean, I now have a better understanding of how important a museum is to the preservation, research and display of human cultural heritage. Its aesthetic value often surpasses time, culture, race or belief. I like to treat the artwork of different periods or cultures as nutrition in the soil of my art, and, although my art is rooted in the Chinese tradition, I am passionate about European art, prehistoric art and others, and I like to let all these influences become embedded naturally in my work.

Some sketches have been developed into woodblock prints. Black-and-white woodblock printing uses the simplest elements of pictorial language, and thus for me it was the ideal art form to express the strength of the builders and the building in the course of its development. However, instead of recording the redevelopment project by making one or two massive pieces, I have chosen to use smaller woodblock prints to depict the ever-growing building. The viewpoints that may seem to have been selected at random reflect the different stages of the redevelopment, with the builders as the main focus. In my woodcuts, I use one flat chisel to cut; this simplest of tools gives me maximum freedom in cutting. I regard the woodcut as a sigilliographical language, which is largely derived from the study of the seals of the Han dynasty (206 BC–220 AD) and the Han calligraphy of stele inscriptions, which are pristine, bold and forceful in style.

For both drawing and printmaking, I do not reject the use of modern technology, such as camera and digital facilities. However, observing with the naked eye, and drawing and cutting with the hand, are essential in the production of my work, and I believe that artists' hands are the antennae of inner perception in the creation of artwork. They cannot be replaced by any machine.

This eight-month project (though in practice, the work continued until 2009) could reflect only certain aspects or stages of the magnificent redevelopment, and the images I created are not a comprehensive record of the rebuilding project – there were more than 5,000 people involved in the building of the new Museum. Rather, I would like these works to be regarded as a few drops of water, partially reflecting the progress of this historic rebuilding project of one of the oldest museums in the world.

Weimin He

Glossary

***Pi* paper**, lit. skin paper, is handmade from fibres of the paper mulberry (*Broussonetia papyrifera*) in large sizes for painting, calligraphy and printmaking. *Pi* paper is usually translucent, thin but very tough and absorbent. The use of *pi* paper can be traced back to the Tang dynasty (618–907 AD).

***Xuan* paper**, is made primarily from the bark of the Tan tree (Pteroceltis tartarinowii). *Xuan* paper is renowned for being soft and fine textured, suitable for conveying the atristic expression of both Chinese calligraphy and ink painting. *Xuan* paper features a smooth surface, a pure and clean texture, a great resistance to creasing, decay and attack from moths and mold, it has a reputation for lasting thousands of years.

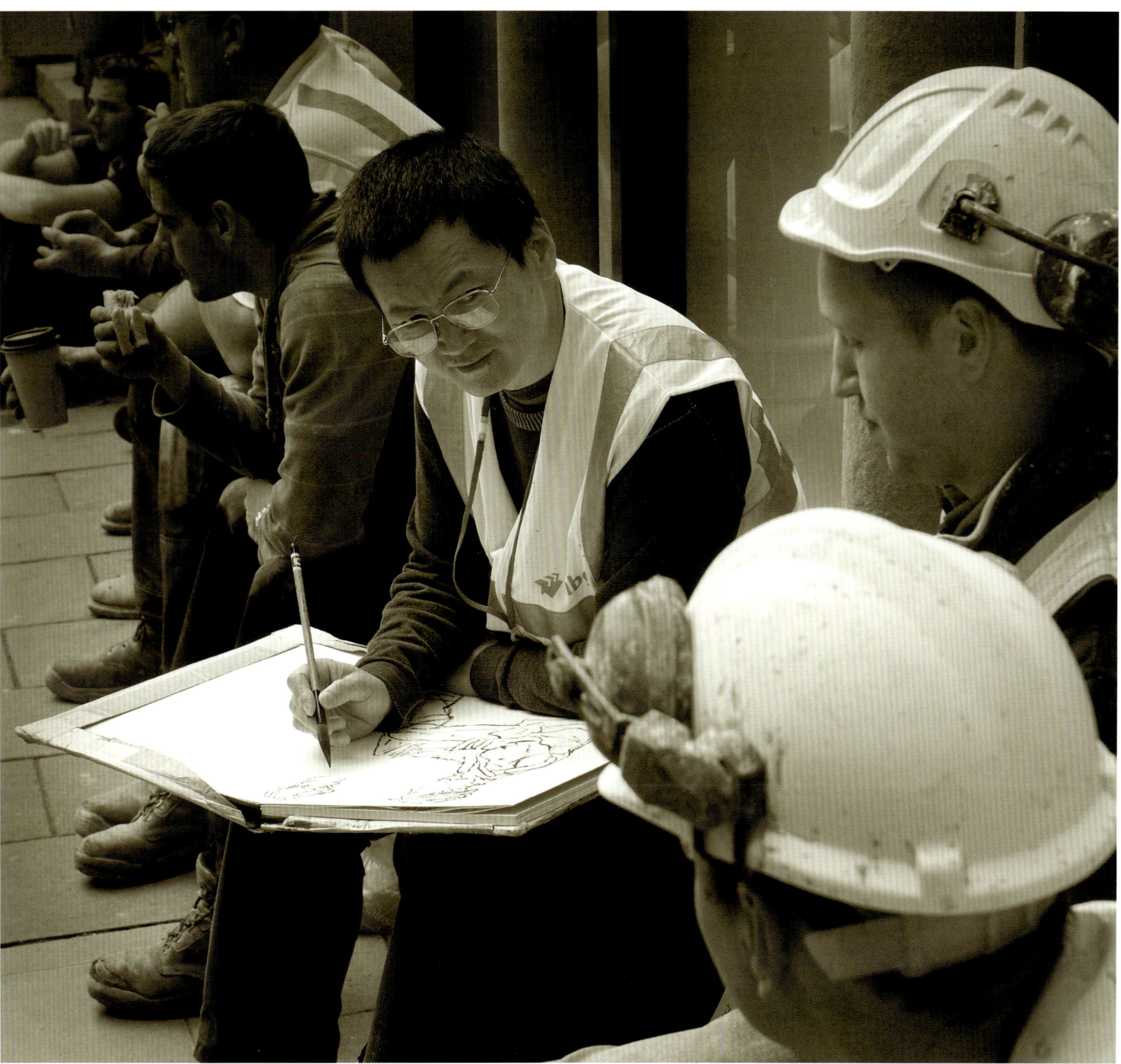

Weimen He at work on site with constuction workers. *Photo courtesy of David Gowers*

Acknowledgements

This body of work has been assembled both to mark the conclusion of my time as artist in residence at the Ashmolean, and, particularly, to coincide with the historic reopening of the Museum. Here I would like to express my gratitude to the people who have offered such enormous support to this project. First, I wish to express my heartfelt gratitude to Dr Christopher Brown, Director of the Ashmolean Museum, and Dr Andrew Topsfield, Keeper of Eastern Art, for their constant support. Thanks are also due to Professor David Barker of the Muban Educational Trust in London for kindly contributing an introduction to this volume and for his continued supervision. In addition, I wish to thank Dr John Hood, Vice Chancellor of the University of Oxford, for his encouragement and kind support.

The building company, BAM Construct UK (previously HBG UK Ltd), kindly offered me full cooperation and unrestricted access to the site, which provided me with tremendous opportunies for the project. I would especially like to thank BAM Construct UK for its generous financial support for the editing of the catalogue. Individual staff members – Anthony Nagle, Construction Manager, Tony O'Keeffe, Project Manager, David Hawkins, Senior Site Manager, Amy Dunford, Site Administrator, Nick Gardner, Gateman, Vince Finn, Gangerman, and Adam Hawkins, Assistant Site Manager – all showed their great enthusiasm for the project and gave me valuable support in every way.

I feel greatly indebted to Ms Jennifer Wood, Director of the Oxford University Estates Directorate (OUED) and to Mike Wigg, Head of Capital Projects OUED, also to Jane Court, Guy Graham and Gill Collett of the OUED, where my current position as artist in residence is based. I am grateful to them all for their support and flexibility with my time schedule.

In the Museum, I have benefited from the enthusiasm and professionalism of many members of the Museum staff: Declan McCarthy, Emily Jolliffe, Nick Mayhew, Henry Kim, Gillian Morrison, Jane Wastie, Aimée Payton, David Gowers, Paul Groves, Jo-Hung Tang, Sigolene Loizeau, Agnes Valençak, Antony Green, Susie Gault, Alan Kitchen, Ally Greathead and Anne Walker. In particular I wish to thank all the staff of the Eastern Art Department, who have made me feel I am still one of the family members.

I also wish to express my gratitude to Dr Anne Farrer, Sotheby's Institute of Art; Dr Oliver Watson, former Keeper of Eastern Art; Professor Gao Yike, Beijing Forestry University; Jane and Simon Mollison, Oxford; Jiang Yan, St Cross College, Oxford University; and Wuon-Gean Ho, printmaker in London, all of whom supported this project in various ways.

My sister, He Yan, fashion designer and Director of Heyan'er Ethical Fashion Ltd, and her husband, Gao Junfeng, generously supported the project by printing the catalogue.

Finally, I feel greatly indebted to all the Museum staff and the BAM staff and construction workers whom I have drawn, for kindly allowing me to depict them in my own way. I am grateful to them for their tolerance and kindness, and thank them also for allowing me to publish their portraits and names. In fact, without the support of all those I have mentioned above, and many who are not named, this project would have been impossible to complete.

Weimin He

The Catalogue

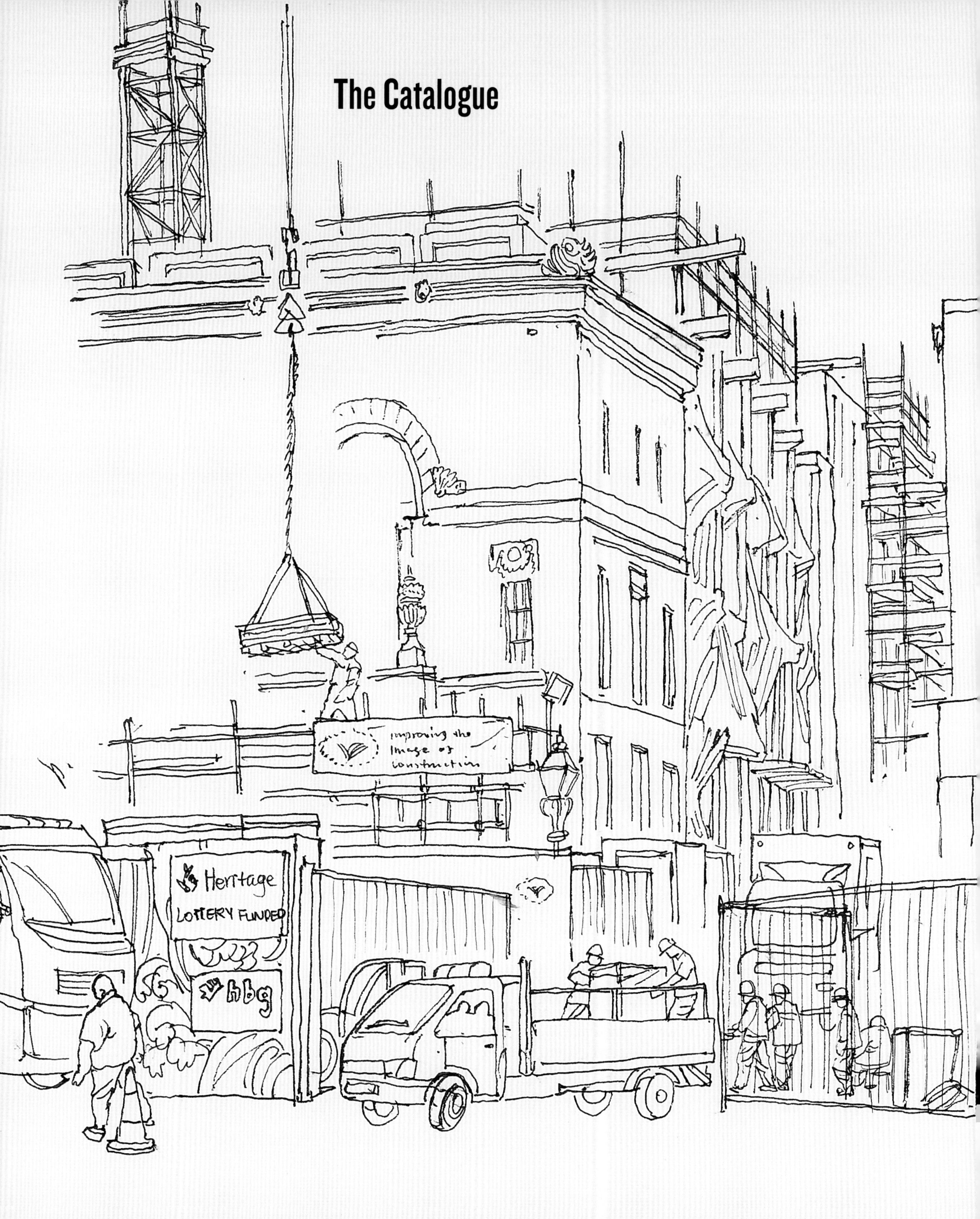

Museum Staff Portraits

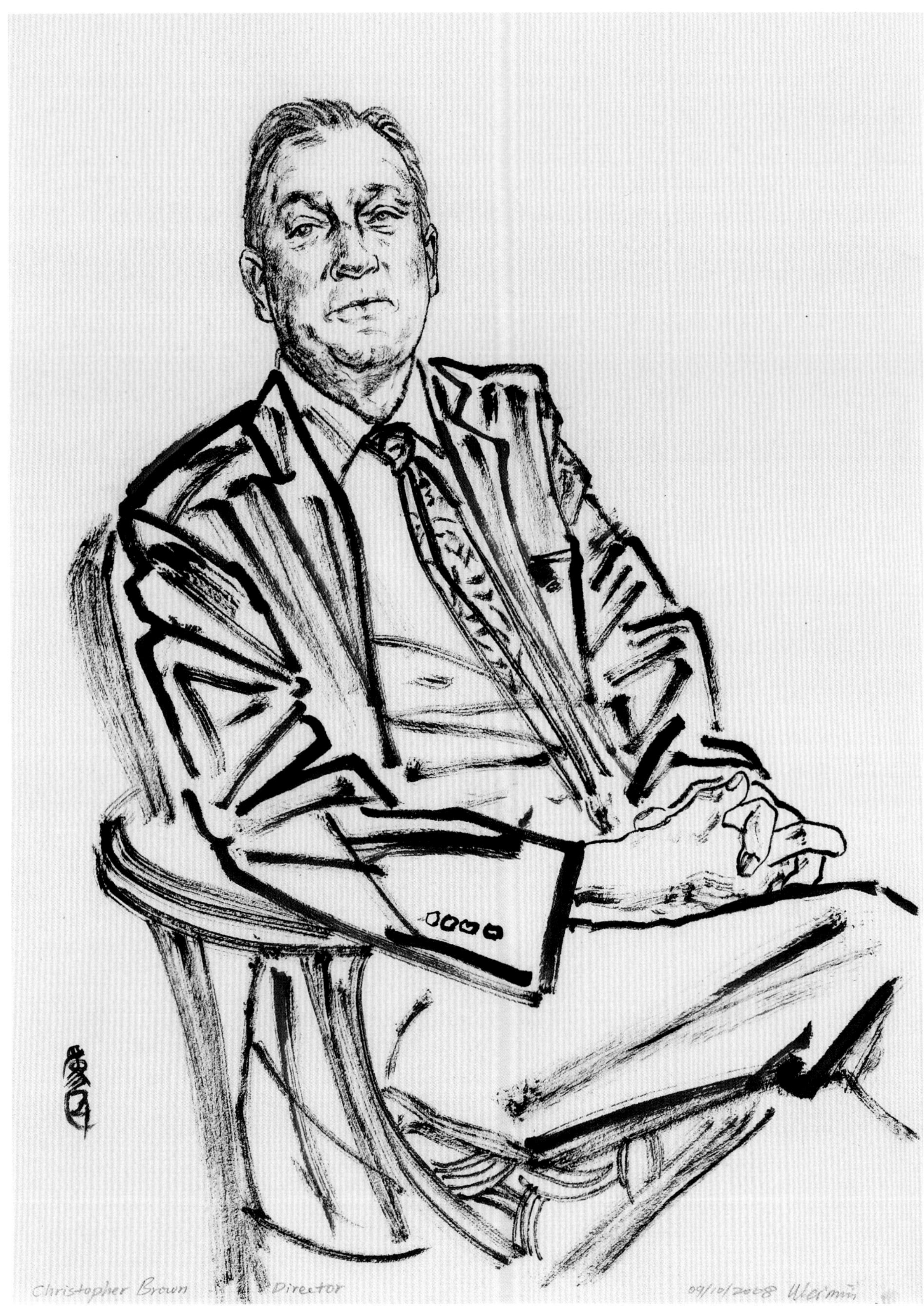

1

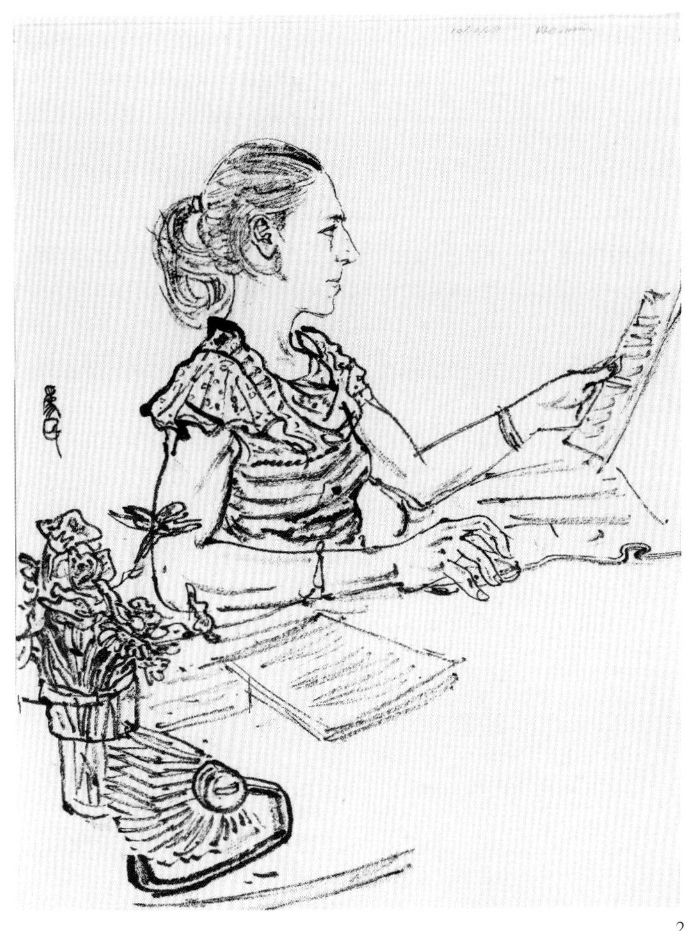

2

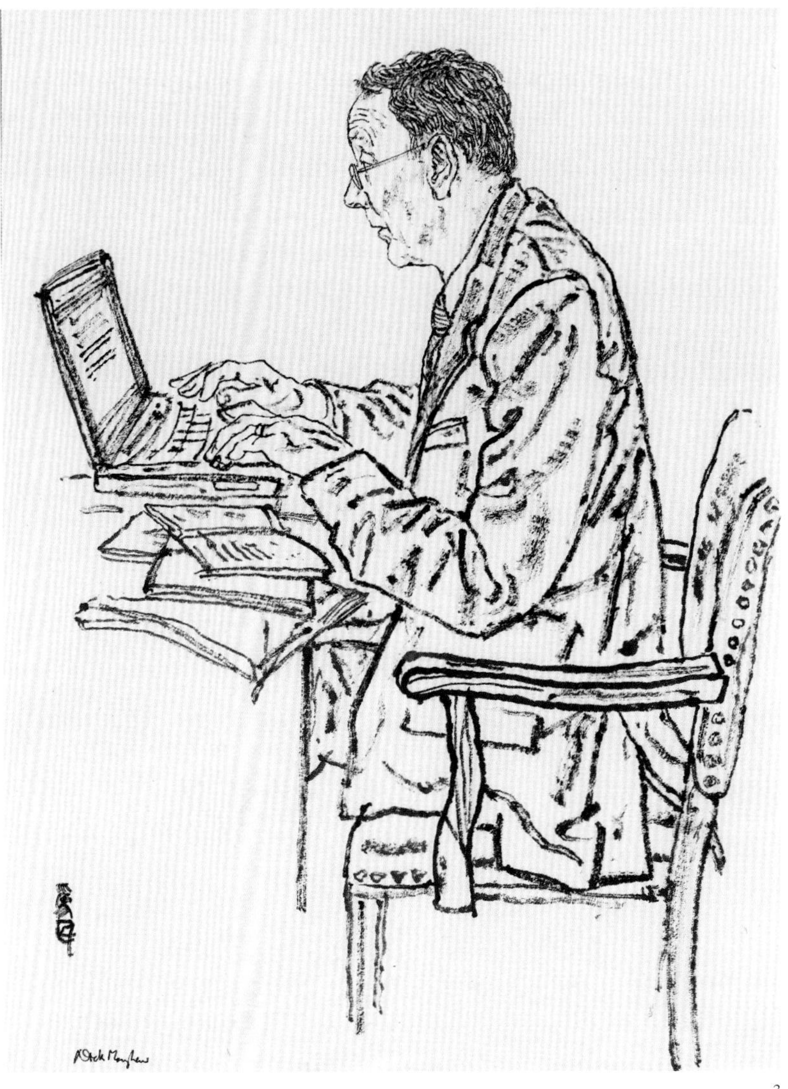

3

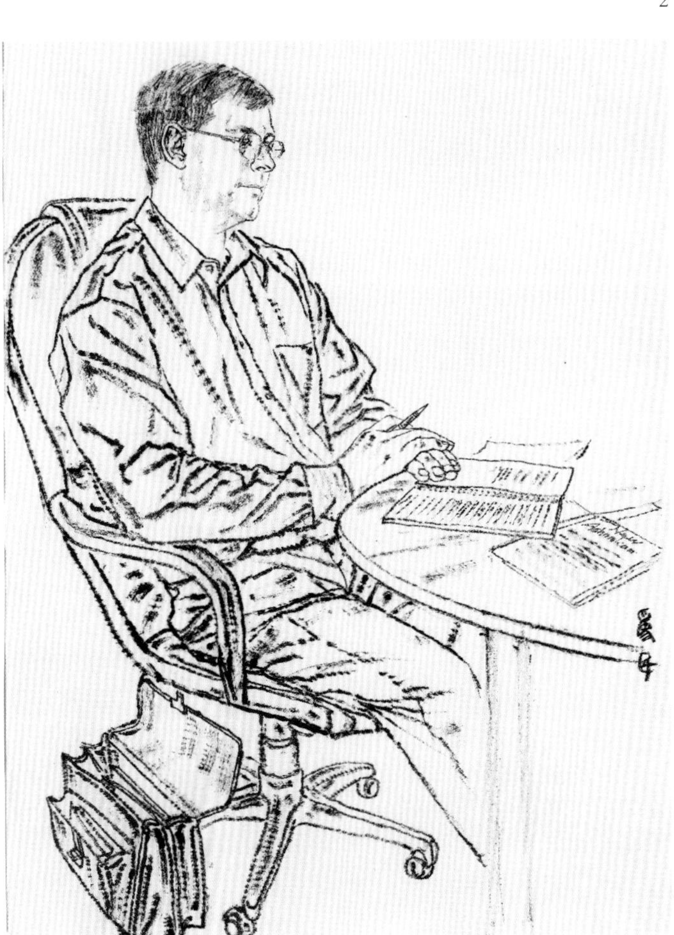

4

1 **Christopher Brown** *Director*
2008. Brush and ink on *pi* paper. Paper size: 46.1 × 33.2 cm

2 **Rachel Lindenbaum** *Personal Assistant to the Director*
2008. Brush and ink on *xuan* paper. Paper size: 44.8 × 34 cm

3 **Nick Mayhew** *Deputy Director (Collections)*
2009. Brush and ink on *xuan* paper. Paper size: 44.8 × 34 cm

4 **Robert Thorpe** *Operations Director*
2009. Brush and ink on *xuan* paper. Paper size: 44.8 × 34 cm

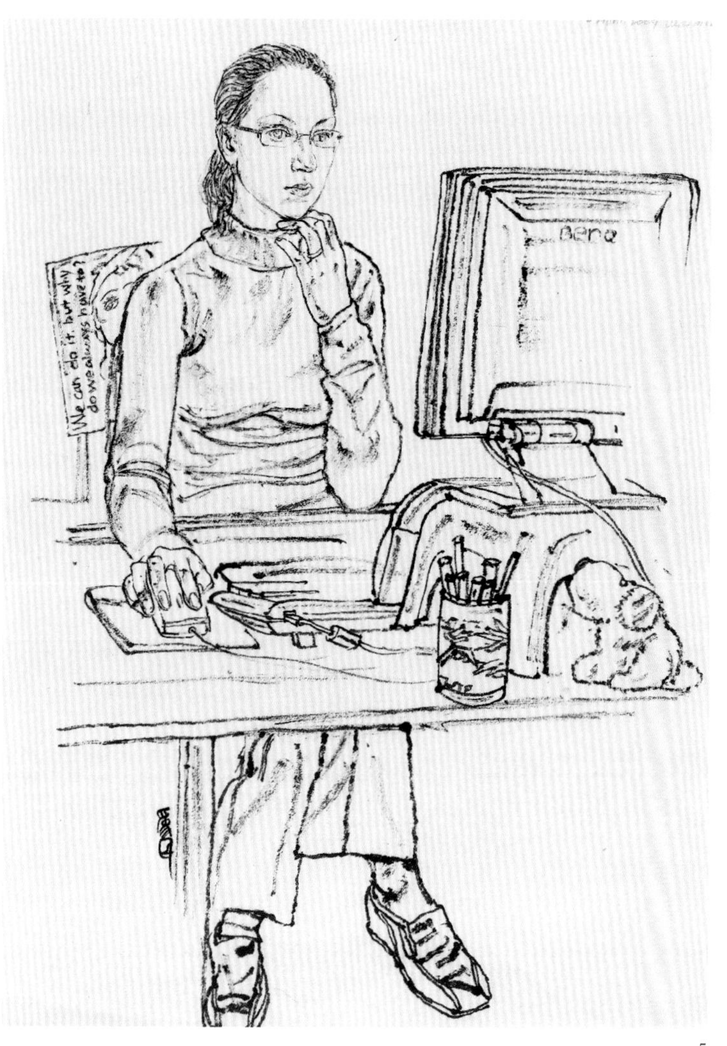

5

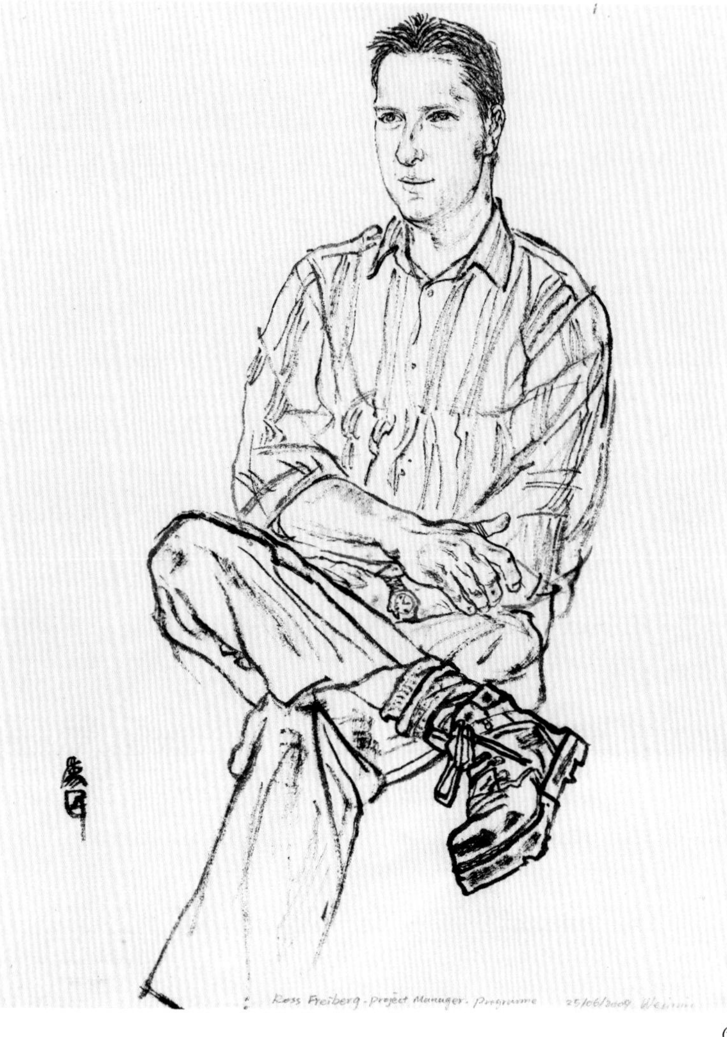

6

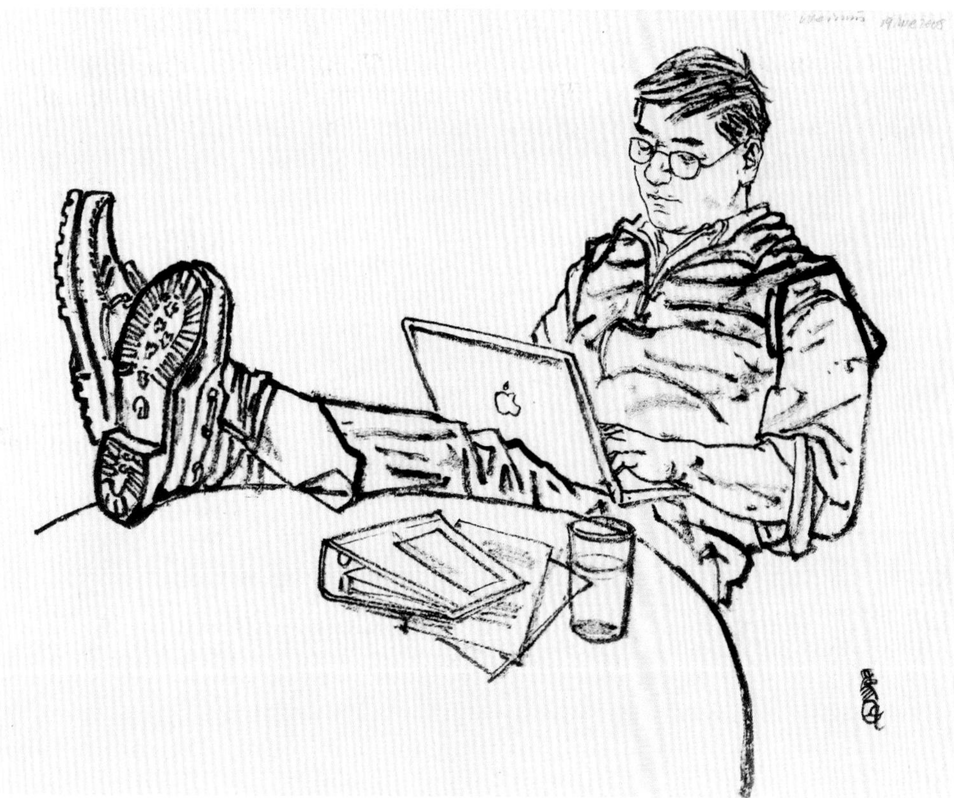

7

5 Victoria McGuinness *Recant Projects Manager*
2009. Brush and ink on *xuan* paper.
Paper size: 44.8 × 34 cm

6 Ross Freiberg *Project Manager (Ashmolean Museum Programme)*
2009. Brush and ink on *xuan* paper.
Paper size: 44.8 × 34 cm

7 Henry Kim *Project Director*
2009. Brush and ink on *pi* paper.
Paper size: 38.3 × 48.8 cm

8 Edith Prak *Deputy Director (Development and Outreach)*
2009. Brush and ink on *xuan* paper.
Paper size: 44.8 × 34 cm

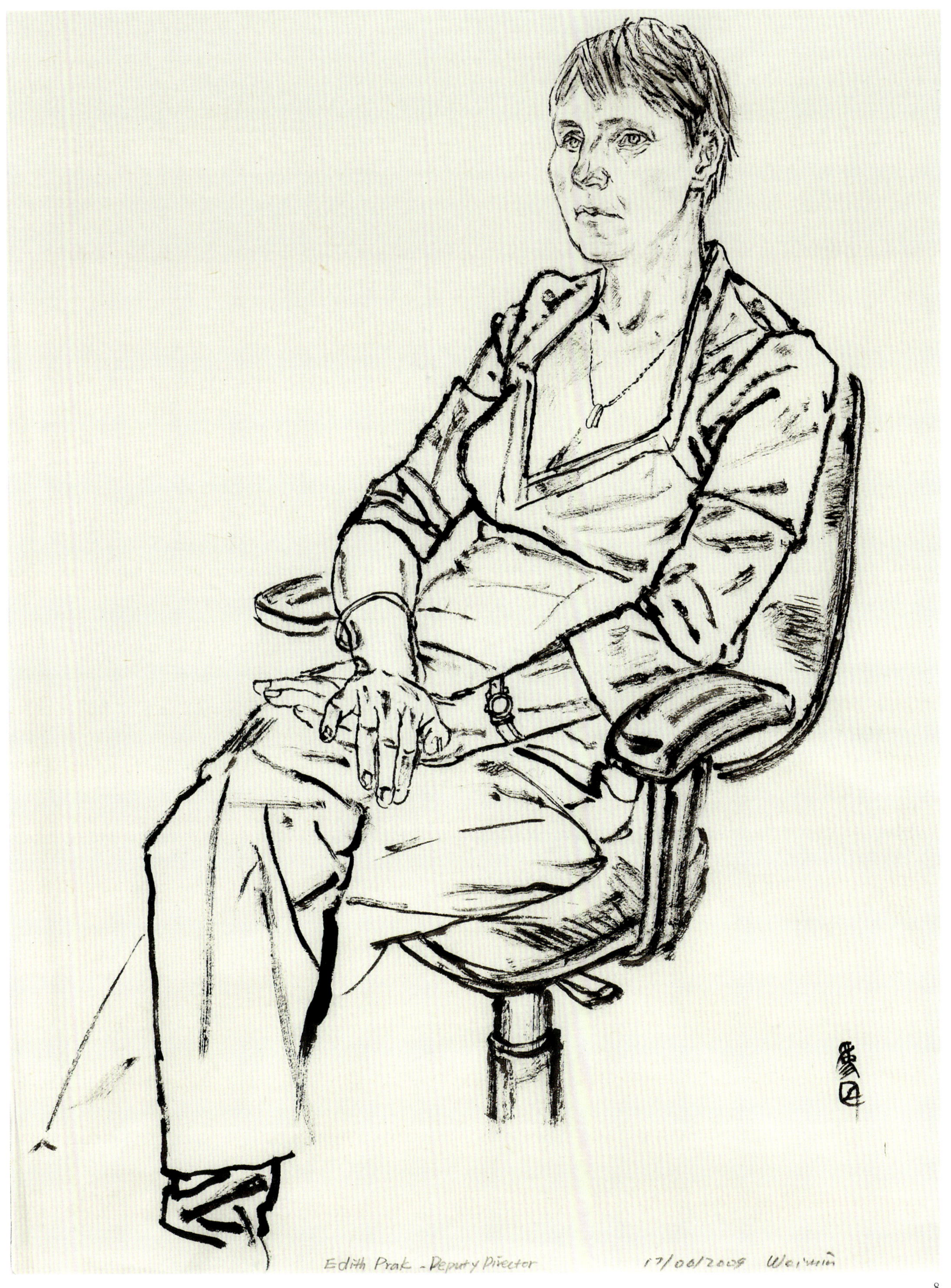

8

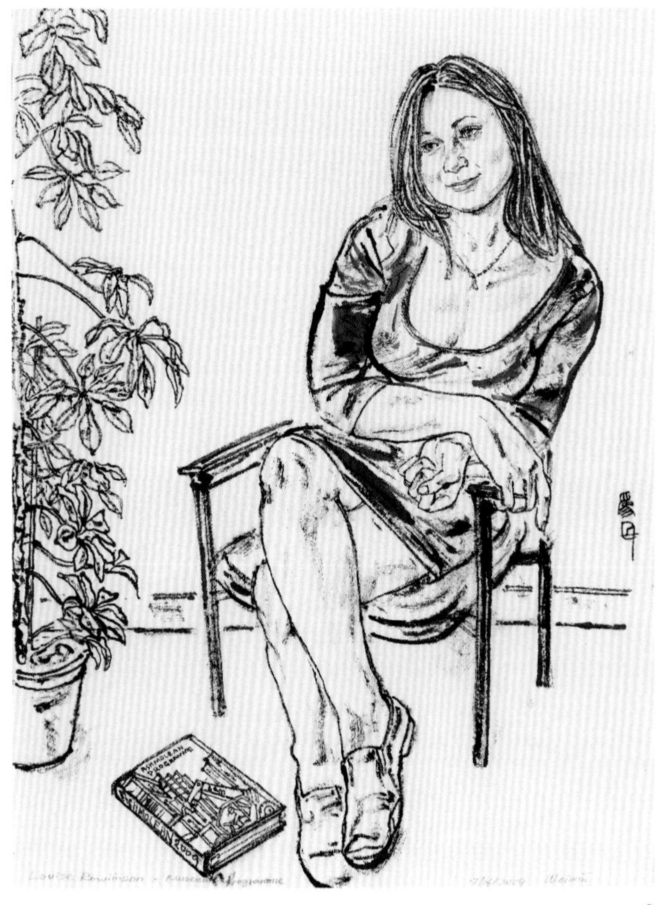

9

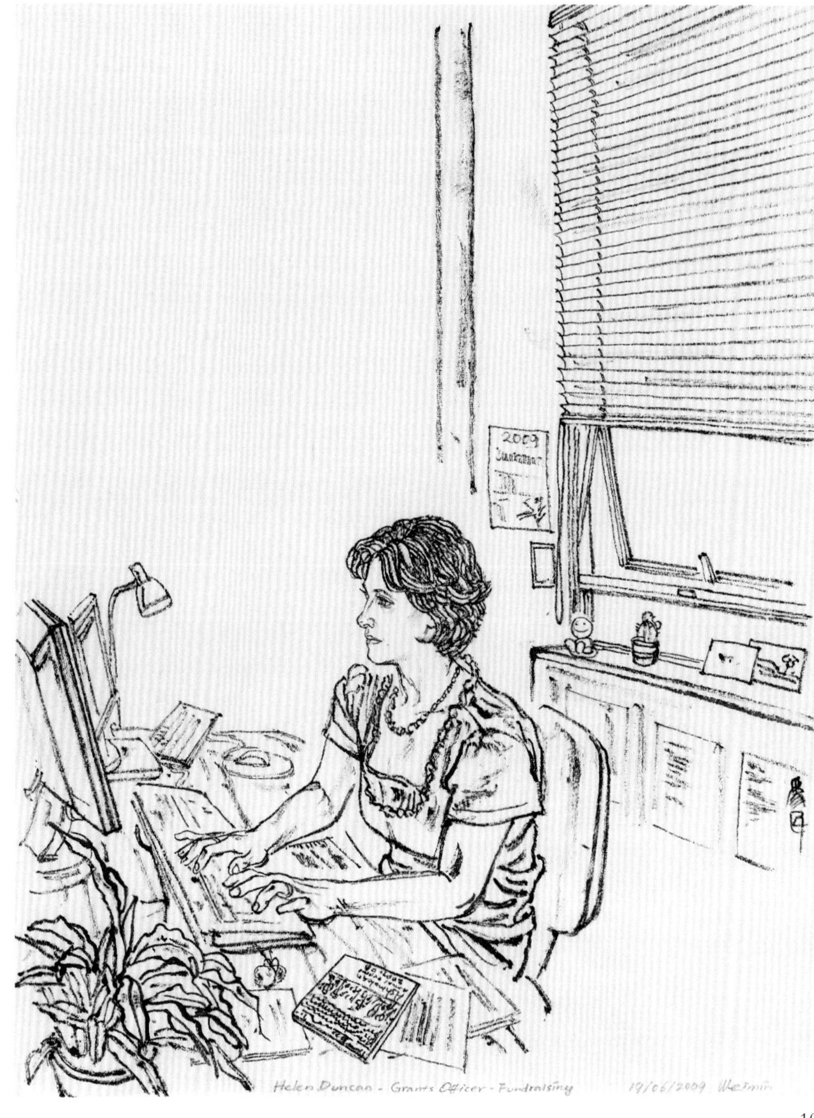

10

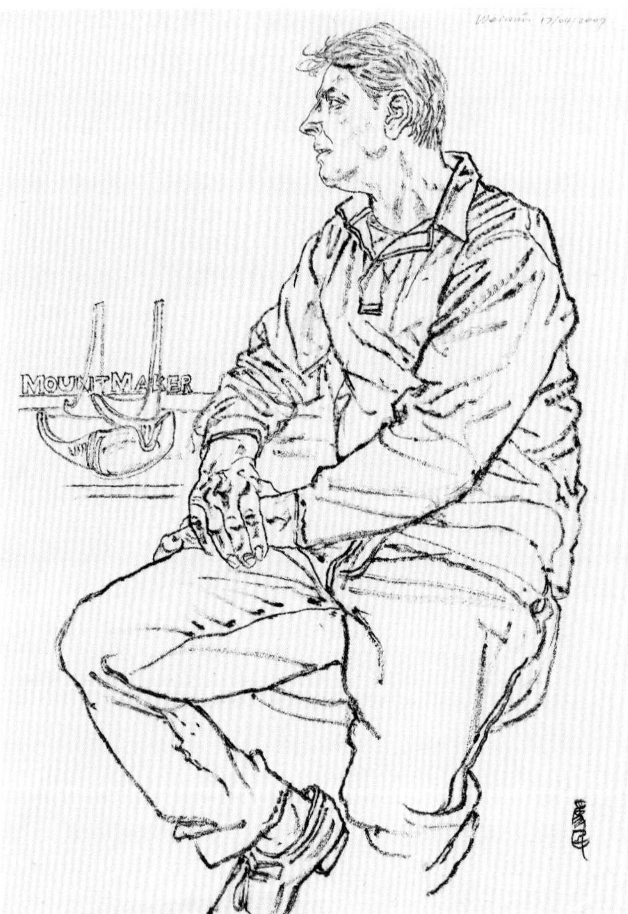

11

9 **Louise Rawlinson** *Project Manager (Ashmolean Museum Programme)*
2009. Brush and ink on *xuan* paper. Paper size: 44.8 × 34 cm

10 **Helen Duncan** *Trusts and Foundations Manager*
2009. Brush and ink on *xuan* paper. Paper size: 44.8 × 34 cm

11 **David Provan** *Mount Maker, Design and Display Project and RI Team*
2009. Brush and ink on *xuan* paper. Paper size: 44.8 × 34 cm

12 **Antony Green** *Senior Campaign Manager*
2009. Brush and ink on *xuan* paper. Paper size: 44.8 × 34 cm

13 **Lizzie Higginson** *Patrons and Friends Manager*
2009. Brush and ink on *xuan* paper. Paper size: 44.8 × 34 cm

14 **Sarah Casey** *Research and Information Officer*
2009. Brush and ink on *xuan* paper. Paper size: 44.8 × 34 cm

15 **Theresa Nicolson** *Corporate Partnerships Manager*
2009. Brush and ink on *xuan* paper. Paper size: 44.8 × 34 cm

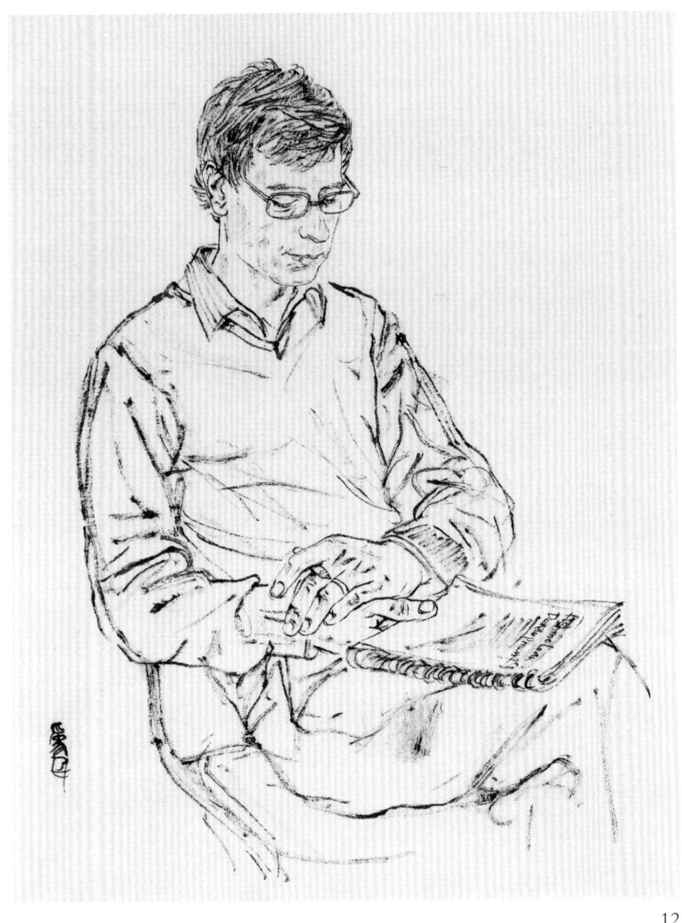

12

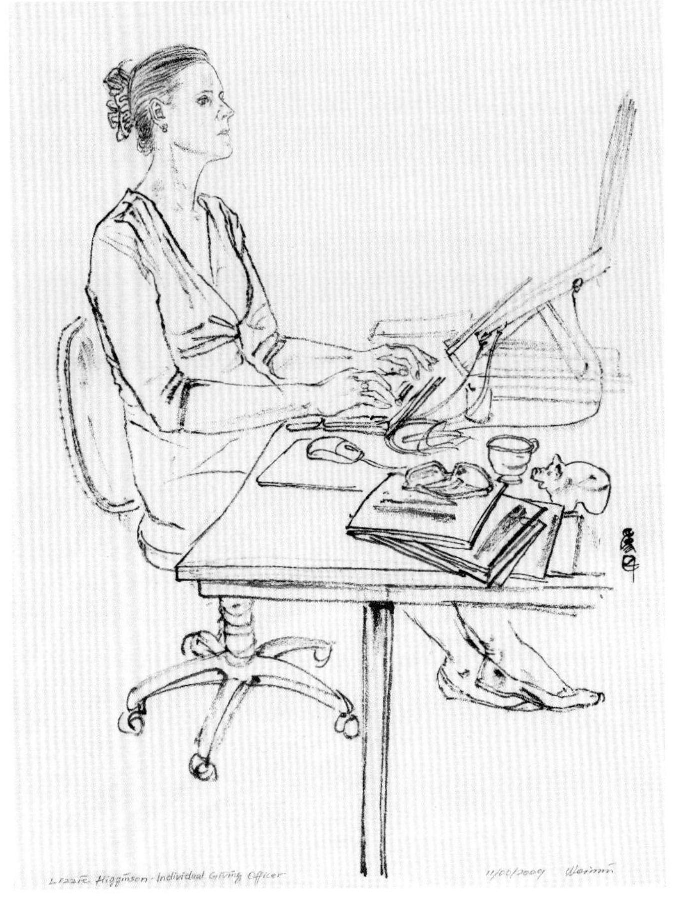

13

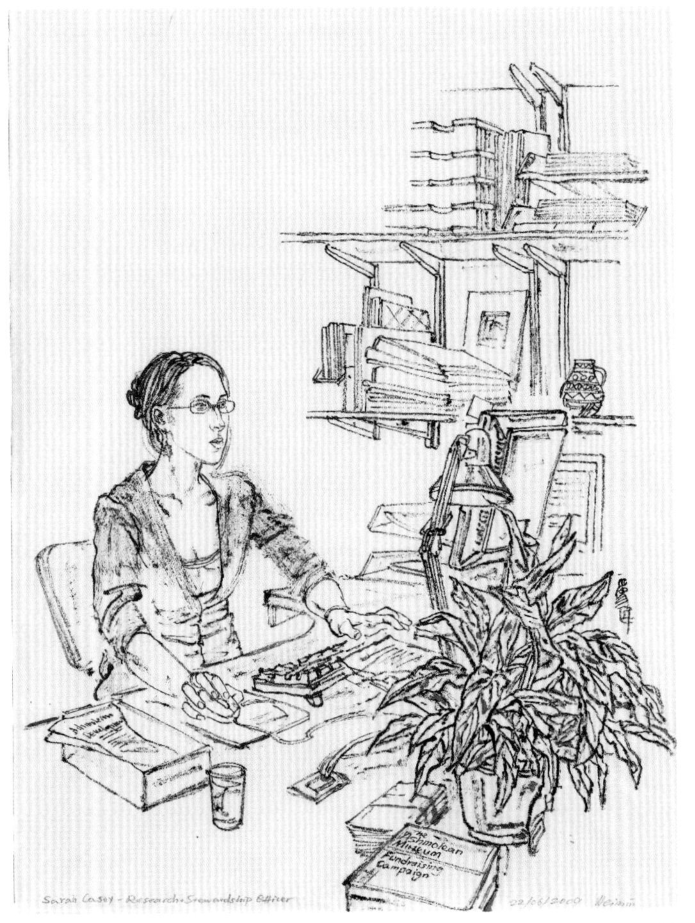

14

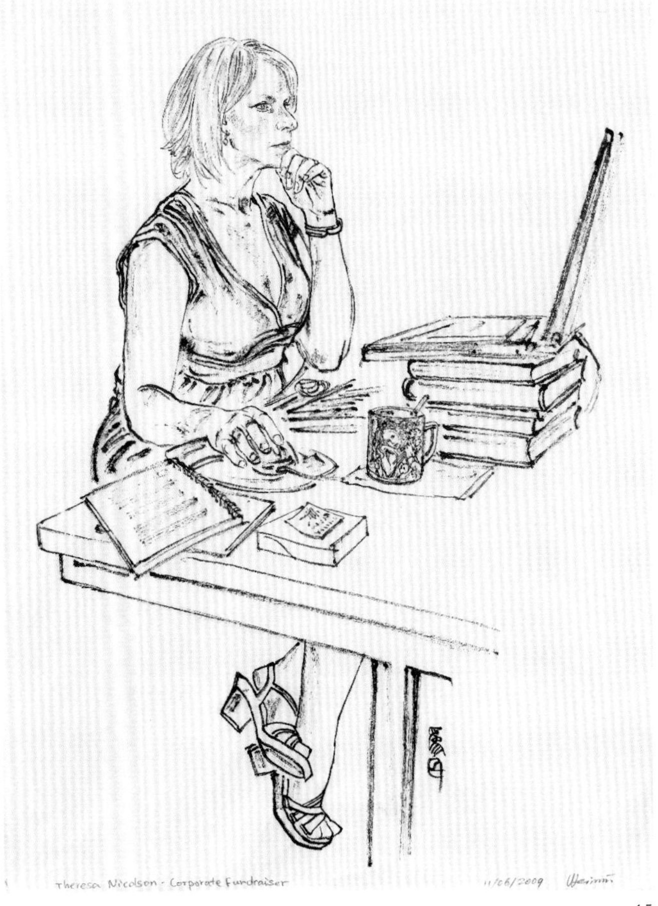

15

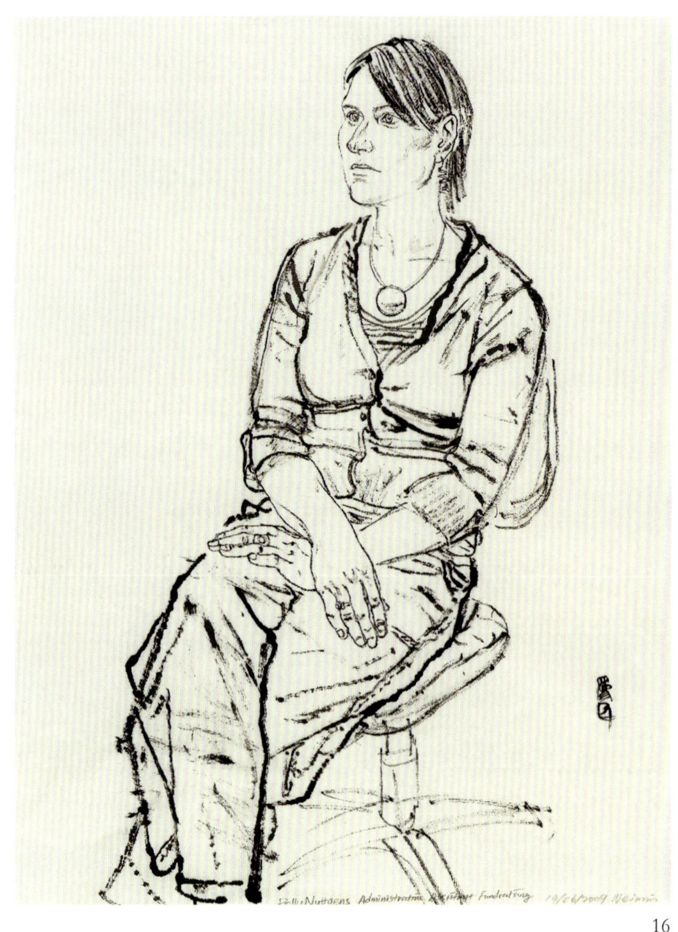

16

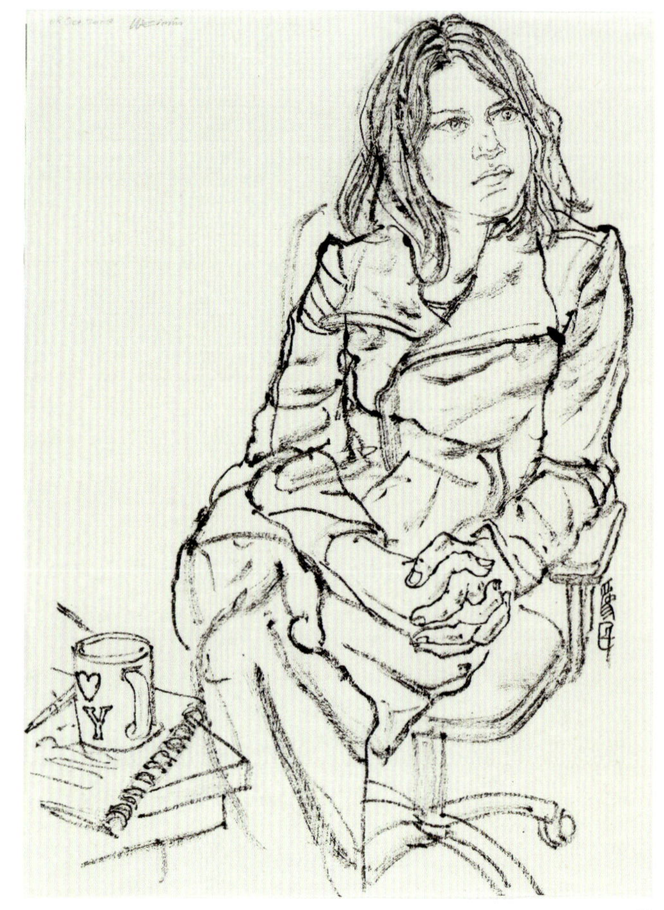

17

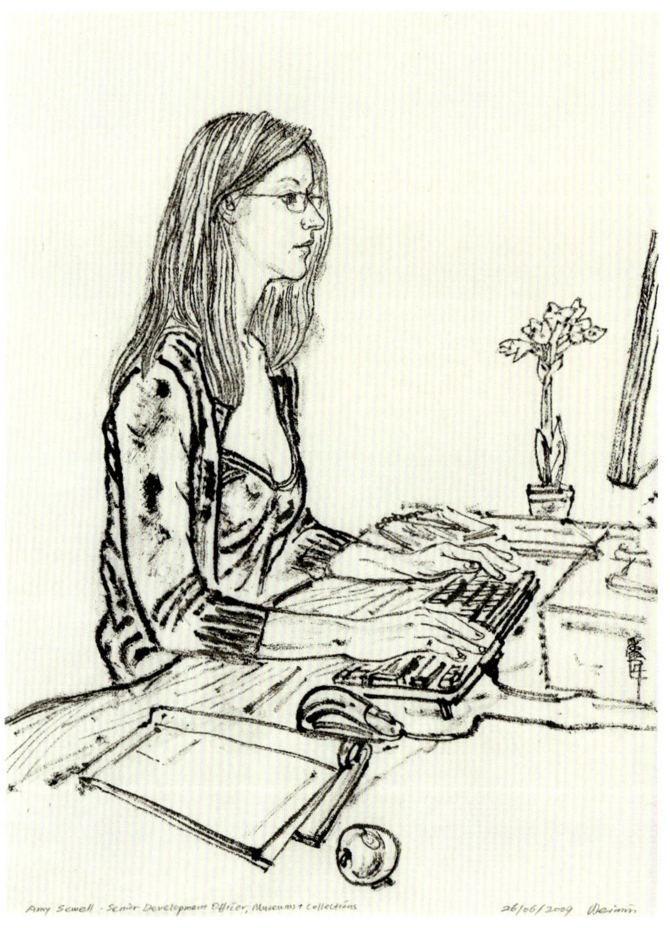

18

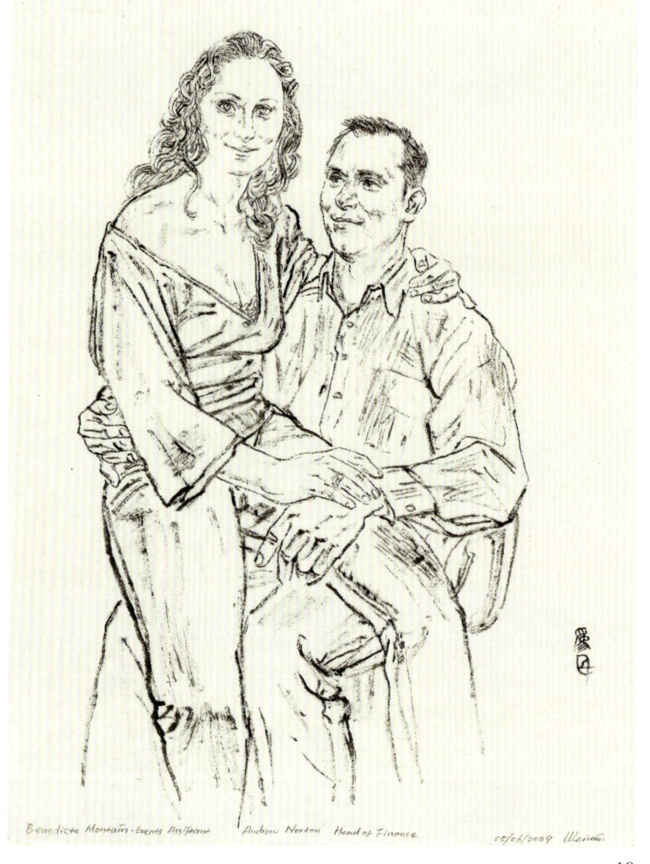

19

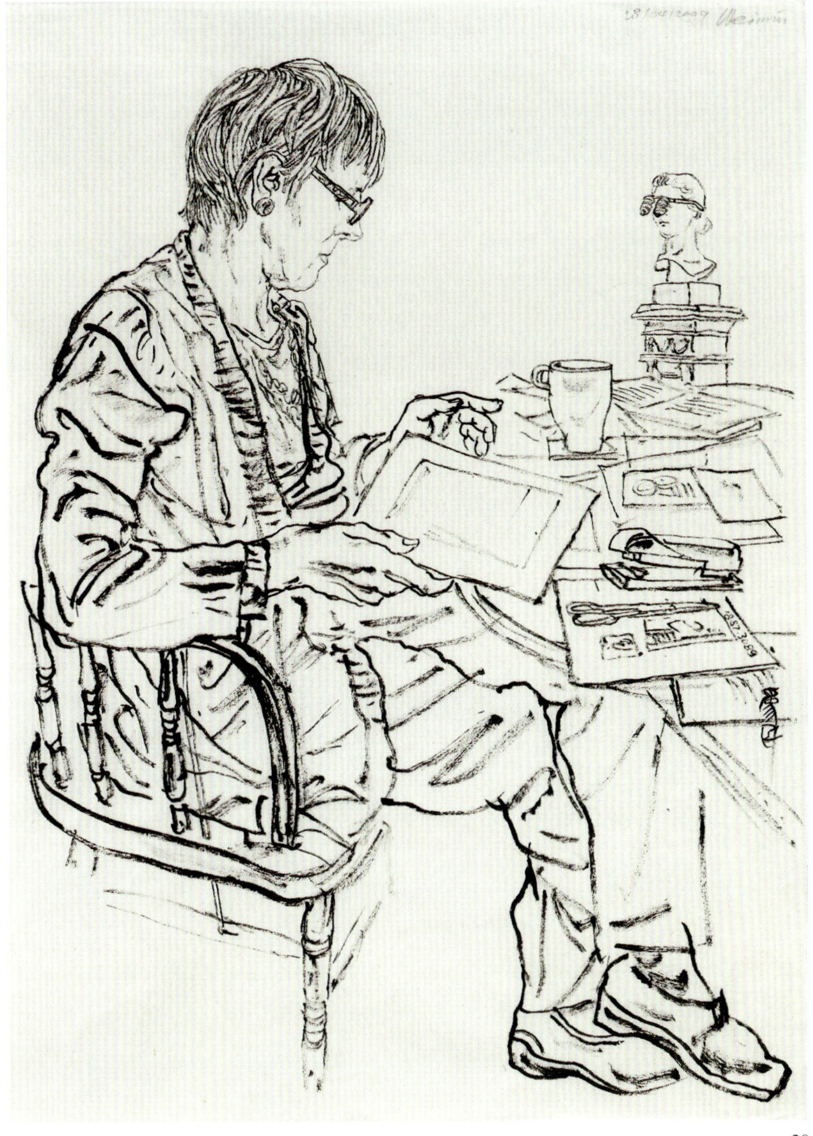

20

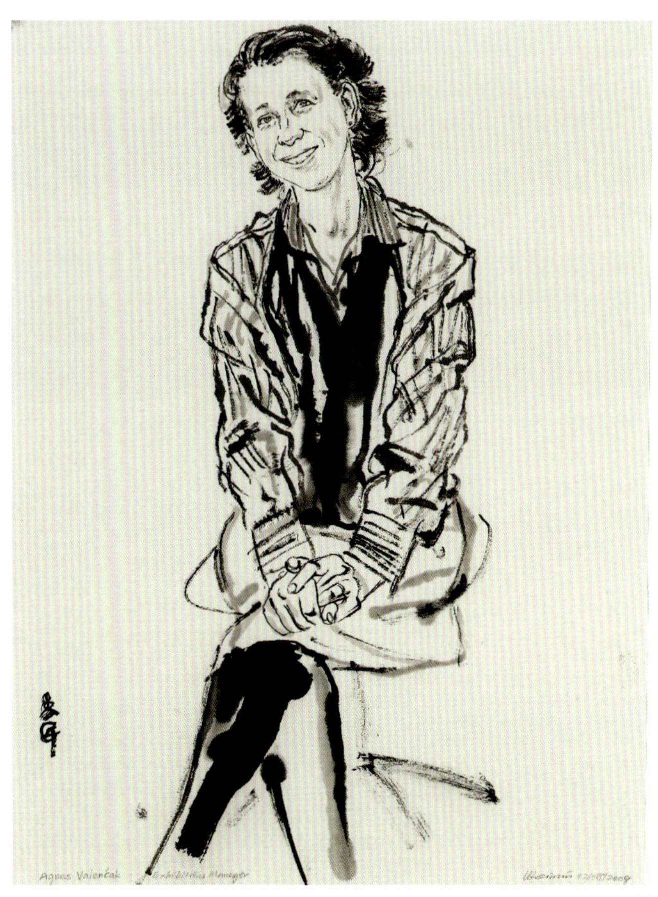

21

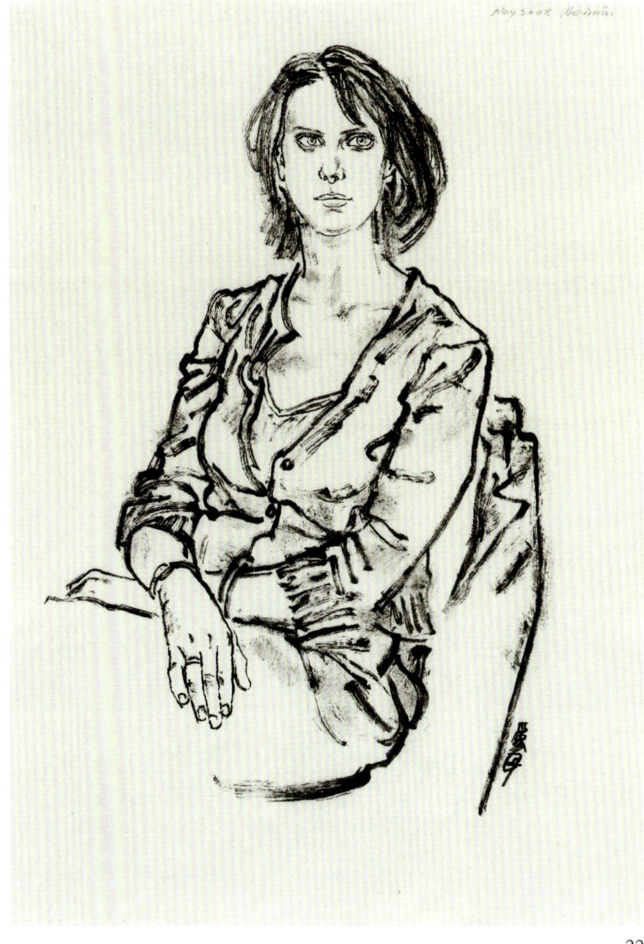

22

16 Polly Nuttgens *Administrative Assistant, Fundraising Office*
2009. Brush and ink on *xuan* paper. Paper size: 44.8 × 34 cm

17 Penny *Former Museum staff*
2008. Brush and ink on *xuan* paper. Paper size: 44.8 × 34 cm

18 Amy Sewell *Senior Development Officer, Museum and Collections*
2009. Brush and ink on *xuan* paper. Paper size: 44.8 × 34 cm

19 Andrew Norton *Head of Finance*
Benedicte Montain *Events Assistant*
2009. Brush and ink on *xuan* paper. Paper size: 44.8 × 34 cm

20 Susan Walker *Keeper, Department of Antiquities (Greek and Roman Antiquities)*
2009. Brush and ink on *xuan* paper. Paper size: 44.8 × 34 cm

21 Agnes Valencak *Exhibitions Manager*
2009. Brush and ink on *xuan* paper. Paper size: 44.8 × 34 cm

22 Susie Gault *Press and Programme Manager*
2008. Brush and ink on *pi* paper. Paper size: 46.1 × 34.7 cm

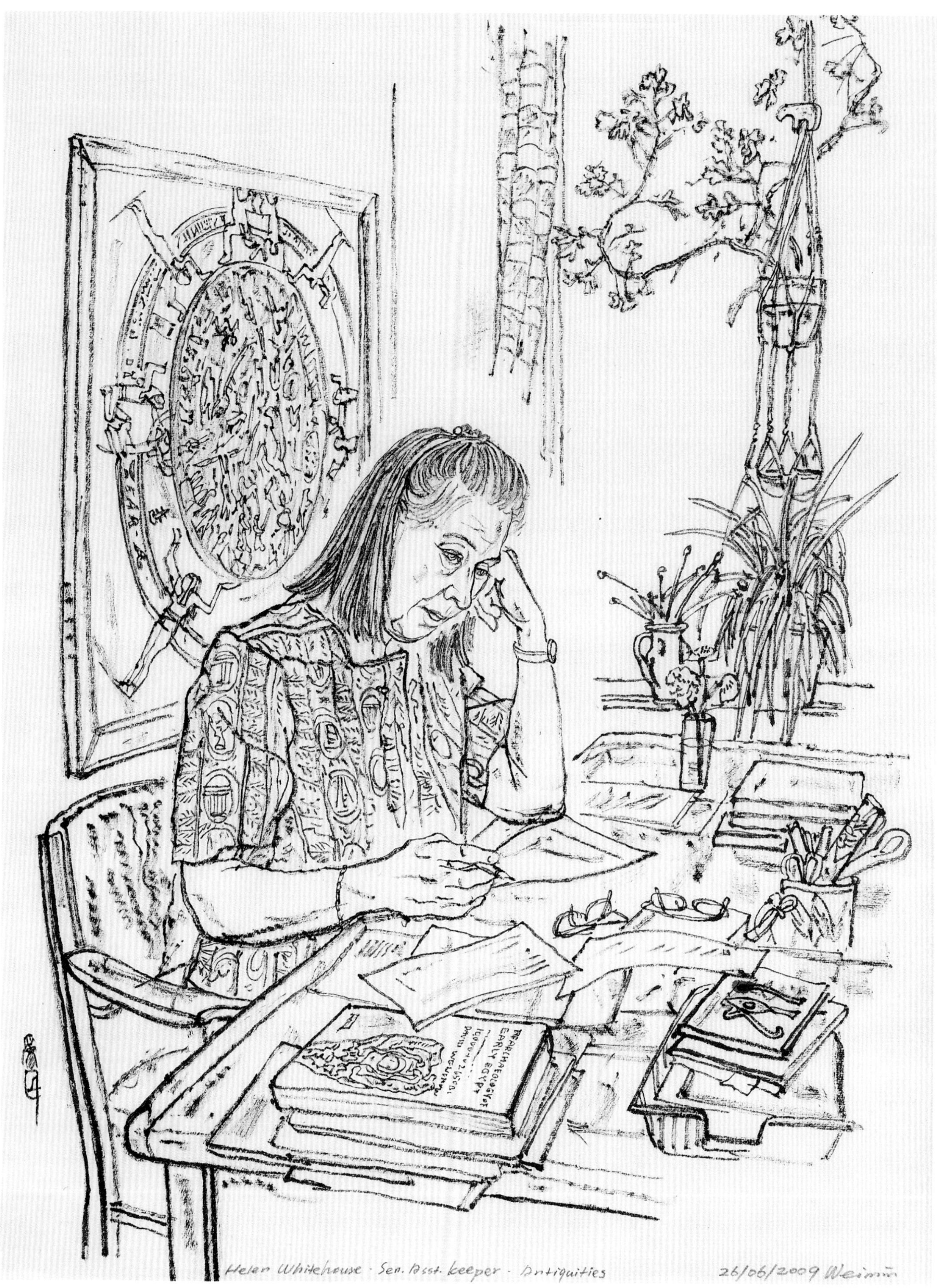
Helen Whitehouse · Sen. Asst. keeper · Antiquities
26/06/2009 Weimin
23

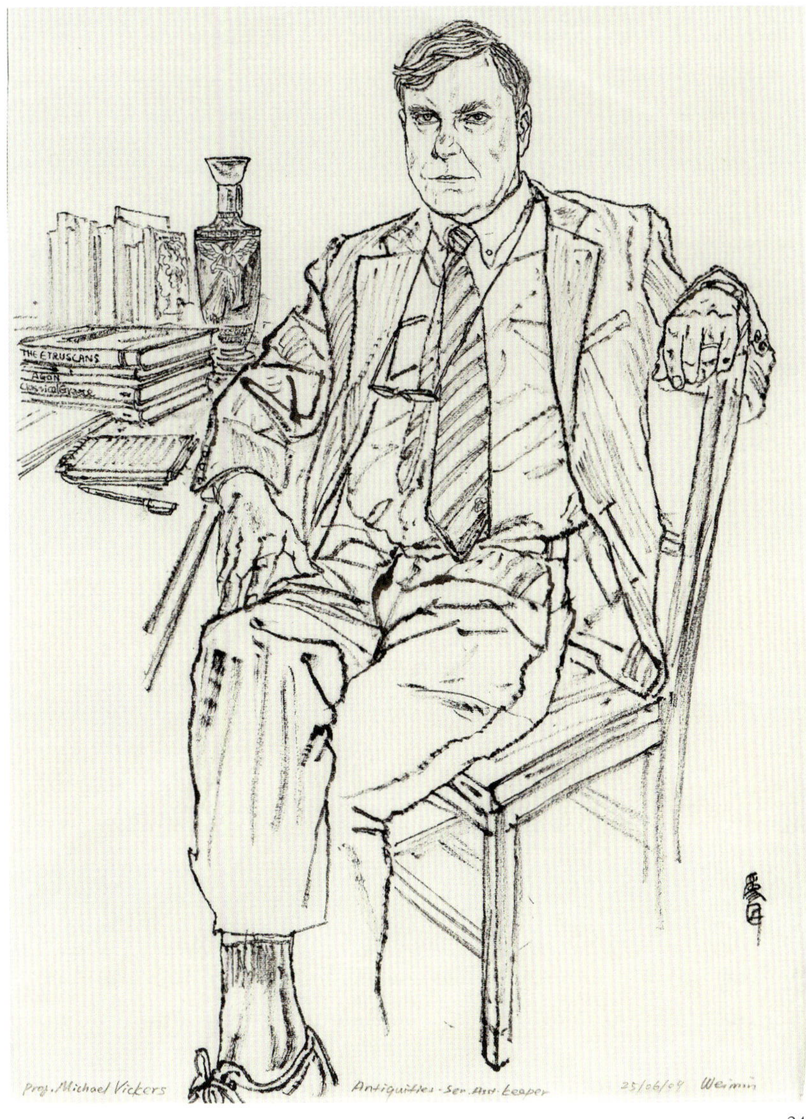

24

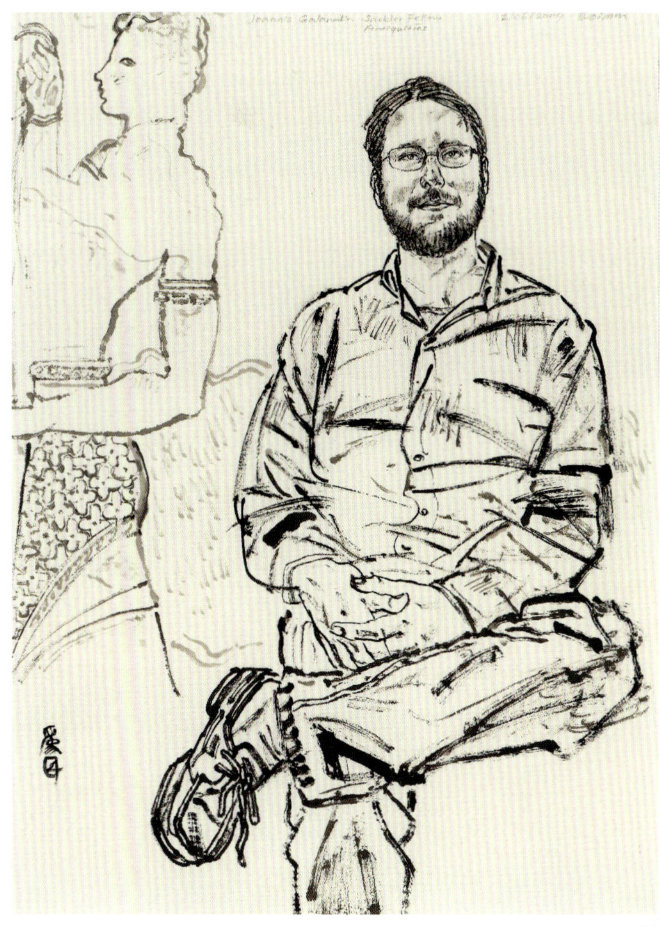

25

26

23 Helen Whitehouse *Senior Assistant Keeper, Department of Antiquities (Ancient Egypt and Sudan)*
2009. Brush and ink on *xuan* paper. Paper size: 44.8 × 34 cm

24 Michael Vickers *Senior Assistant Keeper, Department of Antiquities (Greek, Roman and Byzantine Antiquities)*
2009. Brush and ink on *xuan* paper. Paper size: 44.8 × 34 cm

25 Yannis Galanakis *Sackler Junior Research Fellow in Archaeology (Worcester College) and Project Curator for the Aegean World Gallery, Department of Antiquities*
2009. Brush and ink on *xuan* paper. Paper size: 44.8 × 34 cm

26 David Berry *Ashmolean Project Curator, Department of Antiquities*
2009. Brush and ink on *xuan* paper. Paper size: 44.8 × 34 cm

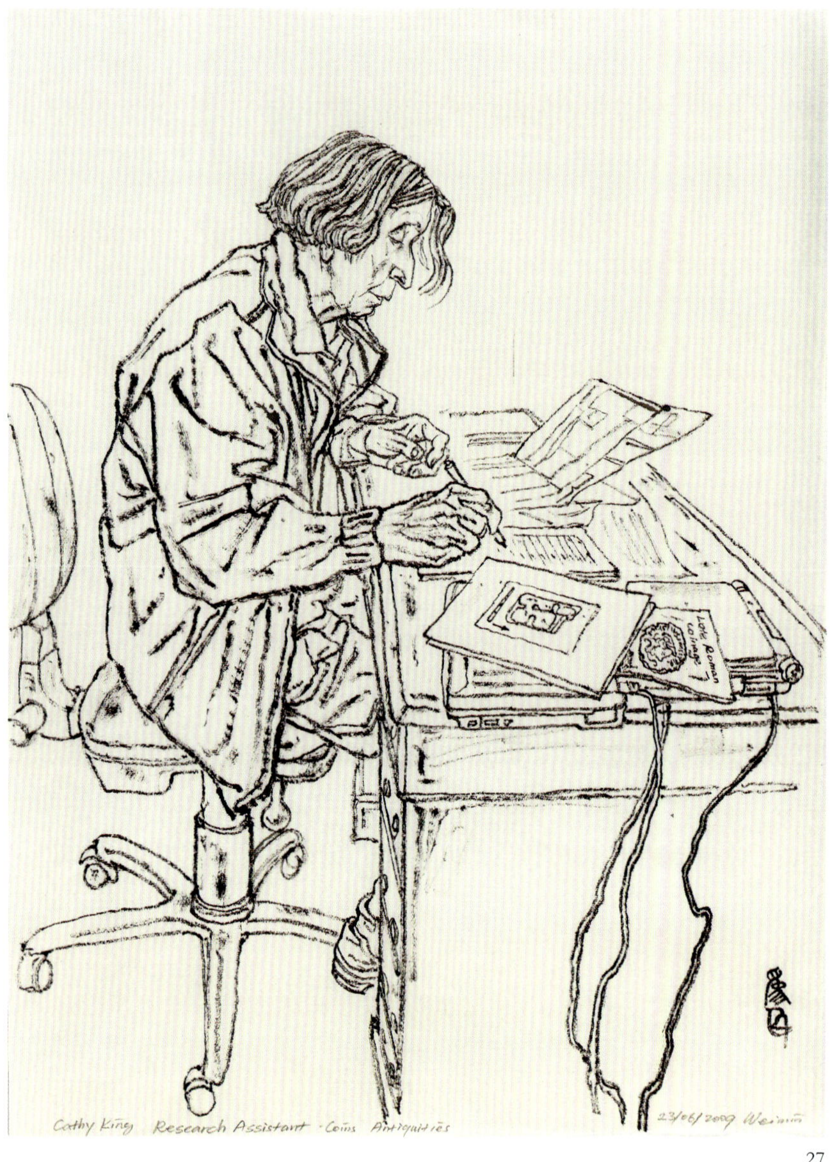

27

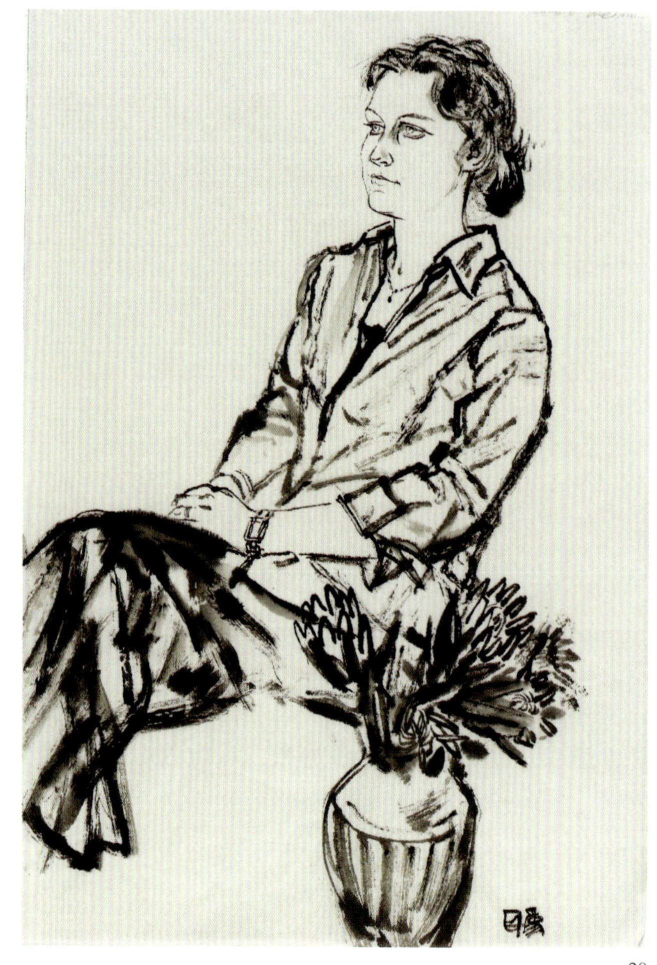

28

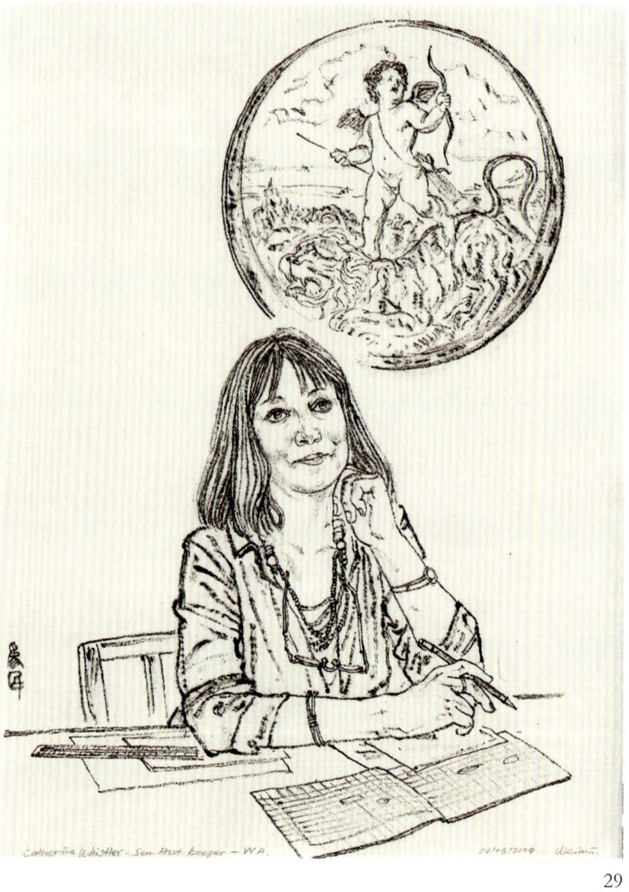

29

27 Cathy King *Research Associate in the Heberden Coin Room, Department of Antiquities*
2009. Brush and ink on *xuan* paper. Paper size: 44.8 × 34 cm

28 Helen Hovey *Documentation Officer, Department of Antiquities*
2006. Brush and ink on *pi* paper. Paper size: 46.1 × 31.5 cm

29 Catherine Whistler *Senior Assistant Keeper, Department of Western Art*
2009. Brush and ink on *xuan* paper. Paper size: 44.8 × 34 cm

30 Jack Green *Project Curator for the Ancient Near East, Department of Antiquities*
2009. Brush and ink on *xuan* paper. Paper size: 44.8 × 34 cm

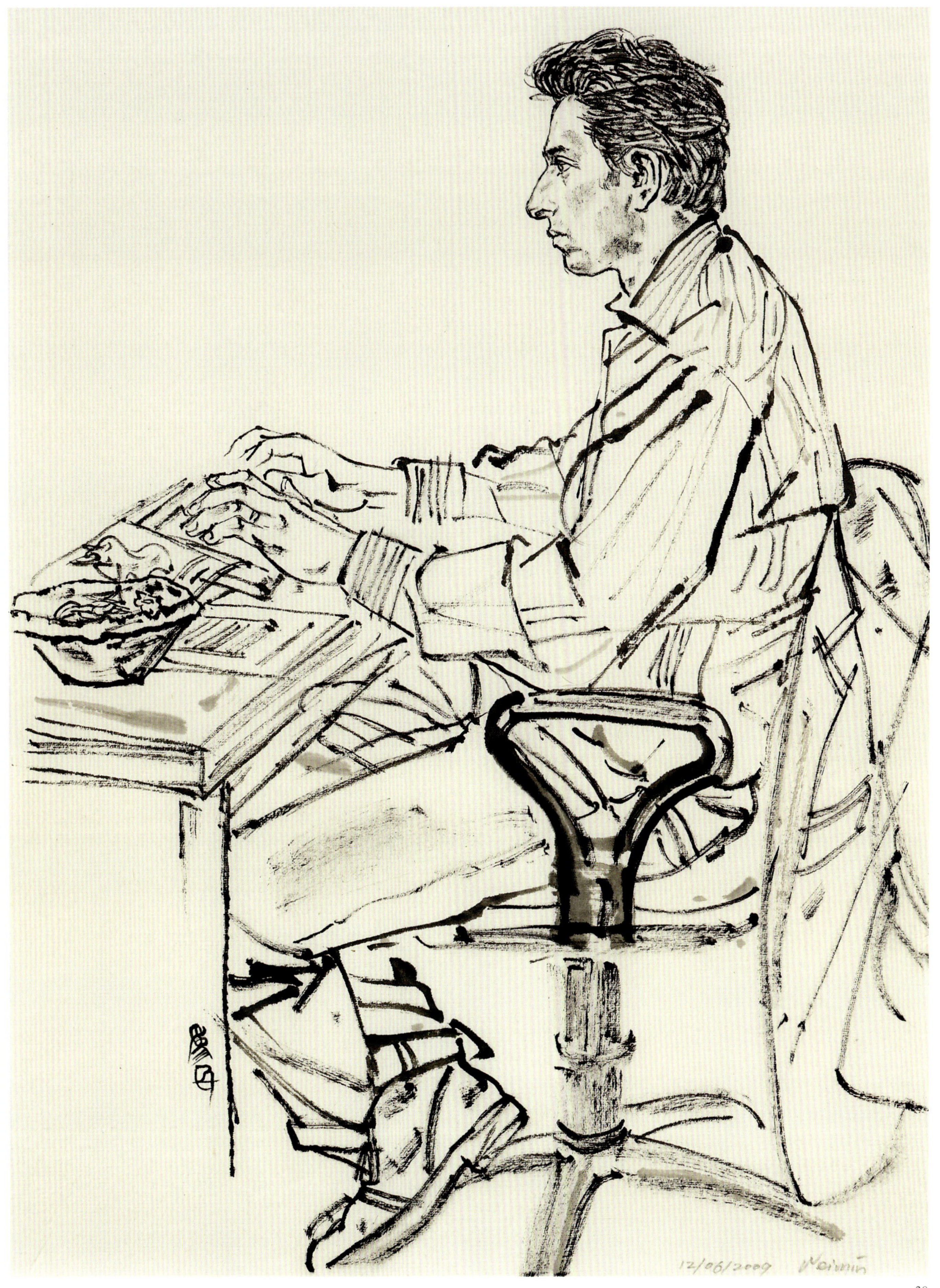

30

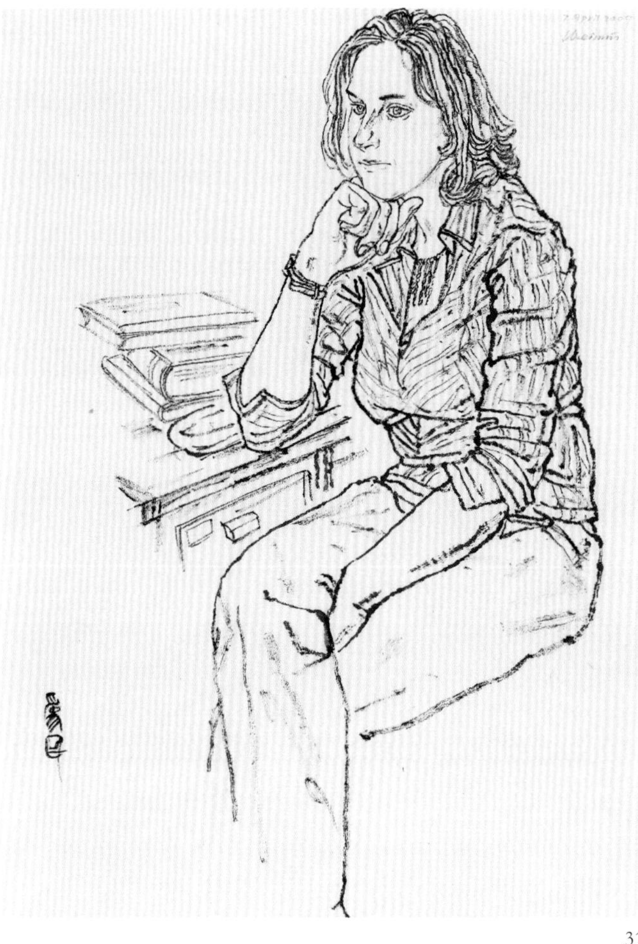

31

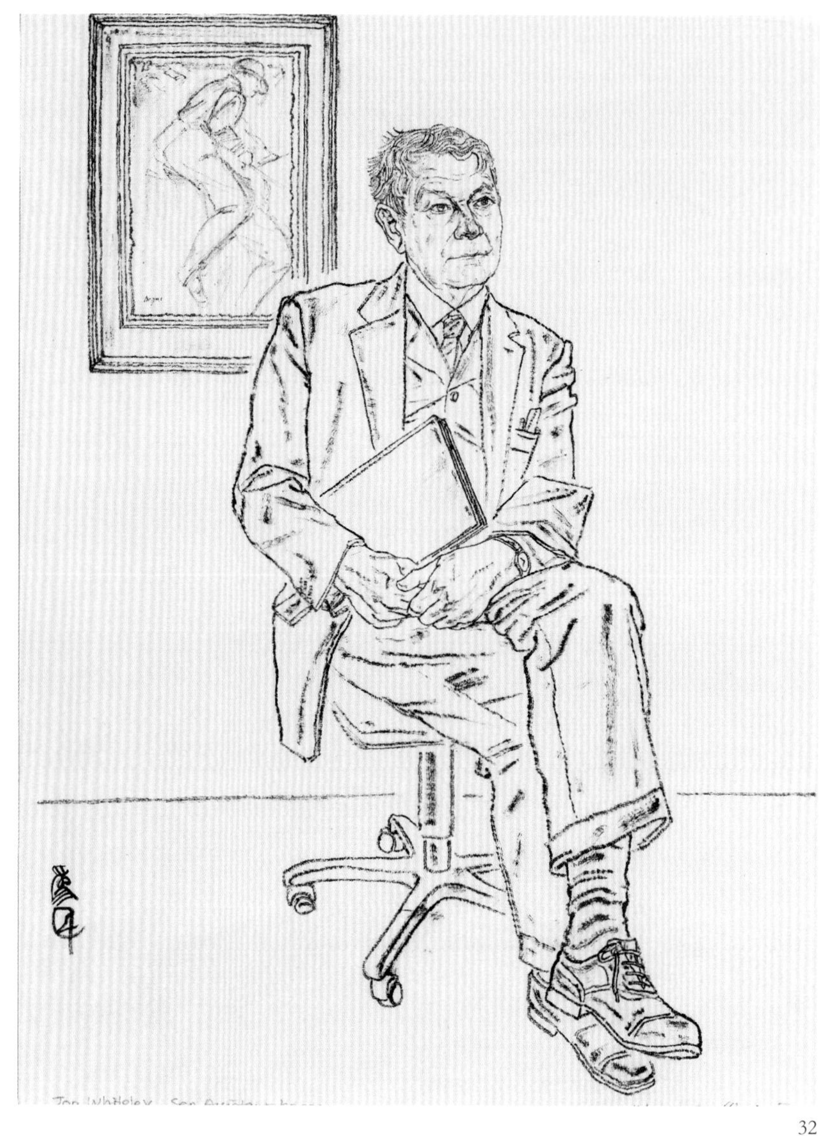

32

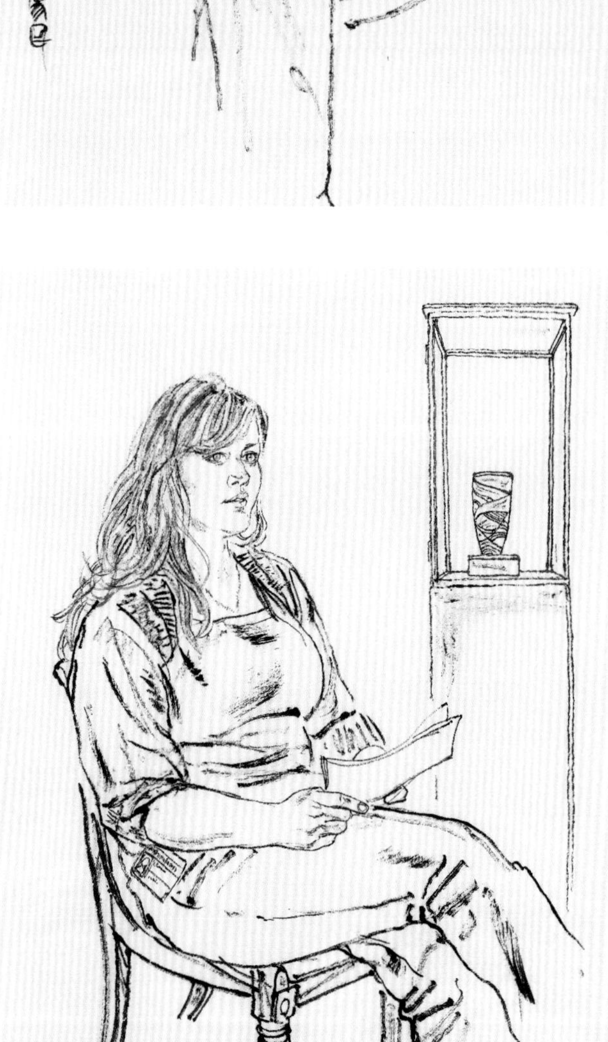

33

31 **Karine Sauvignon** *Print Room Supervisor, Department of Western Art*
2009. Brush and ink on *xuan* paper. Paper size: 44.8 × 34 cm

32 **Jon Whiteley** *Senior Assistant Keeper, Department of Western Art*
2009. Brush and ink on *xuan* paper. Paper size: 44.8 × 34 cm

33 **Christina Chilcott** *Western Art Refurbishment and Documentation*
2009. Brush and ink on *xuan* paper. Paper size: 44.8 × 34 cm

34 **Chris Howgego** *Keeper, Heberden Coin Room (Roman)*
2009. Brush and ink on *xuan* paper. Paper size: 44.8 × 34 cm

The Ashmolean
Money Gallery
Chris Howgego - Keeper - Heberden Coin Room
25/06/2009 Weimin

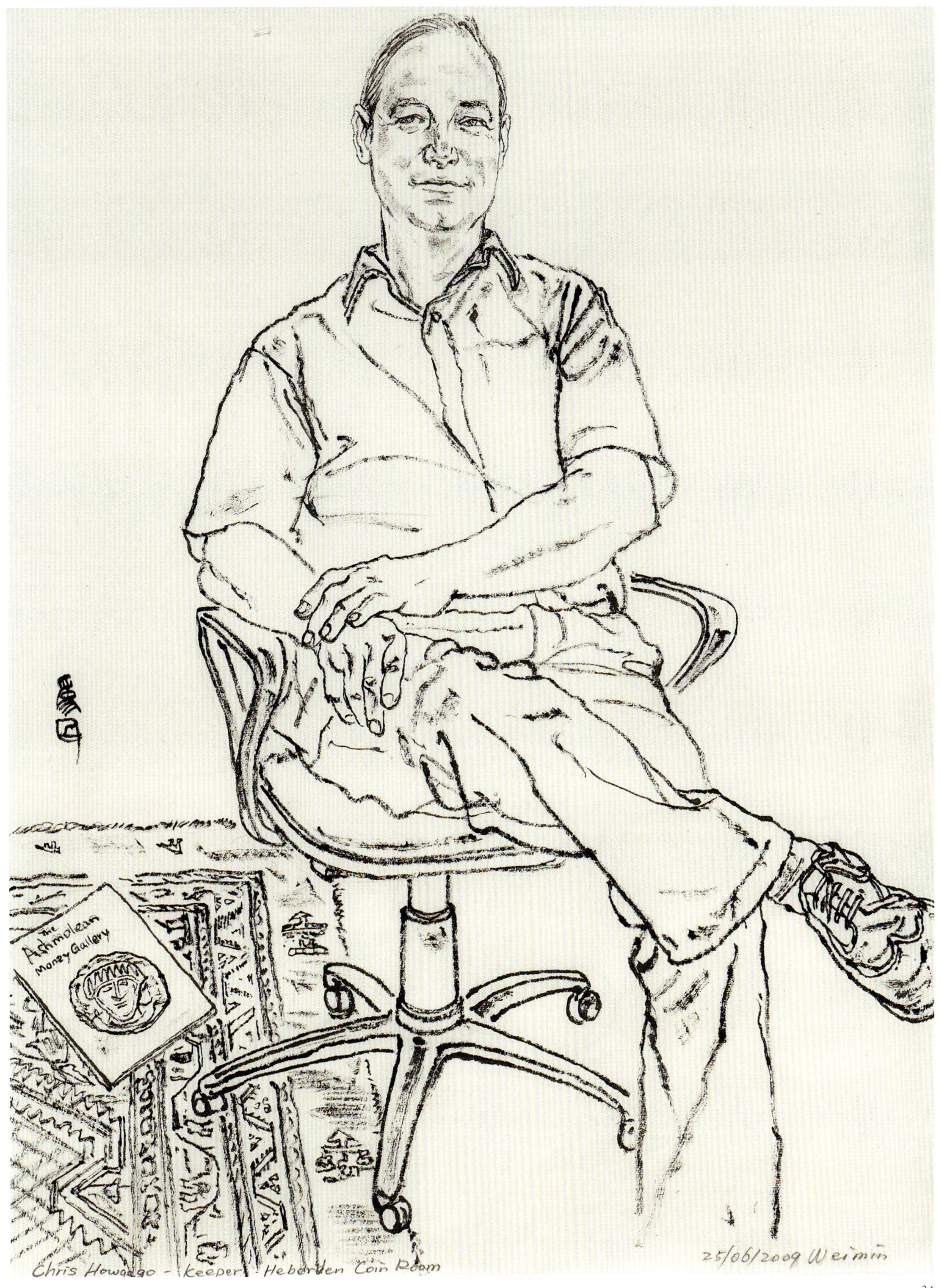

34

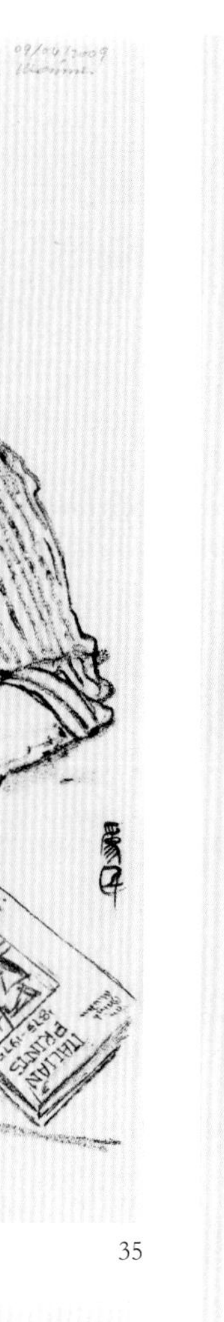

35

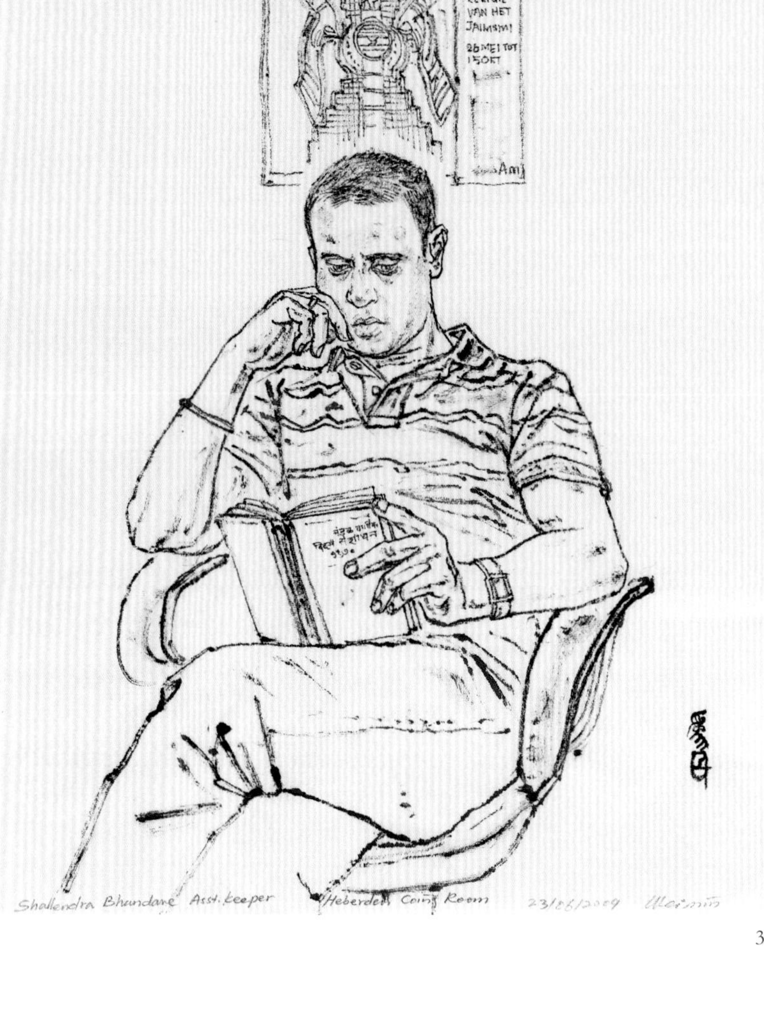

36

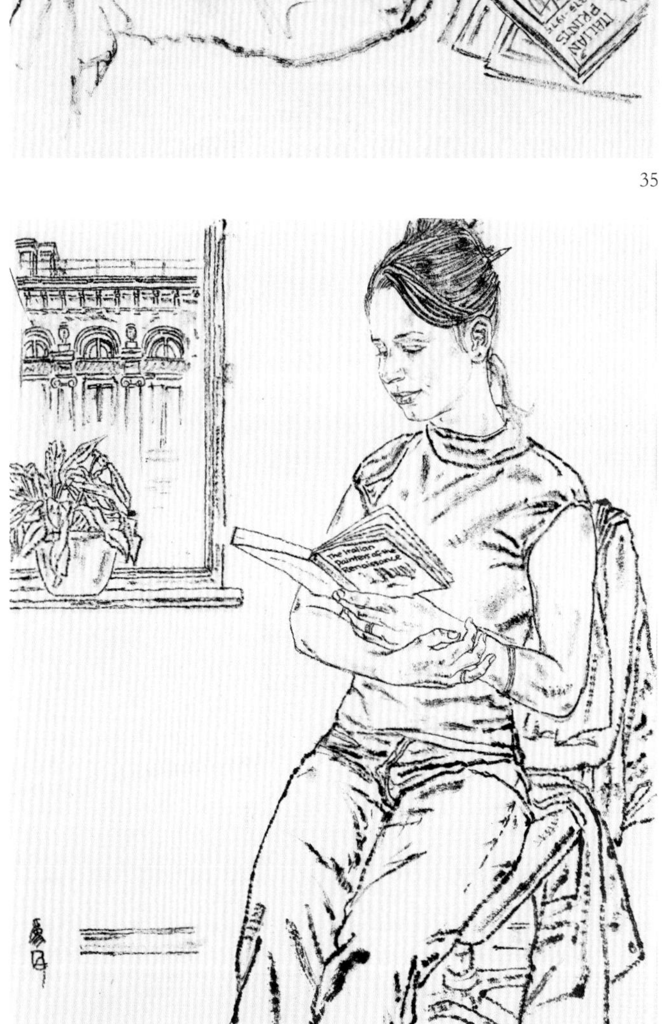

37

35 Angelamaria Aceto *Print Room Assistant , Department of Western Art*
2009. Brush and ink on *xuan* paper. Paper size: 44.8 × 34 cm

36 Shailendra Bhandare *Assistant Keeper (South Asian and Oriental Numismatics), Heberden Coin Room*
2009. Brush and ink on *xuan* paper. Paper size: 44.8 × 34 cm

37 Beth West *Museum Assistant, Department of Western Art*
2009. Brush and ink on *xuan* paper. Paper size: 44.8 × 34 cm

38 Roz Britton-Strong *Administrator of Heberden Coin Room*
2009. Brush and ink on *xuan* paper. Paper size: 44.8 × 34 cm

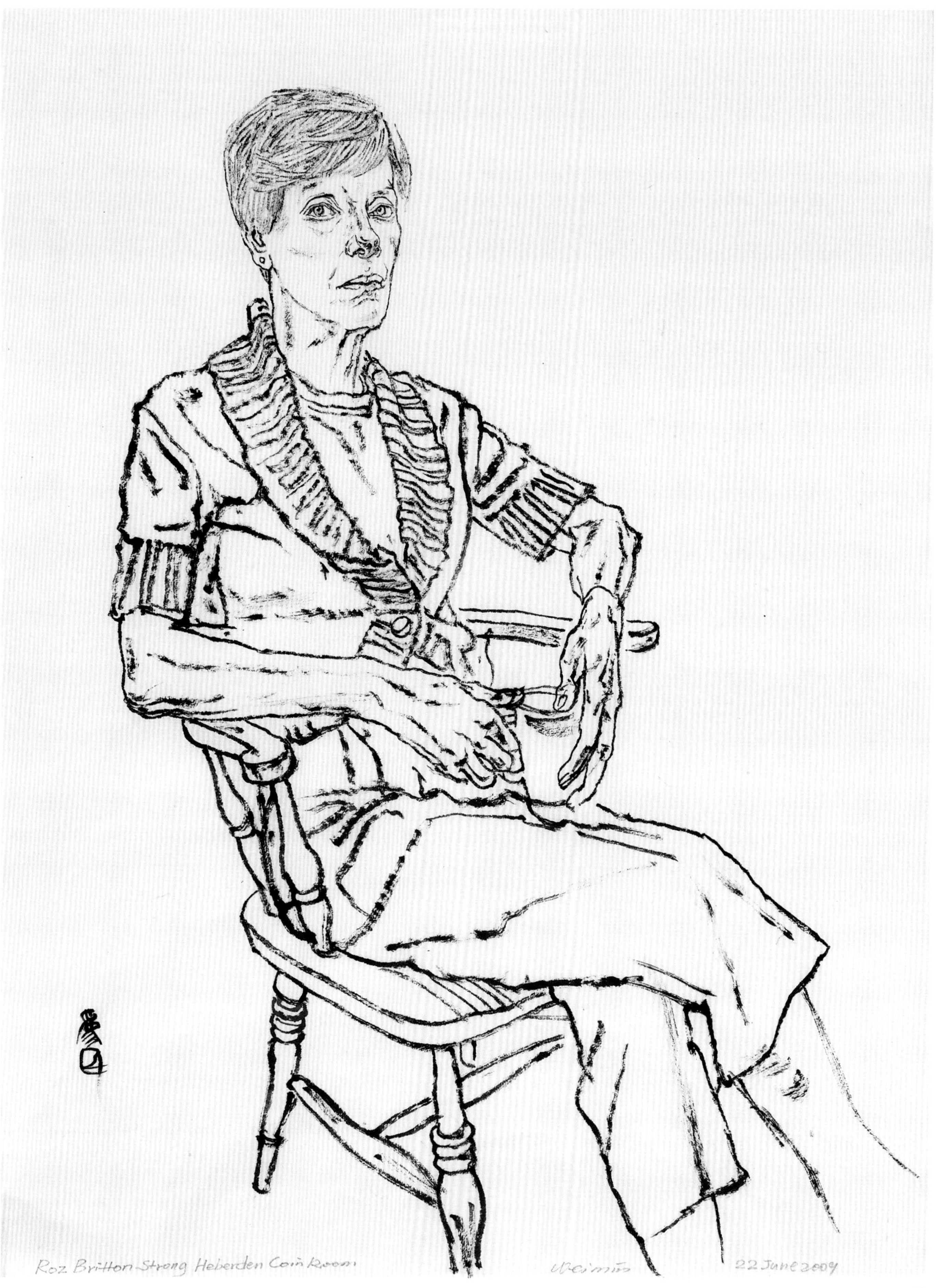

38

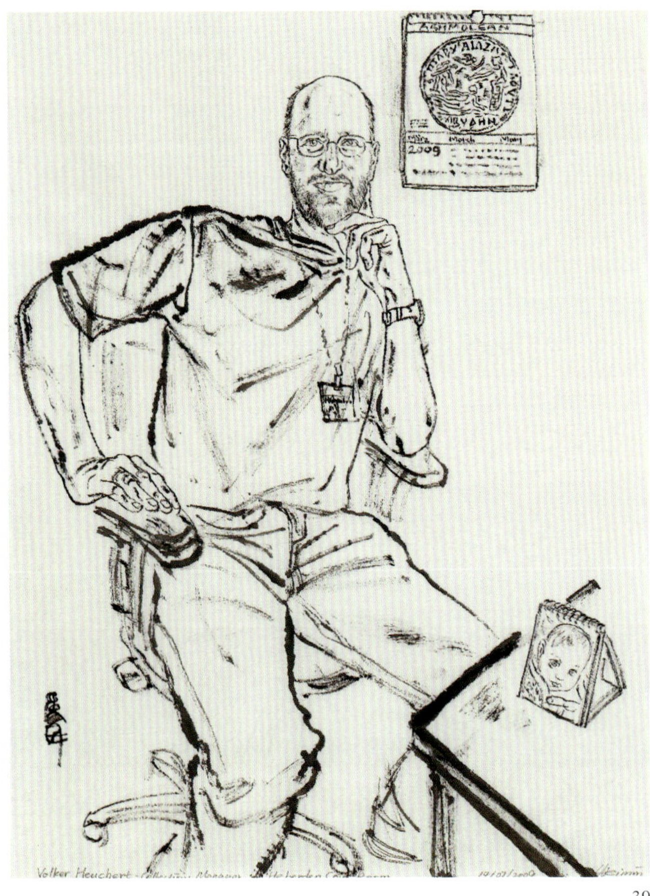

39

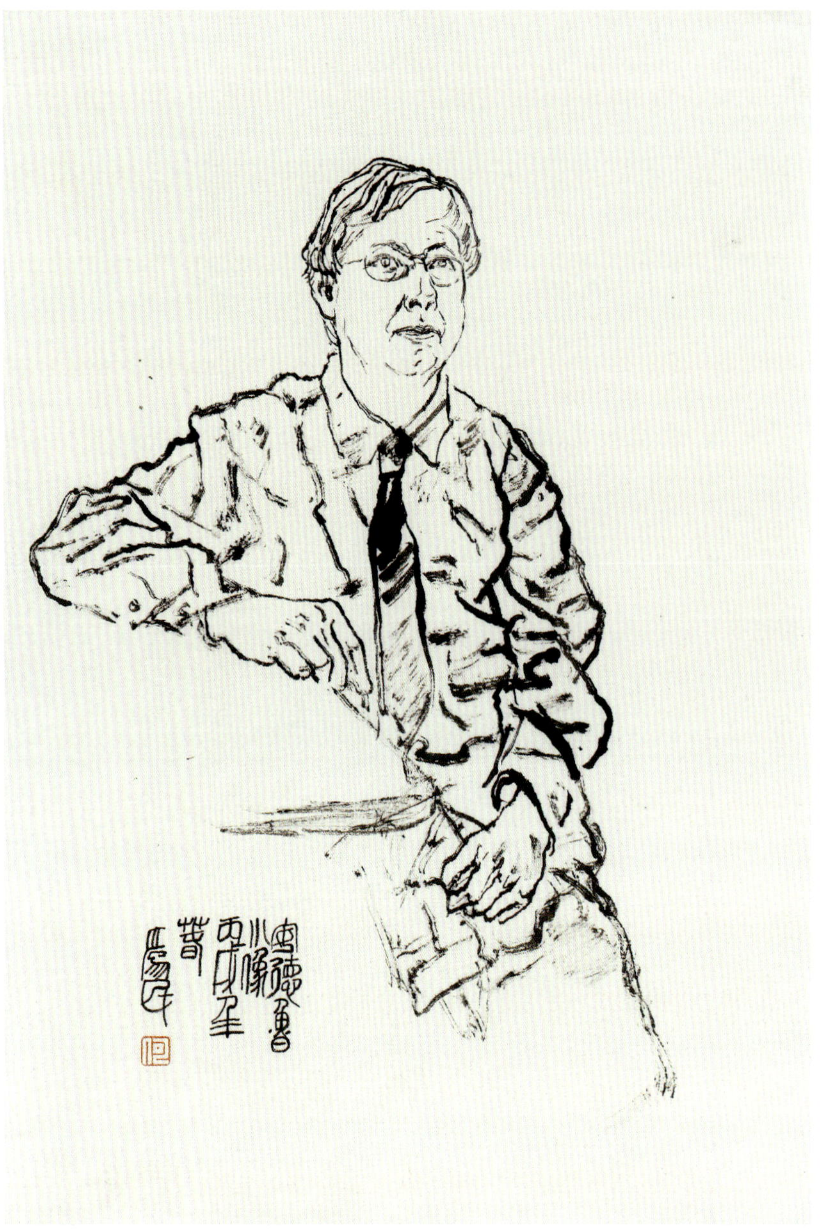

40

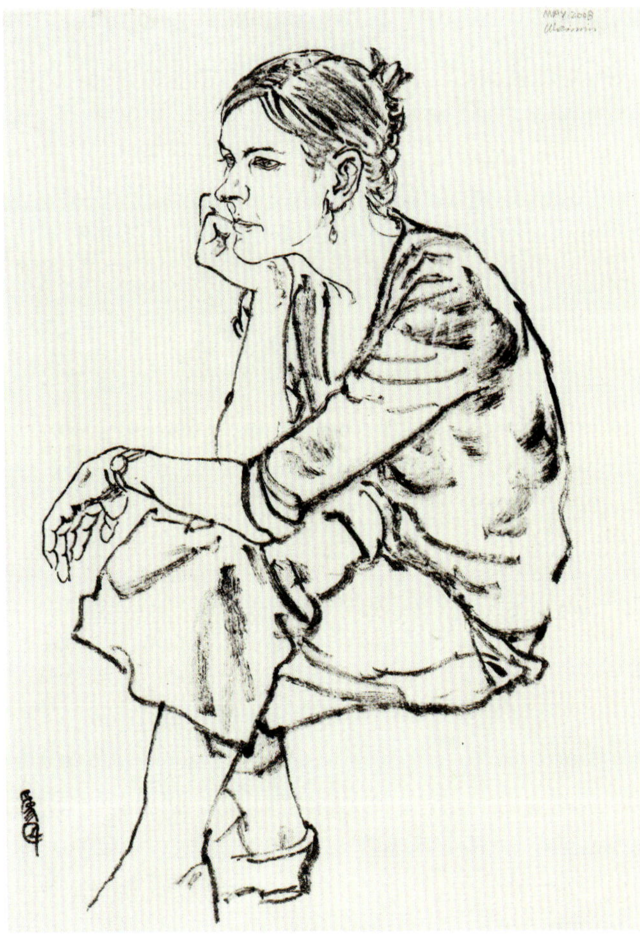

41

39 Volker Heuchert *Collections Manager, Heberden Coin Room*
2009. Brush and ink on *xuan* paper. Paper size: 44.8 × 34 cm

40 Andrew Topsfield *Keeper, Department of Eastern Art (art and archaeology of India and South East Asia)*
2006. Brush and ink on *pi* paper. Paper size: 46.1 × 31.3 cm

41 Clare Pollard *Assistant Keeper, Department of Eastern Art (Japanese art)*
2008. Brush and ink on *pi* paper. Paper size: 46.1 × 34 cm

42 Shelagh Vainker *Assistant Keeper, Department of Eastern Art (art and archaeology of China and Korea)*
2009. Brush and ink on *xuan* paper. Paper size: 44.8 × 34 cm

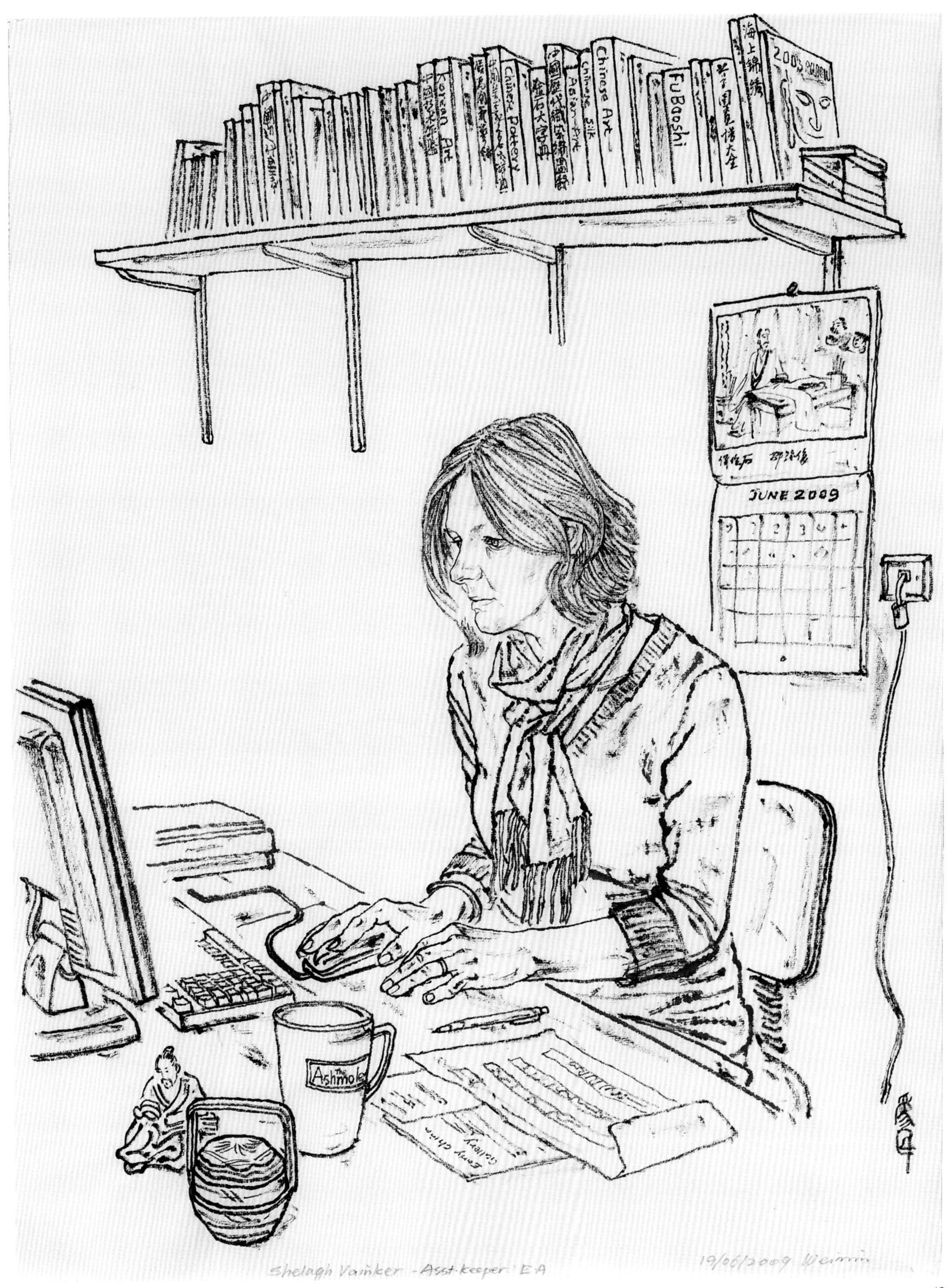

Chinese Art
FU Baoshi
Chinese Pottery
Korean Art
Asian Art
Chinese Silk
JUNE 2009
The Ashmolean
Early China Gallery
Shelagh Vainker - Asst. keeper EA
19/06/2009 Weimin

42

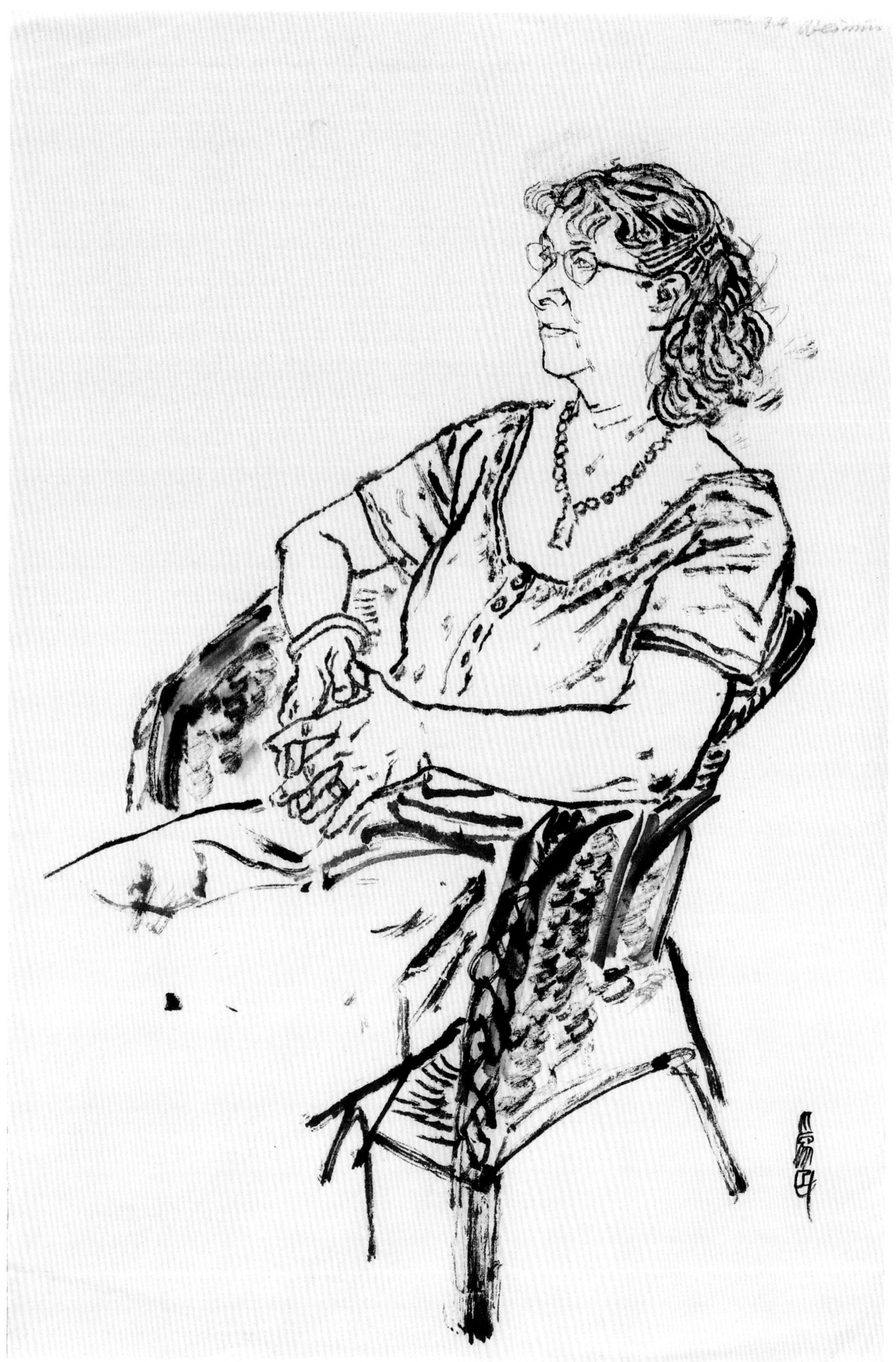

43

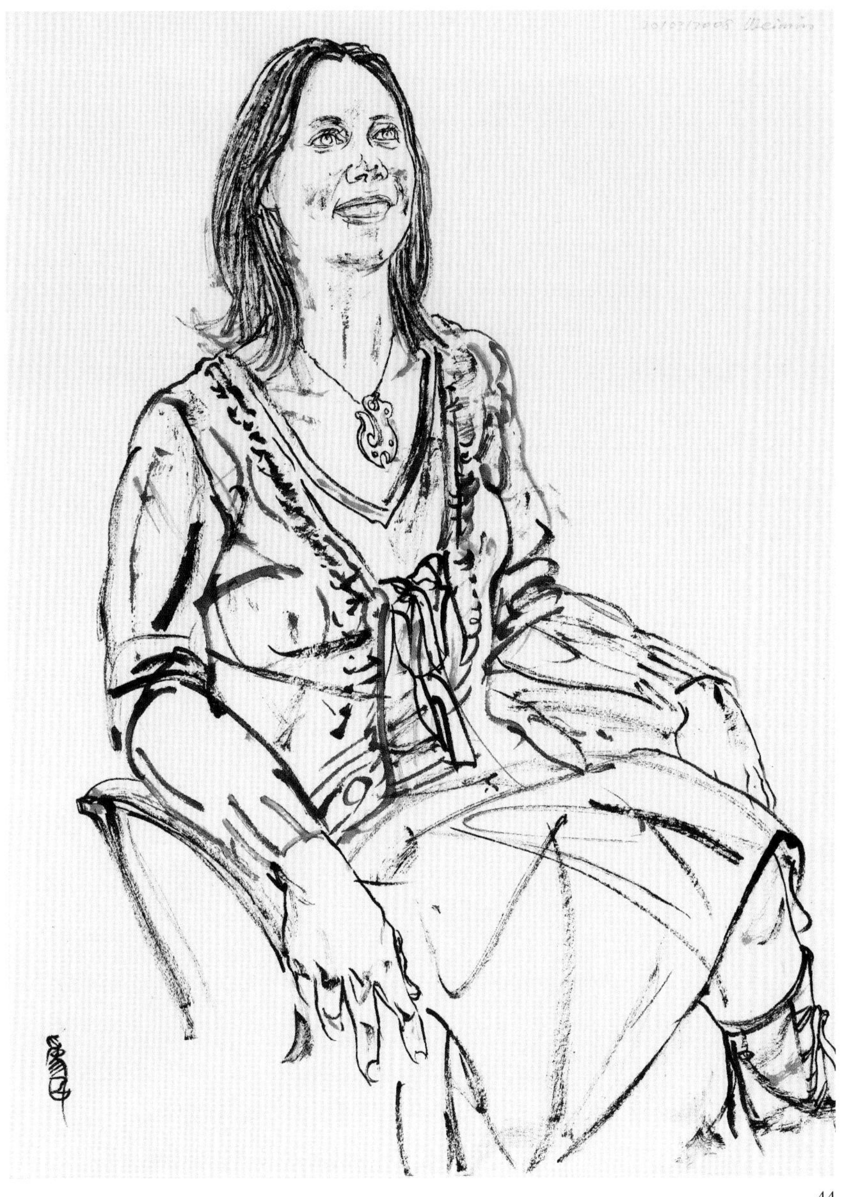

44

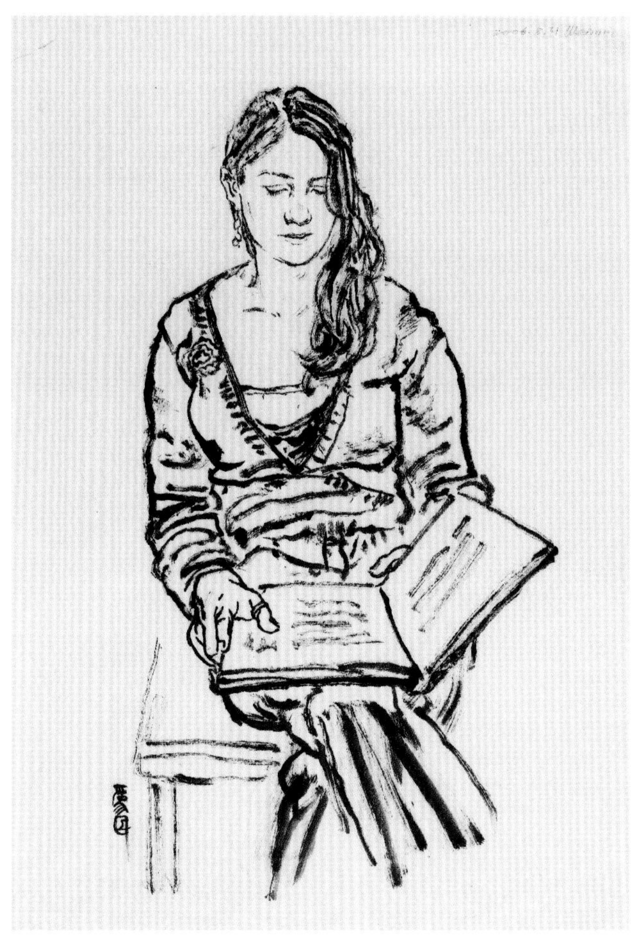

45

46

43 **Ruth Barnes** *Textile Curator, Department of Eastern Art (Textiles Gallery)*
2006. Brush and ink on *pi* paper. Paper size: 46.1 × 31.1 cm

44 **Zena McGreevy** *Documentation Officer, Department of Eastern Art*
2009. Brush and ink on *xuan* paper. Paper size: 44.8 × 34 cm

45 **Aimée Payton** *Administrator, Department of Eastern Art*
2006. Brush and ink on *pi* paper. Paper size: 46.1 × 33.5 cm

46 **Teresa Fitzherbert** *Curator, Creswell Archive, Department of Eastern Art*
2008. Brush and ink on *xuan* paper. Paper size: 44.8 × 34 cm

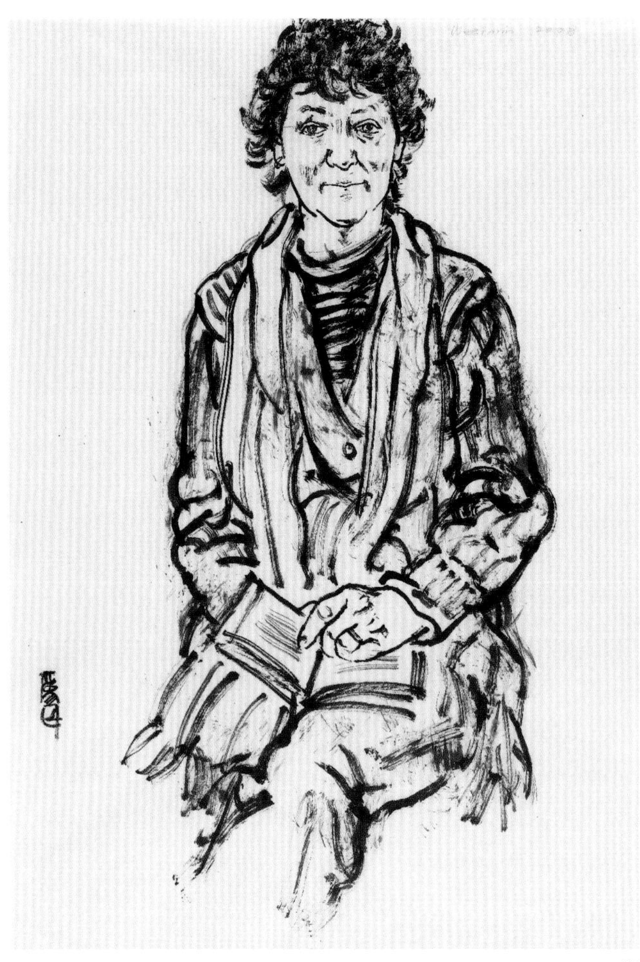

47

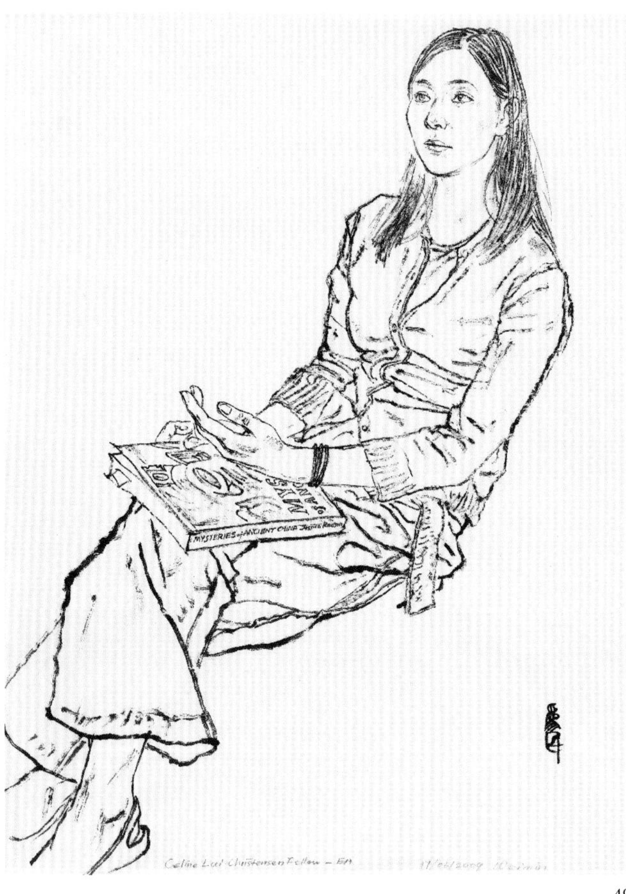

49

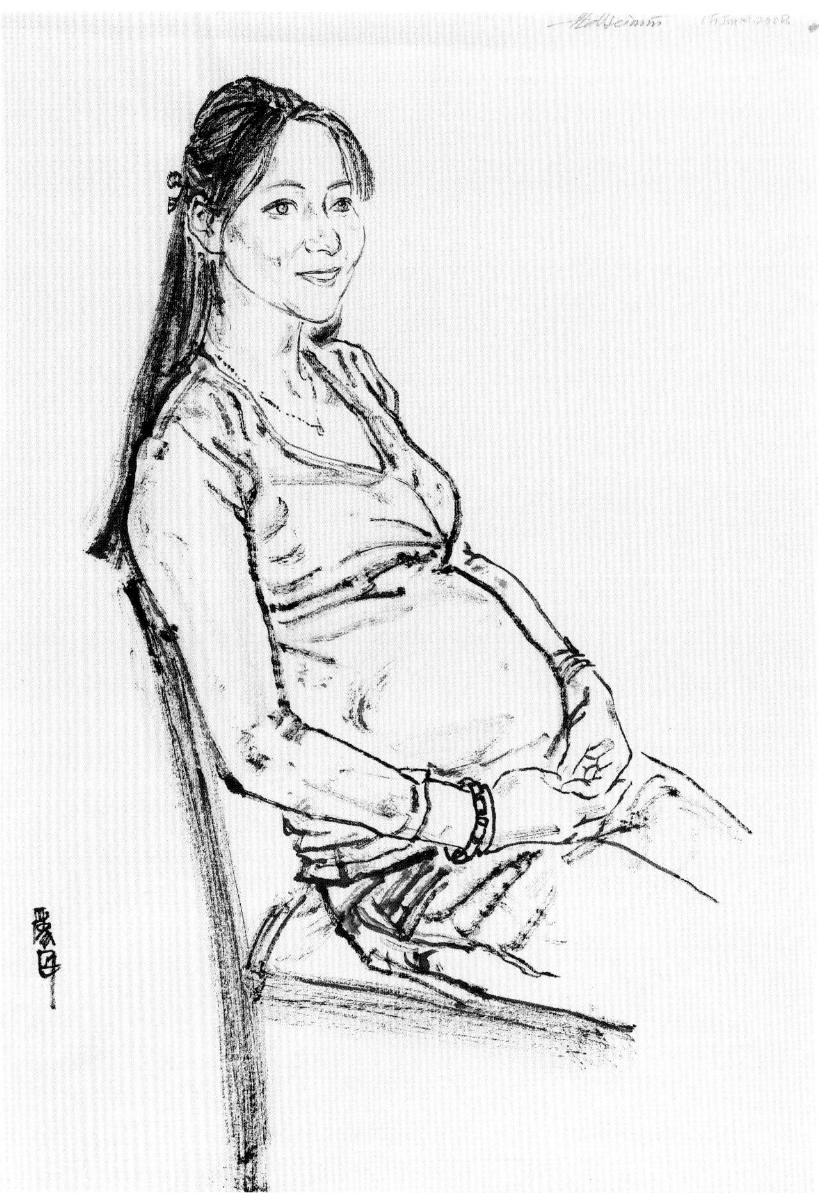

48

47 **Joyce Seaman** *Research Associate, Department of Eastern Art (art of Japan)*
2008. Brush and ink on *pi* paper. Paper size: 46.1 × 32.7 cm

48 **Mitsuko Watanabe** *Research Assistant, Department of Eastern Art (art of Japan)*
2008. Brush and ink on *xuan* paper. Paper size: 47.7 × 35.5 cm

49 **Celine Lai** *Christensen Fellow of Chinese Painting, Department of Eastern Art*
2009. Brush and ink on *xuan* paper. Paper size: 44.8 × 34 cm

50 **Paul Groves** *Project Manager, Yousef Jameel Online Centre, Department of Eastern Art*
2009. Brush and ink on *xuan* paper. Paper size: 44.8 × 34 cm

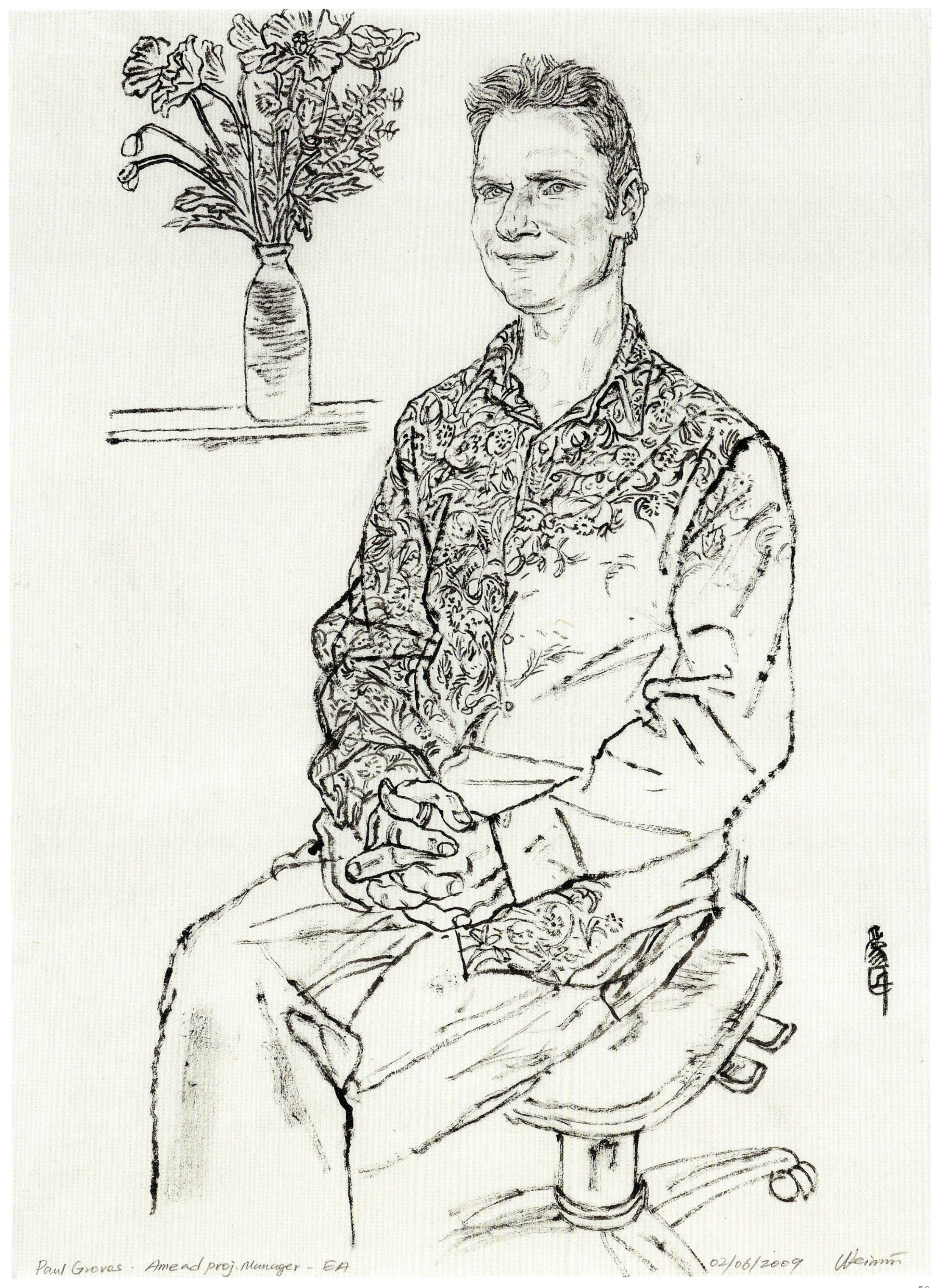

50

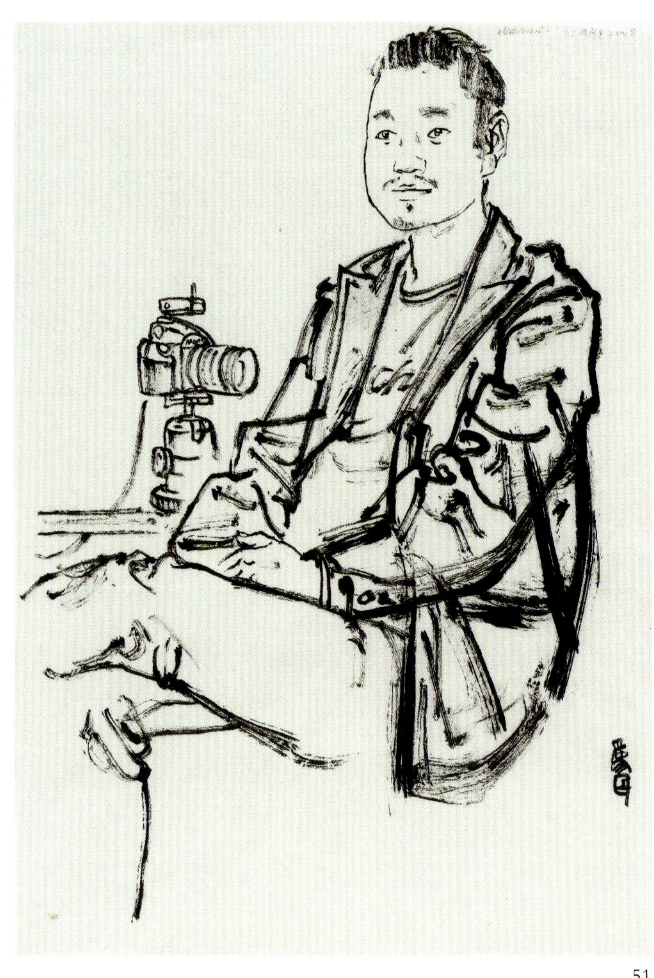

51

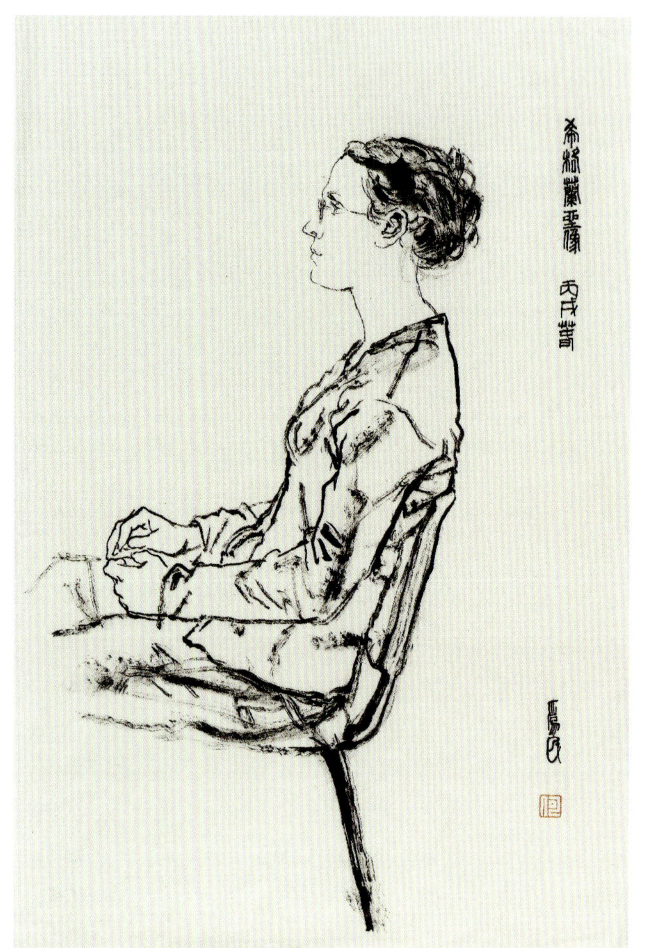

52

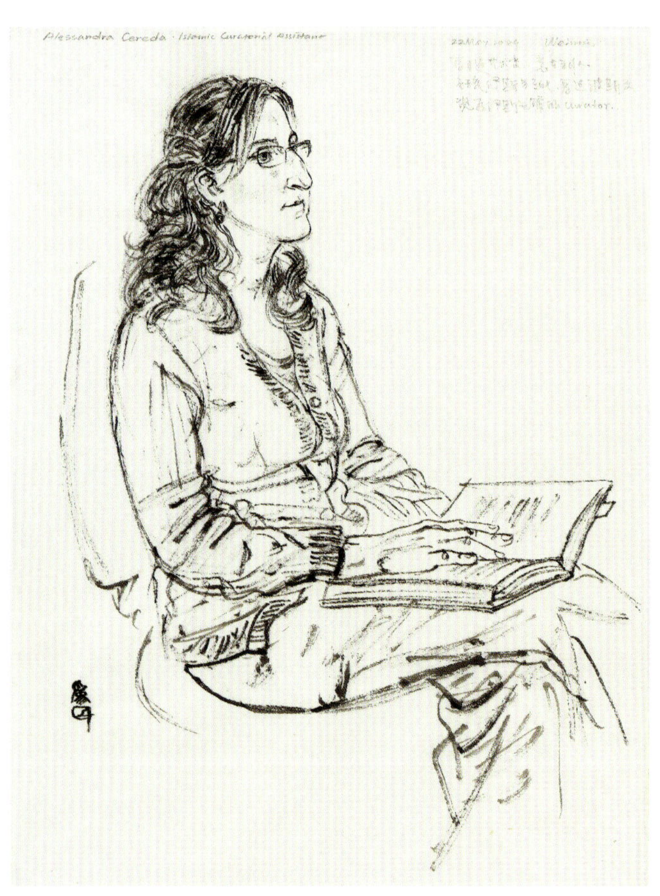

Alessandra Cereda · Islamic Curatorial Assistant

29/05/2009

53

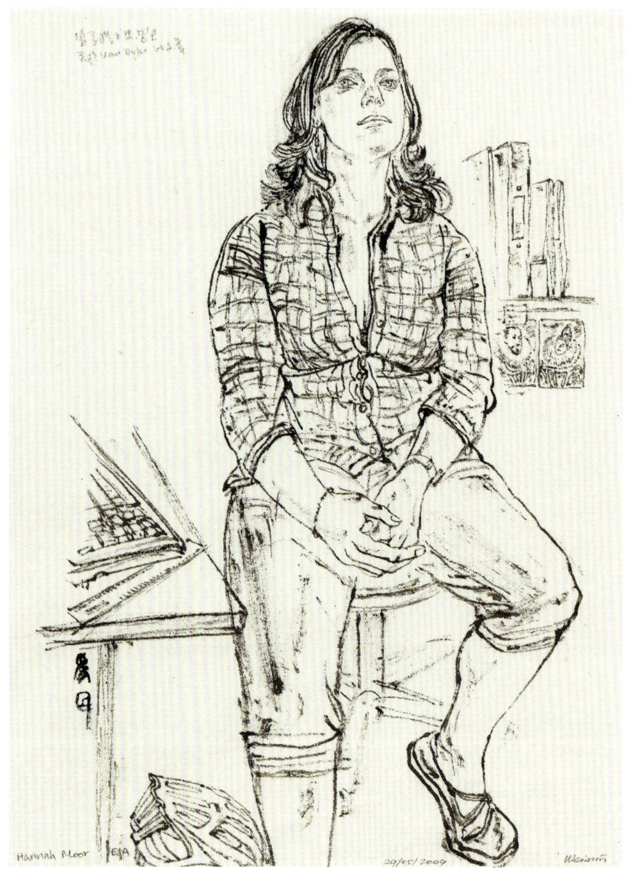

54

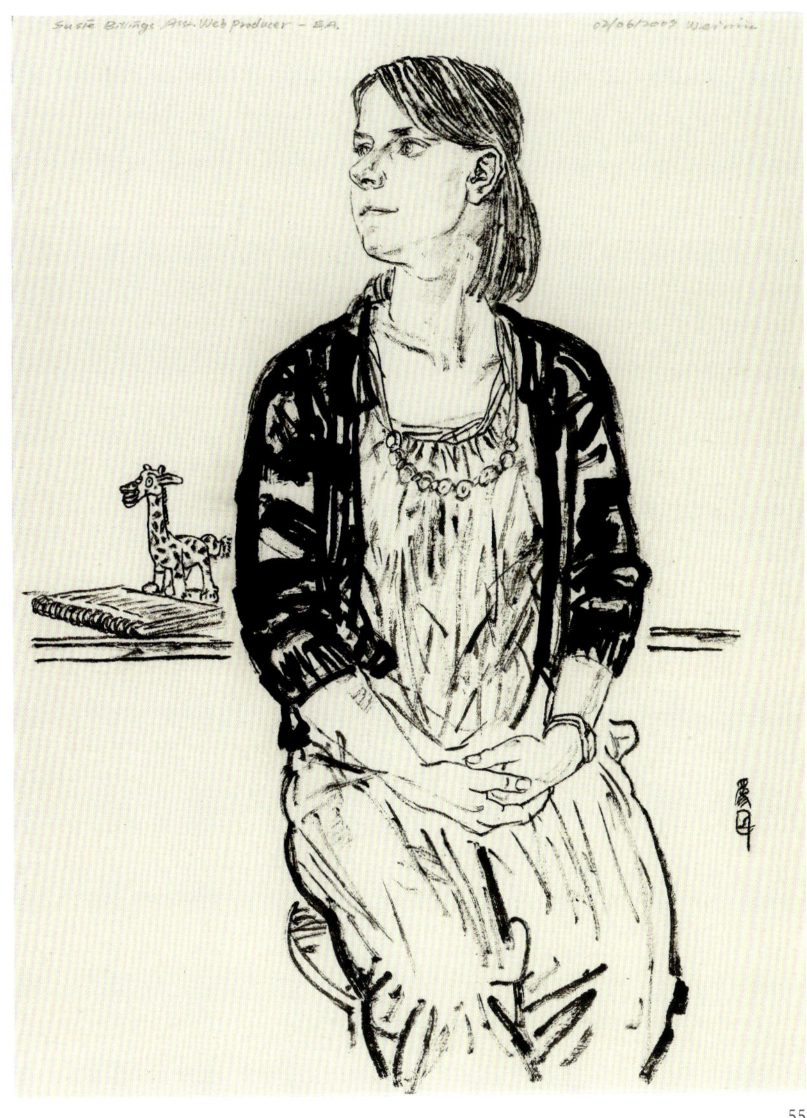

55

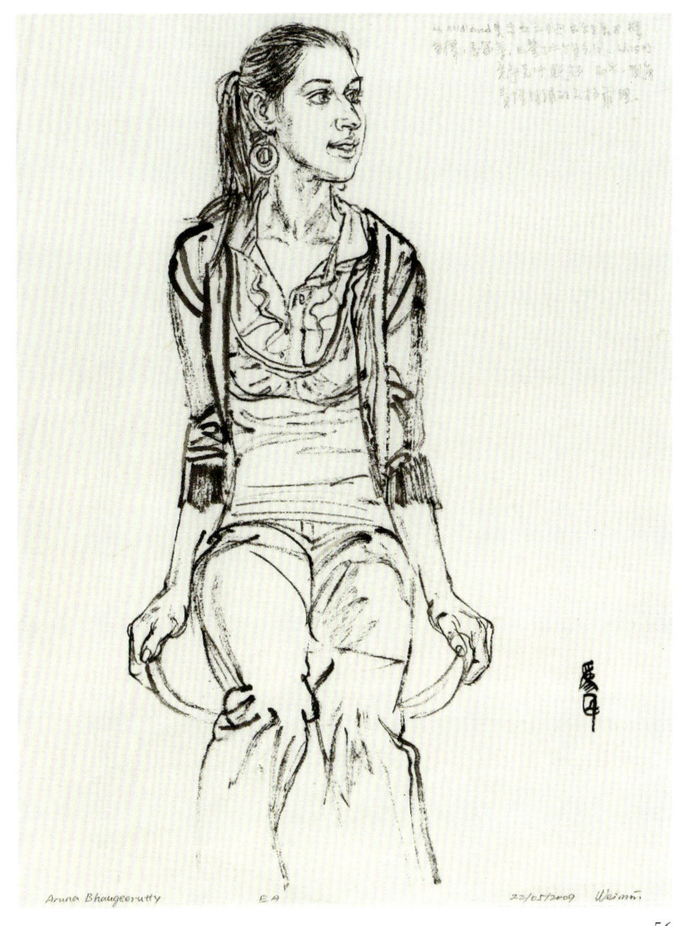

56

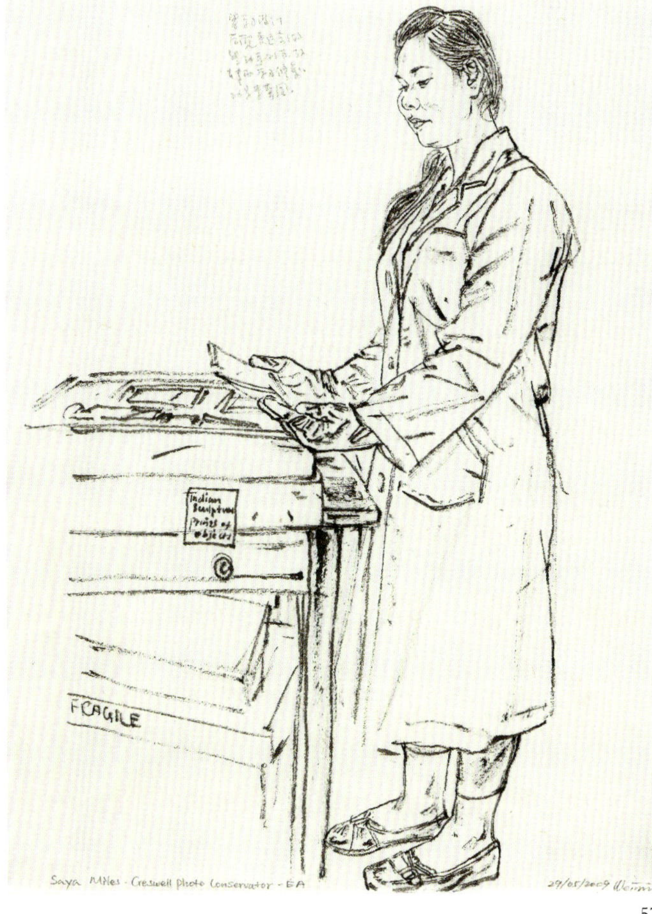

57

51 **Jo-Hung Tang** *Studio Photographer, Yousef Jameel Online Centre, Department of Eastern Art*
2008. Brush and ink on *pi* paper. Paper size: 46.1 × 33.3 cm

52 **Sigolene Loizeau** *Collections Coordinator, Yousef Jameel Online Centre, Department of Eastern Art*
2006. Brush and ink on *pi* paper. Paper size: 46.1 × 31.2 cm

53 **Alessandra Cereda** *Curatorial Assistant in Islamic Art, Department of Eastern Art*
2009. Brush and ink on *xuan* paper. Paper size: 44.8 × 34 cm

54 **Hannah Moor** *Project Documentation Assistant, Yousef Jameel Online Centre, Department of Eastern Art*
2009. Brush and ink on *xuan* paper. Paper size: 44.8 × 34 cm

55 **Susie Billings** *Content Editor, Yousef Jameel Online Centre, Department of Eastern Art*
2009. Brush and ink on *xuan* paper. Paper size: 44.8 × 34 cm

56 **Aruna Bhaugeerutty** *Project Documentation Assistant, Yousef Jameel Online Centre, Department of Eastern Art*
2009. Brush and ink on *xuan* paper. Paper size: 44.8 × 34 cm

57 **Saya Miles** *Photographic Conservator, Department of Eastern Art*
2009. Brush and ink on *xuan* paper. Paper size: 44.8 × 34 cm

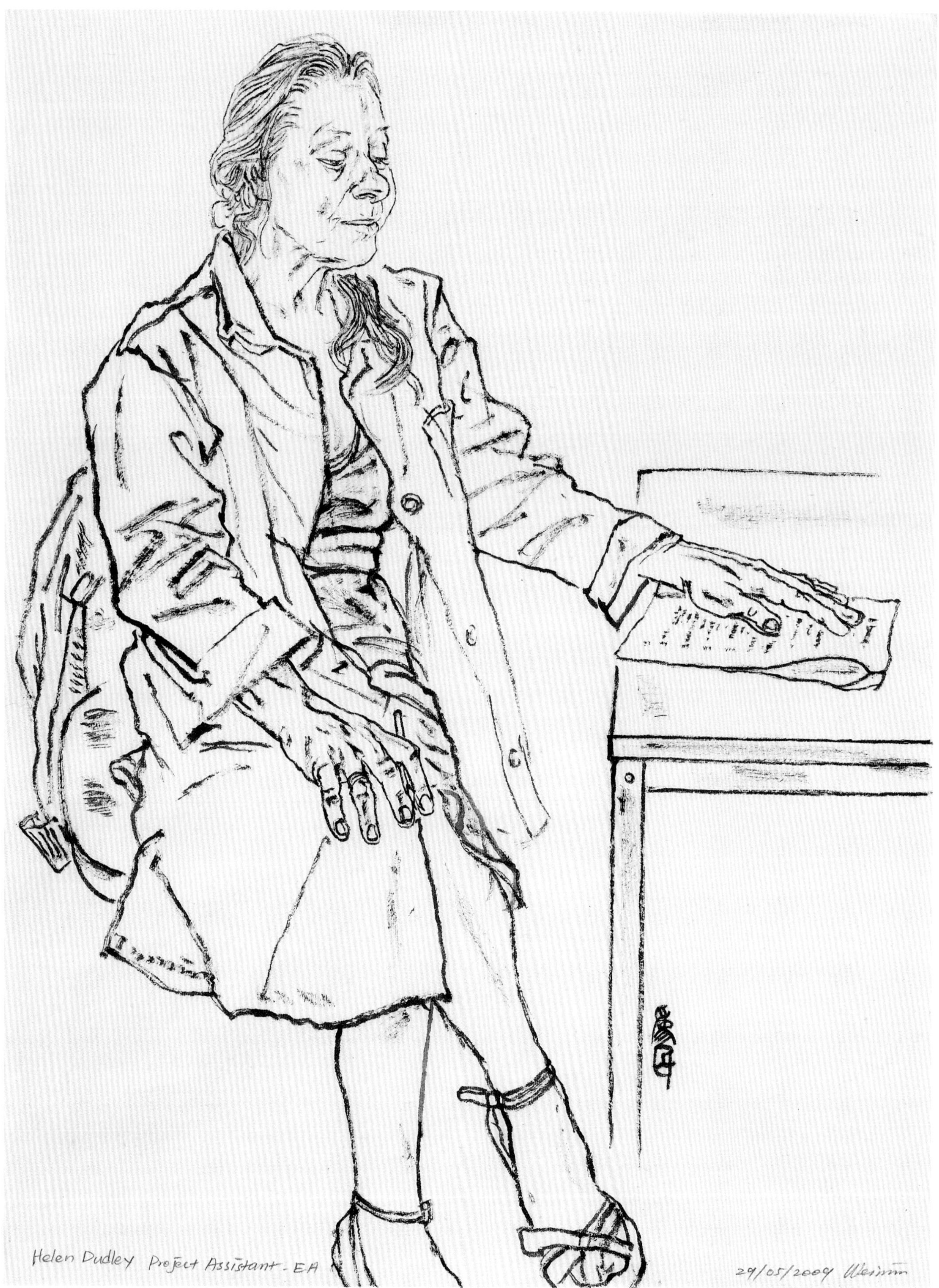

58

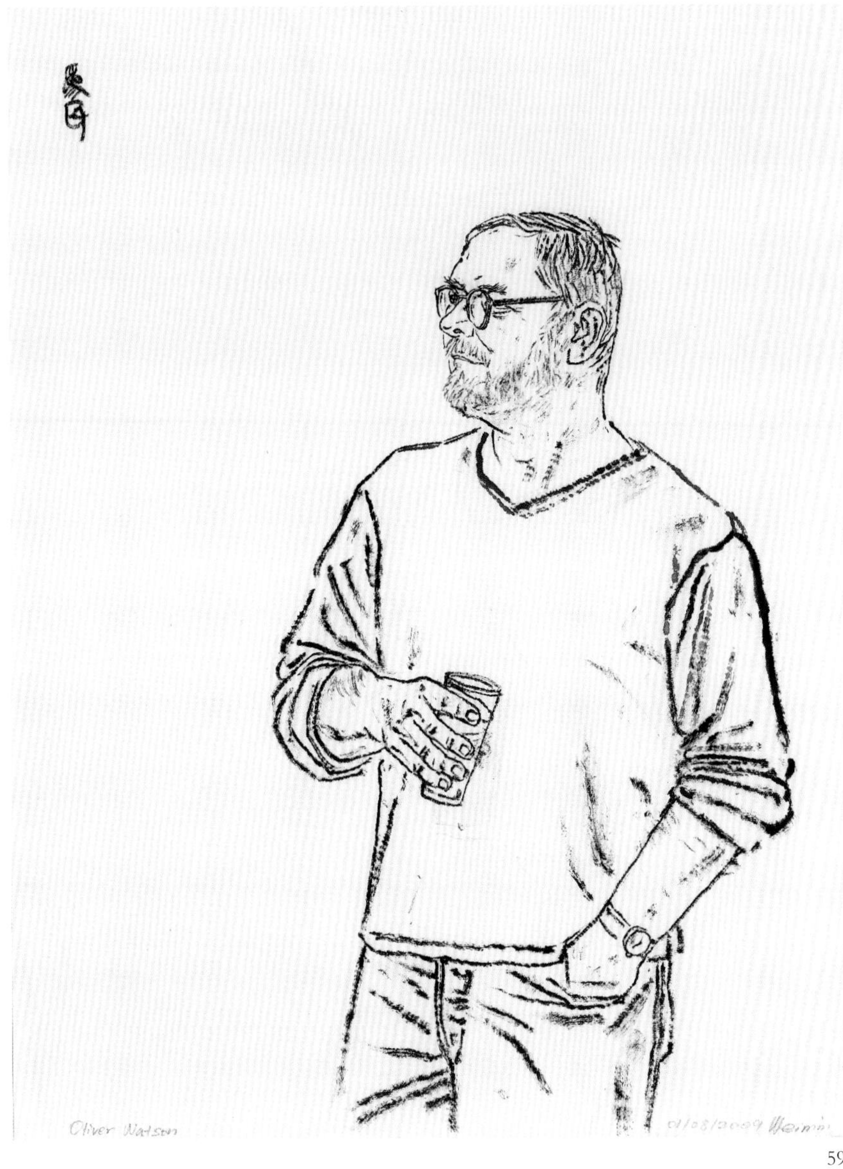
59

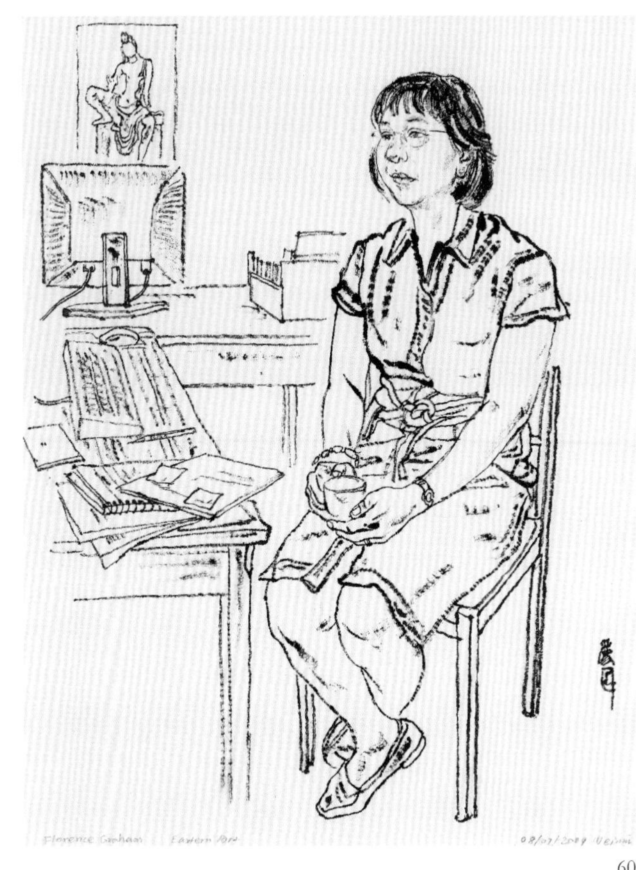
60

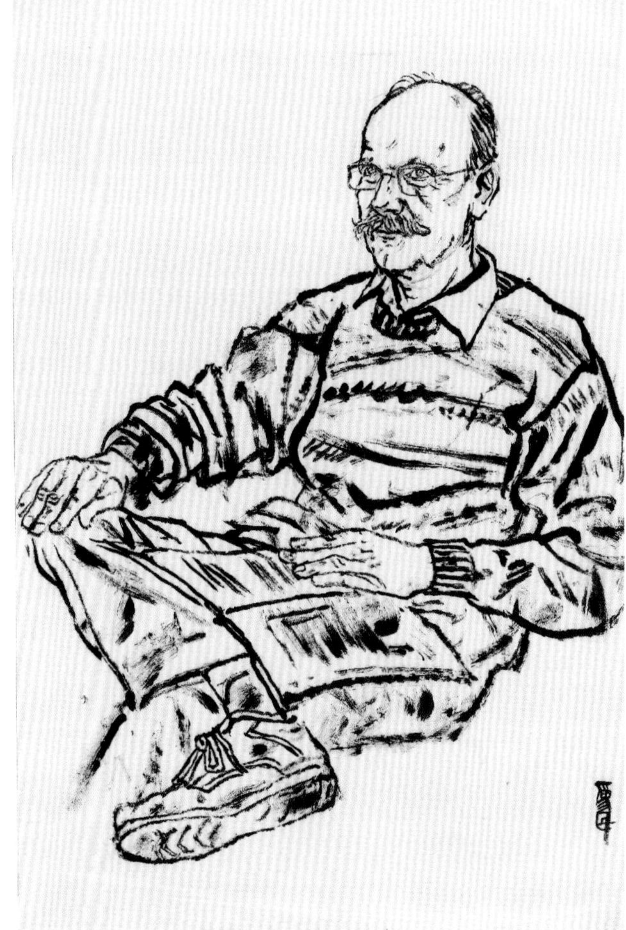
61

58 **Helen Dudley** *Project Assistant, Creswell Archive, Department of Eastern Art*
2009. Brush and ink on *xuan* paper. Paper size: 44.8 × 34 cm

59 **Oliver Watson** *Former Keeper of Department of Eastern Art*
2009. Brush and ink on *xuan* paper. Paper size: 44.8 × 34 cm

60 **Florence Graham** *Assistant Administrator, Department of Eastern Art*
2009. Brush and ink on *xuan* paper. Paper size: 46.1 × 30.3 cm

61 **John** *Former Museum staff*
2006. Brush and ink on *pi* paper. Paper size: 46.1 × 30.3 cm

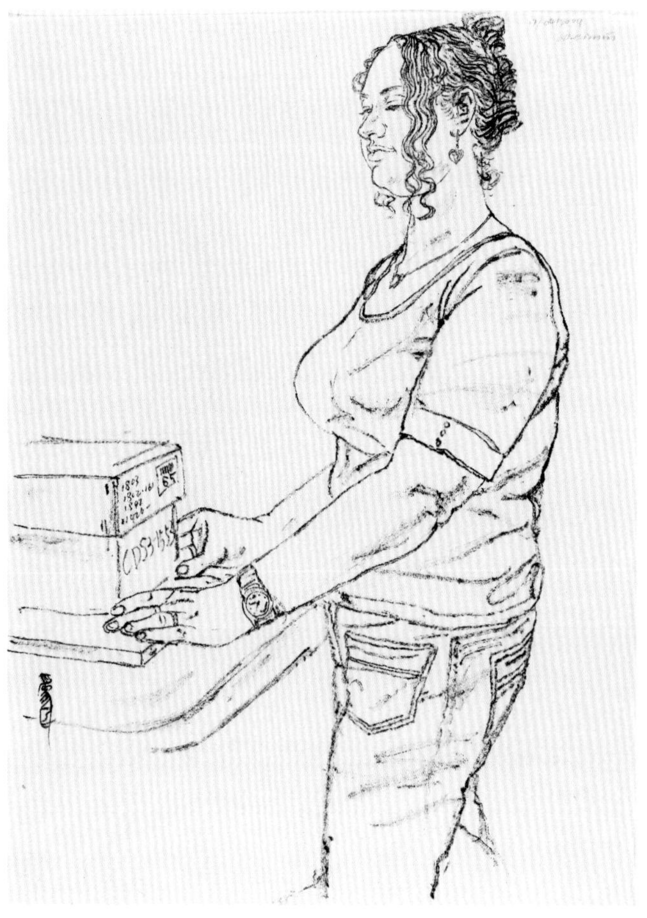

62

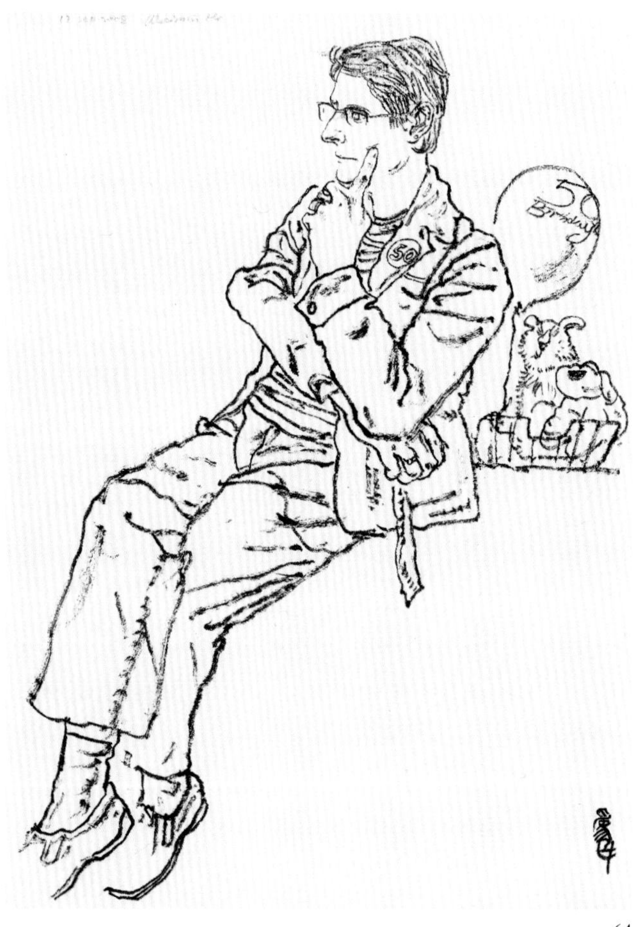

64

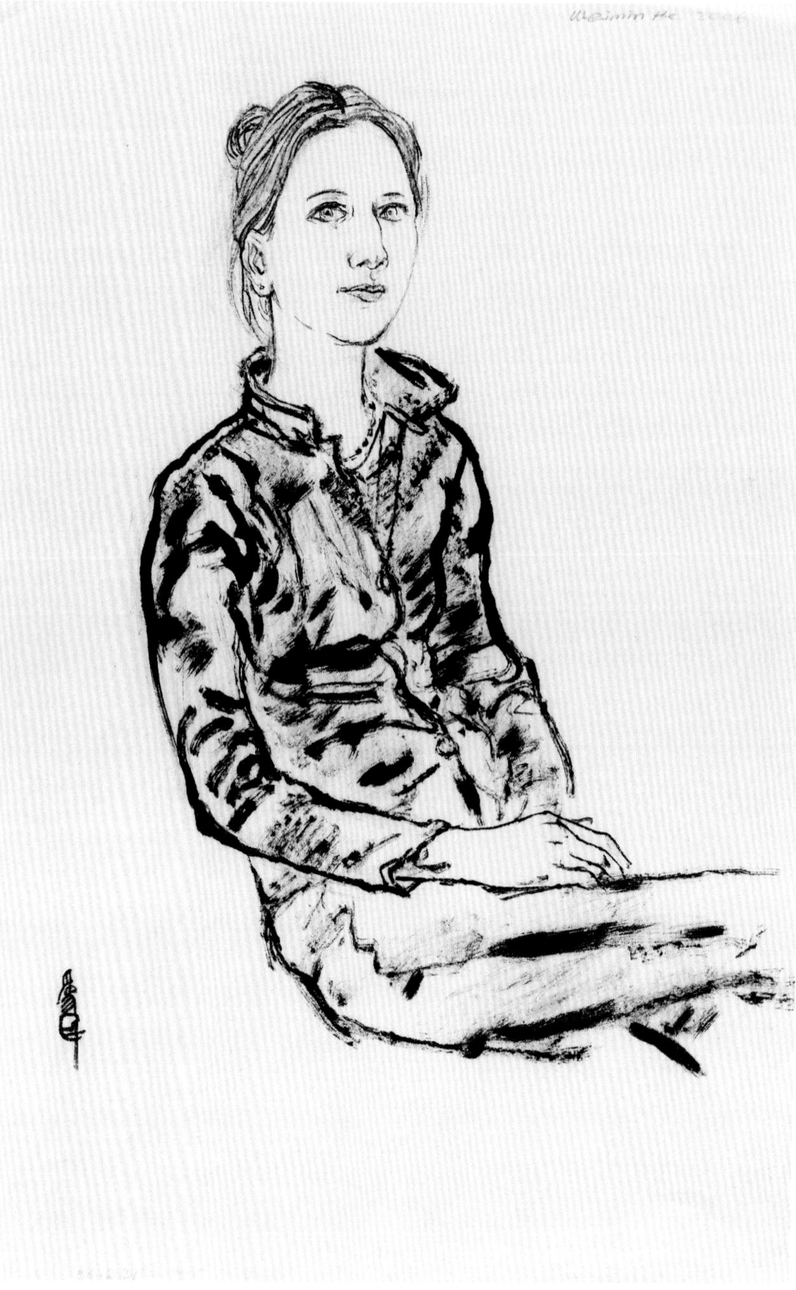

63

62 Sarah Debenham *Team Leader, Retrieval Team, Ashmolean Development Project*
2009. Brush and ink on *xuan* paper. Paper size: 44.8 × 34 cm

63 Ann Katrin *Former Museum staff*
2006. Brush and ink on *pi* paper. Paper size: 46.1 × 30 cm

64 Helen Cooper *Accounts Assistant, Finance Department*
2008. Brush and ink on *xuan* paper. Paper size: 44.8 × 34 cm

65 Claudia Van Deventer *Management Accountant, Finance Department*
2008. Brush and ink on *xuan* paper. Paper size: 44.8 × 34 cm

66 Jonathan Moffett *Head of ICT Department*
2009. Brush and ink on *xuan* paper. Paper size: 44.8 × 34 cm

67 Radka Mecheri *Finance Officer, Finance Department*
2008. Brush and ink on *xuan* paper. Paper size: 44.8 × 34 cm

68 Alan Russell *ICTSO (Apps.) ICT Department*
2009. Brush and ink on *xuan* paper. Paper size: 44.8 × 34 cm

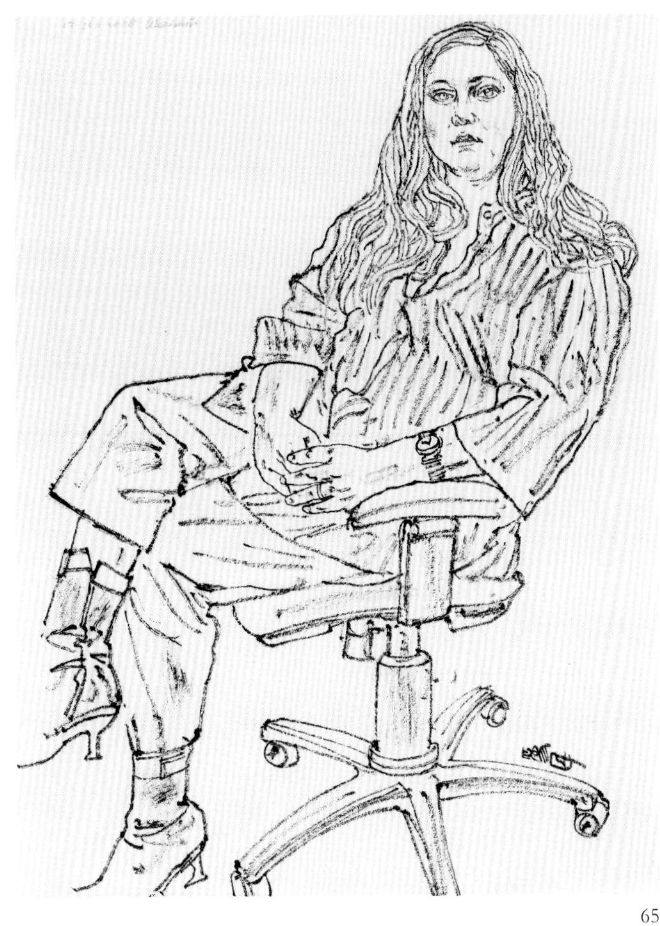

65

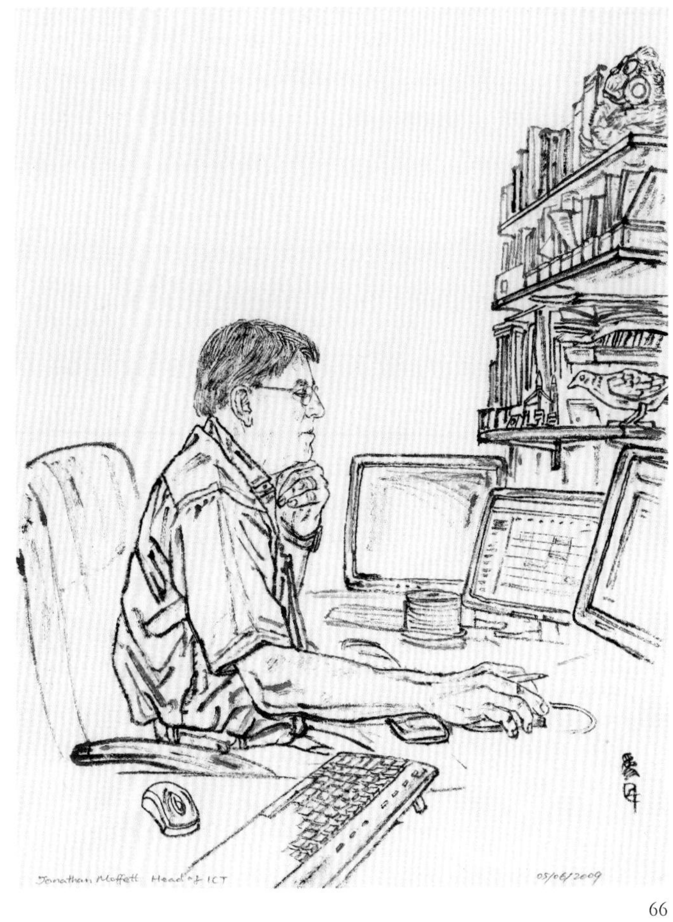

66

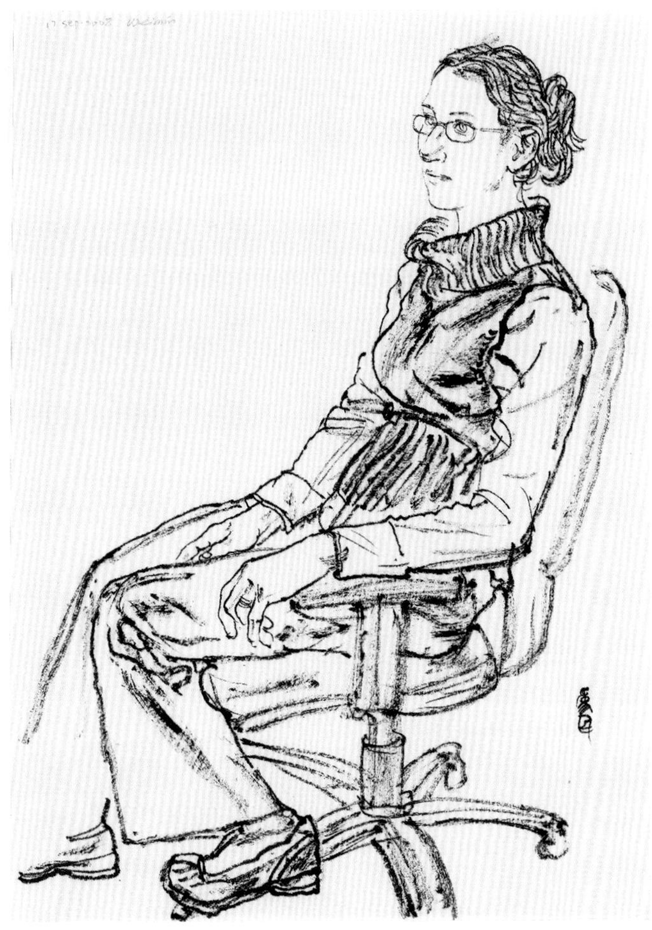

67

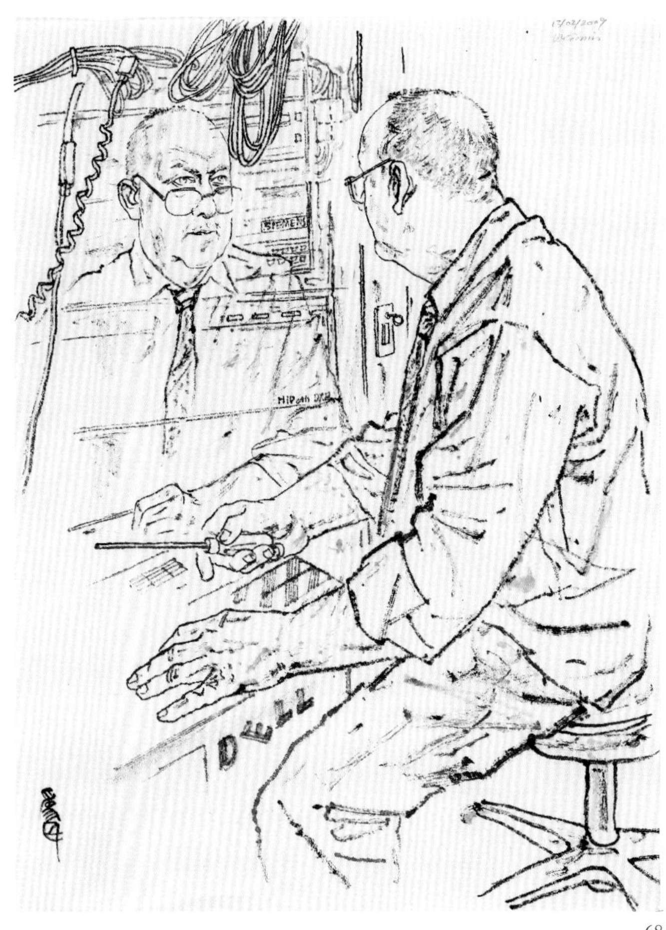

68

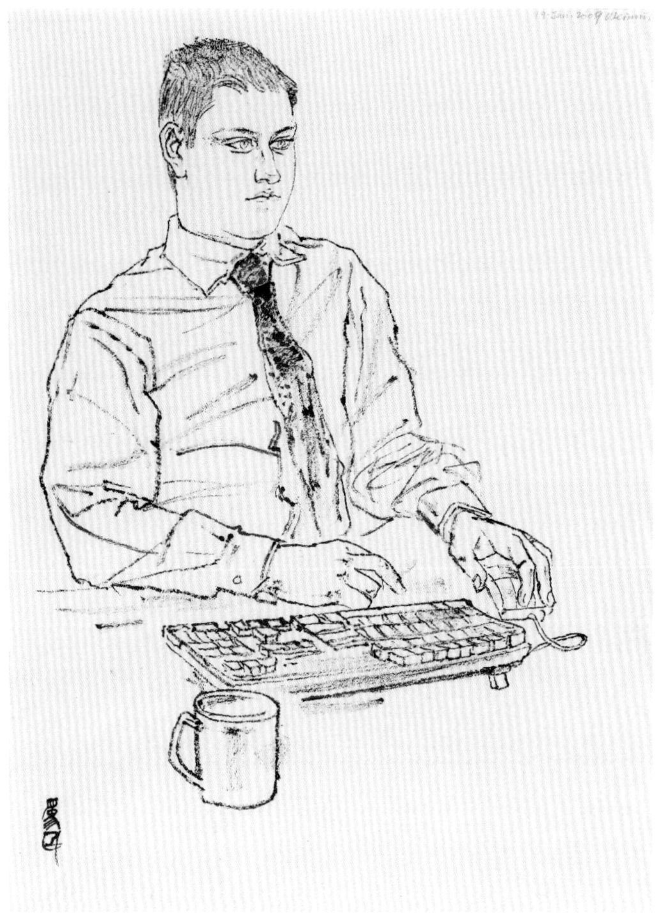

69

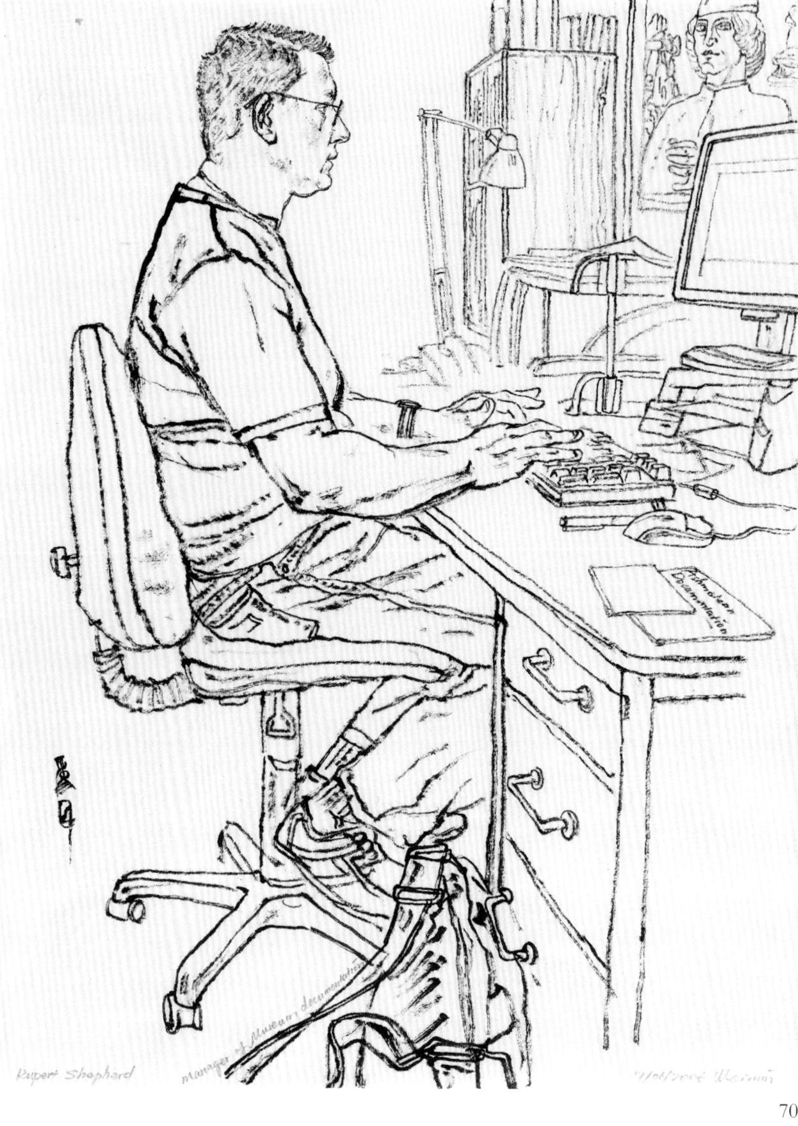

70

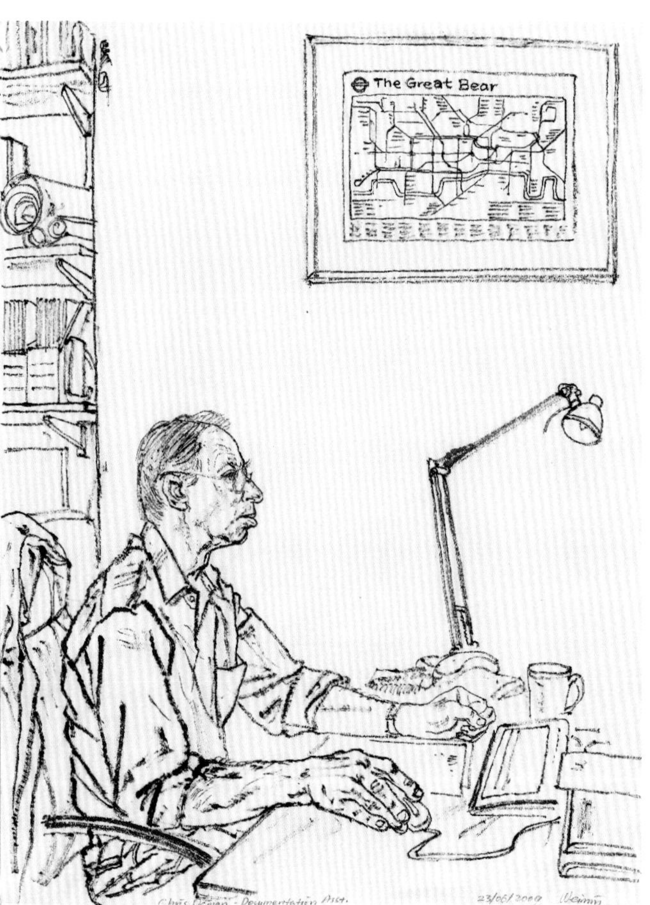

71

69 **Ian** *Former Museum staff*
2009. Brush and ink on *xuan* paper. Paper size: 44.8 × 34 cm

70 **Rupert Shepherd** *Manager of Museum Documentation, Documentation Department*
2009. Brush and ink on *xuan* paper. Paper size: 44.8 × 34 cm

71 **Chris Osman** *Documentation Assistant, Documentation Department*
2009. Brush and ink on *xuan* paper. Paper size: 44.8 × 34 cm

72 **Chris Powell** *ICTSO (Digital), ICT Department*
2009. Brush and ink on *xuan* paper. Paper size: 44.8 × 34 cm

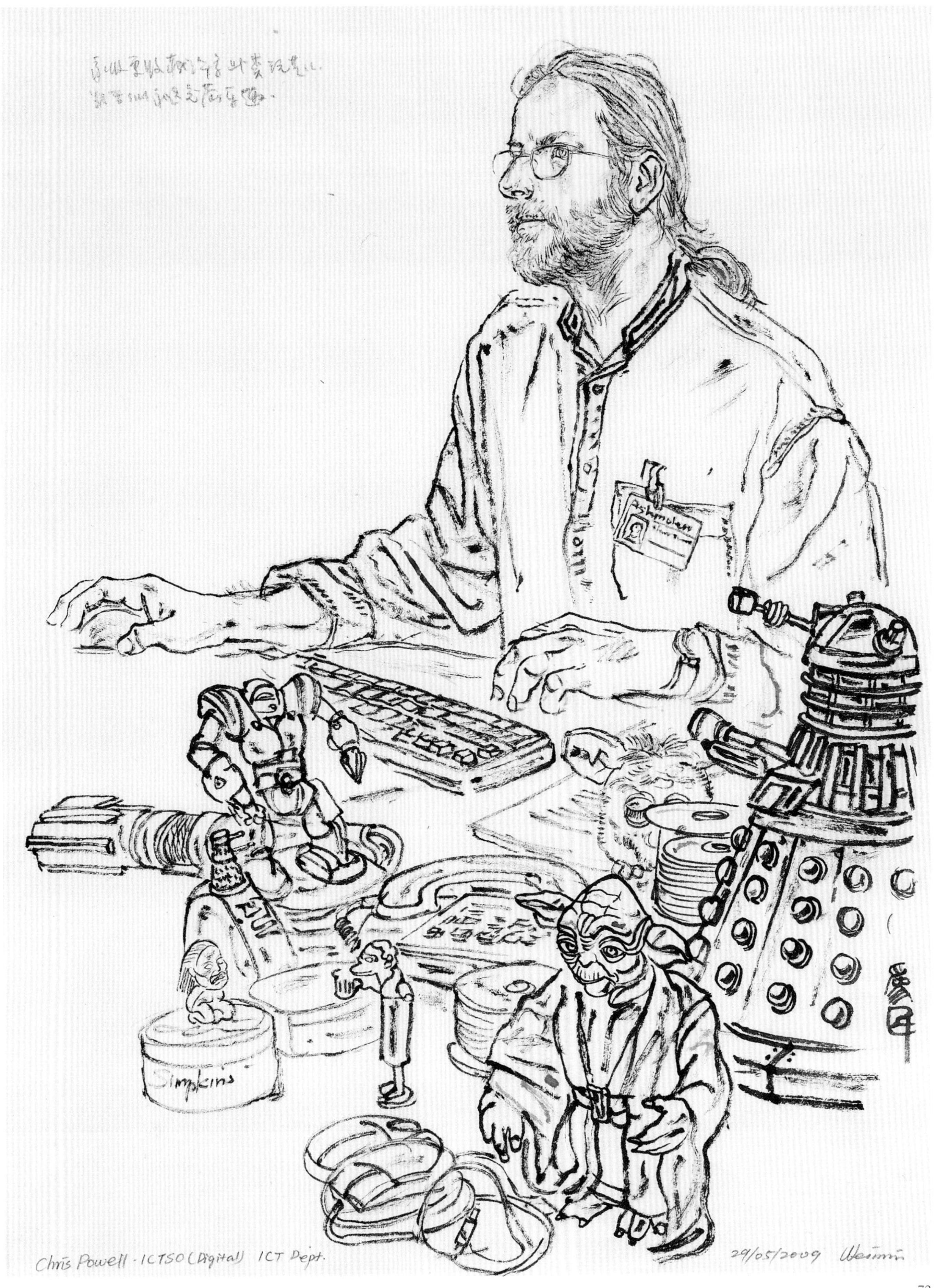

72

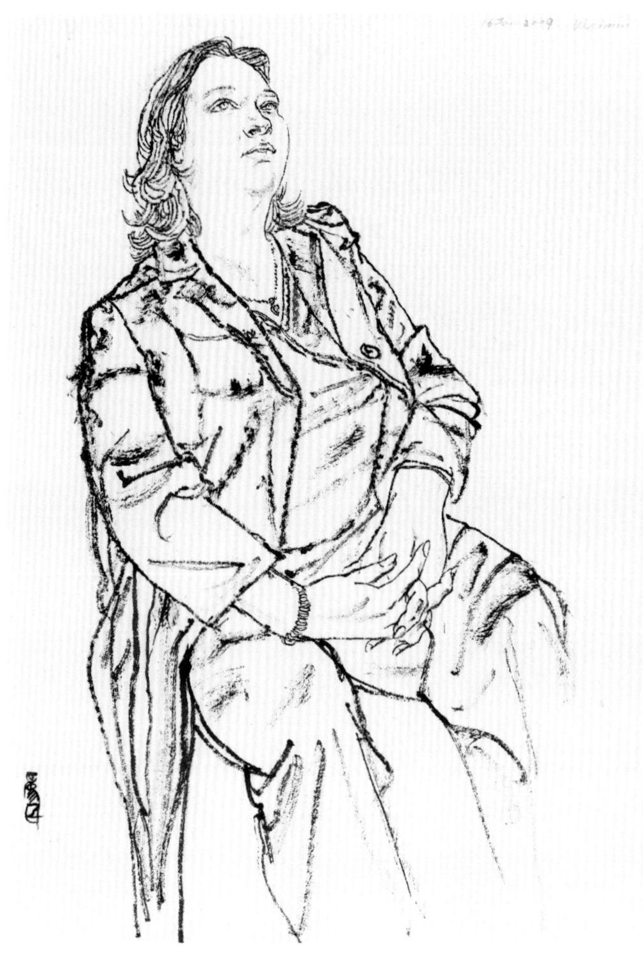

73

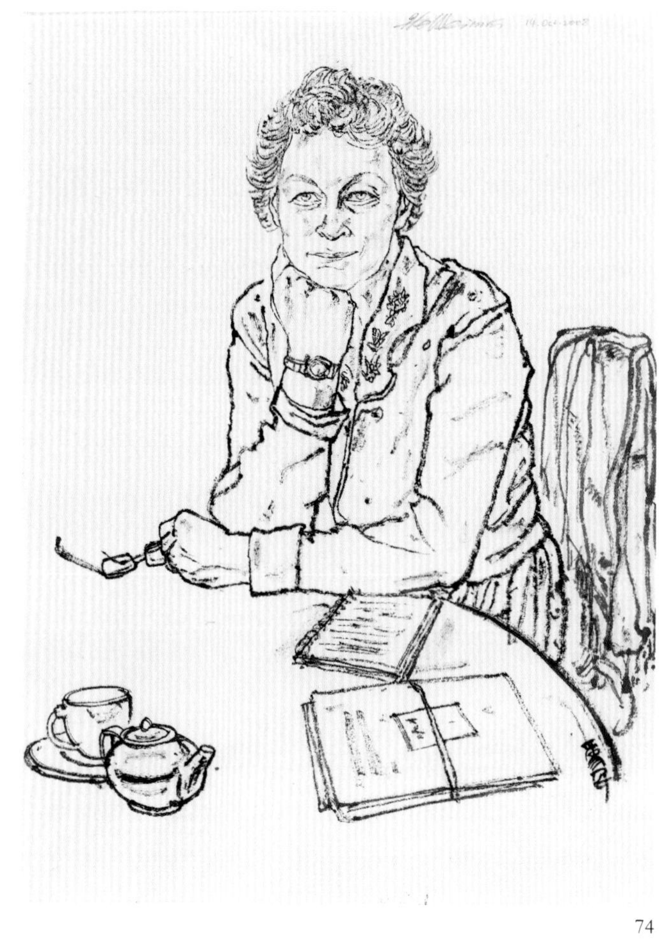

74

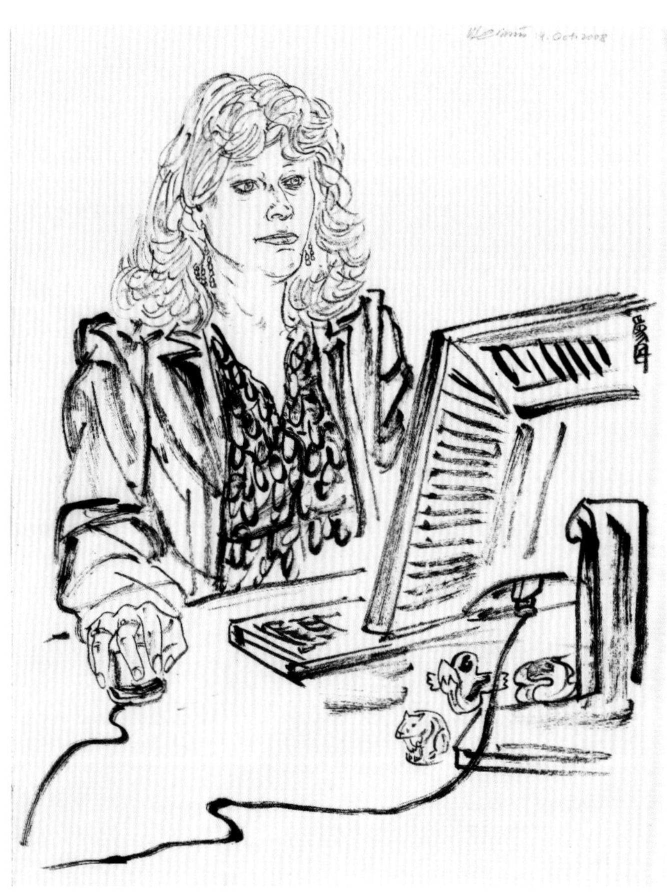

75

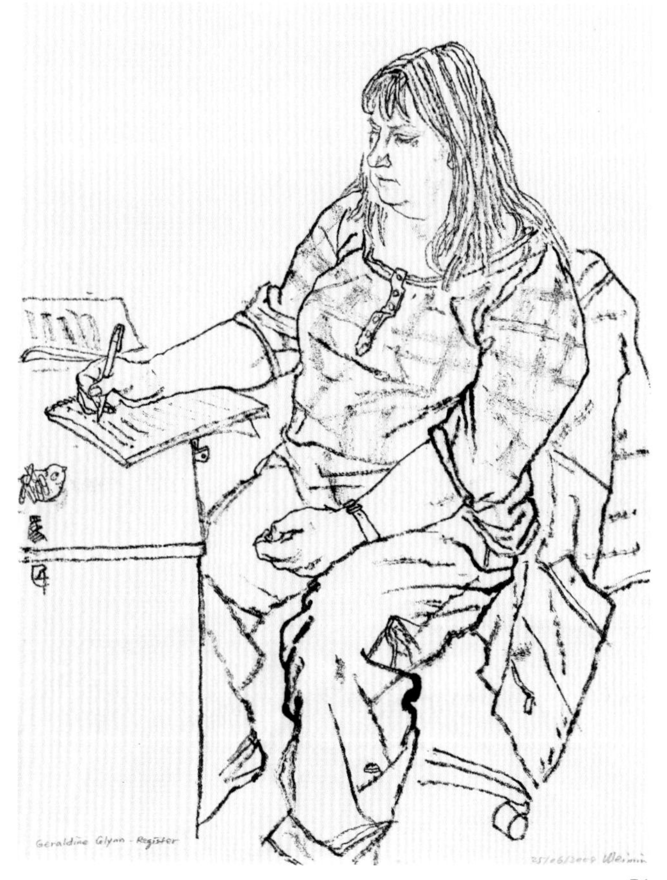

76

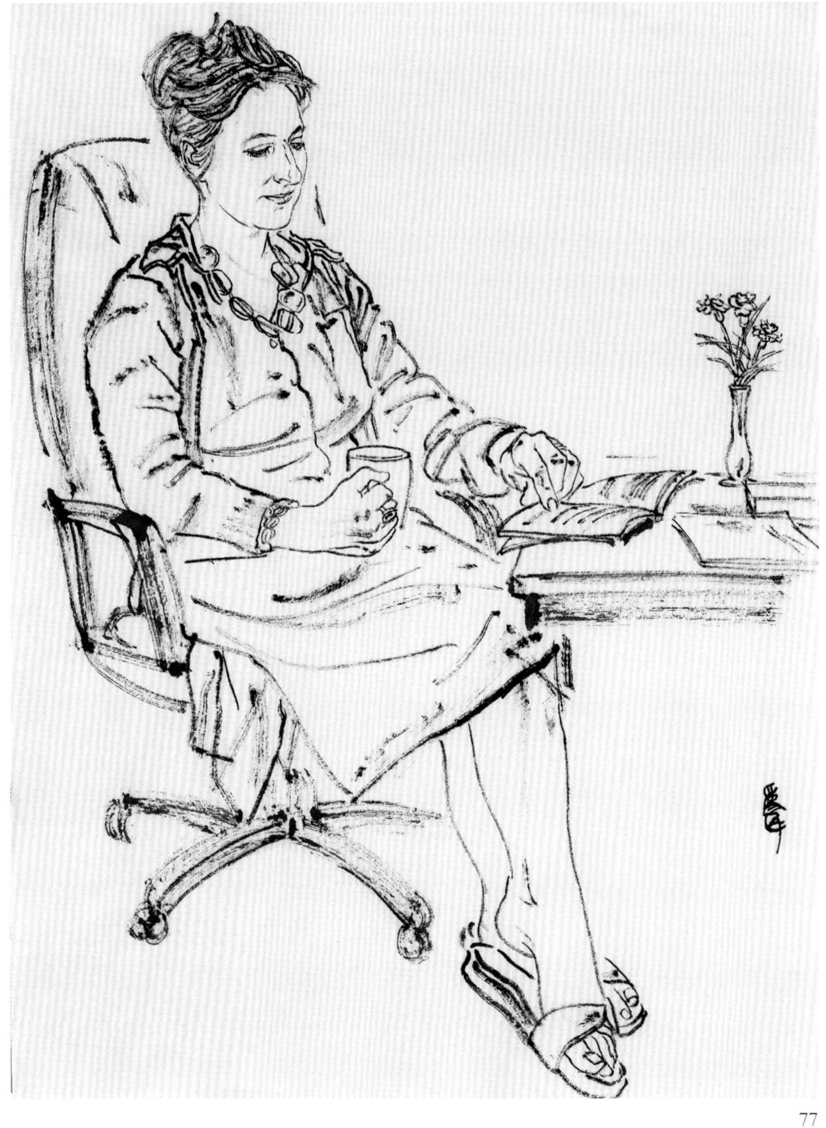

77

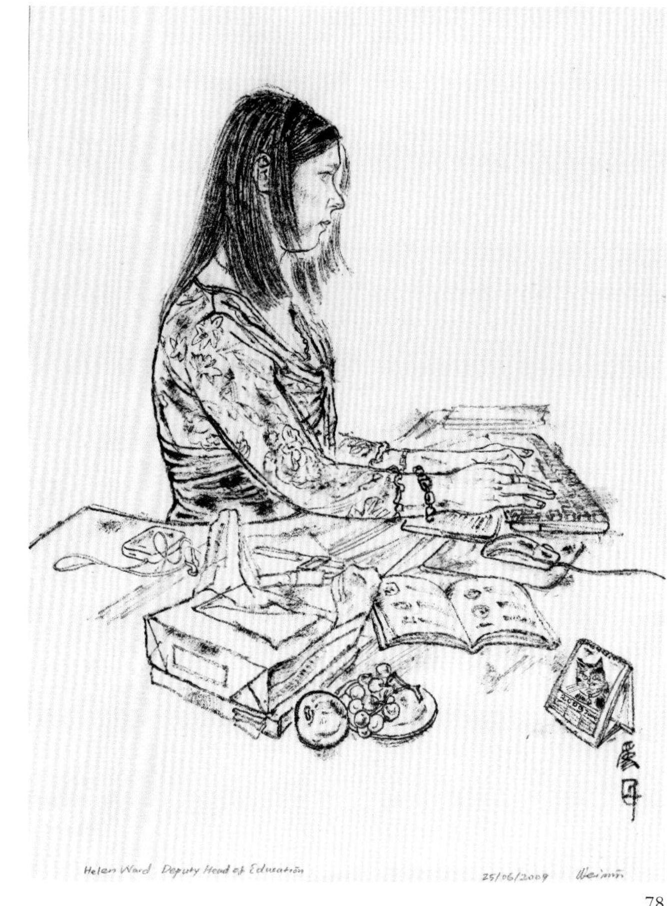

78

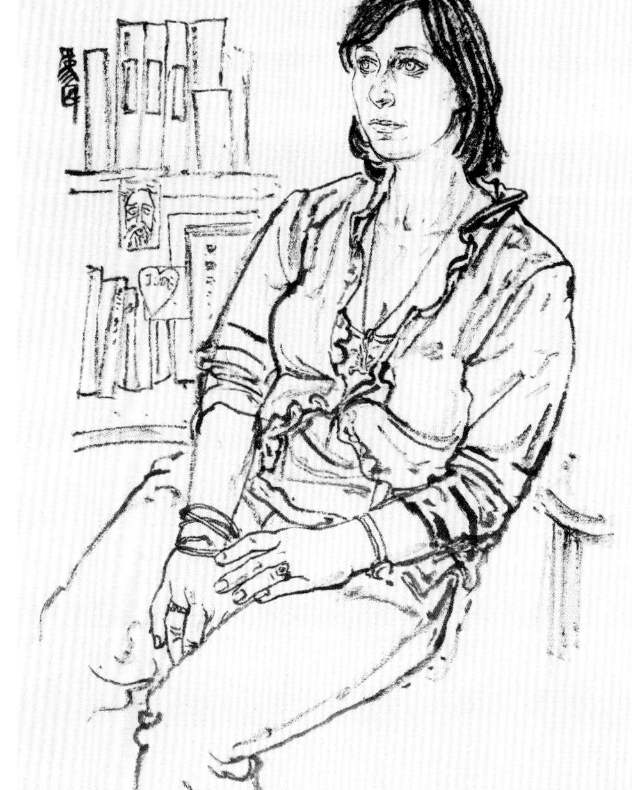

79

73 **Gillian Morris** *Head of Human Resources*
2009. Brush and ink on *xuan* paper. Paper size: 44.8 × 34 cm

74 **Sarah** *Former Museum staff*
2008. Brush and ink on *xuan* paper. Paper size: 44.8 × 34 cm

75 **Jane Wastie** *Human Resources Manager*
2008. Brush and ink on *pi* paper. Paper size: 46.1 × 34 cm

76 **Geraldine Glynn** *Registrar*
2009. Brush and ink on *xuan* paper. Paper size: 44.8 × 34 cm

77 **Jo Rice** *Head of Education Department*
2009. Brush and ink on *xuan* paper. Paper size: 44.8 × 34 cm

78 **Helen Ward** *Deputy Head of Education Department*
2009. Brush and ink on *xuan* paper. Paper size: 44.8 × 34 cm

79 **Jude Barrett** *Education Officer, Education Department*
2008. Brush and ink on *pi* paper. Paper size: 48.8 × 38.3 cm

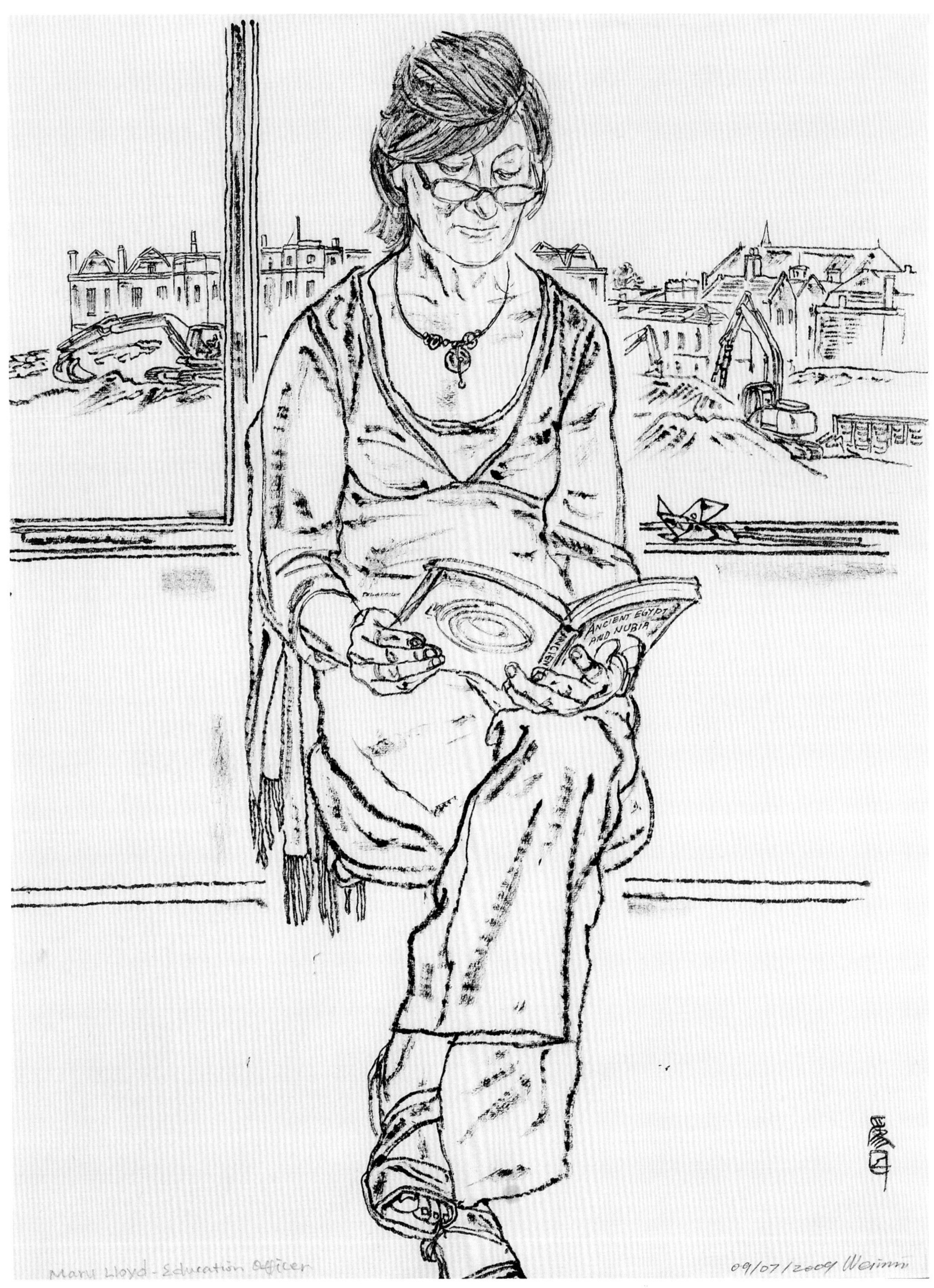

80 Mary Lloyd *Education Officer for Schools, Education Department*
2009. Brush and ink on *xuan* paper. Paper size: 44.8 × 34 cm

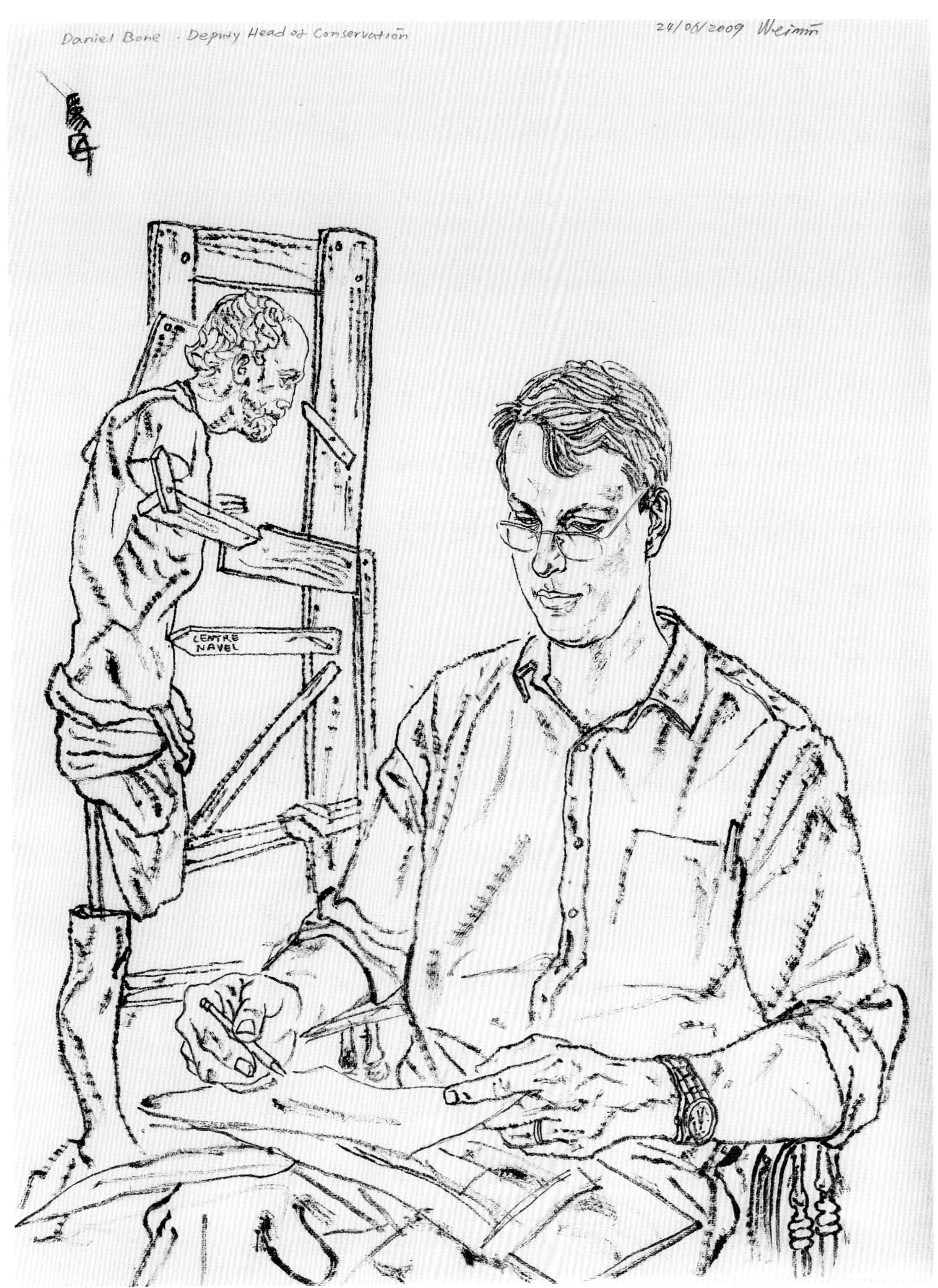

81 Daniel Bone *Deputy Head of Conservation*
2009. Brush and ink on *xuan* paper. Paper size: 44.8 × 34 cm

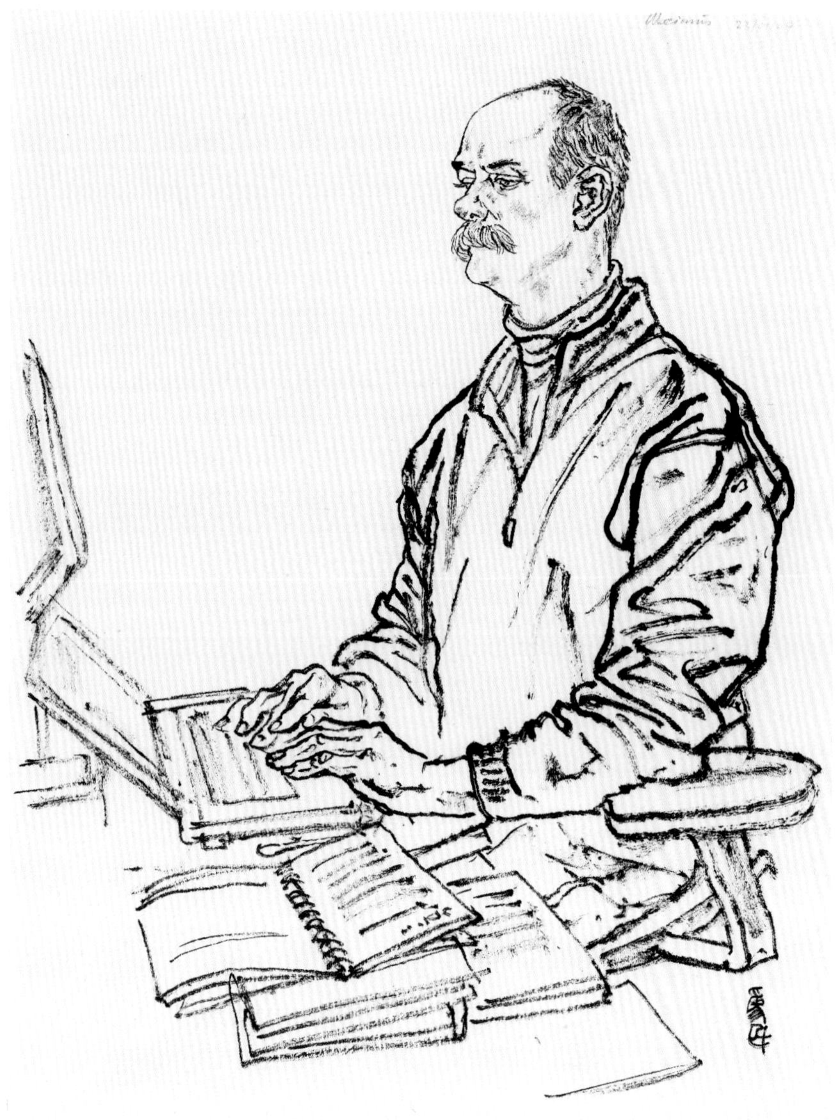

82

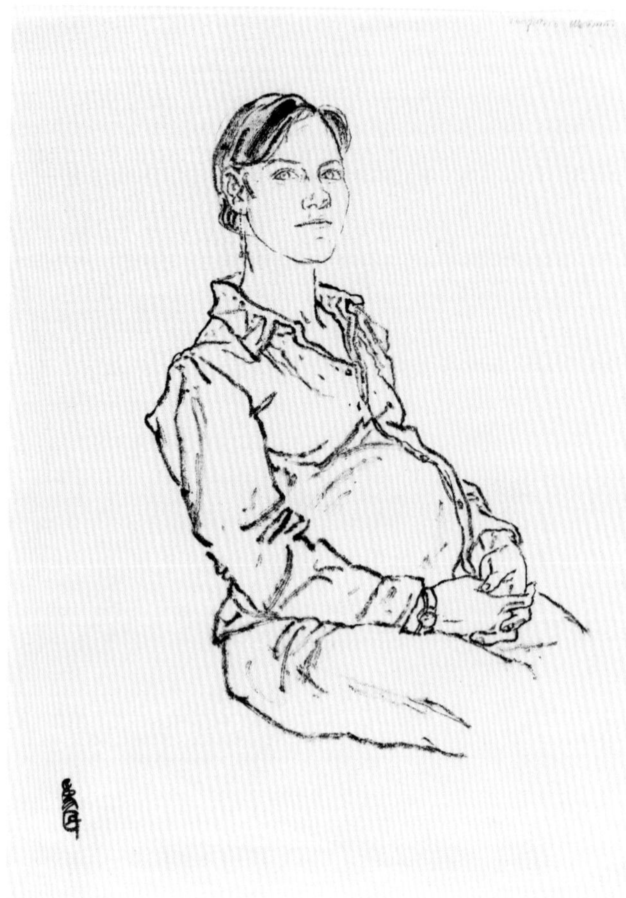

83

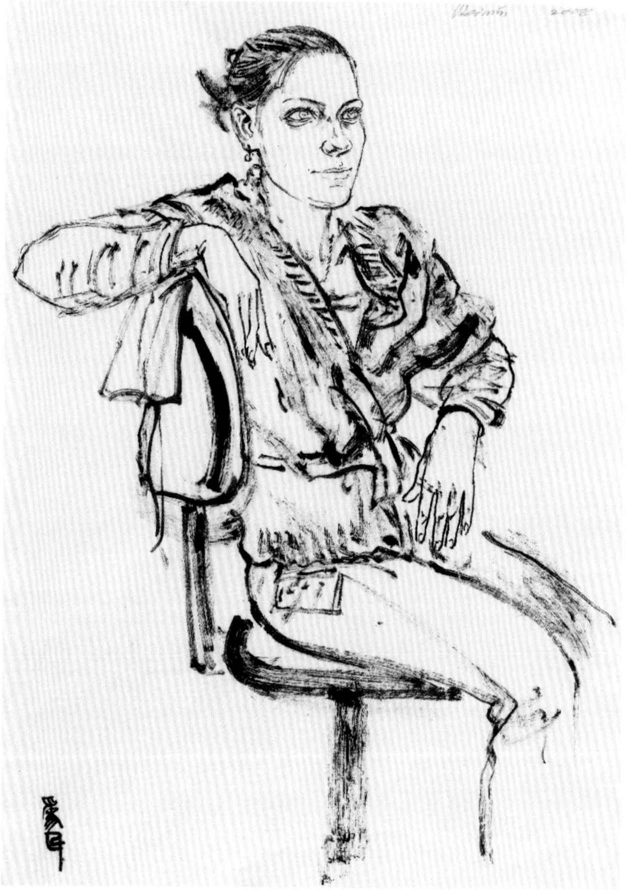

84

82 Mark Norman *Head of Conservation*
2009. Brush and ink on *xuan* paper. Paper size: 44.8 × 34 cm

83 Alexandra Greathead *Paper Conservator*
2007. Brush and ink on *pi* paper. Paper size: 46.1 × 32.2 cm

84 Stella Ditschkowski *Assistant Paper Conservator*
2008. Brush and ink on *pi* paper. Paper size: 46.1 × 34.4 cm

85 Paulina Lobaton *Objects Conservator*
2009. Brush and ink on *xuan* paper. Paper size: 44.8 × 34 cm

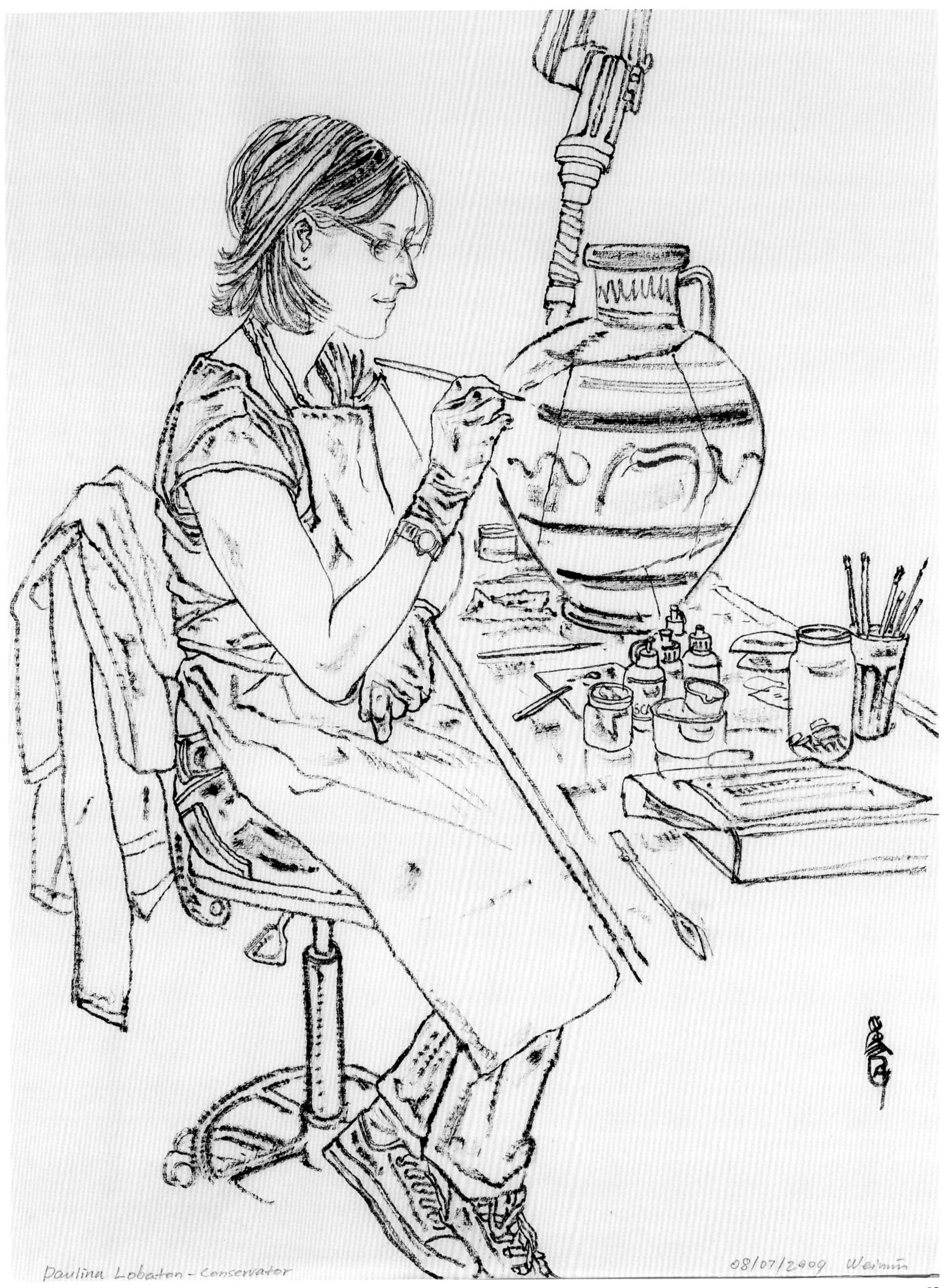

85

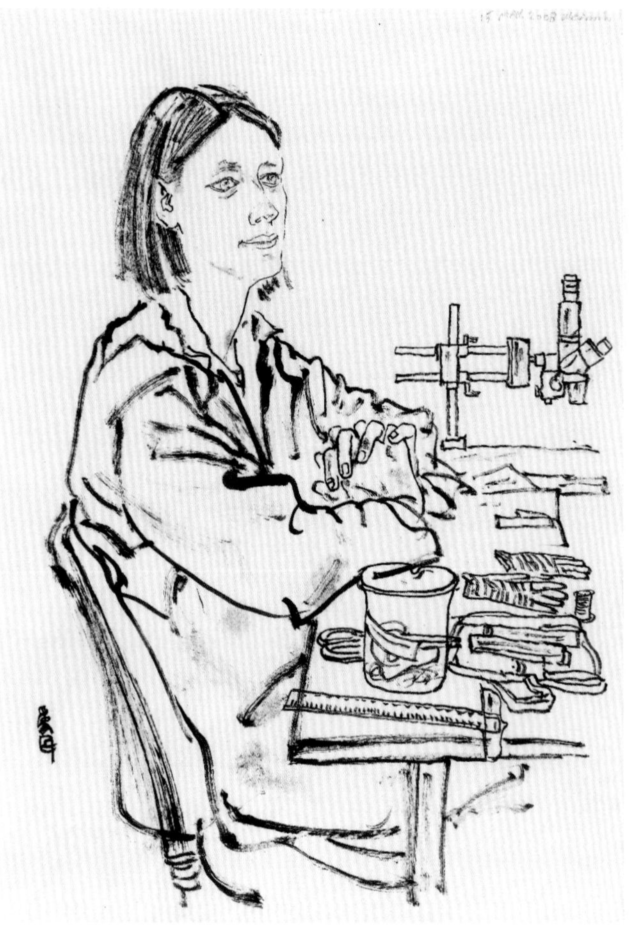

86

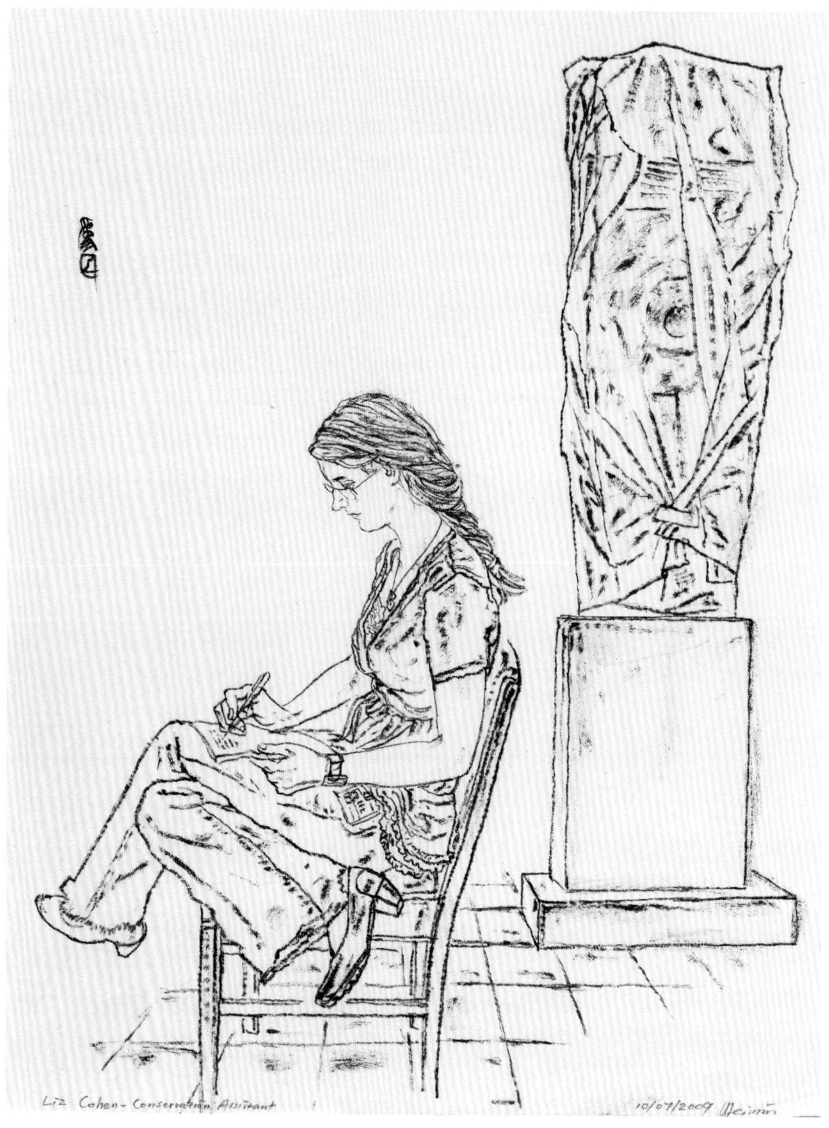

87

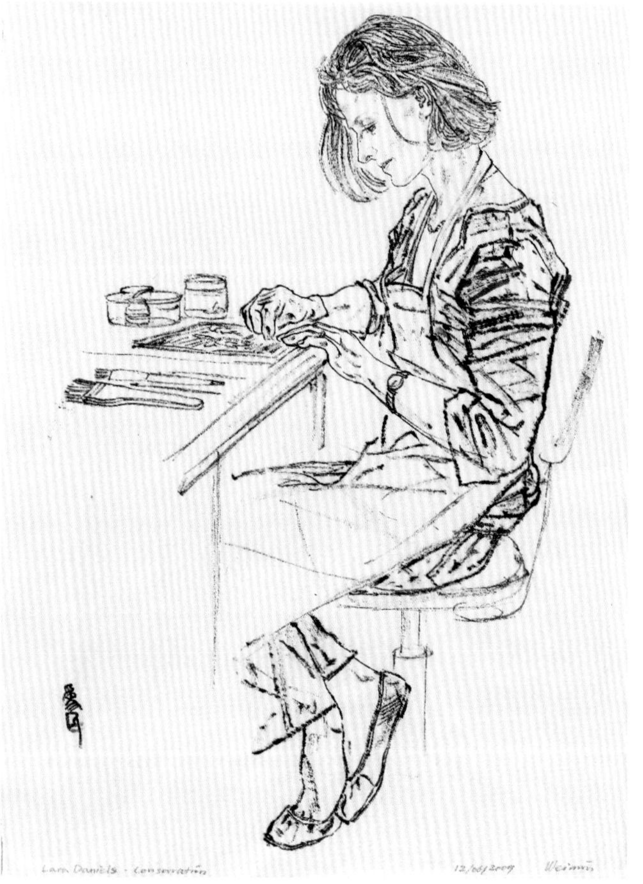

88

86 Sue Stanton *Textile Conservator*
2008. Brush and ink on *pi* paper. Paper size: 46.1 × 32.8 cm

87 Liz Cohen *Conservation Assistant*
2009. Brush and ink on *xuan* paper. Paper size: 44.8 × 34 cm

88 Lara Daniels *Paper Conservator*
2009. Brush and ink on *xuan* paper. Paper size: 44.8 × 34 cm

89 Graeme Campbell *Head of Design, Design Office*
2009. Brush and ink on *xuan* paper. Paper size: 44.8 × 34 cm

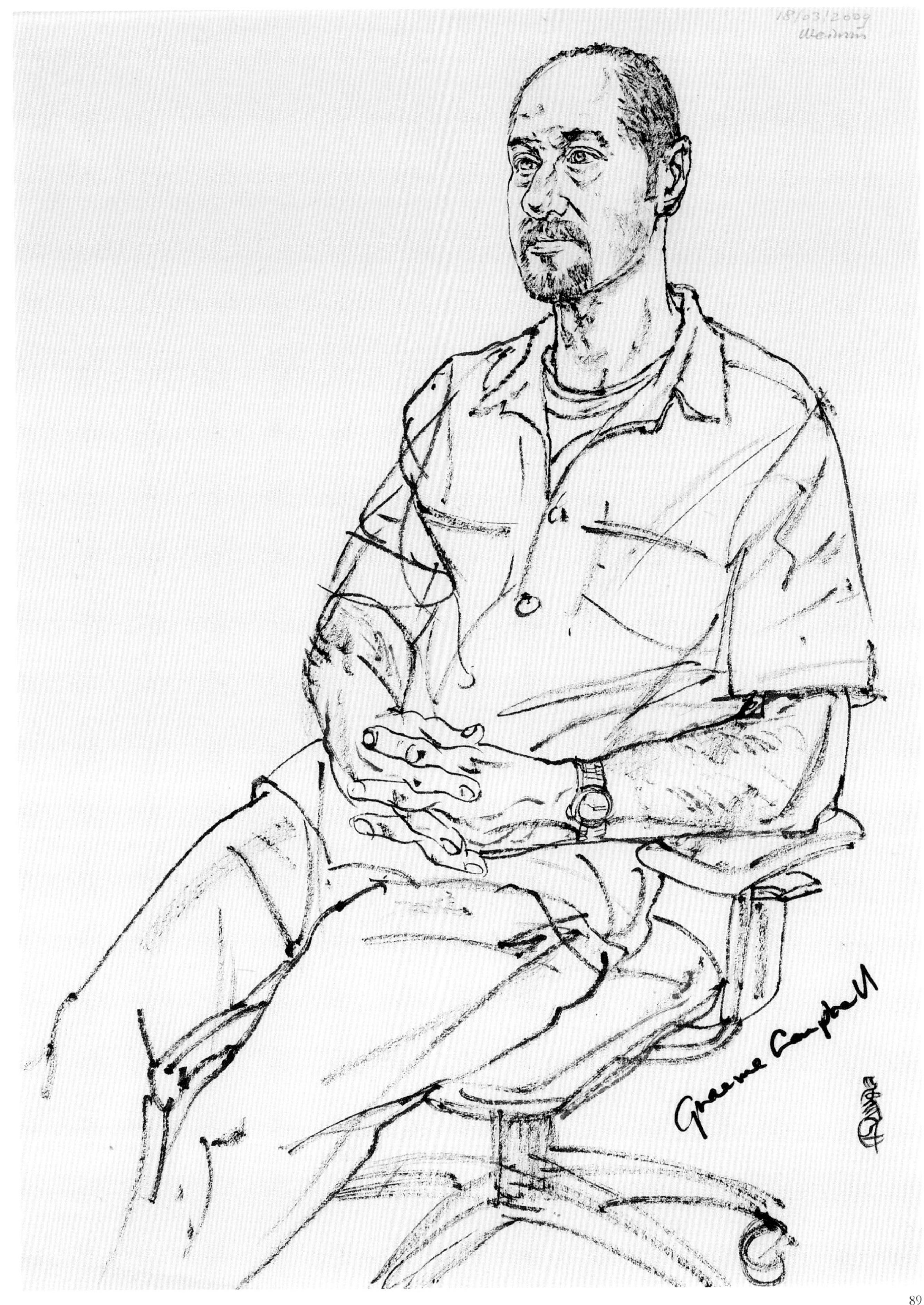
18/03/2009
Graeme Campbell

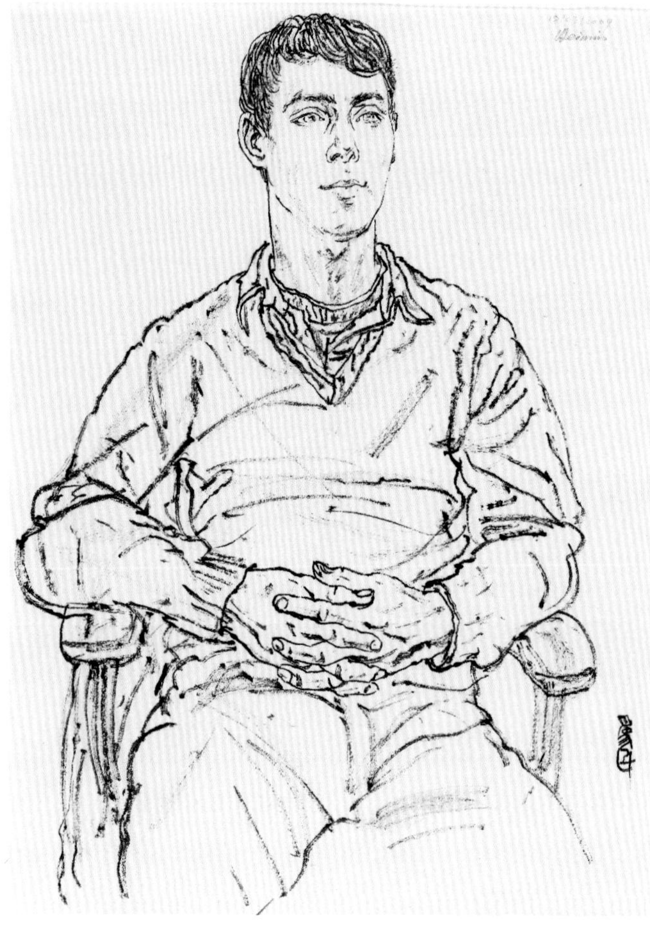

90

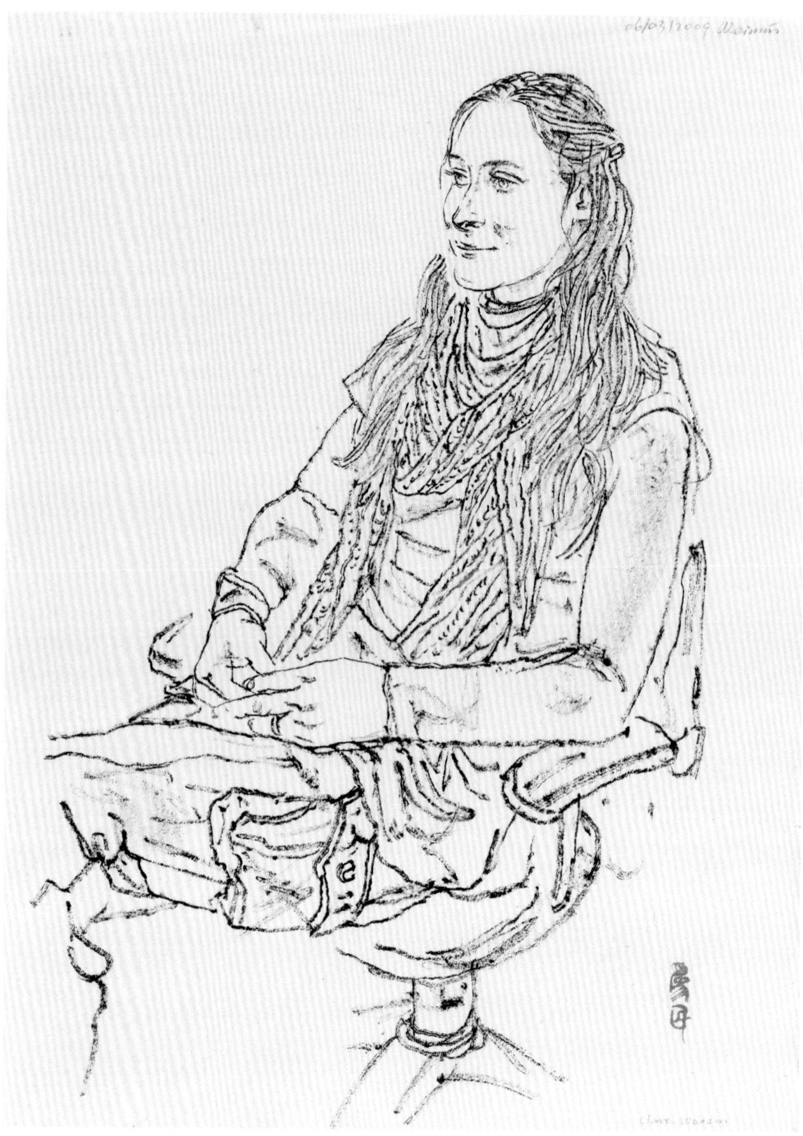

91

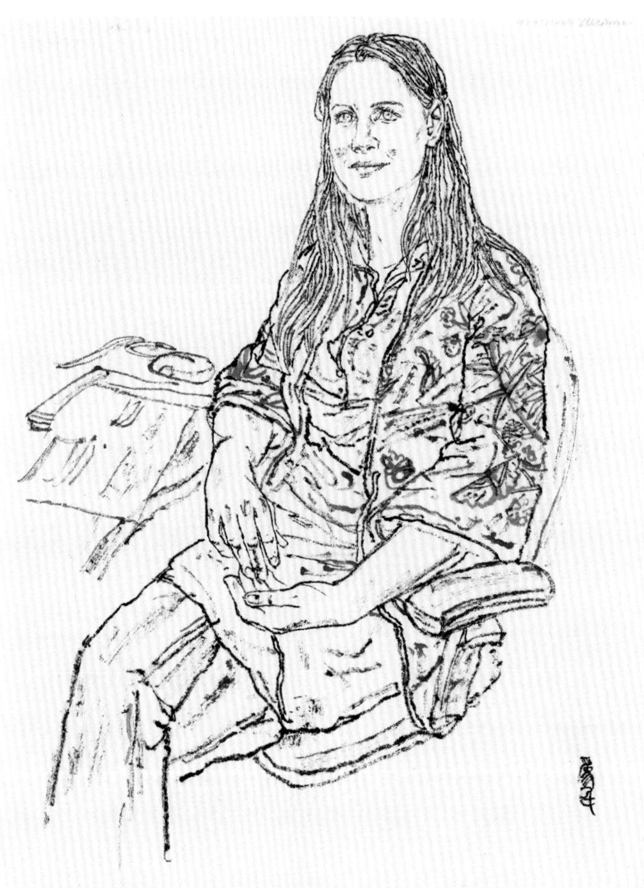

92

90 Greg Jones *Assistant Designer, Design Office*
2009. Brush and ink on *xuan* paper. Paper size: 44.8 × 34 cm

91 Clare Watson *Exhibition Designer, Design Office*
2009. Brush and ink on *xuan* paper. Paper size: 44.8 × 34 cm

92 Gesa Döerfler *Exhibition Designer, Design Office*
2009. Brush and ink on *xuan* paper. Paper size: 44.8 × 34 cm

93 Junia Brown *Graphic Designer, Design Office*
2009. Brush and ink on *xuan* paper. Paper size: 44.8 × 34 cm

94 Amery Gration *Designer, Design Office*
2009. Brush and ink on *xuan* paper. Paper size: 44.8 × 34 cm

95 Karen Luff *Graphic Designer, Design Office*
2009. Brush and ink on *xuan* paper. Paper size: 44.8 × 34 cm

96 Clara Mun *Object Tracer, Design Office*
2009. Brush and ink on *xuan* paper. Paper size: 44.8 × 34 cm

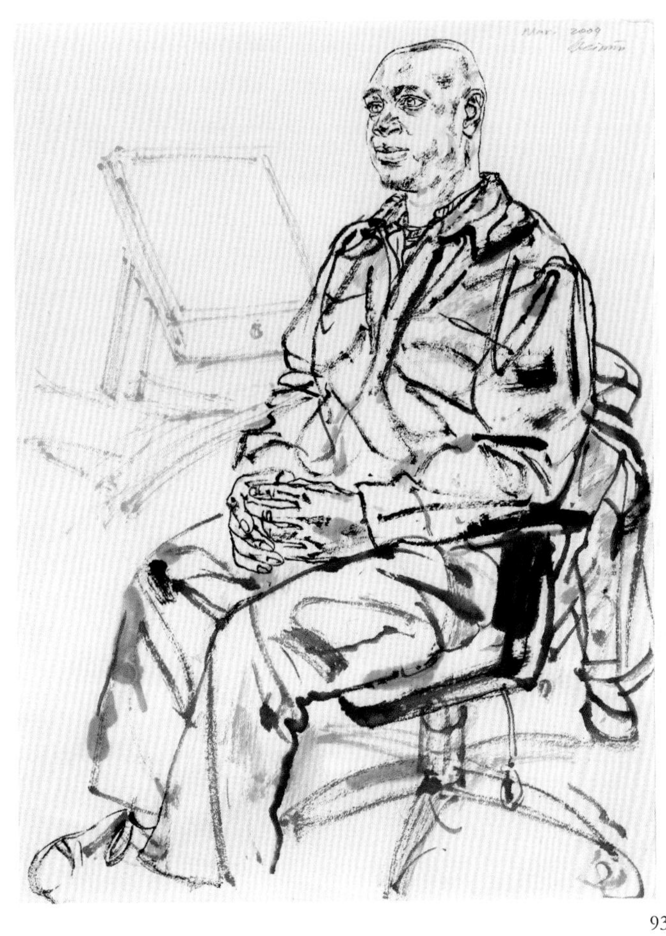

93

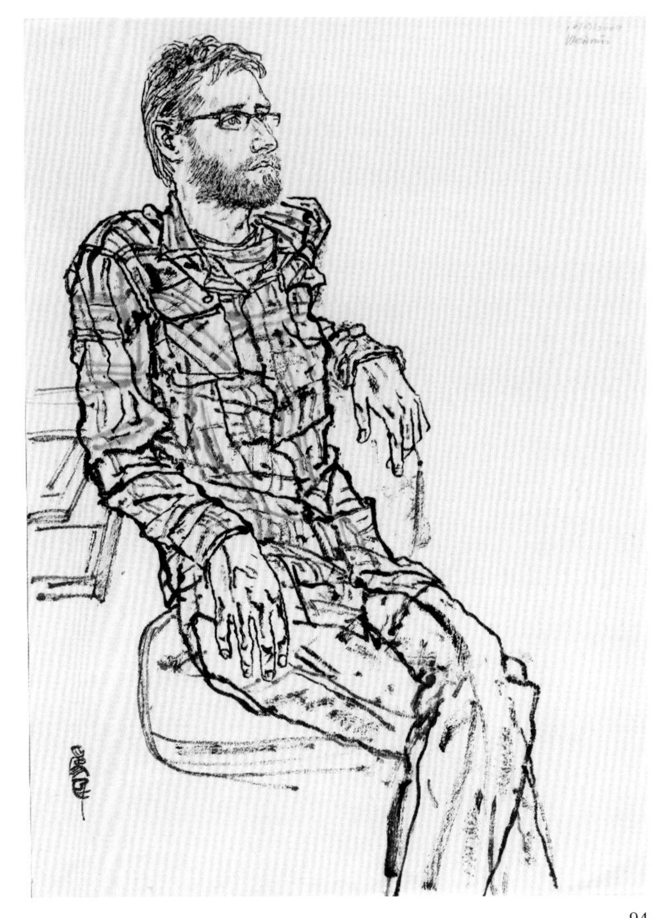

94

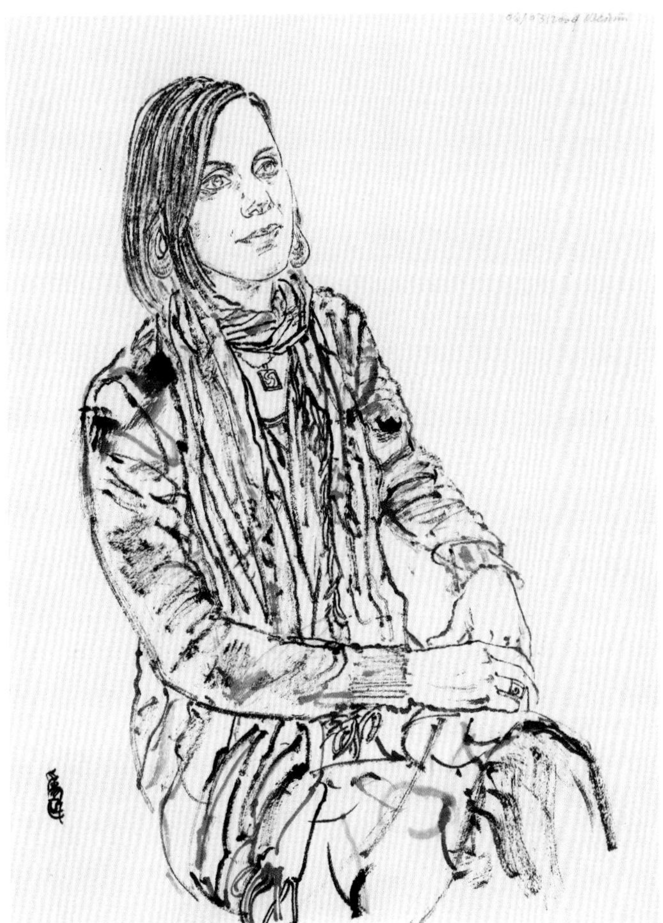

95

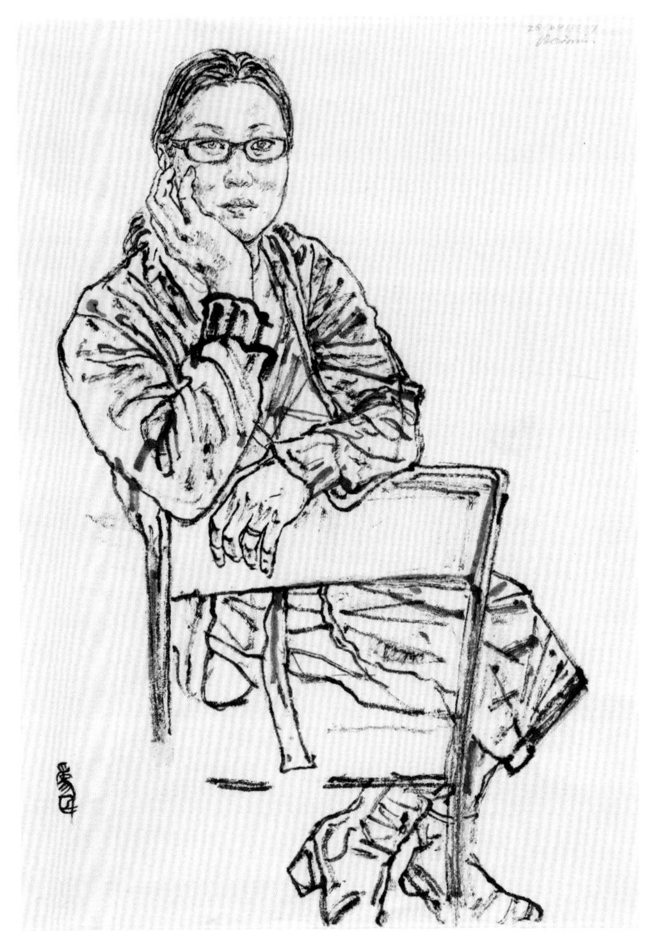

96

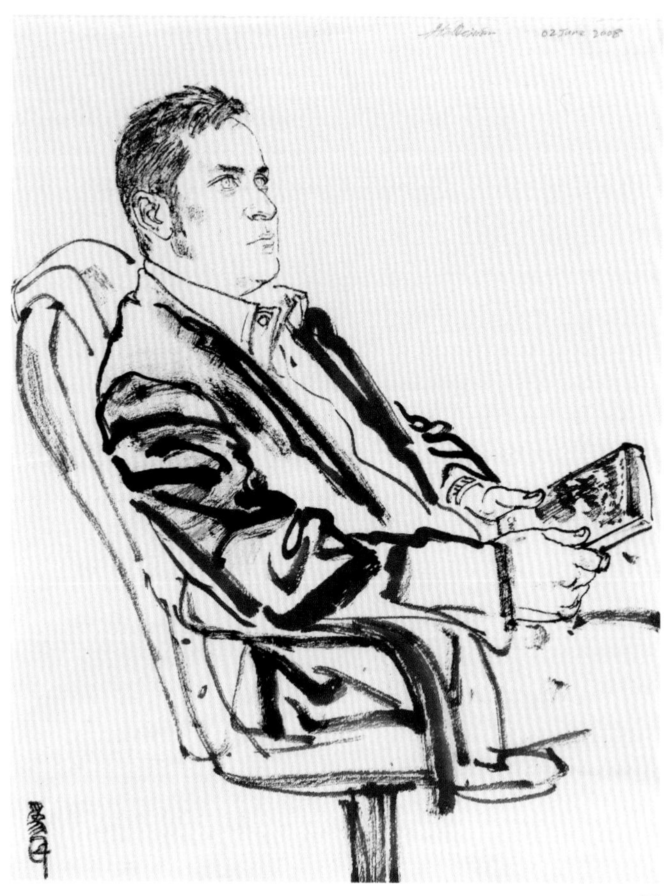

97

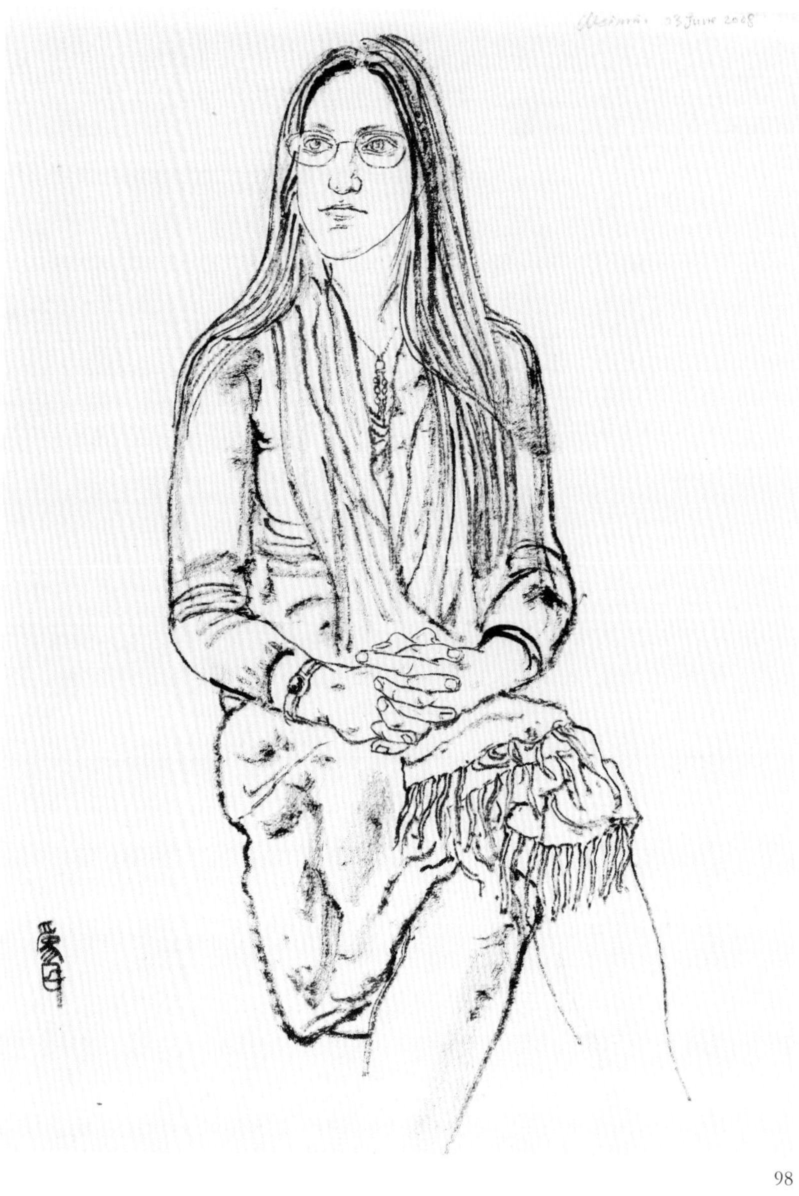

98

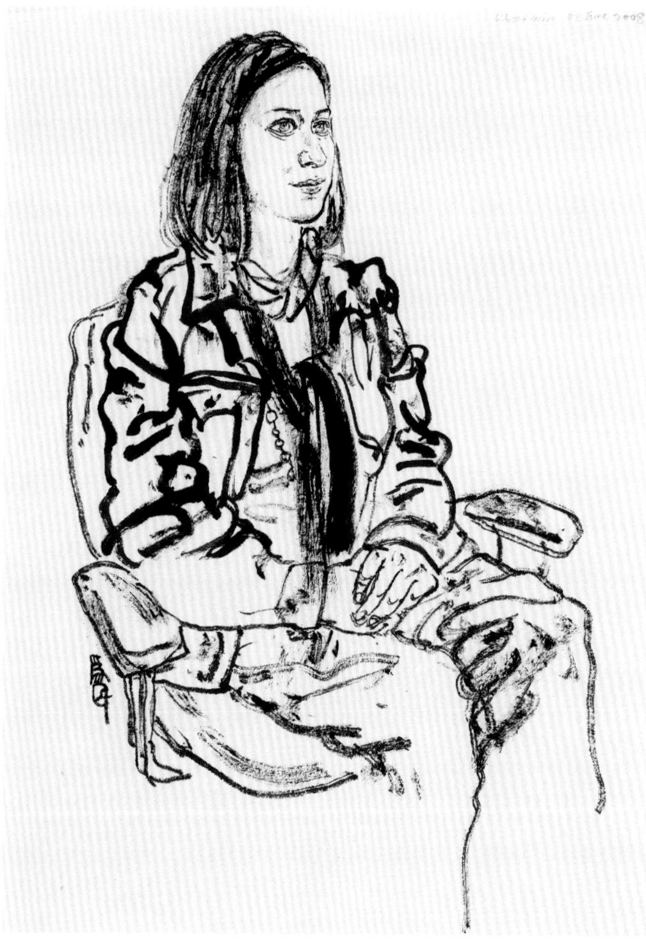

99

97 Declan McCarthy *Publications Manager*
2008. Brush and ink on *xuan* paper. Paper size: 47.9 × 38.7 cm

98 Katherine Wodehouse *Picture Library Manager*
2008. Brush and ink on *pi* paper. Paper size: 47.5 × 38.2 cm

99 Amanda *Former Museum staff*
2008. Brush and ink on *xuan* paper. Paper size: 44.8 × 34 cm

100 Emily Jolliffe *Publications Deputy Manager*
2009. Brush and ink on *xuan* paper. Paper size: 44.8 × 34 cm

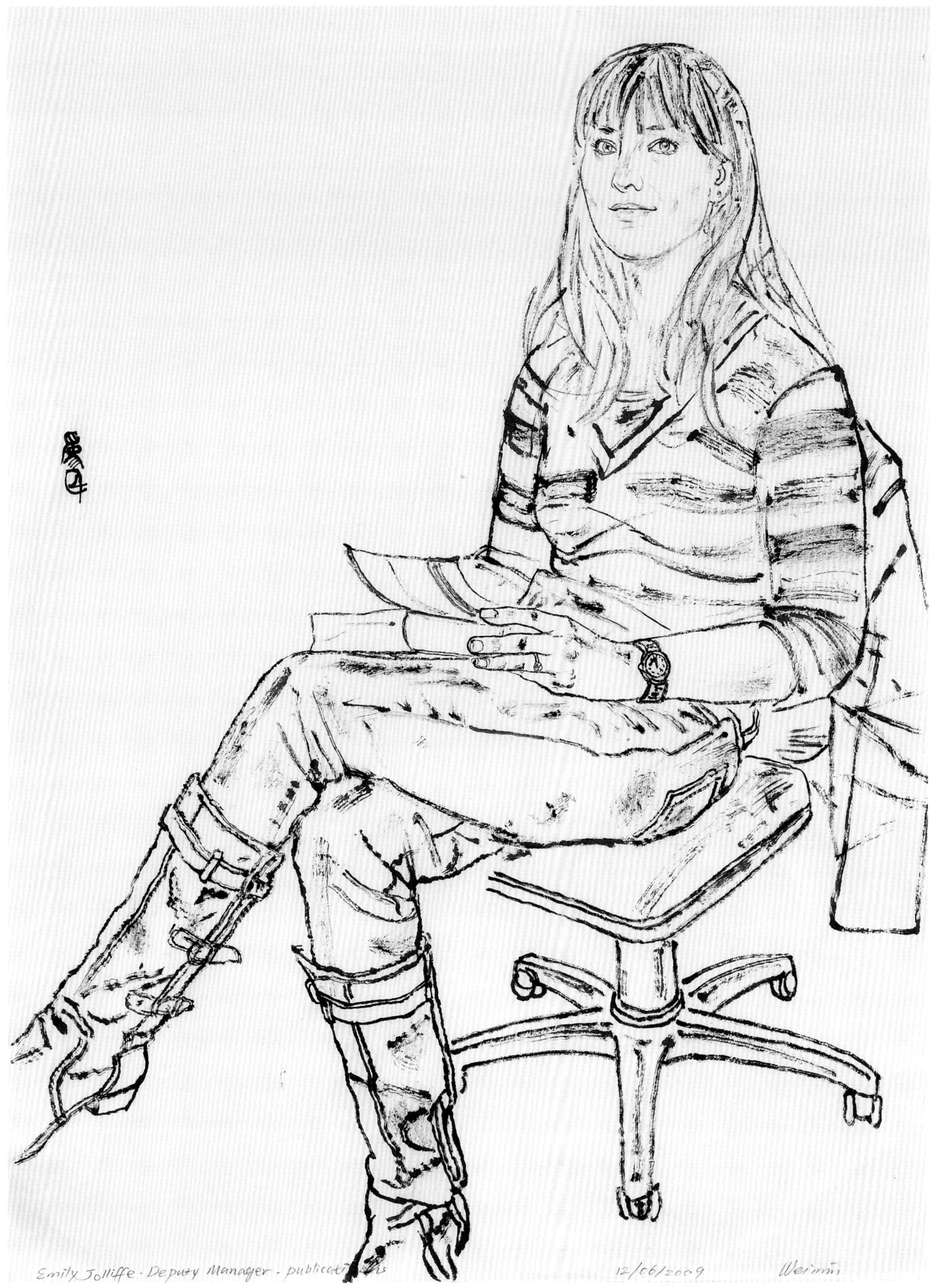

100

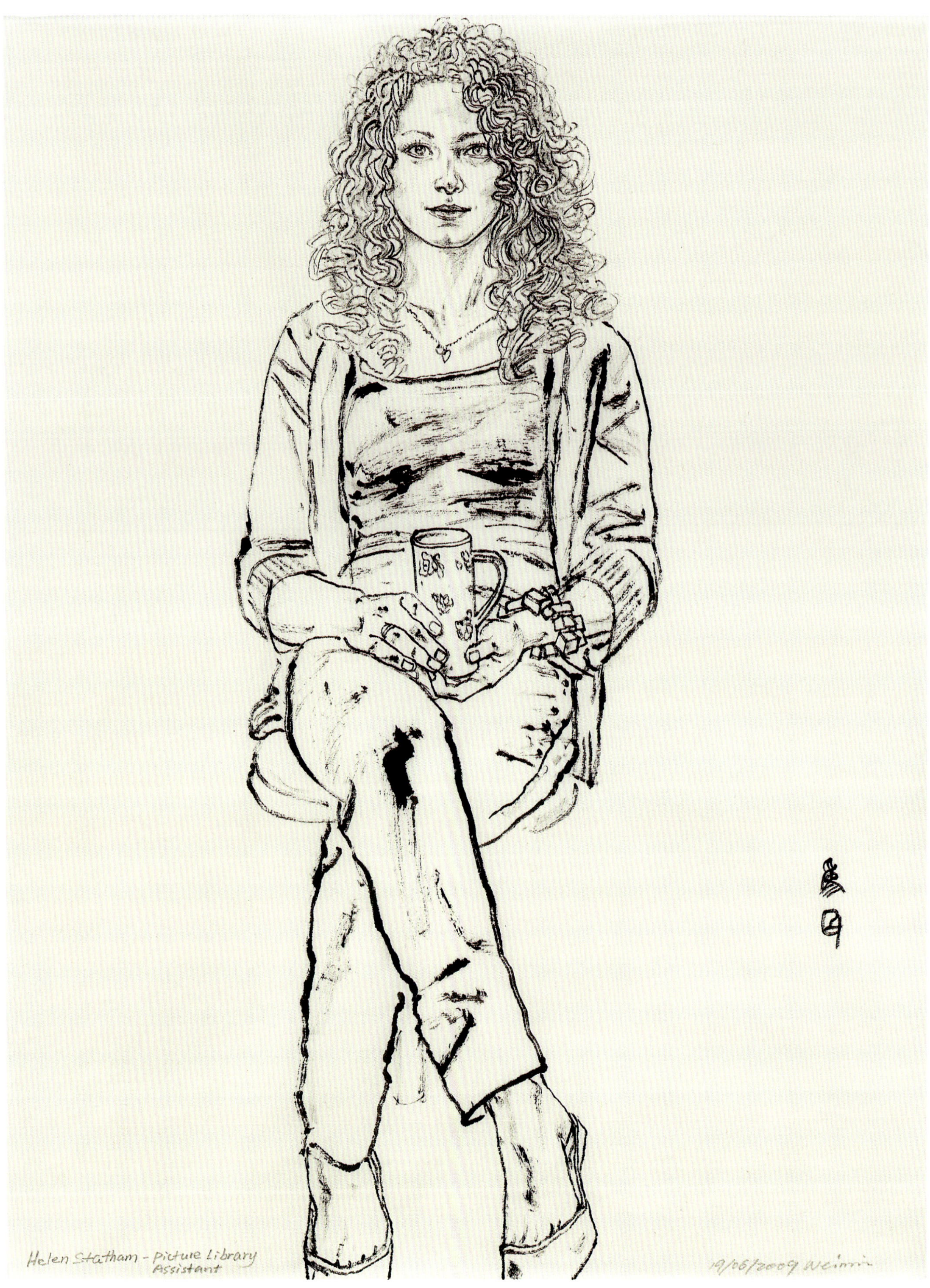

101

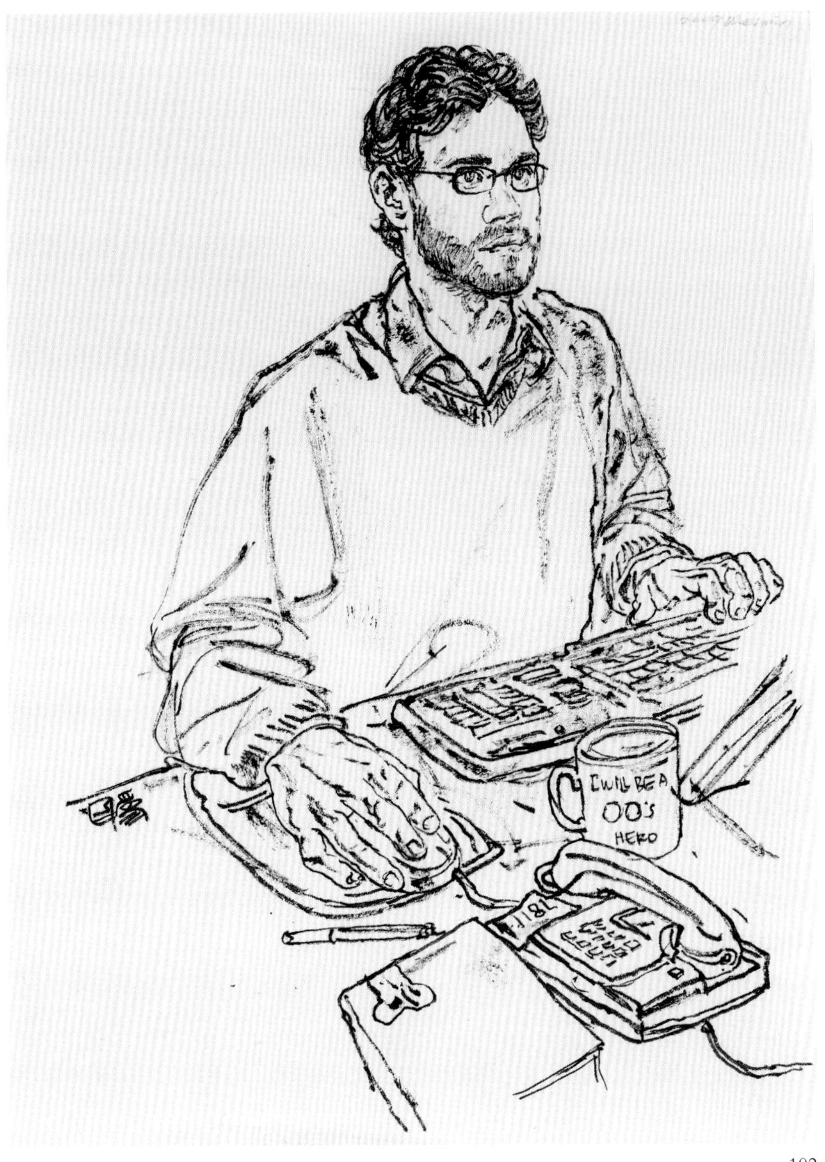

102

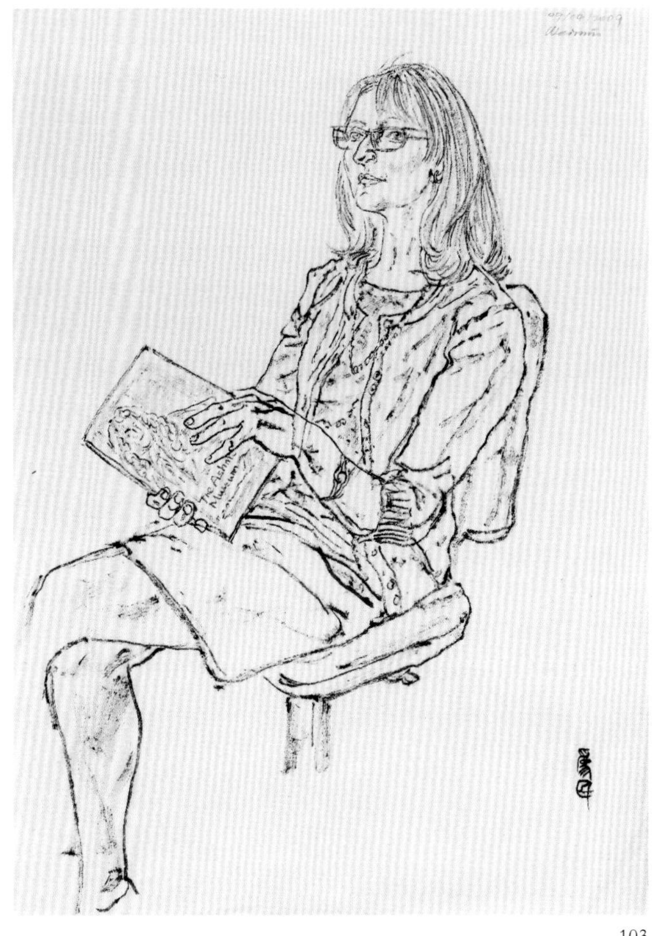

103

104

101 Helen Statham *Picture Library Assistant*
2009. Brush and ink on *xuan* paper. Paper size: 44.8 × 34 cm

102 Nick Butterley *Project Administrator*
2009. Brush and ink on *xuan* paper. Paper size: 44.8 × 34 cm

103 Anne Walker *Museum Shop Manager*
2009. Brush and ink on *xuan* paper. Paper size: 44.8 × 34 cm

104 Gill Vulliamy *Deputy Manager, Museum Shop*
2009. Brush and ink on *xuan* paper. Paper size: 44.8 × 34 cm

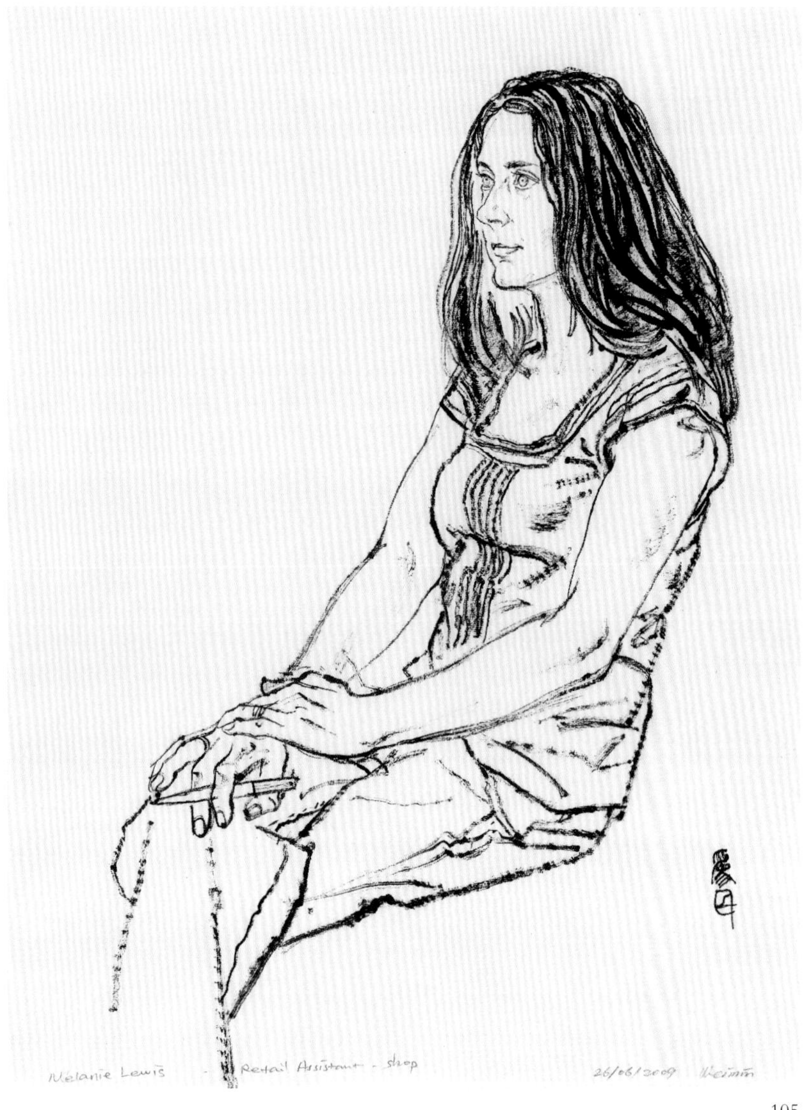

105

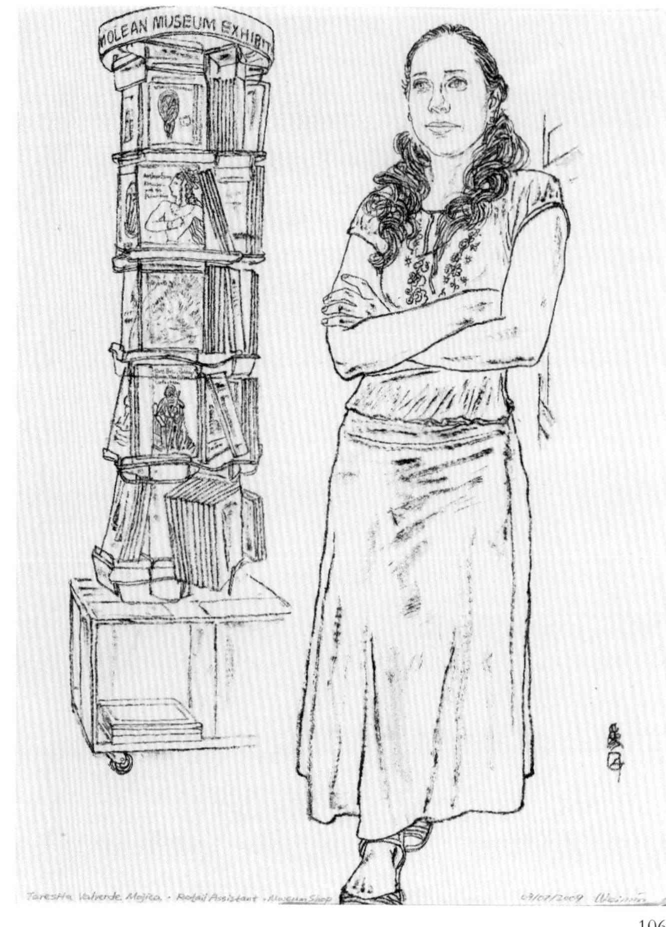

106

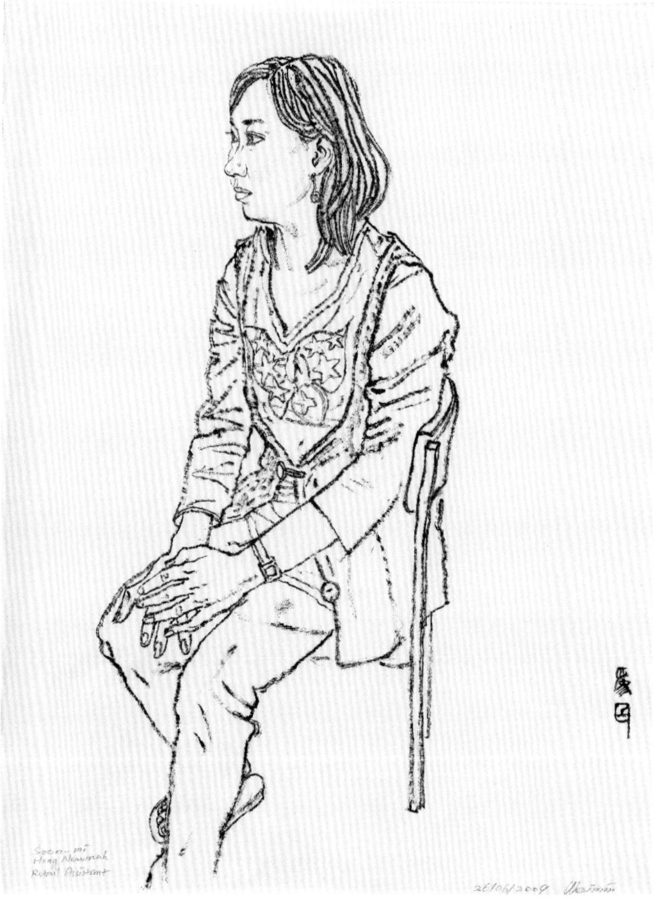

107

105 Melanie Lewis *Admin Assistant, Museum Shop*
2009. Brush and ink on *xuan* paper. Paper size: 44.8 × 34 cm

106 Sagal Esse *Retail Assistant, Museum Shop*
2009. Brush and ink on *xuan* paper. Paper size: 44.8 × 34 cm

107 Soon-mi Hong Newmah *Retail Assistant, Museum Shop*
2009. Brush and ink on *xuan* paper. Paper size: 44.8 × 34 cm

108 Teresita Valverde Mojica *Retail Assistant, Museum Shop*
2009. Brush and ink on *xuan* paper. Paper size: 44.8 × 34 cm

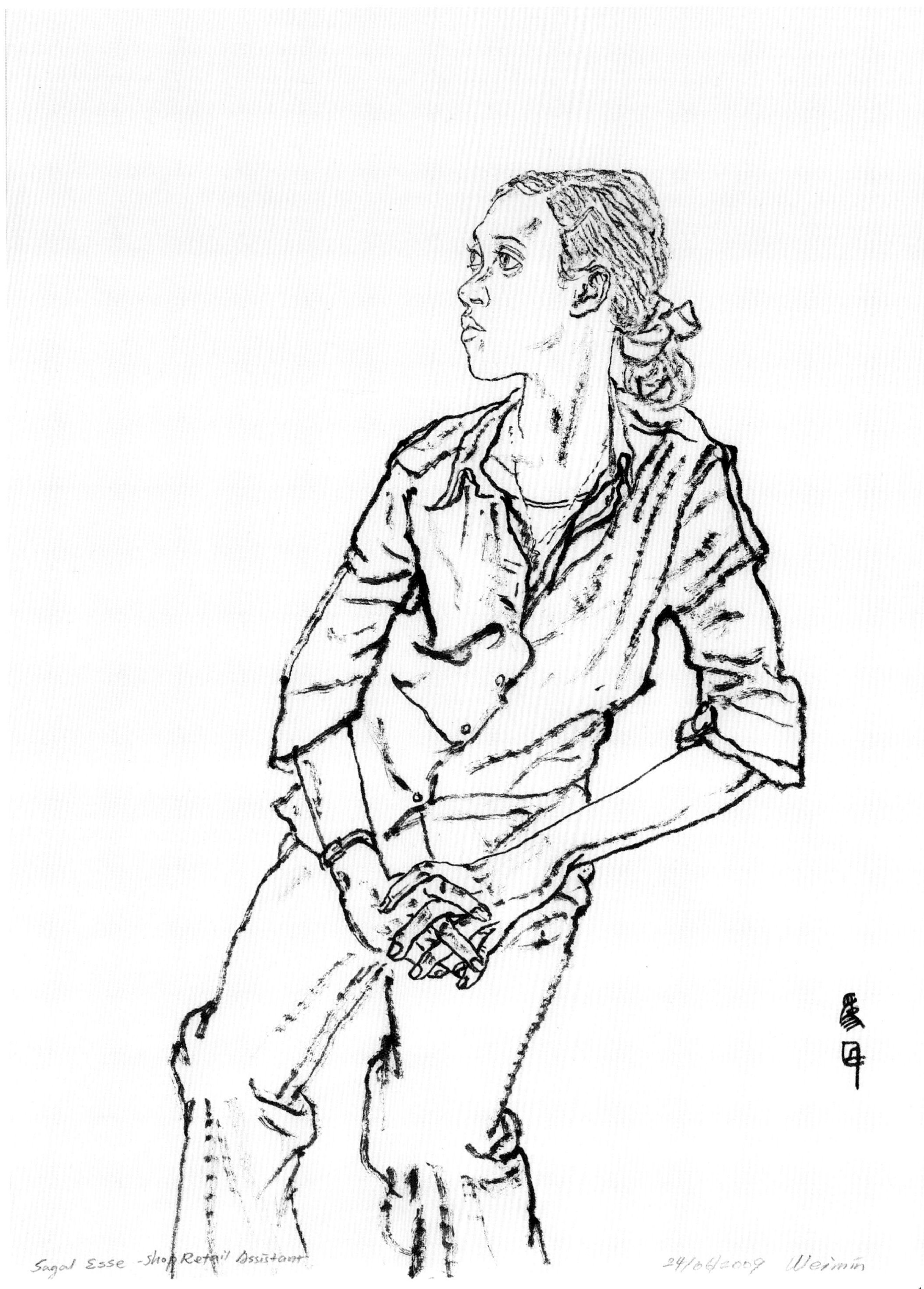

108

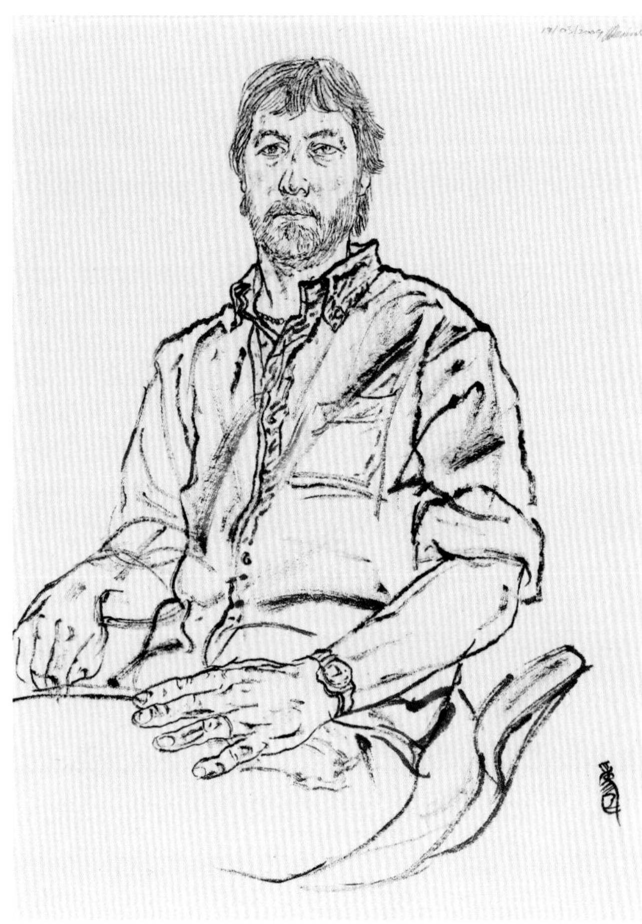

109

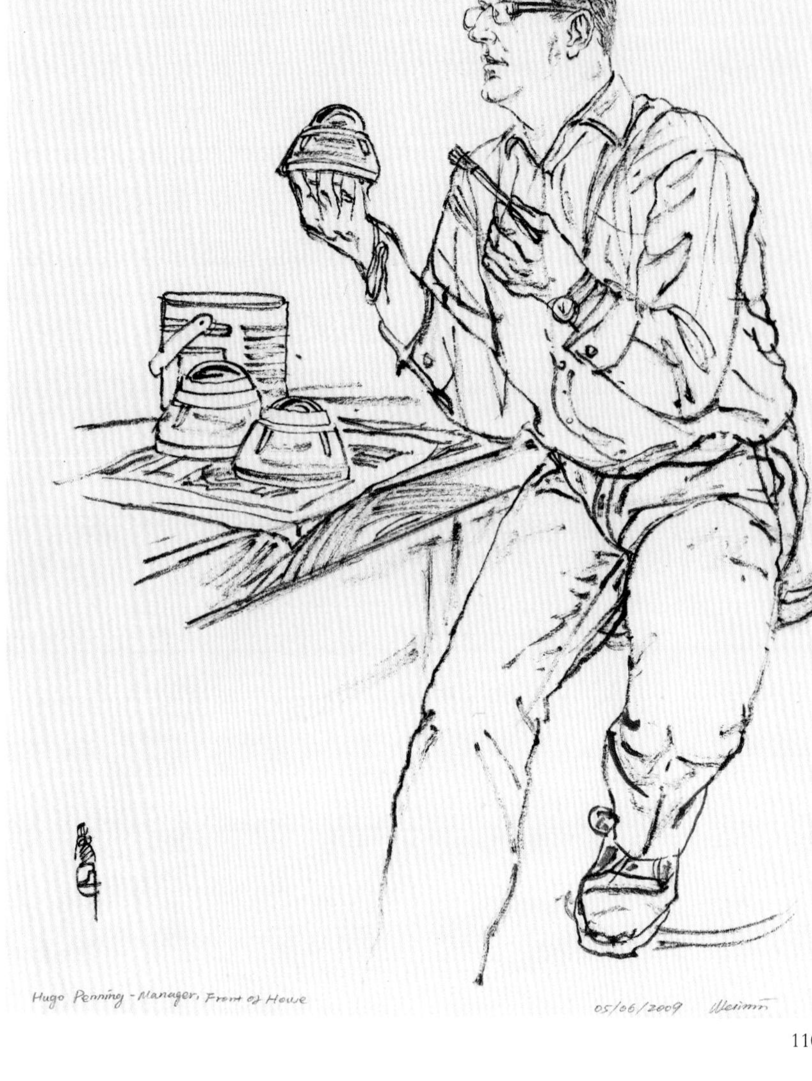

110

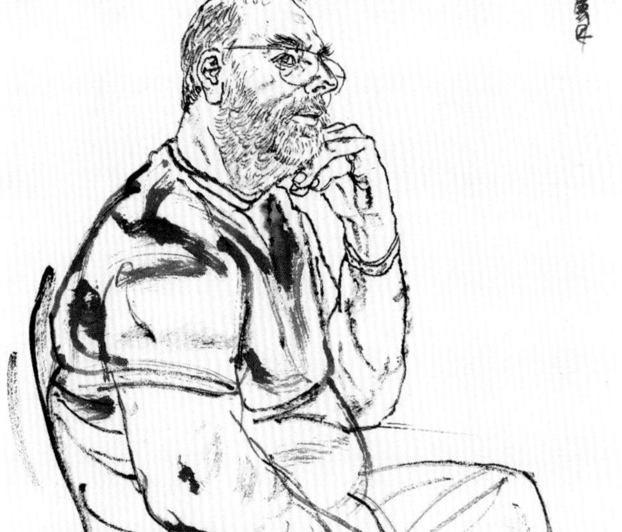

111

109 **David Gowers** *Chief Photographer*
2009. Brush and ink on *xuan* paper. Paper size: 44.8 × 34 cm

110 **Hugo Penning** *Front of House Manager*
2009. Brush and ink on *xuan* paper. Paper size: 44.8 × 34 cm

111 **Nick Pollard** *Photographer*
2009. Brush and ink on *xuan* paper. Paper size: 44.8 × 34 cm

112 **Trevor Stephens** *Front of House Assistant*
2009. Brush and ink on *xuan* paper. Paper size: 44.8 × 34 cm

113 **Ray Ansty** *Deputy Manager, Building Services*
2009. Brush and ink on *xuan* paper. Paper size: 44.8 × 34 cm

114 **Alan Kitchen** *Building Services Manager*
2009. Brush and ink on *xuan* paper. Paper size: 44.8 × 34 cm

115 **Mark Rowbottom** *Technician, Building Services*
2009. Brush and ink on *xuan* paper. Paper size: 44.8 × 34 cm

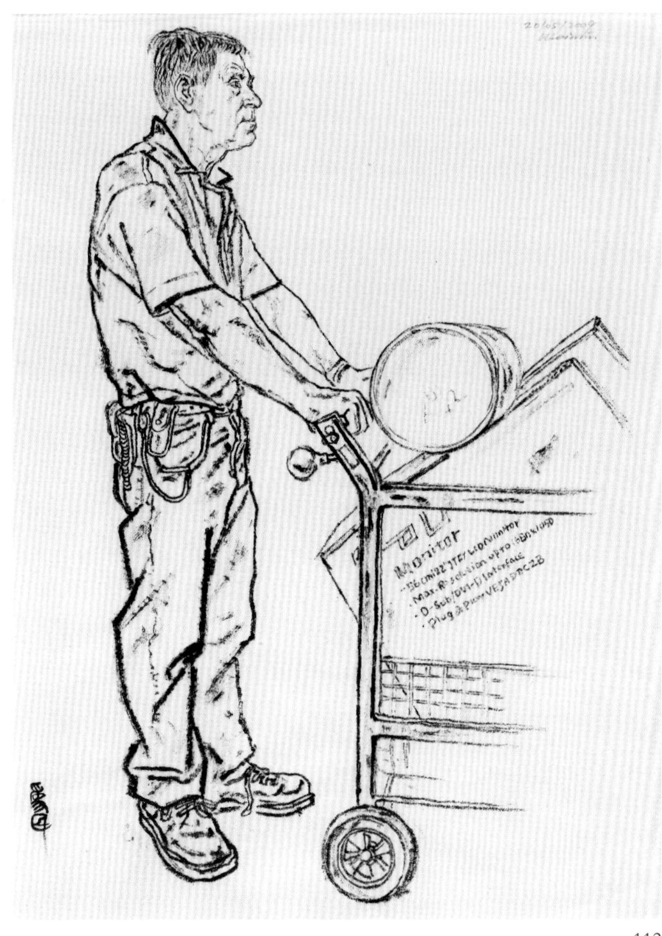

112

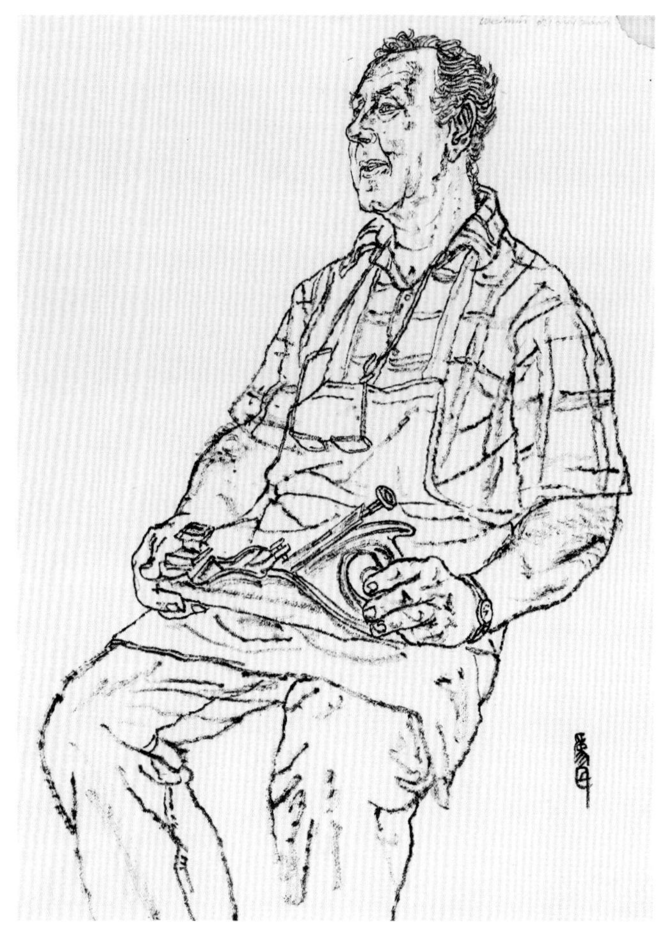

113

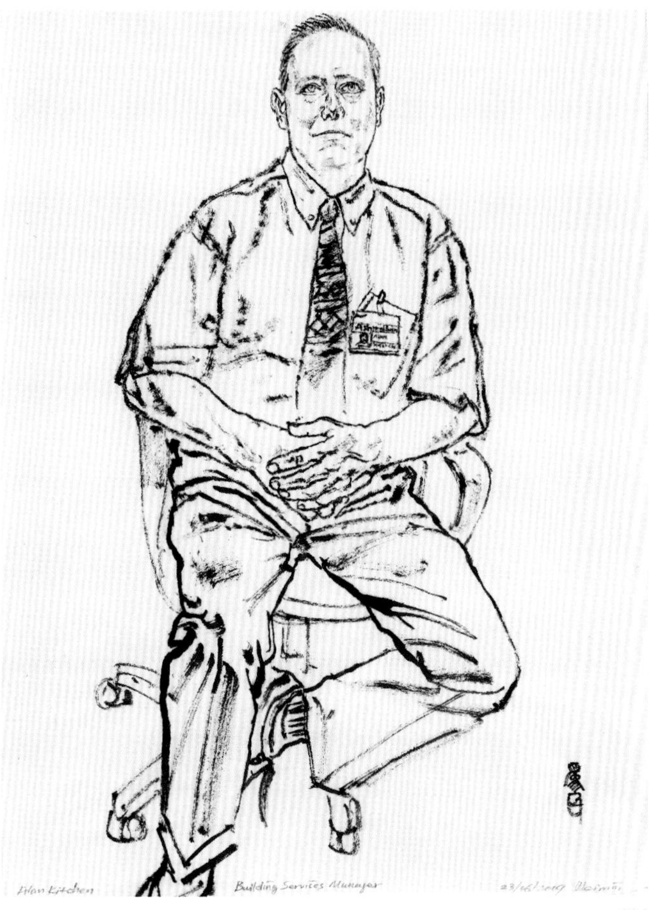

114

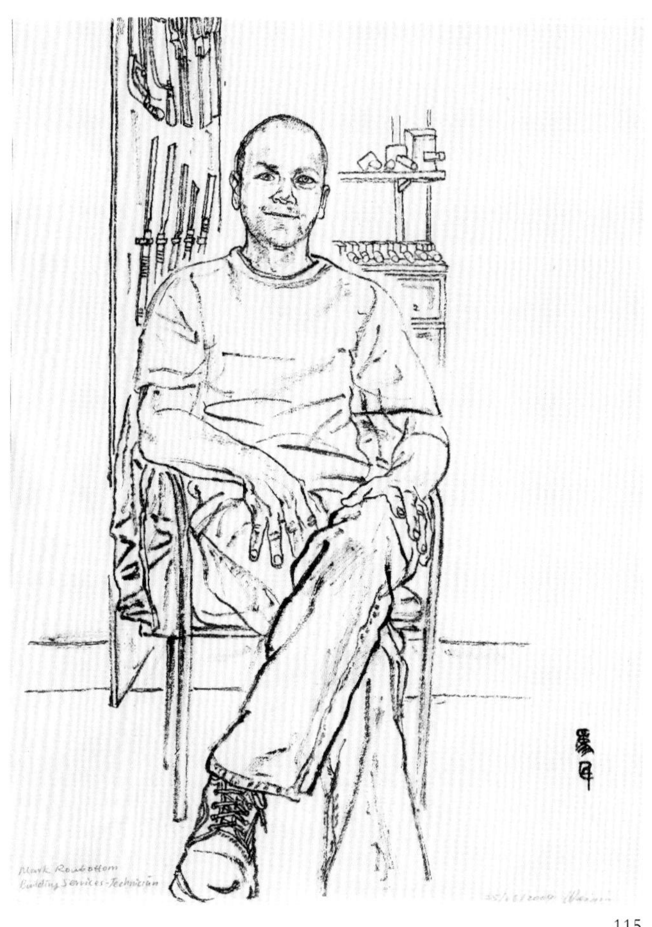

115

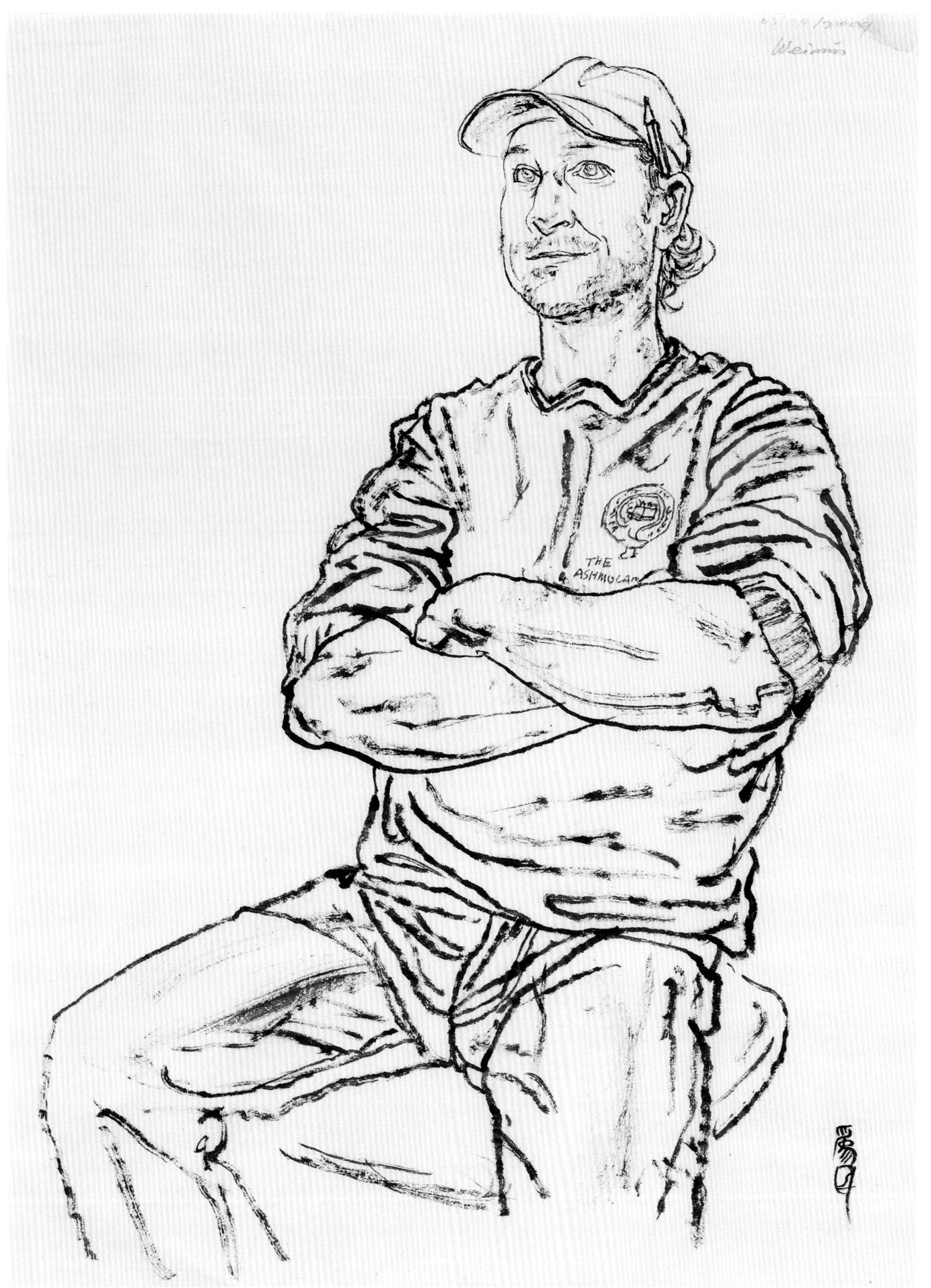

116

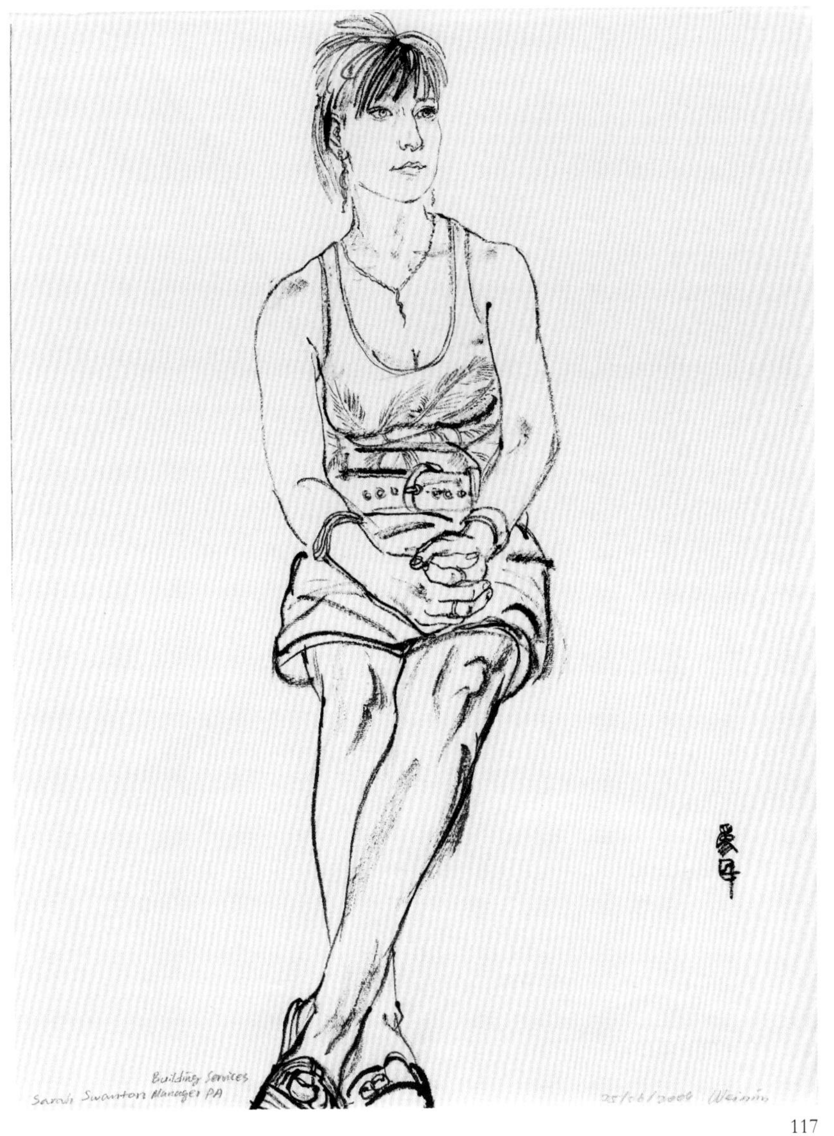

117

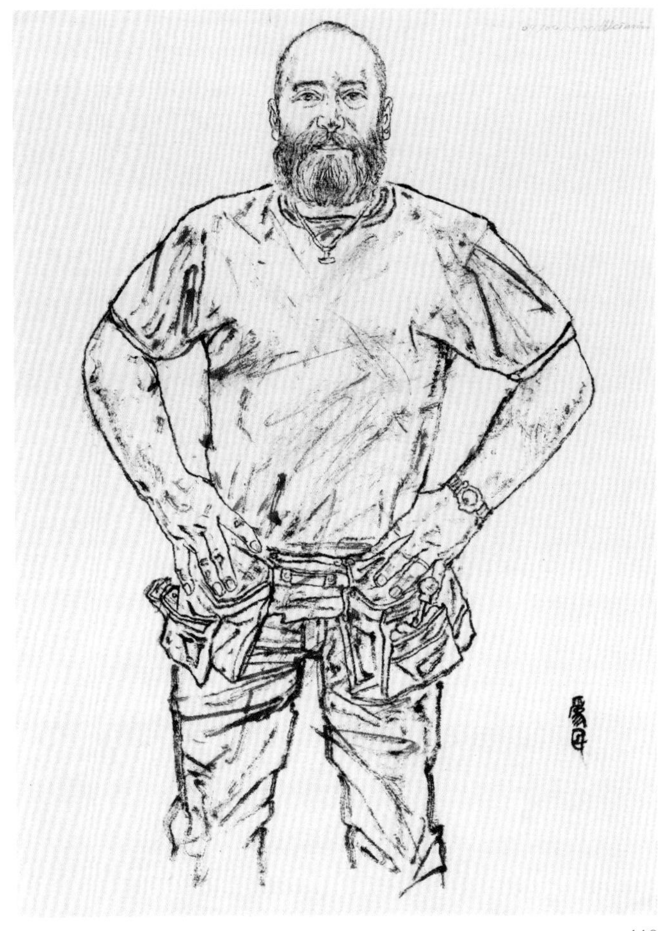

118

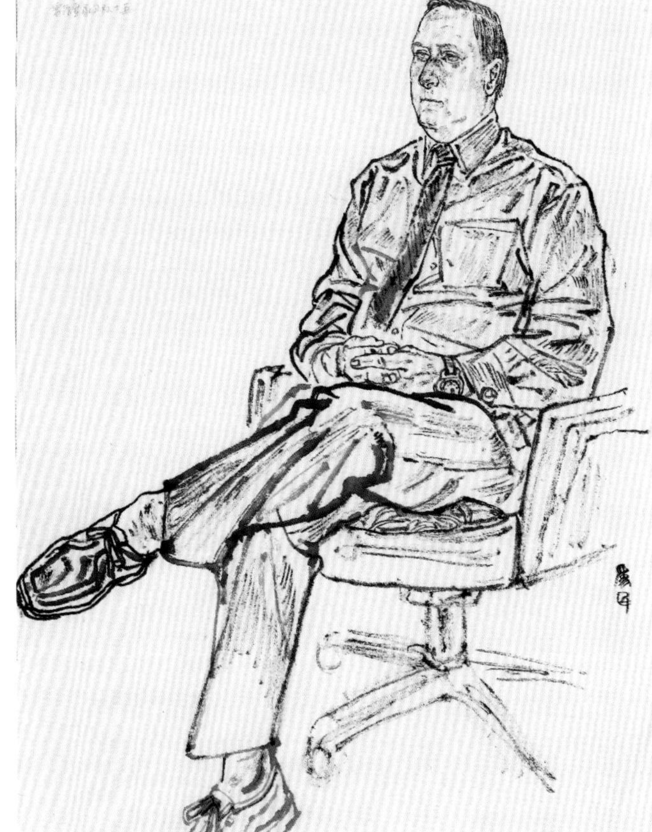

119

116 Paul Evett *Technician, Building Services*
2009. Brush and ink on *xuan* paper. Paper size: 44.8 × 34 cm

117 Sarah Swanton *Manager PA, Building Services*
2009. Brush and ink on *xuan* paper. Paper size: 44.8 × 34 cm

118 Robert Johnson *Technician, Building Services*
2009. Brush and ink on *xuan* paper. Paper size: 44.8 × 34 cm

119 Robert Baker *Security Officer*
2009. Brush and ink on *xuan* paper. Paper size: 44.8 × 34 cm

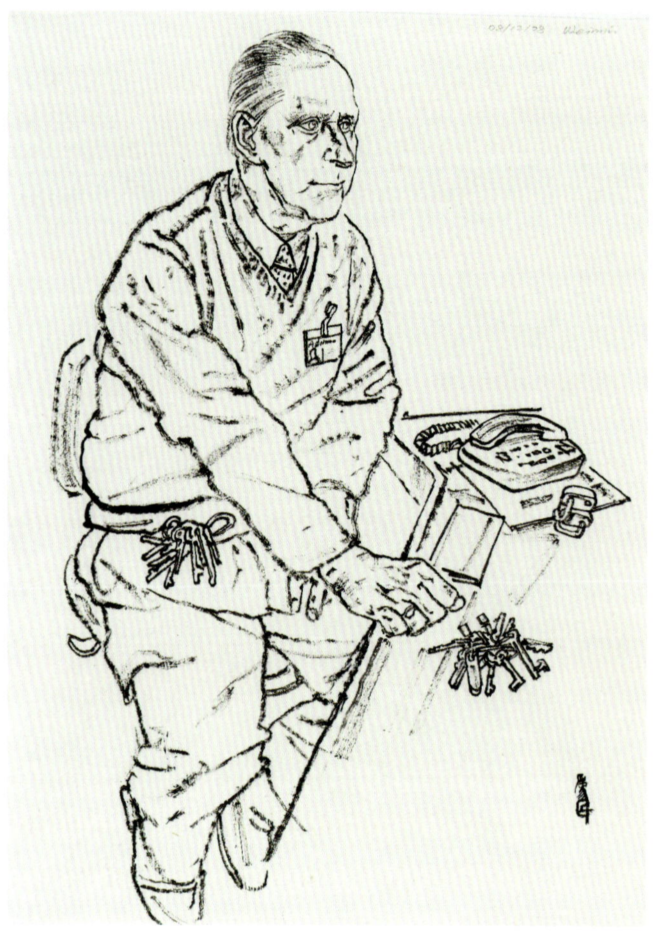

120

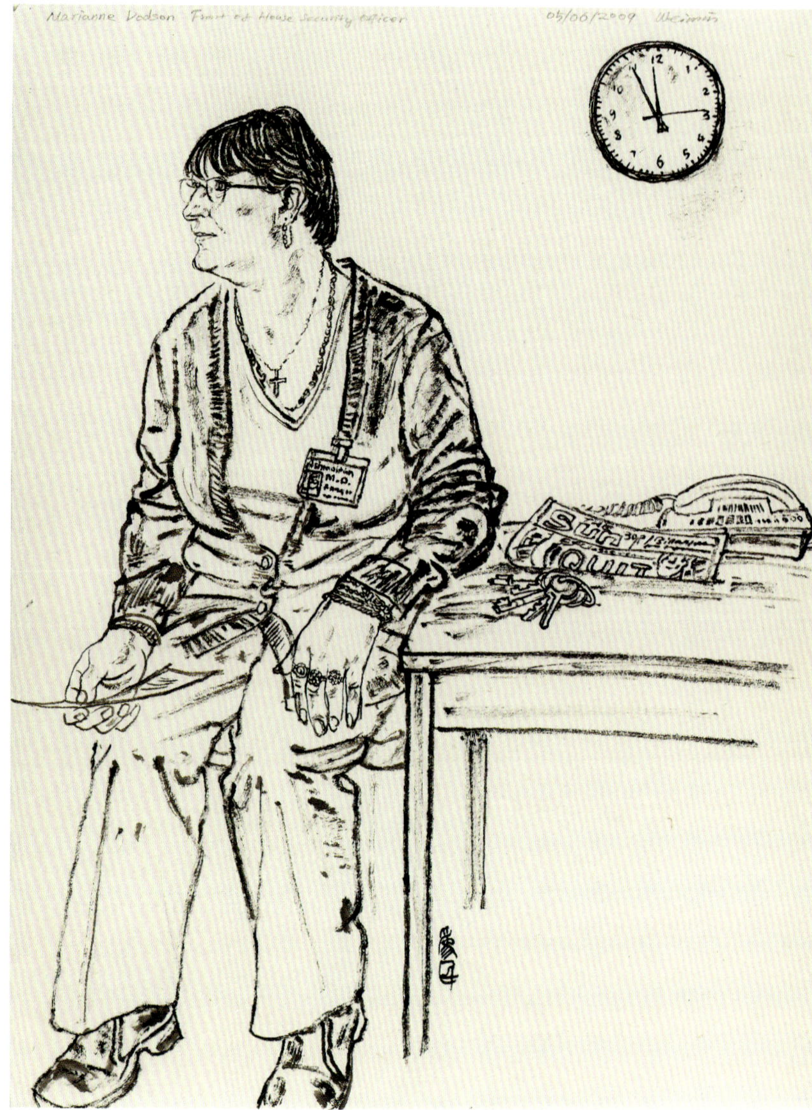

121

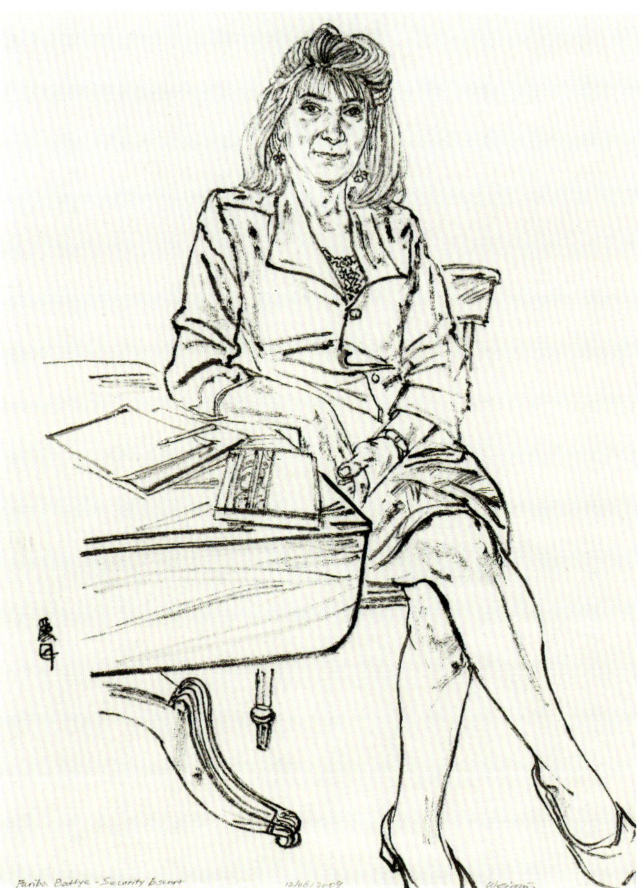

122

120 Joe Hathaway *Security Officer*
2009. Brush and ink on *xuan* paper. Paper size: 44.8 × 34 cm

121 Marianne Dodson *Security Officer*
2009. Brush and ink on *xuan* paper. Paper size: 44.8 × 34 cm

122 Fariba Battye *Museum staff*
2009. Brush and ink on *xuan* paper. Paper size: 44.8 × 34 cm

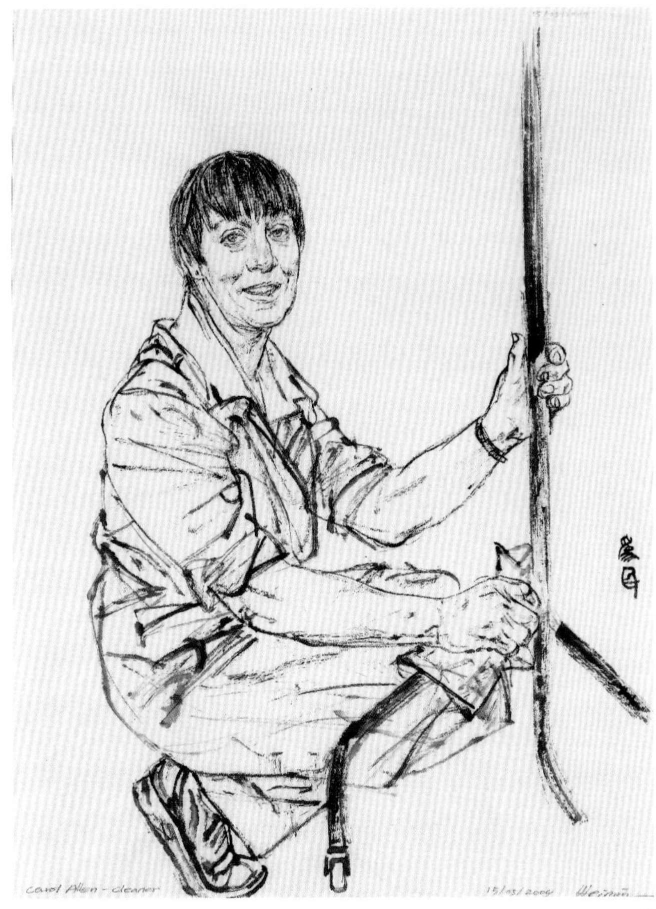

123

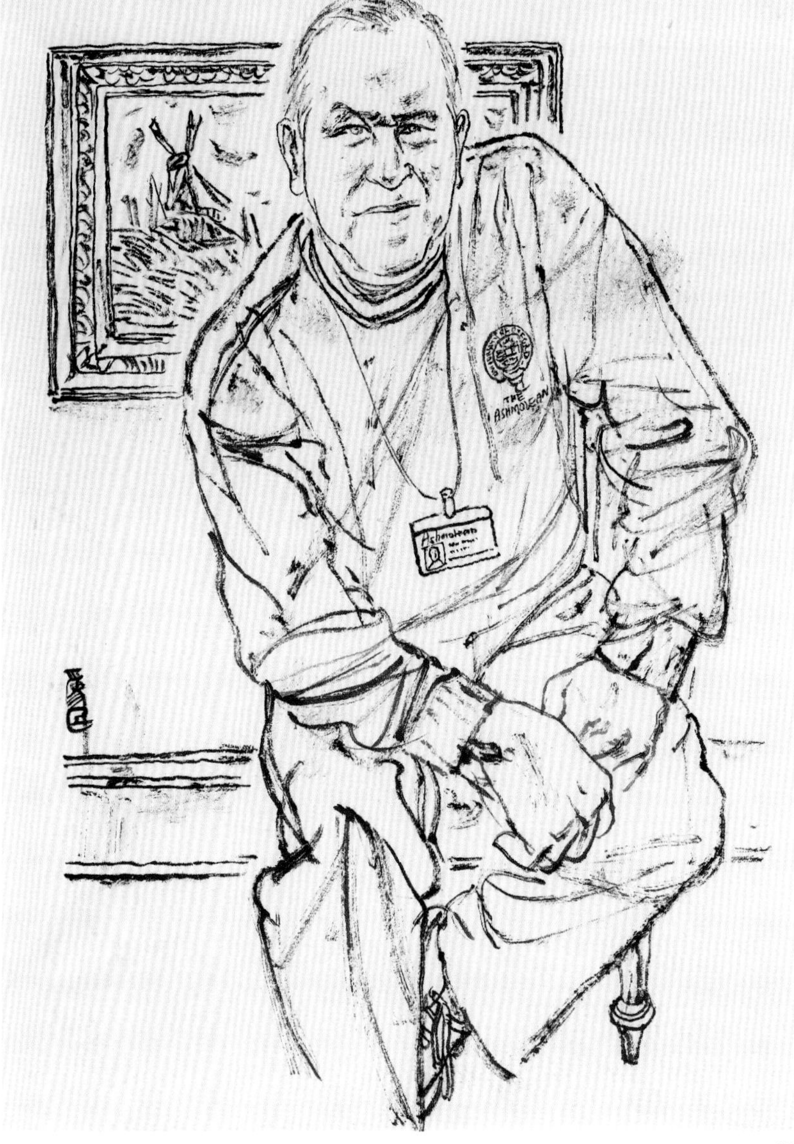

124

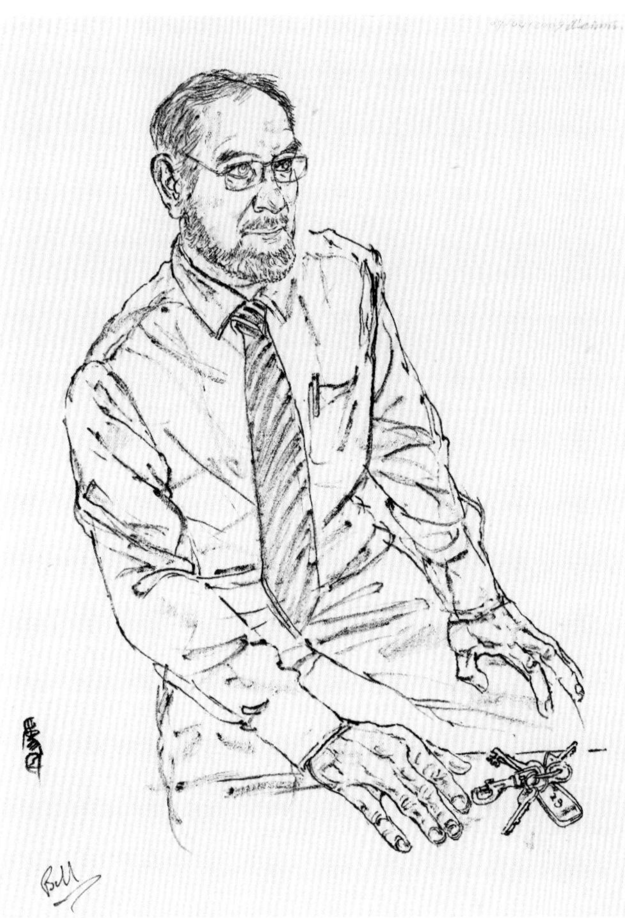

125

123 Carol Allen *Cleaner*
2009. Brush and ink on *xuan* paper. Paper size: 44.8 × 34 cm

124 Moussa *Former Museum staff*
2008. Brush and ink on *xuan* paper. Paper size: 44.8 × 34 cm

125 Bill *Former Museum staff*
2009. Marker on *xuan* paper. Paper size: 44.8 × 34 cm

On the Project

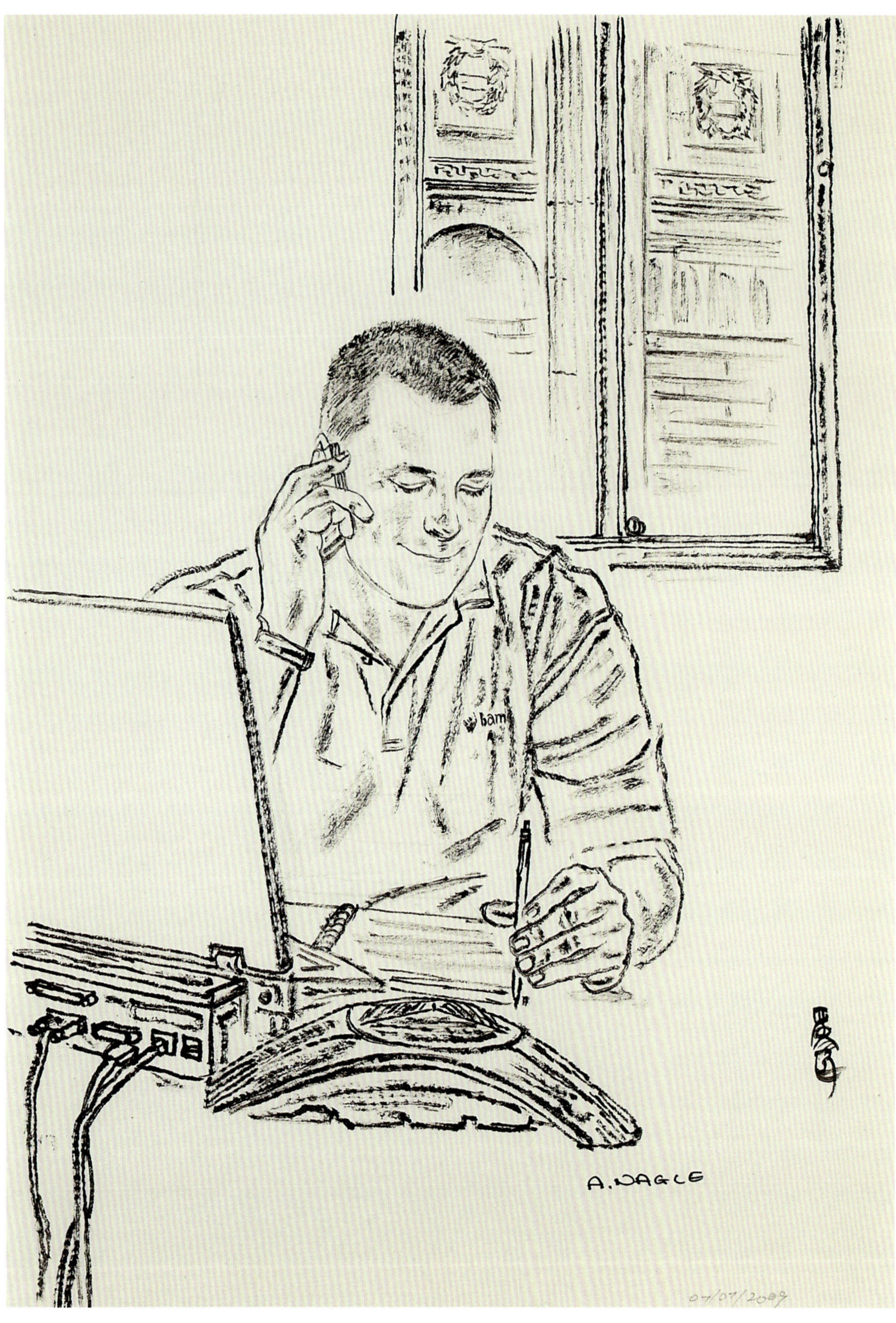

126 Antony Nagle *Construction Manager*
2009. Brush and ink on album leaves. Paper size: 44.2 × 32.3 cm

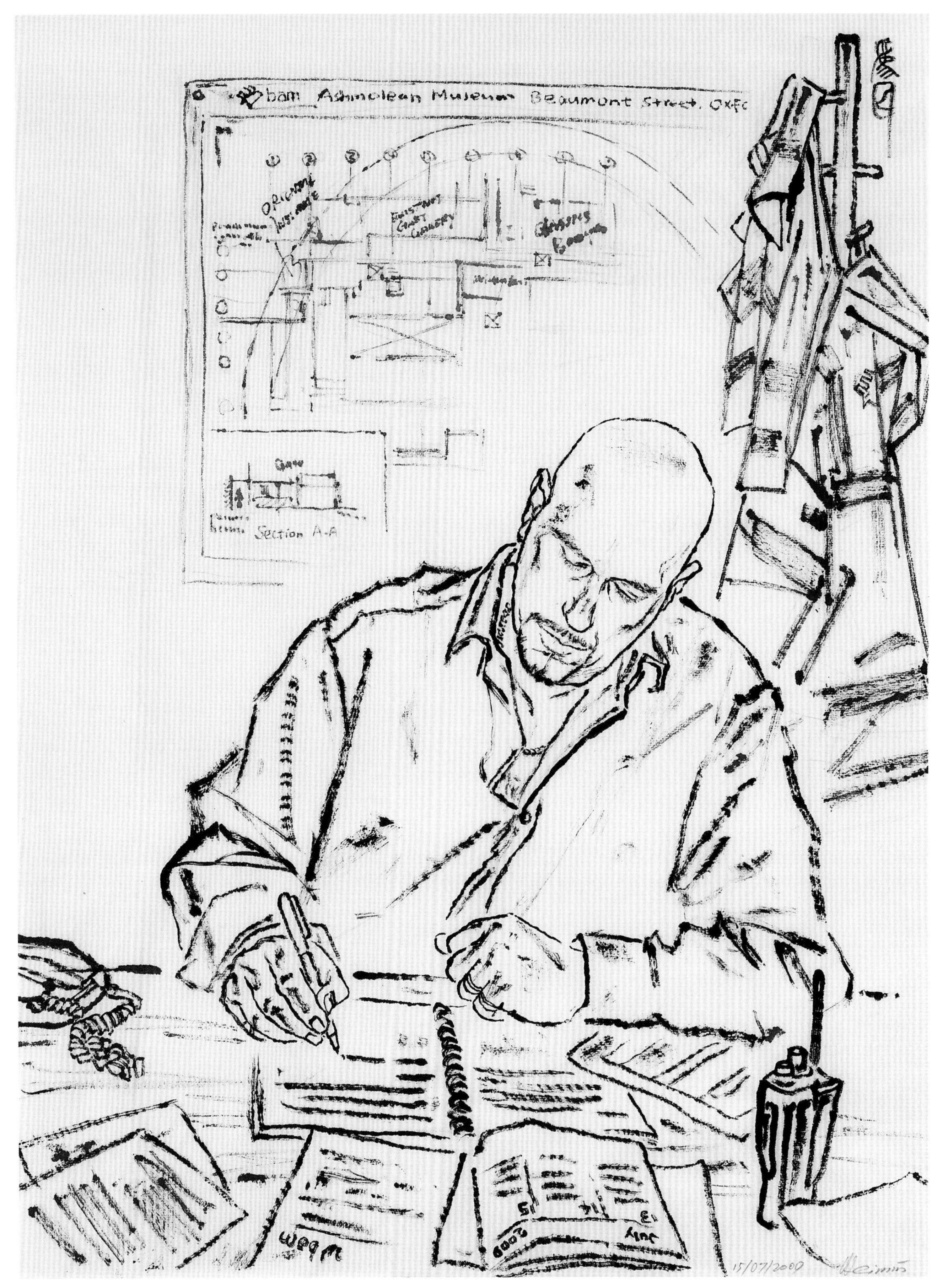

127 Tony O'Keeffe *Project Manager*
2009. Brush and ink on *xuan* paper. Paper size: 44.8 × 34 cm

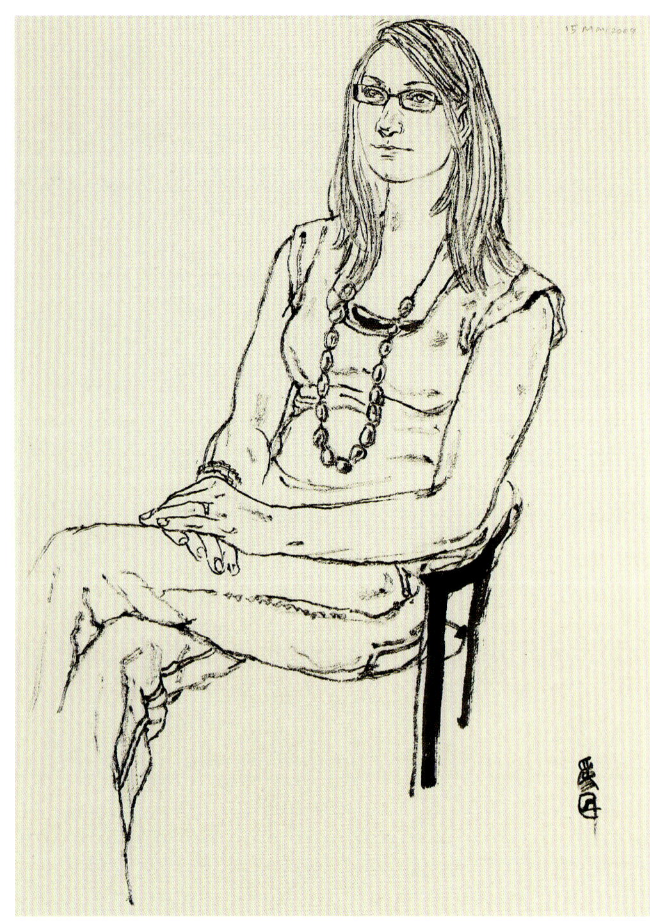

128

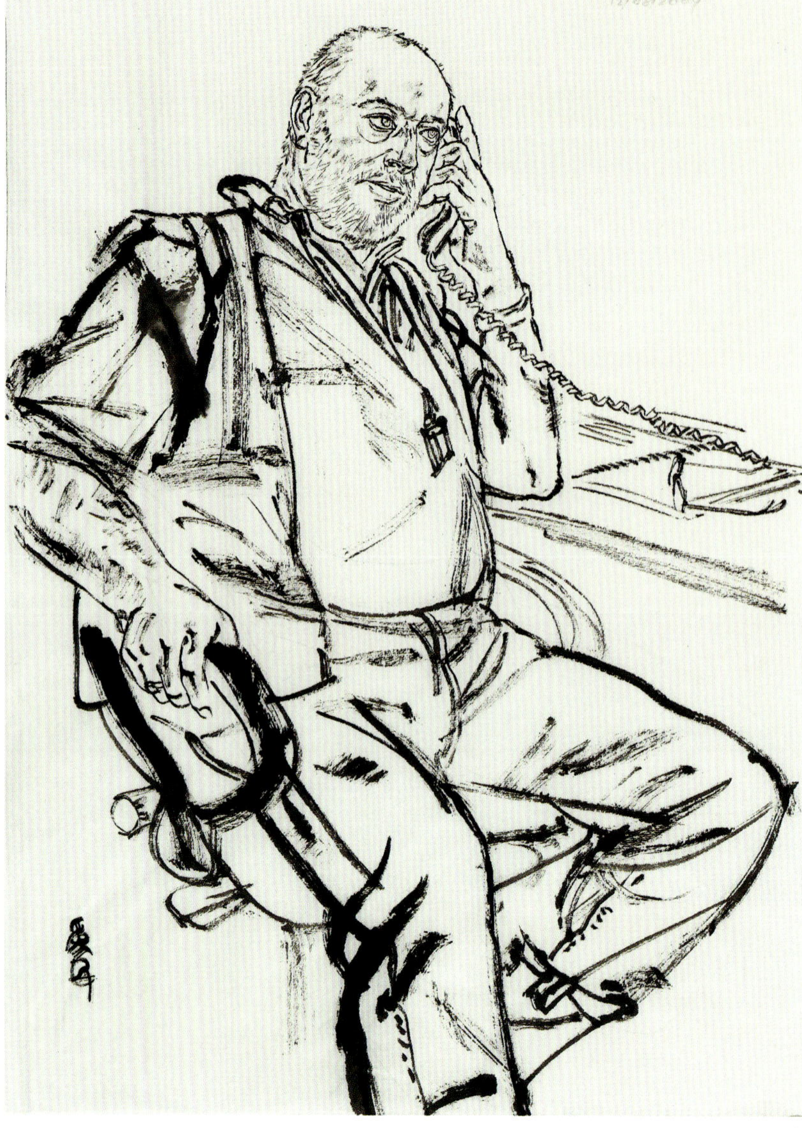

129

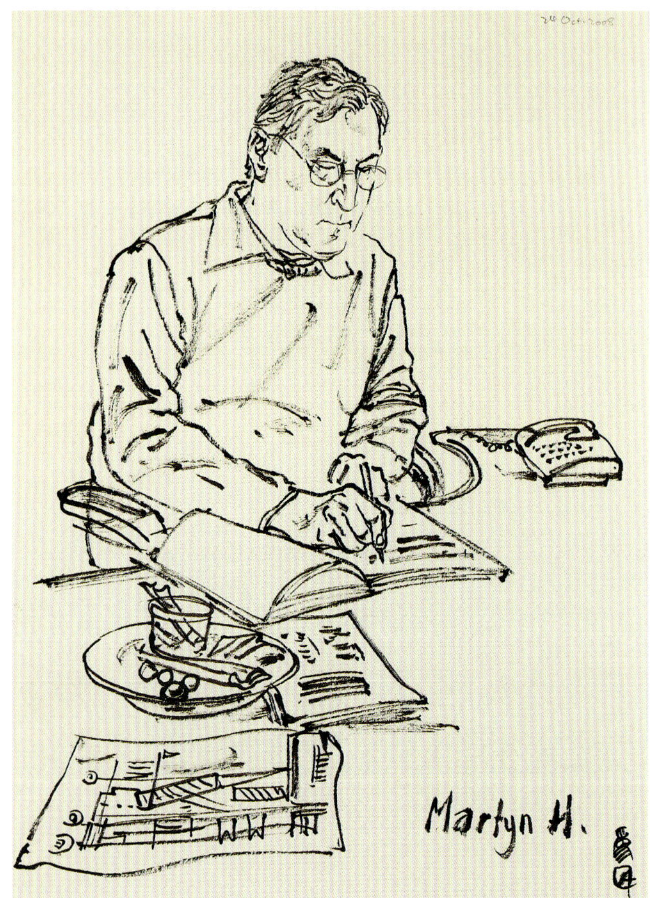

130

128 Amy Dunford *Site Administrator*
2009. Brush and ink on album leaves. Paper size: 44.2 × 32.3 cm

129 David Hawkins *Senior Site Manager*
2009. Brush and ink on paper. Paper size: 44.8 × 34 cm

130 Martyn Howden *Senior Site Manager*
2008. Brush and ink on album leaves. Paper size: 44.2 × 32.3 cm

131 Brett Smith *Building Services Assistant*
2009. Brush and ink on album leaves. Paper size: 44.2 × 32.3 cm

132 Jason Norton *Carpenter*
2008. Brush and ink on album leaves. Paper size: 44.2 × 32.3 cm

133 Adam Hawkins *Assistant Site Manager*
2009. Brush and ink on album leaves. Paper size: 44.2 × 32.3 cm

134 Vince Finn *Gangerman*
2008. Brush and ink on album leaves. Paper size: 44.2 × 32.3 cm

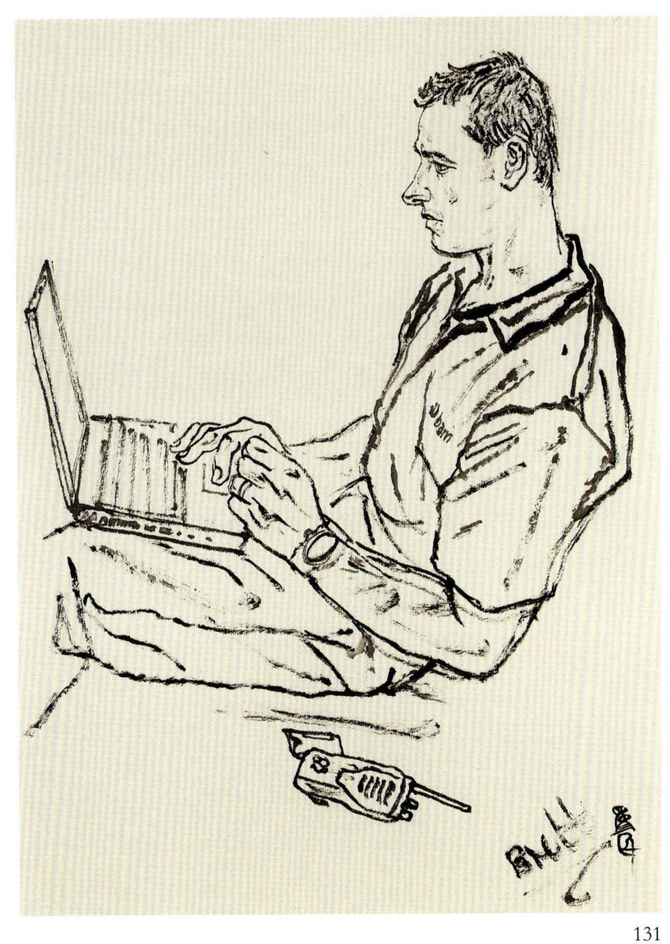
131

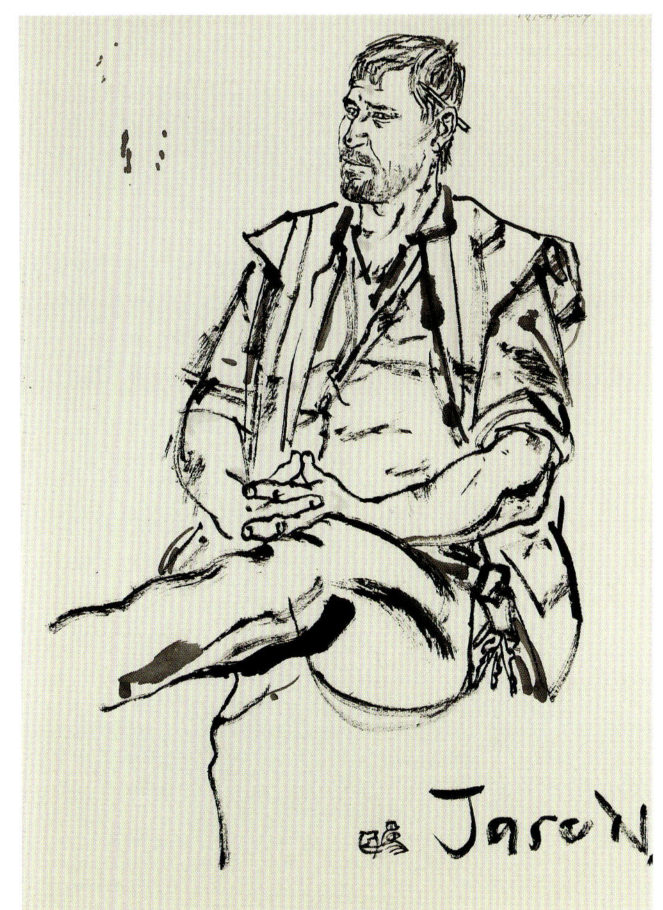

132

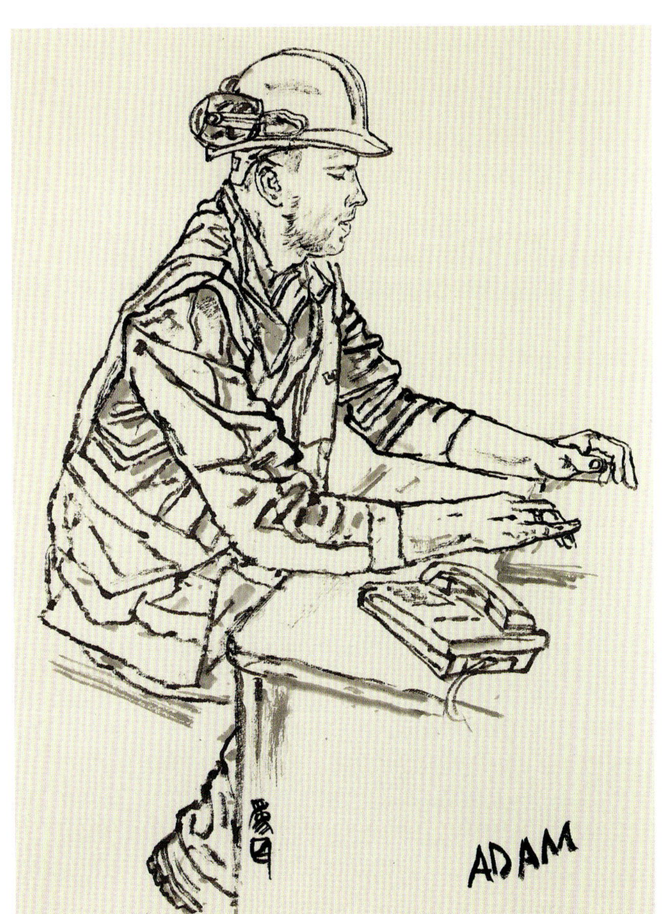

133

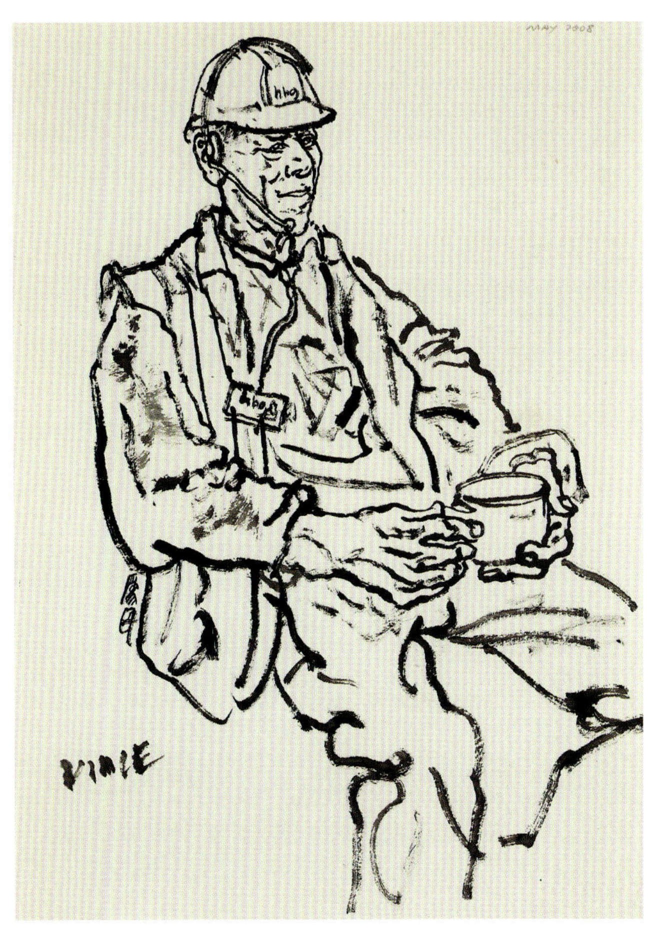
134

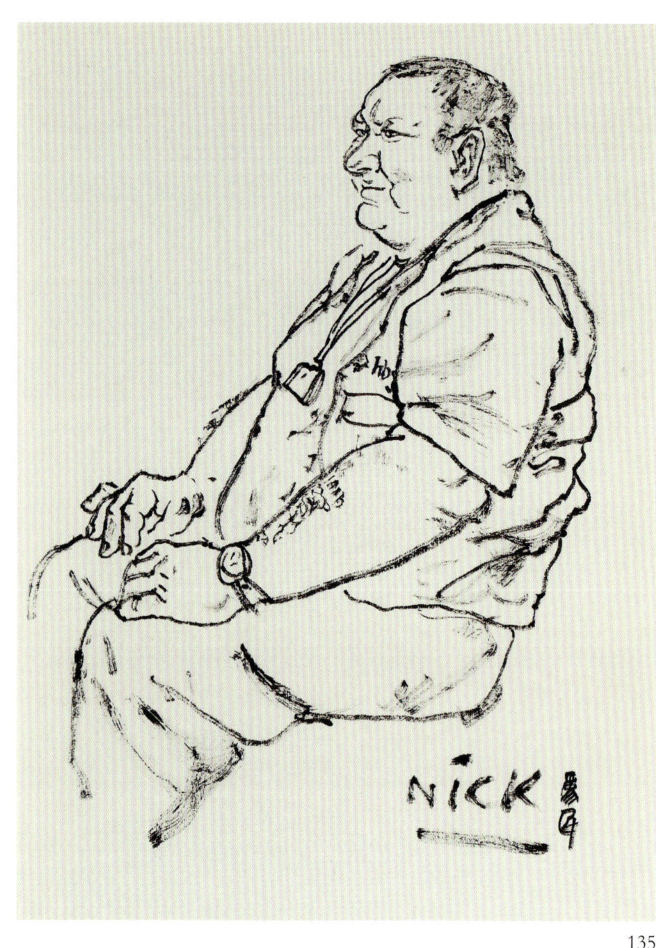

135

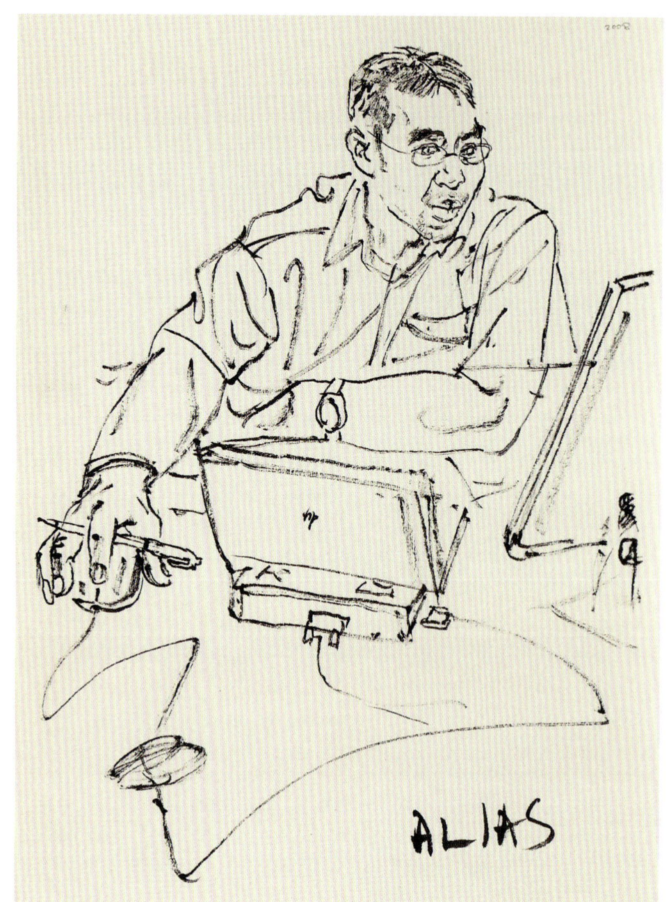

136

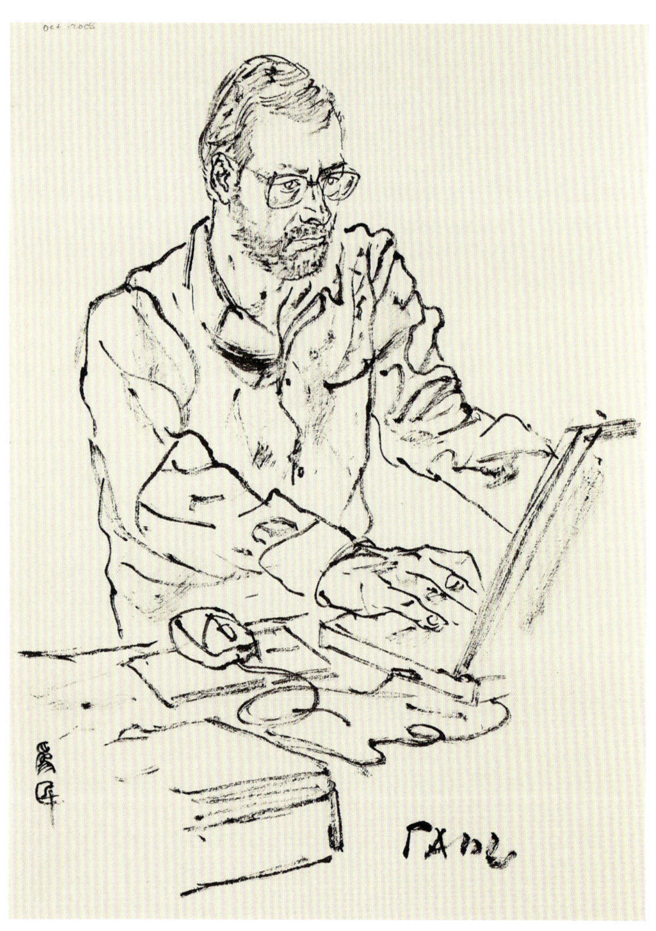

137

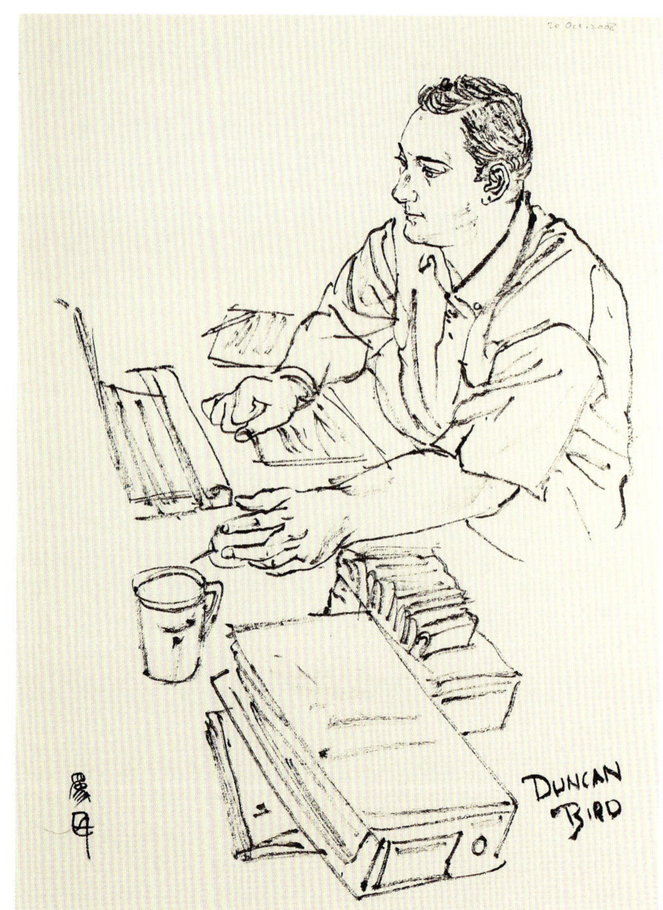

138

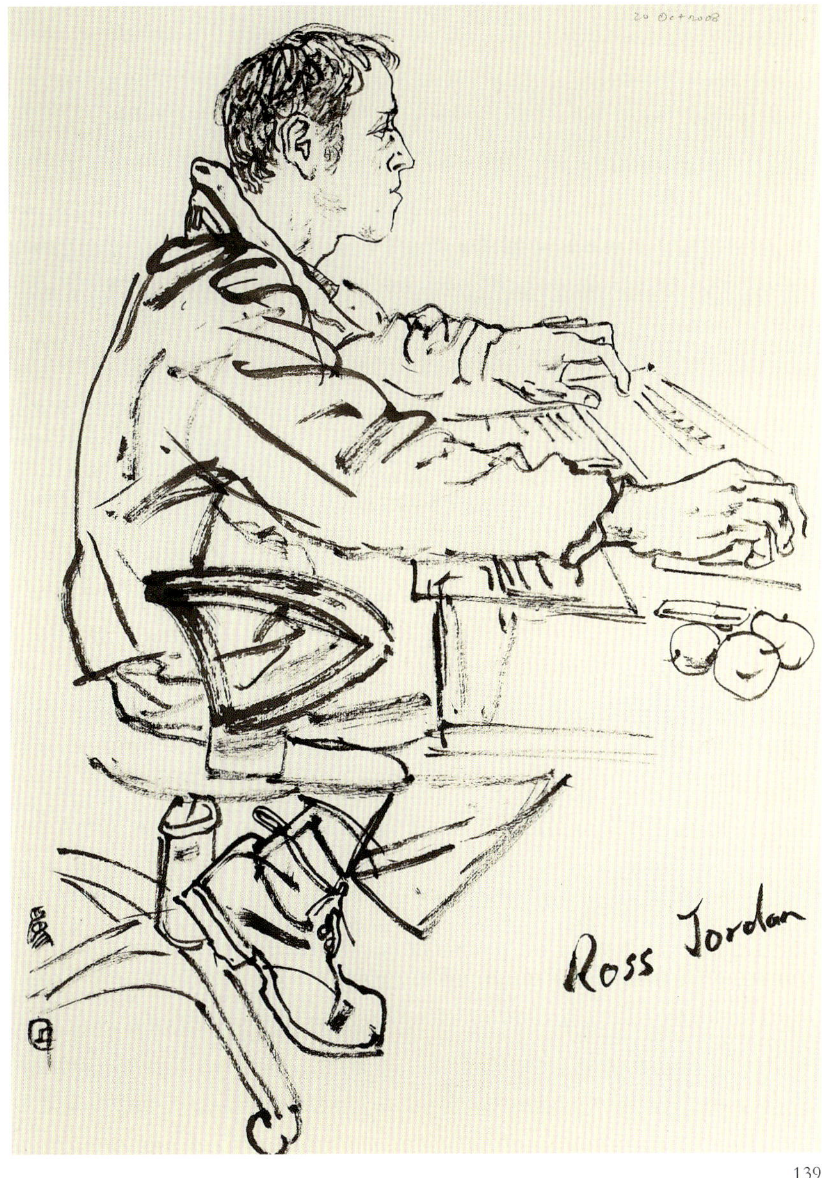

139

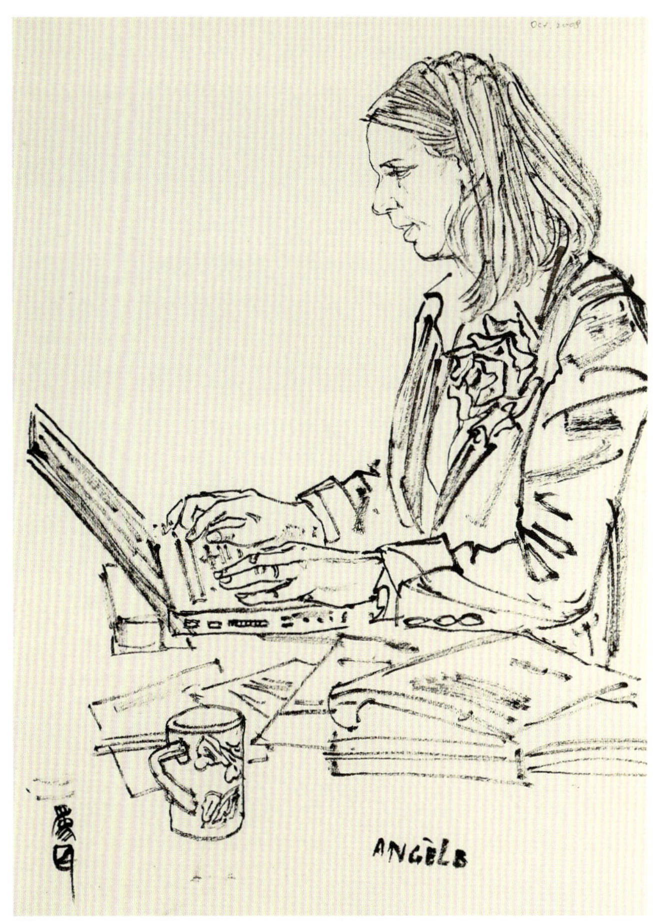

140

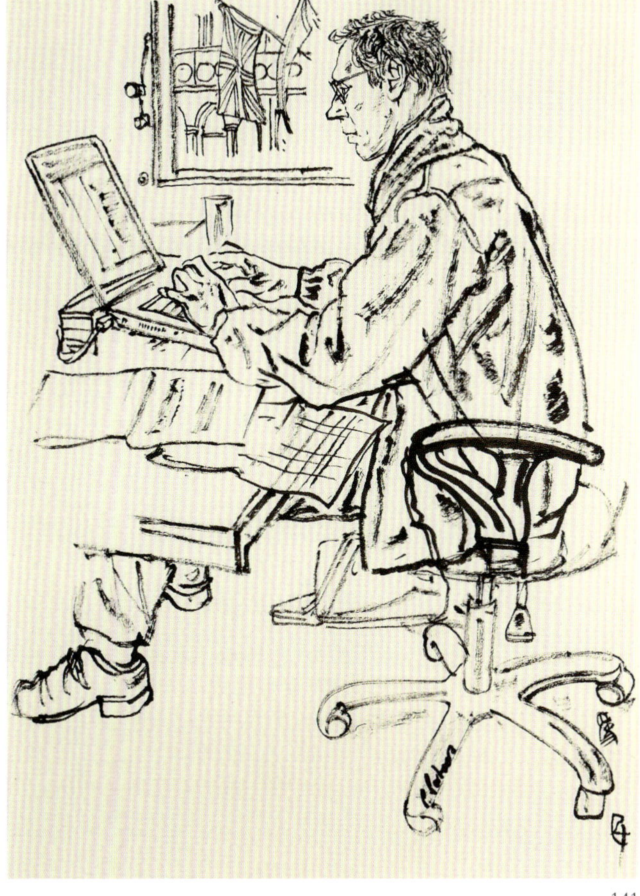

141

135 Nick Gardner *Gateman*
2008. Brush and ink on album leaves. Paper size: 44.2 × 32.3 cm

136 Alias Masud *Project Surveyor*
2008. Brush and ink on album leaves. Paper size: 44.2 × 32.3 cm

137 Paul Durden *Design Manager*
2008. Brush and ink on album leaves. Paper size: 44.2 × 32.3 cm

138 Duncan Bird *M&E Project Surveyor*
2008. Brush and ink on album leaves. Paper size: 44.2 × 32.3 cm

139 Ross Jordan *Project Surveyor*
2008. Brush and ink on album leaves. Paper size: 44.2 × 32.3 cm

140 Angèle Braham *Causeway Administrator*
2008. Brush and ink on album leaves. Paper size: 44.2 × 32.3 cm

141 Colin Allen *Commissioning Manager*
2009. Brush and ink on album leaves. Paper size: 44.2 × 32.3 cm

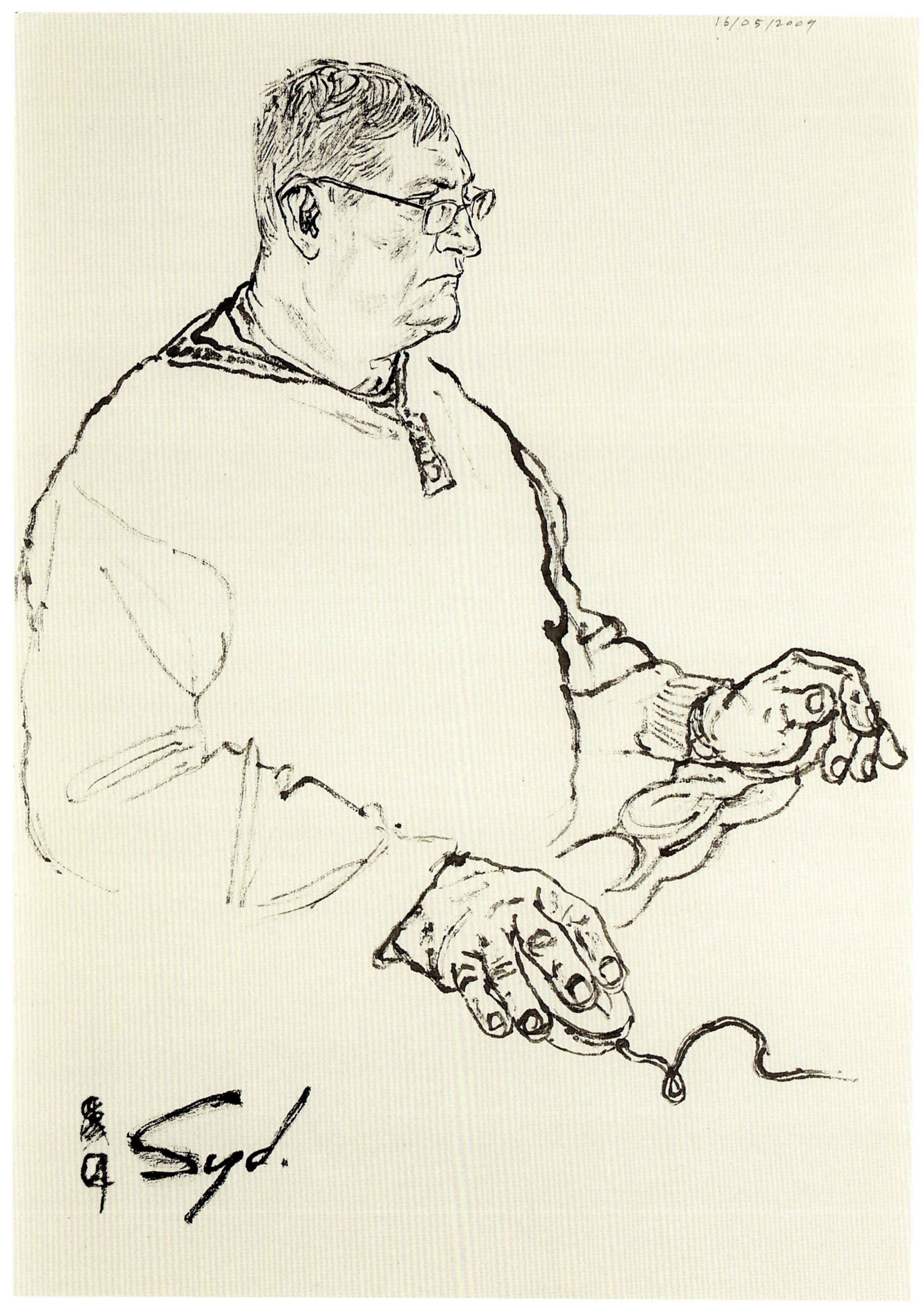

142

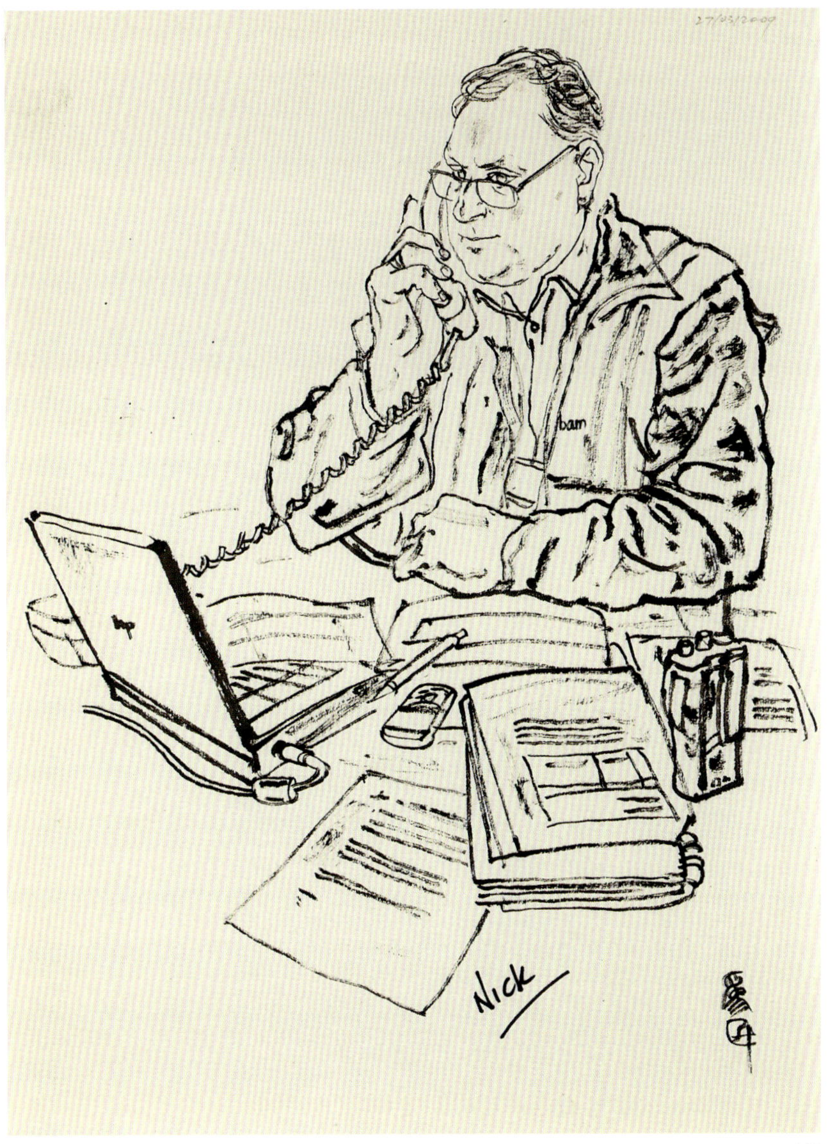

143

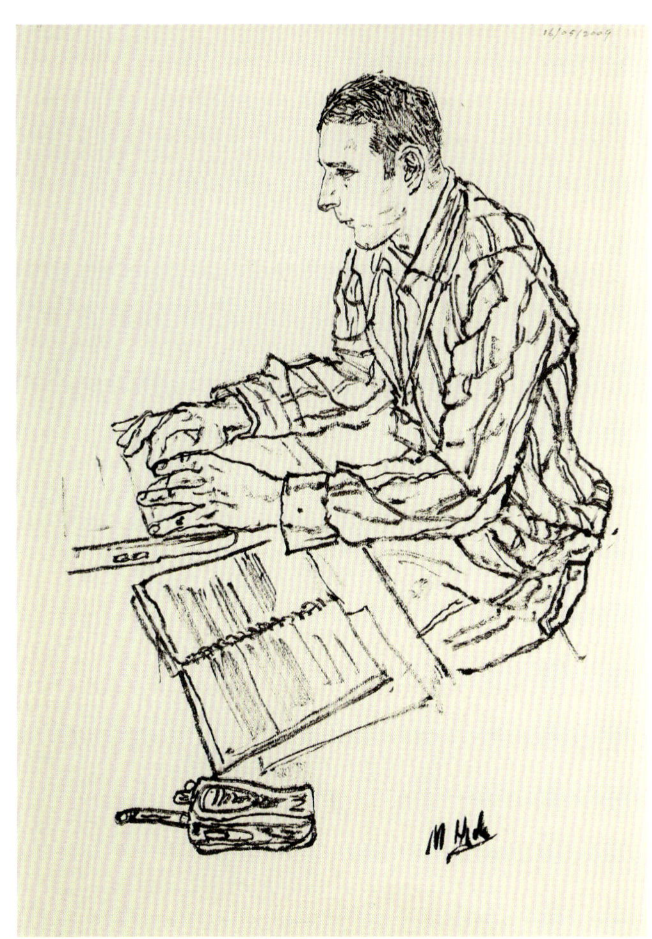

144

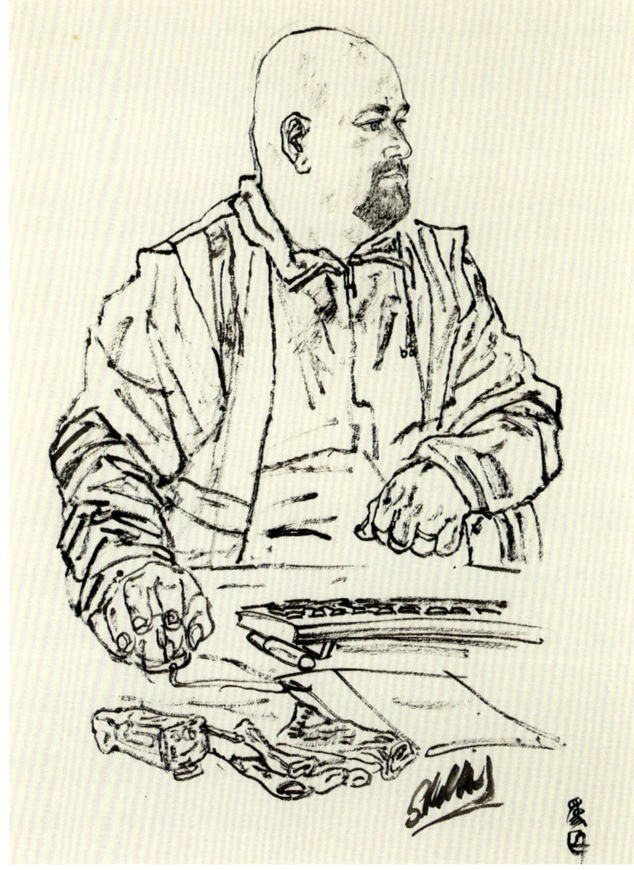

145

142 Syd Pitt *Building Services Manager*
2009. Brush and ink on album leaves. Paper size: 44.2 × 32.3 cm

143 Nick Carpenter *Building Services Project Manager*
2009. Brush and ink on album leaves. Paper size: 44.2 × 32.3 cm

144 Michael Hyde *Senior Site Manager*
2009. Brush and ink on album leaves. Paper size: 44.2 × 32.3 cm

145 Scott Hellaby *Senior Site Manager*
2009. Brush and ink on album leaves. Paper size: 44.2 × 32.3 cm

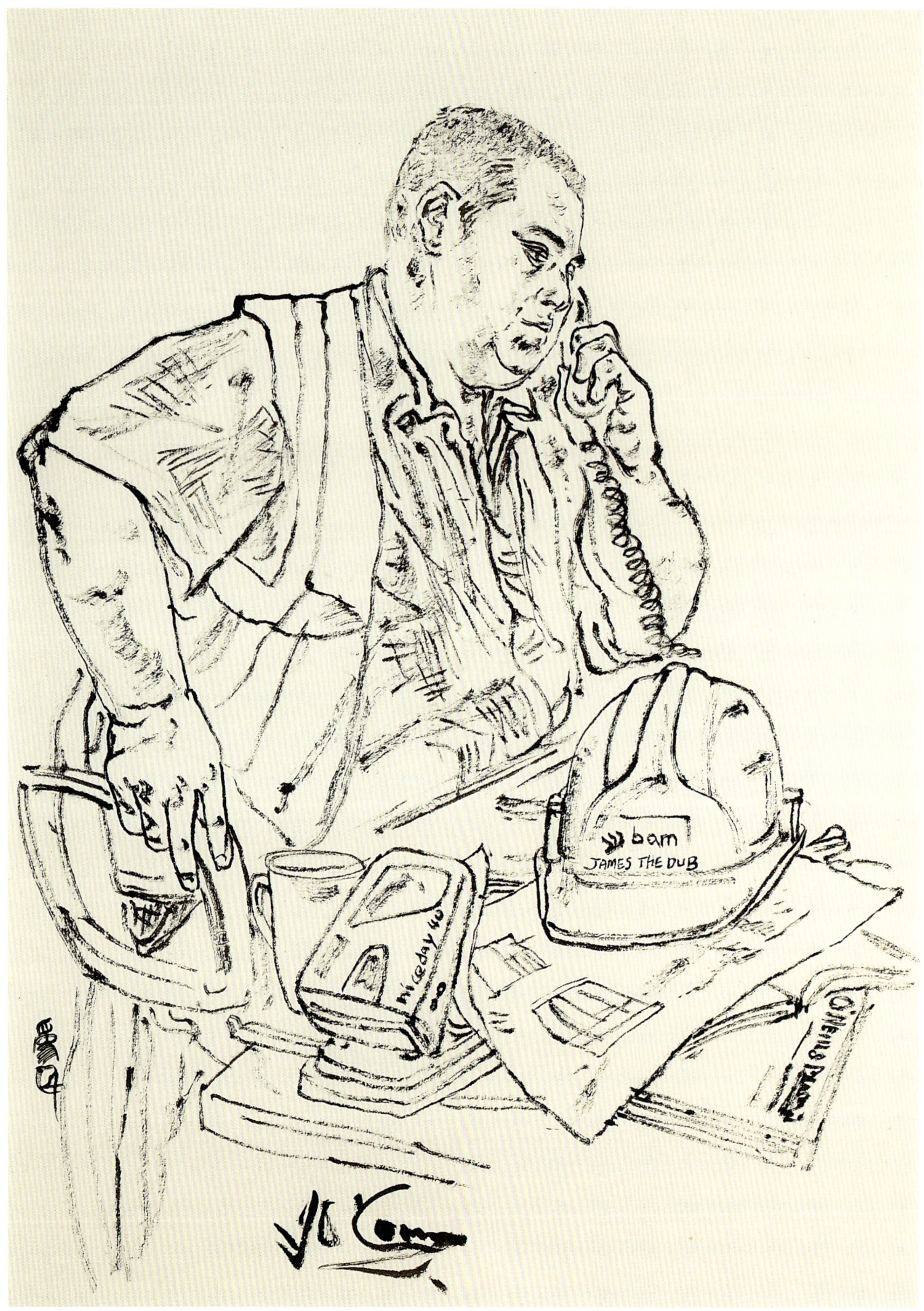

146

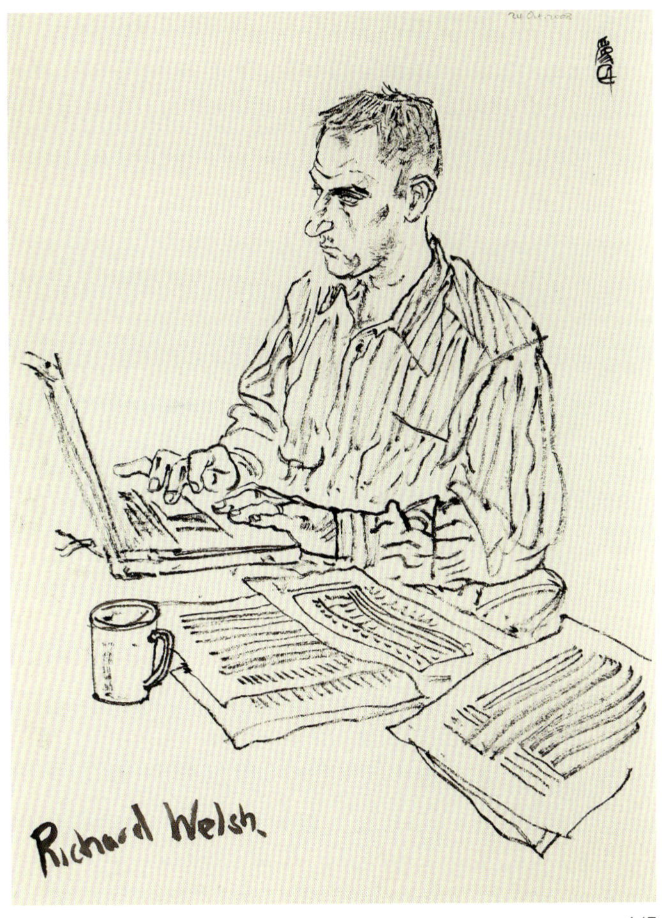

147

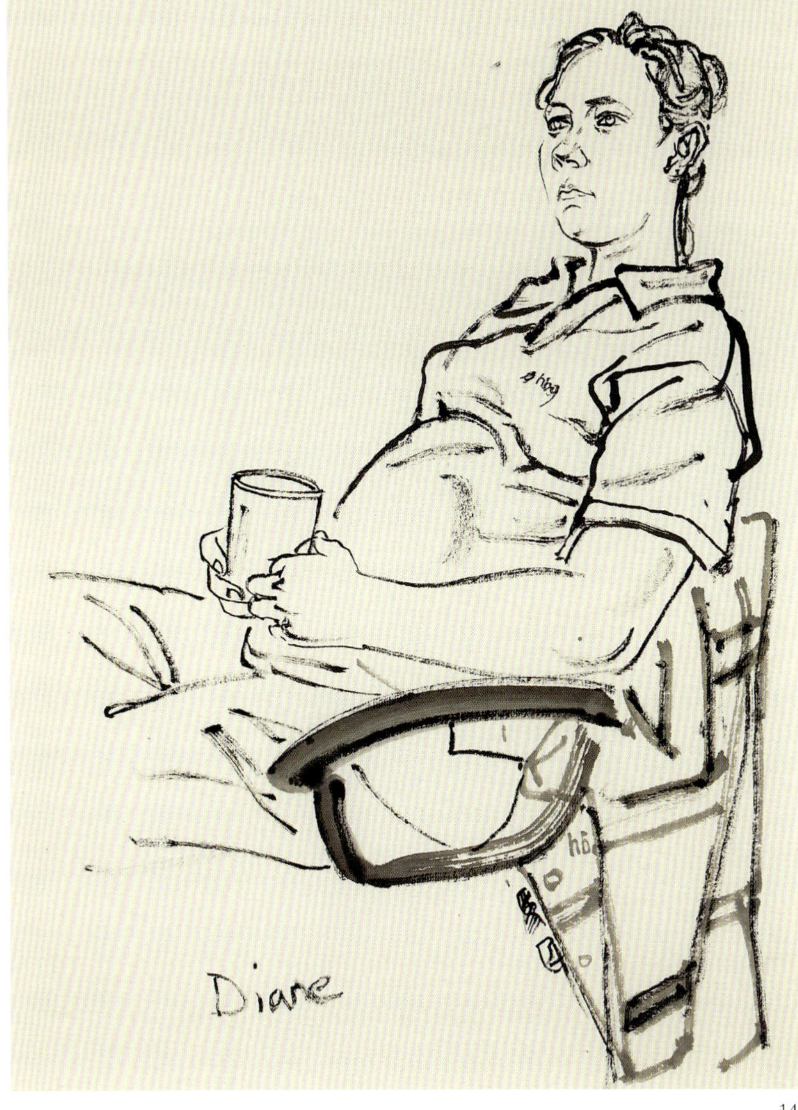

148

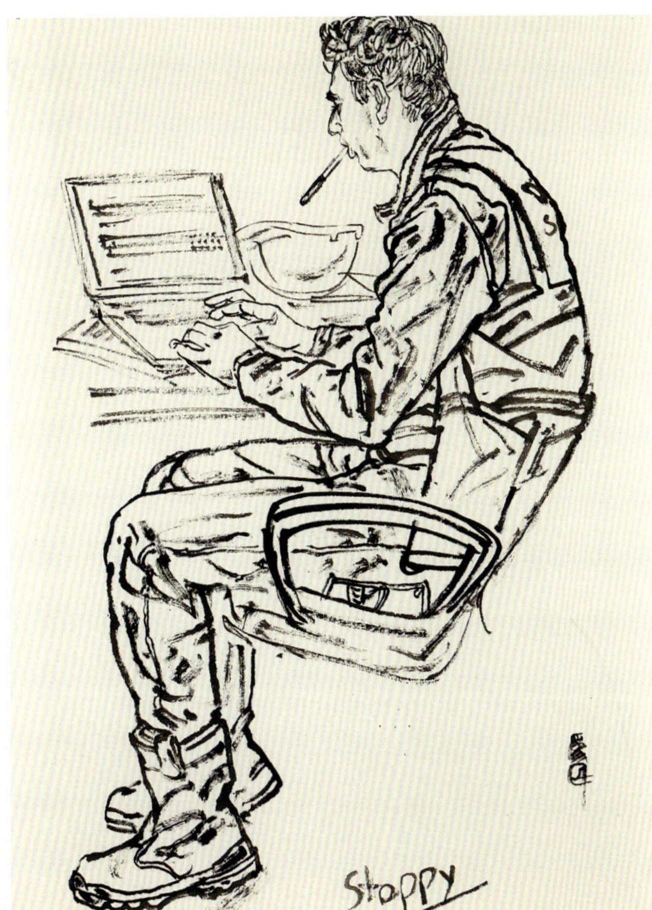

149

146 James O'Connor *Senior Site Manager*
2009. Brush and ink on album leaves. Paper size: 44.2 × 32.3 cm

147 Richard Welch *Planner*
2008. Brush and ink on album leaves. Paper size: 44.2 × 32.3 cm

148 Diane Newman *Senior Site Manager*
2008. Brush and ink on album leaves. Paper size: 44.2 × 32.3 cm

149 Michael Stopp *Assistant Site Manager*
2009. Brush and ink on album leaves. Paper size: 44.2 × 32.3 cm

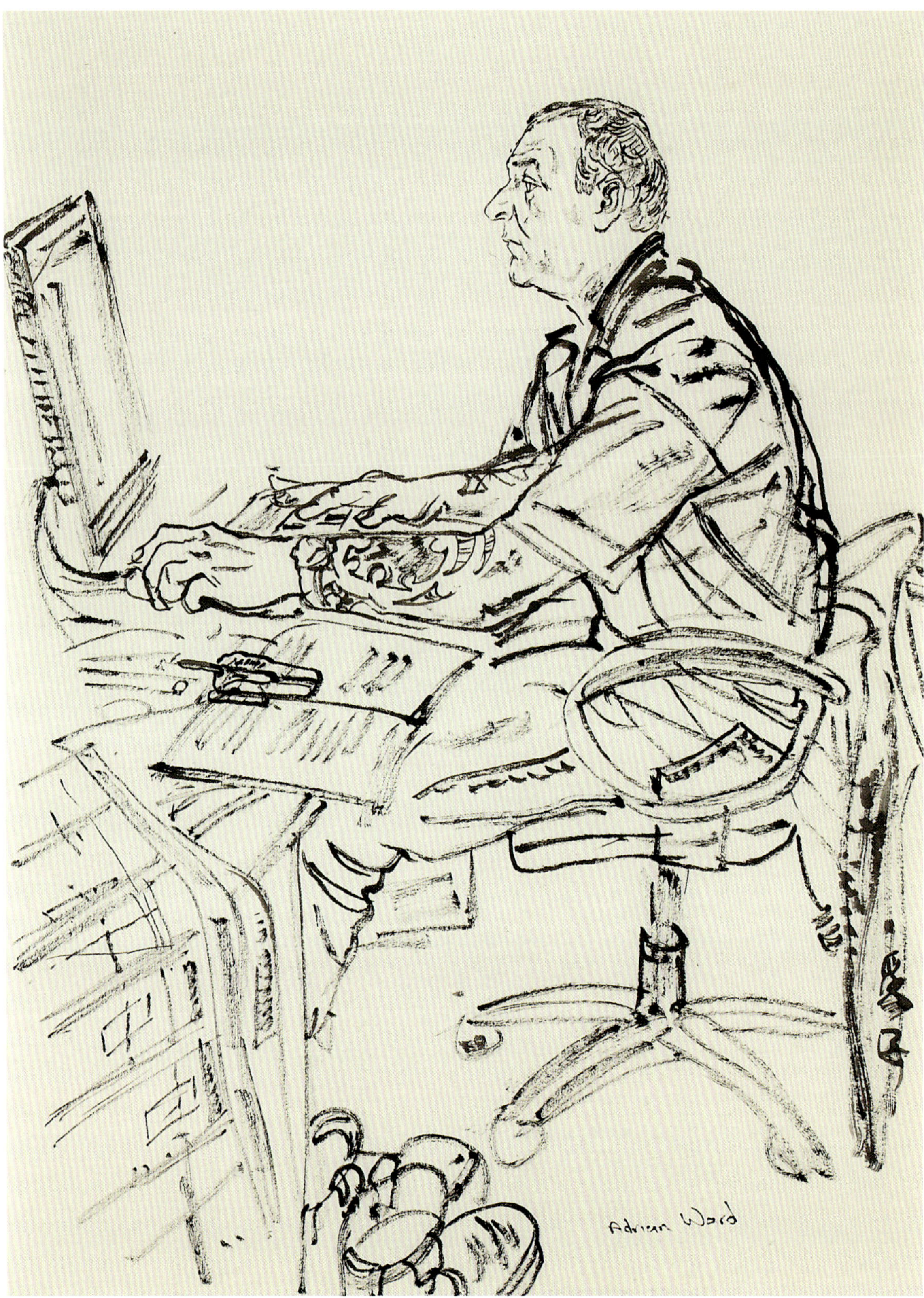

150

150 Adrian Ward *Senior Site Manager*
2009. Brush and ink on album leaves. Paper size: 44.2 × 32.3 cm

151 Brian Mooney *Project Planner*
2009. Brush and ink on album leaves. Paper size: 44.2 × 32.3 cm

152 Stuart Cade *Project Architect*
2009. Brush and ink on *xuan* paper. Paper size: 44.8 × 34 cm

153 Colin Levett *Managing Surveyor*
2009. Brush and ink on album leaves. Paper size: 44.2 × 32.3 cm

154 Steve Pearse *Contract Manager, Meyvaert*
2009. Brush and ink on *xuan* paper. Paper size: 44.8 × 34 cm

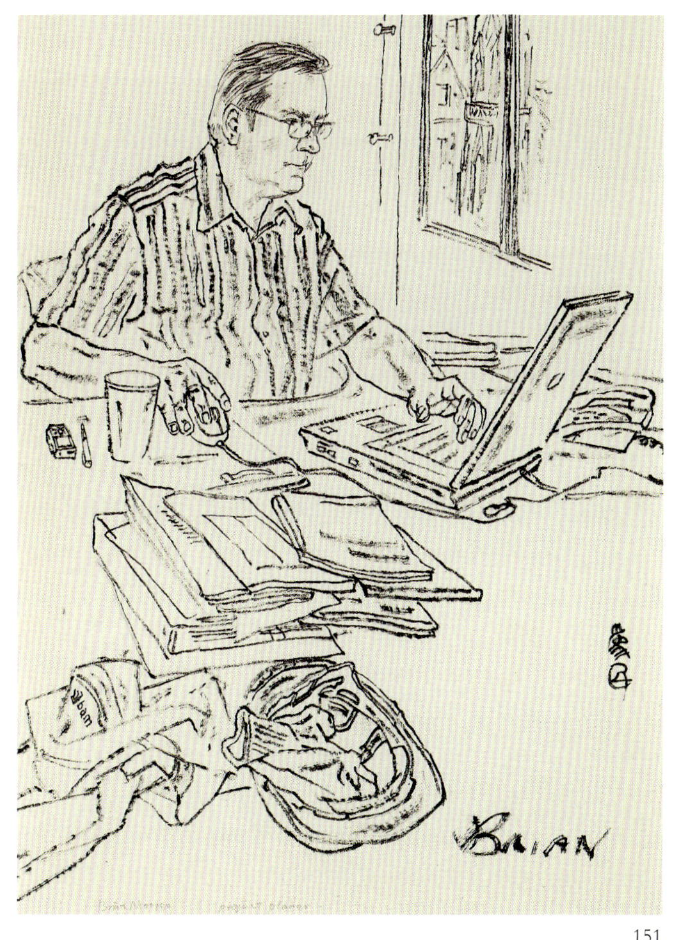

151

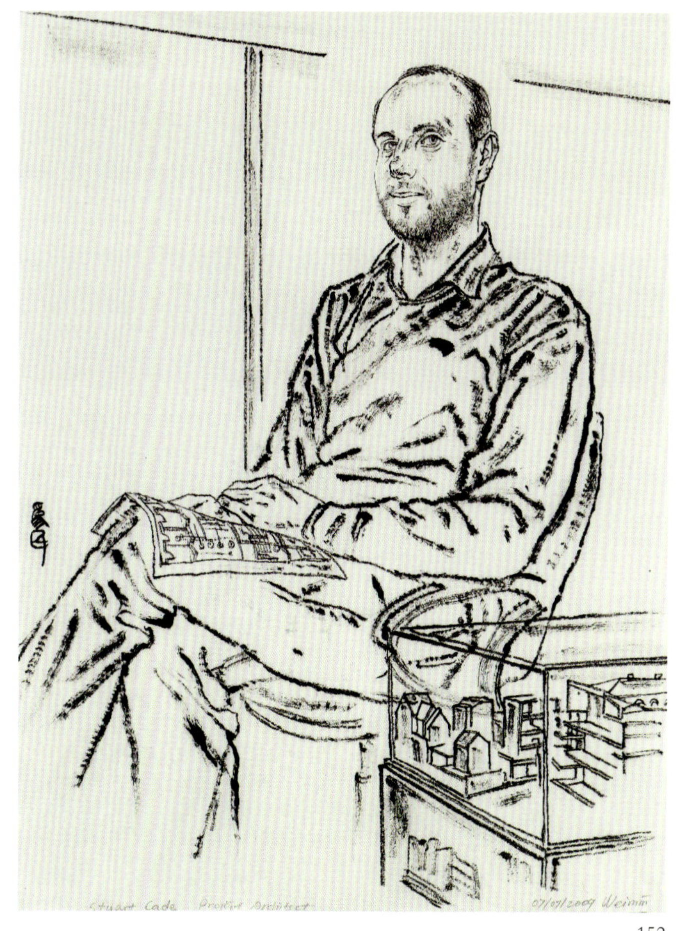

152

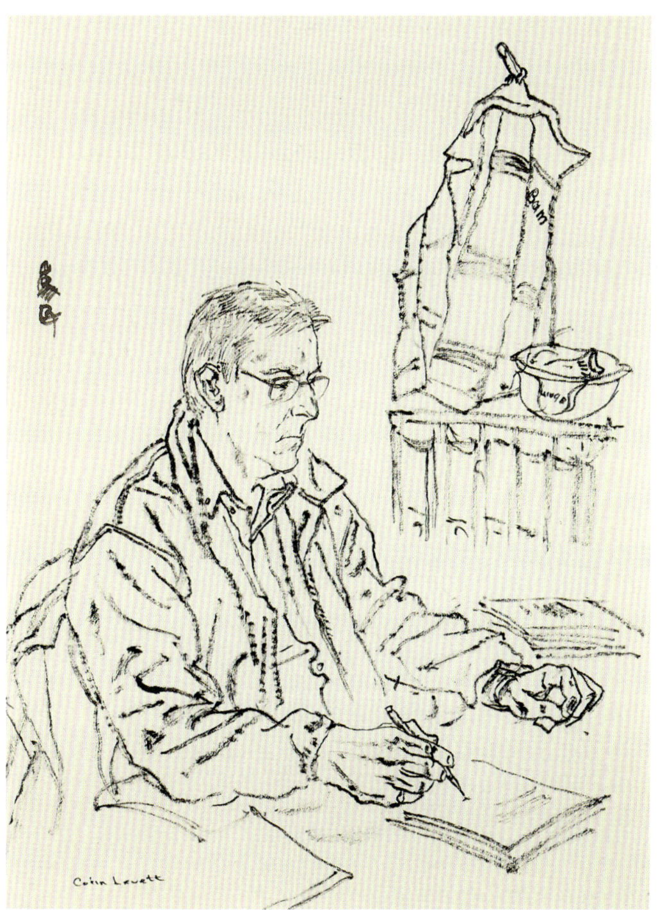

153

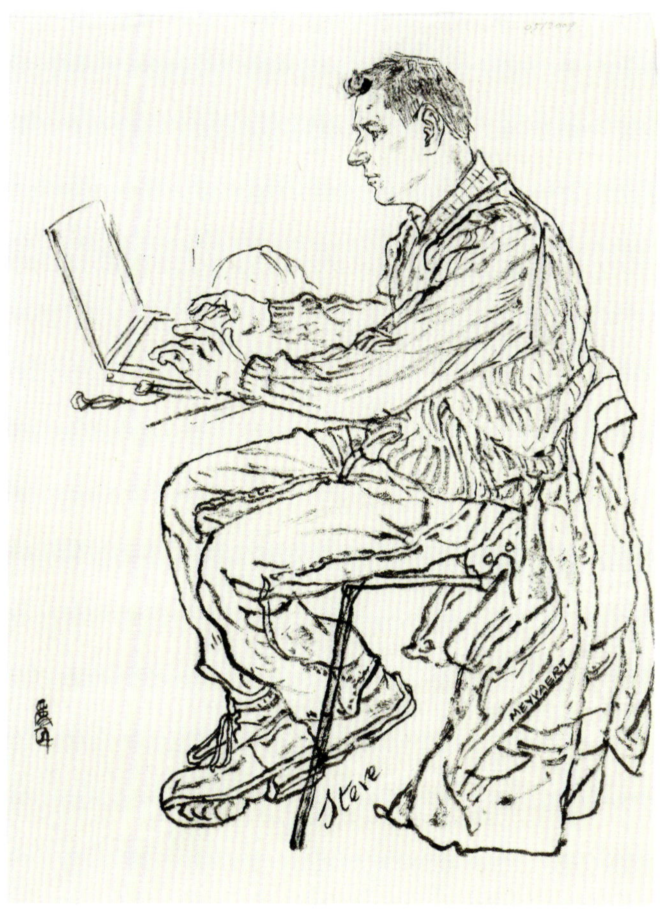

154

Construction Workers

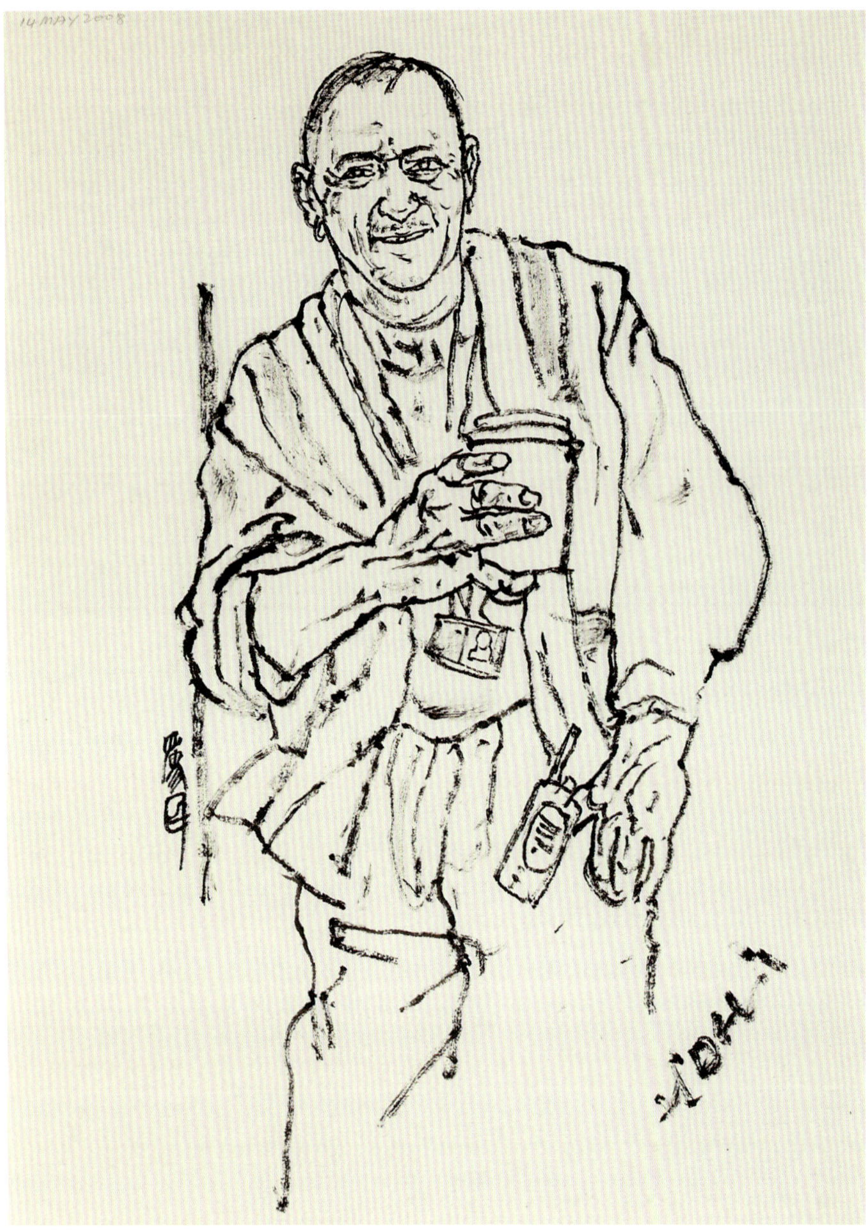

155

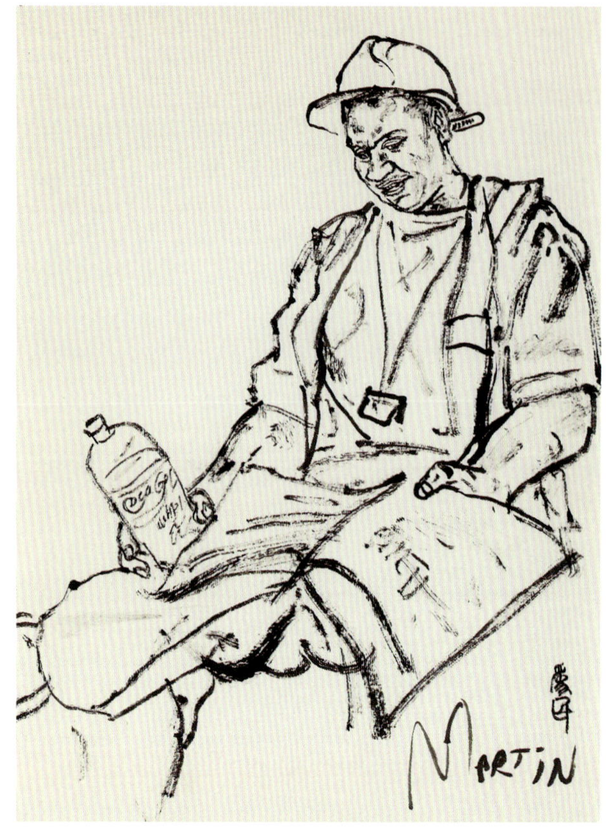

156

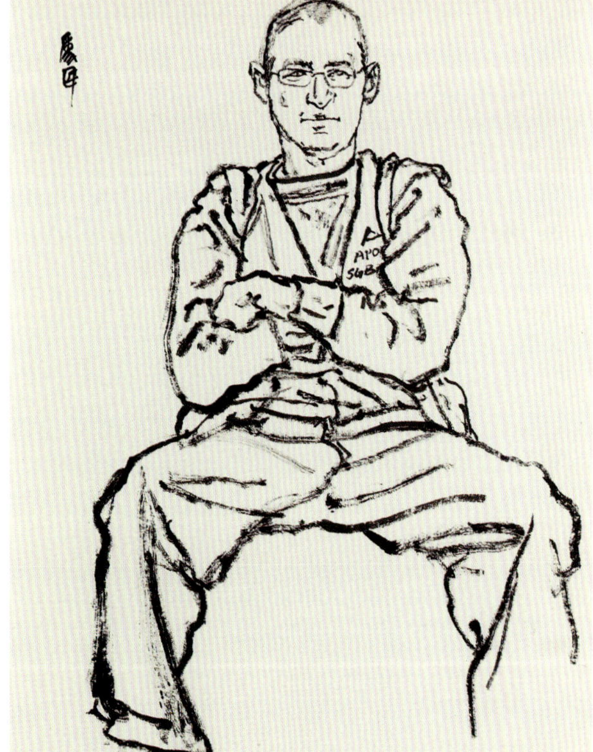
157

155 Construction worker *Banksman*
2008. Brush and ink on album leaves. Paper size: 44.2 × 32.3 cm

156 Martin *Construction worker*
2008. Brush and ink on album leaves. Paper size: 44.2 × 32.3 cm

157 *Construction worker*
2008. Brush and ink on album leaves. Paper size: 44.2 × 32.3 cm

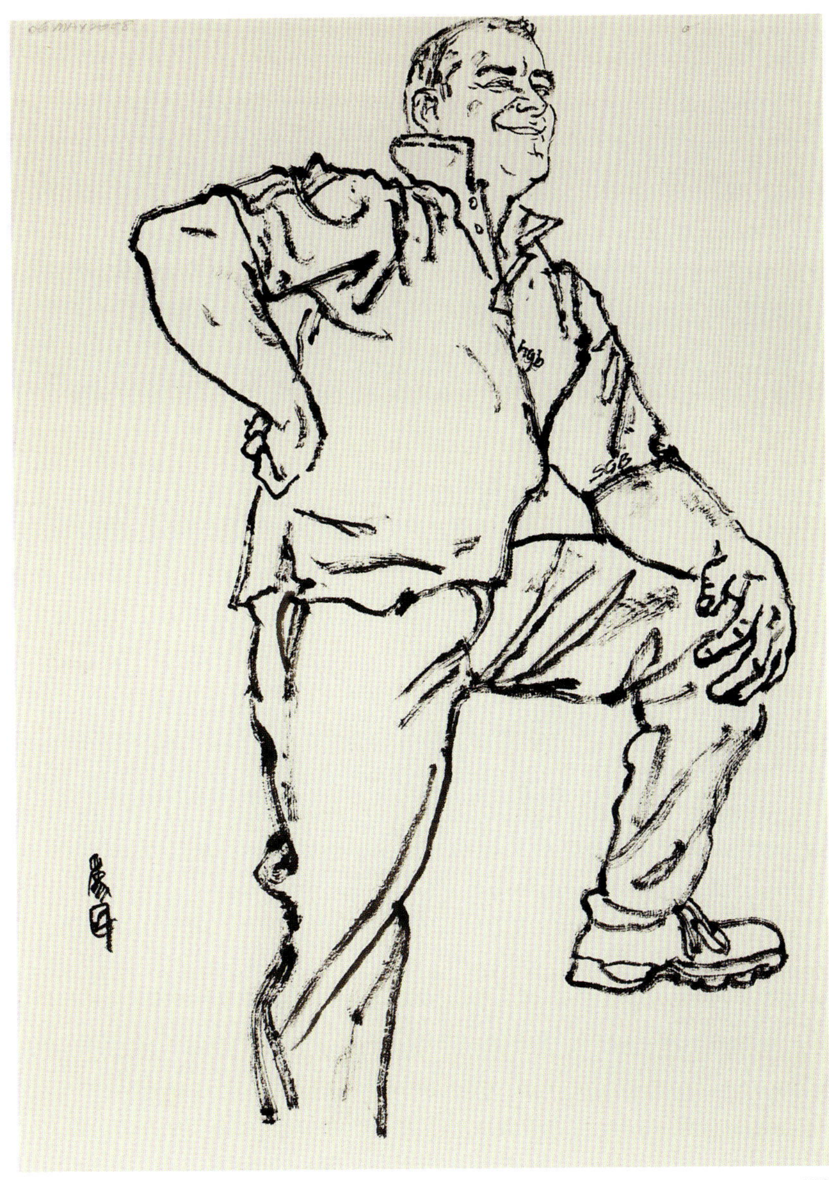

158

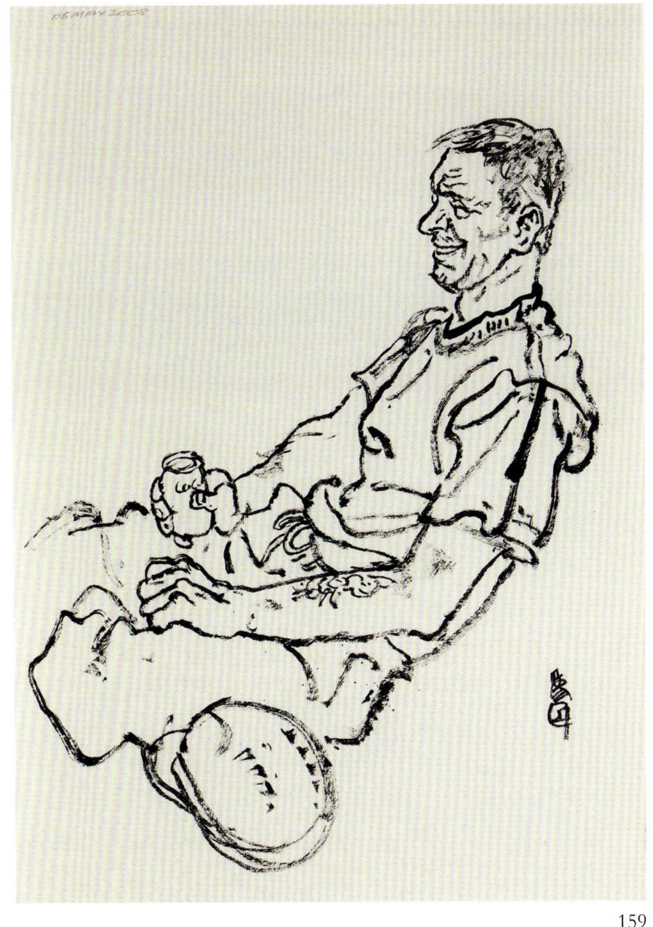

159

160

158 Warren *Scaffolder*
2008. Brush and ink on album leaves. Paper size: 44.2 × 32.3 cm

159 Alan *Bricklayer*
2008. Brush and ink on album leaves. 44.2 × 32.3 cm

160 Rob *Damp-proofing*
2008. Brush and ink on album leaves. Paper size: 44.2 × 32.3 cm

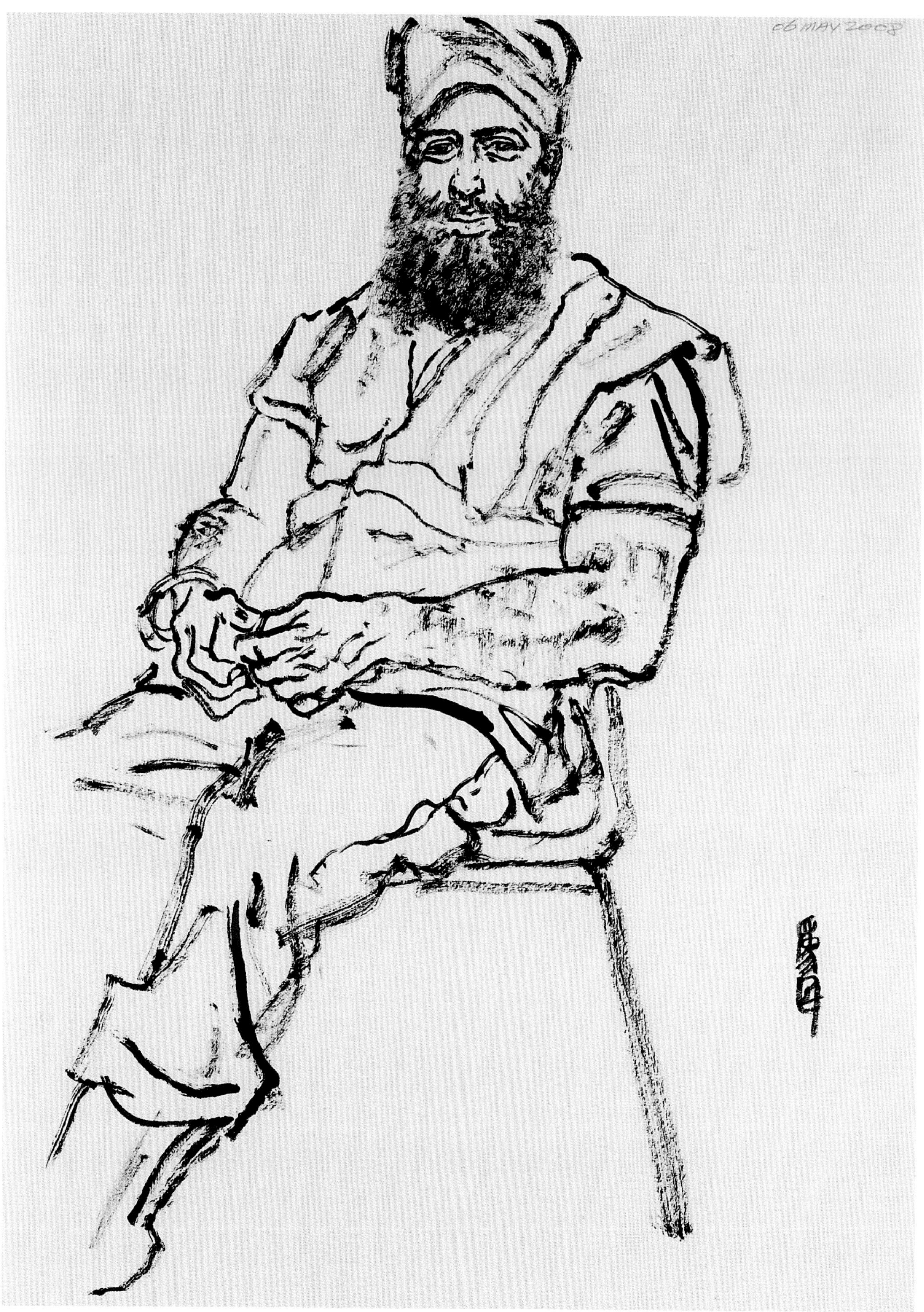

161

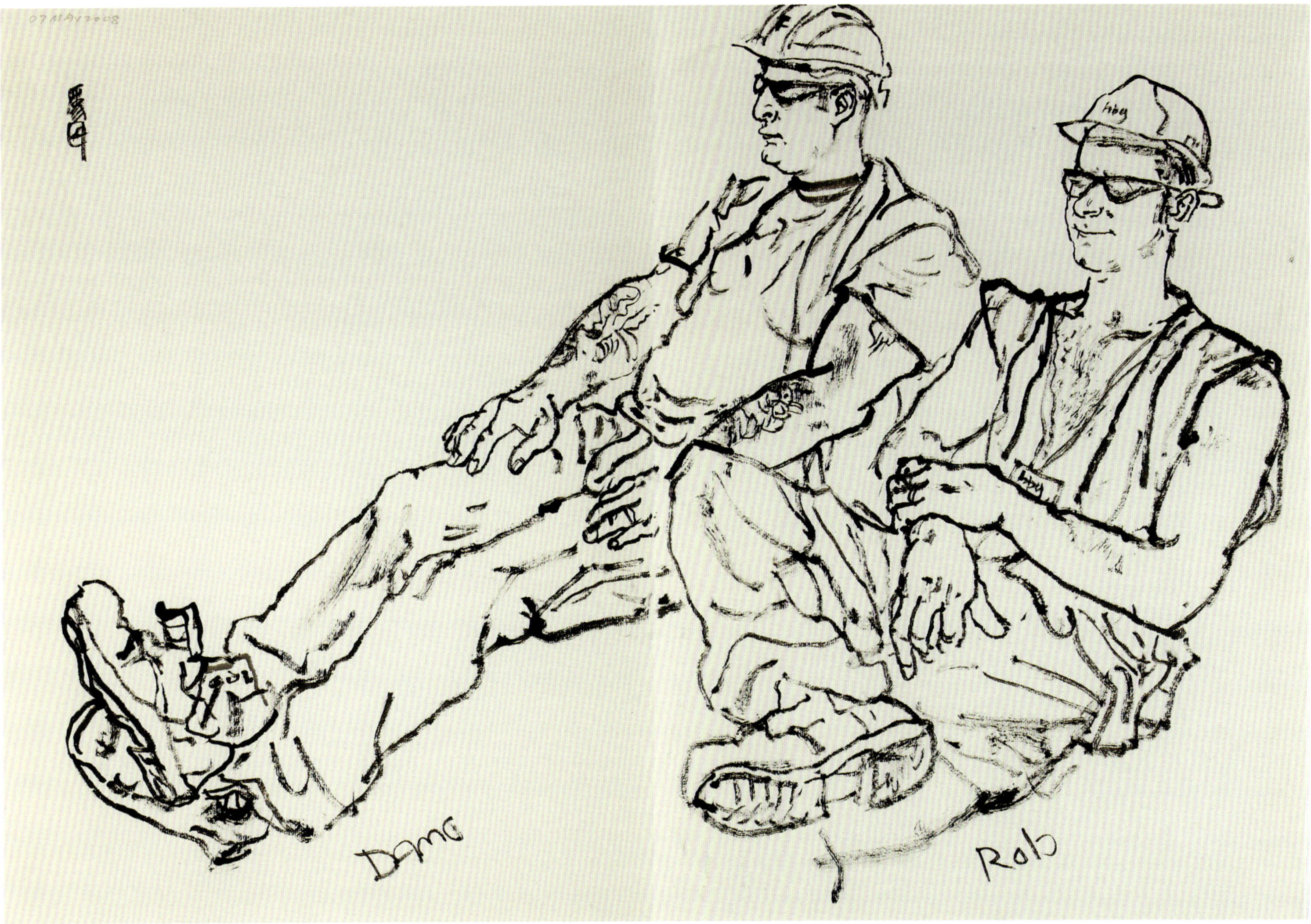

162

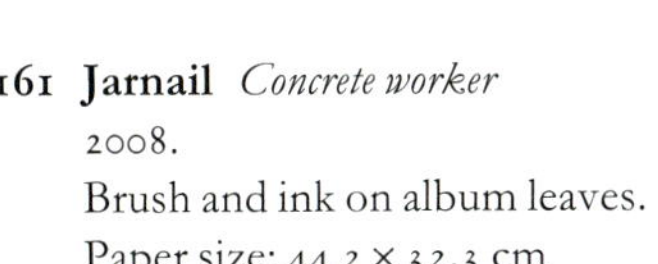

161 Jarnail *Concrete worker*
2008.
Brush and ink on album leaves.
Paper size: 44.2 × 32.3 cm

162 Damadian and Rob *Carpenters*
2008.
Brush and ink on album leaves.
Paper size: 44.2 × 64.6 cm

163 *Construction workers*
2008.
Brush and ink on album leaves.
Paper size: 44.2 × 64.6 cm

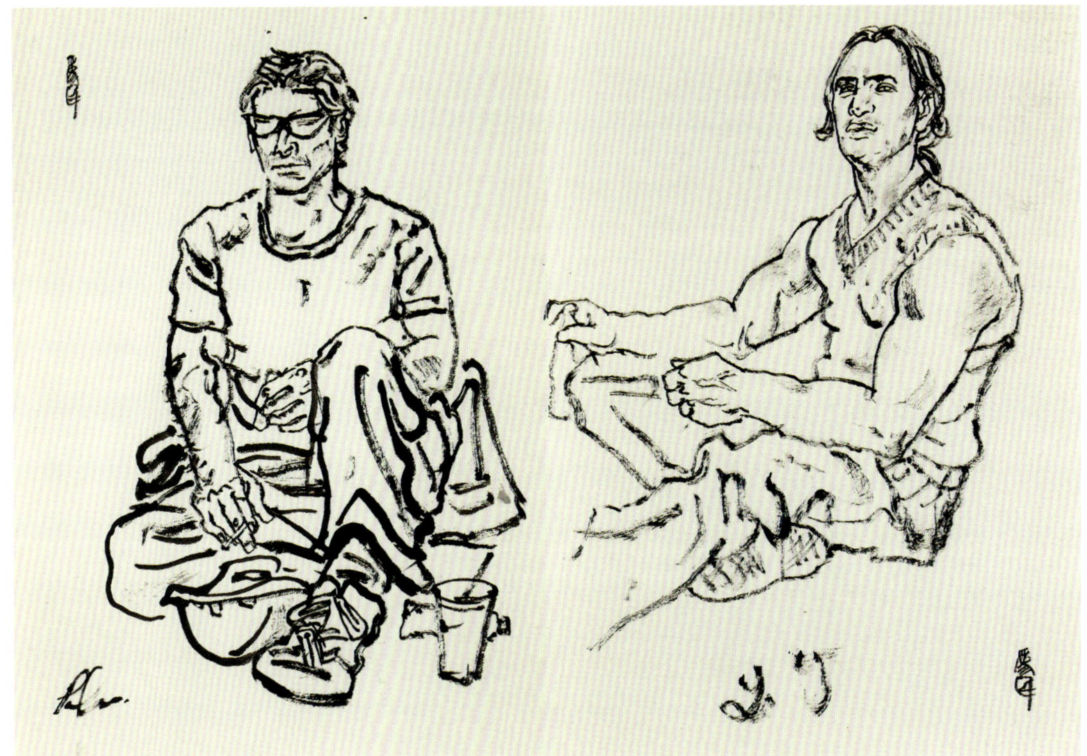

163

164 *Construction workers*
2008.
Brush and ink on album leaves.
Paper size: 44.2 × 64.6 cm

165 **Paul** *Steel fixer*
2008.
Brush and ink on album leaves.
Paper size: 44.2 × 32.3 cm

166 **Robby** *Scaffolder*
2008.
Brush and ink on album leaves.
Paper size: 44.2 × 32.3 cm

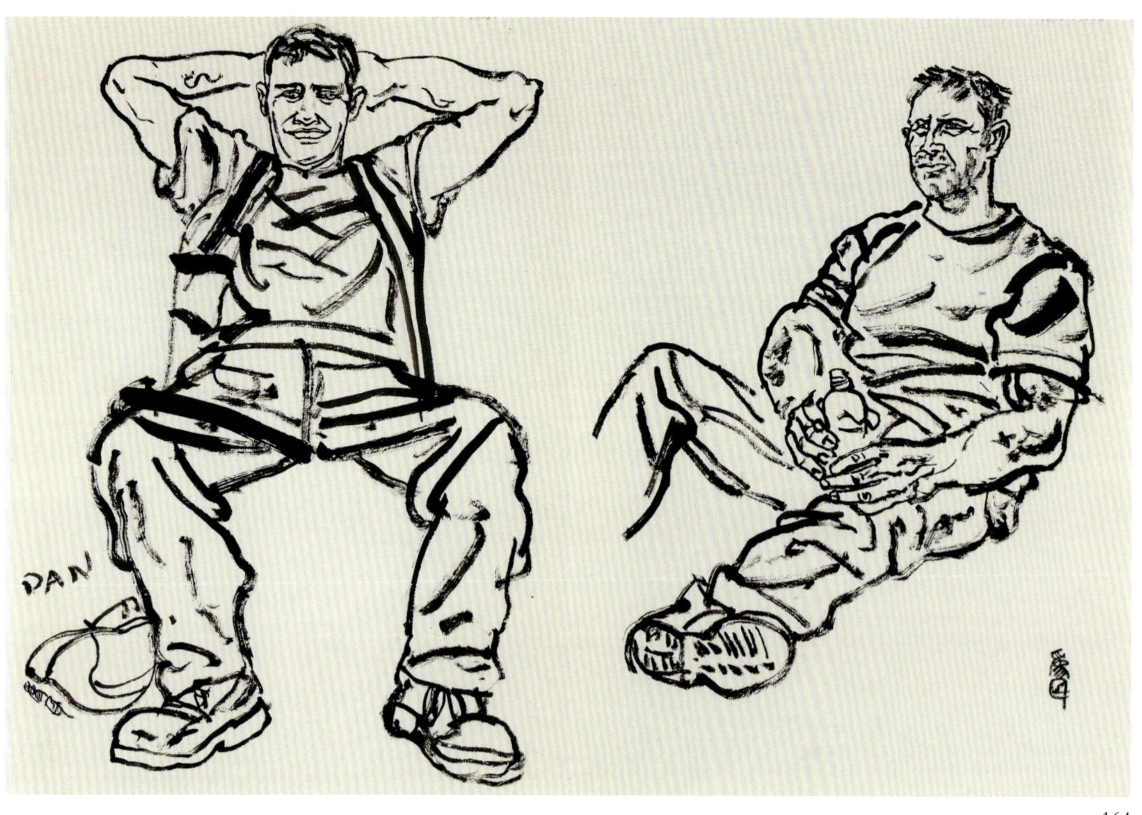

164

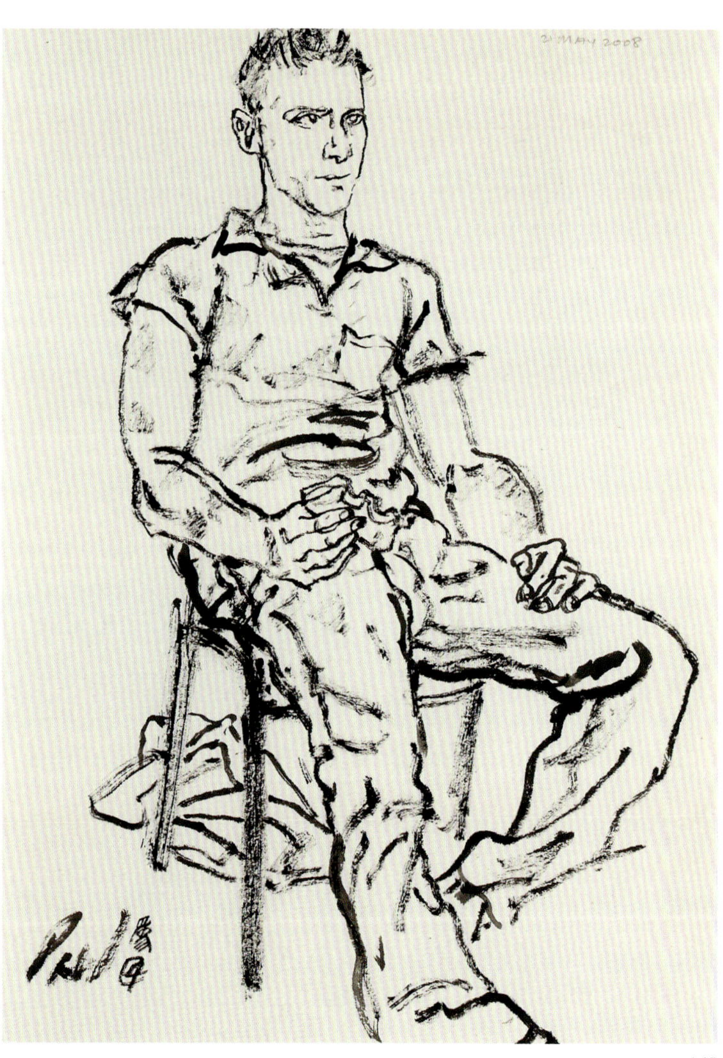

165

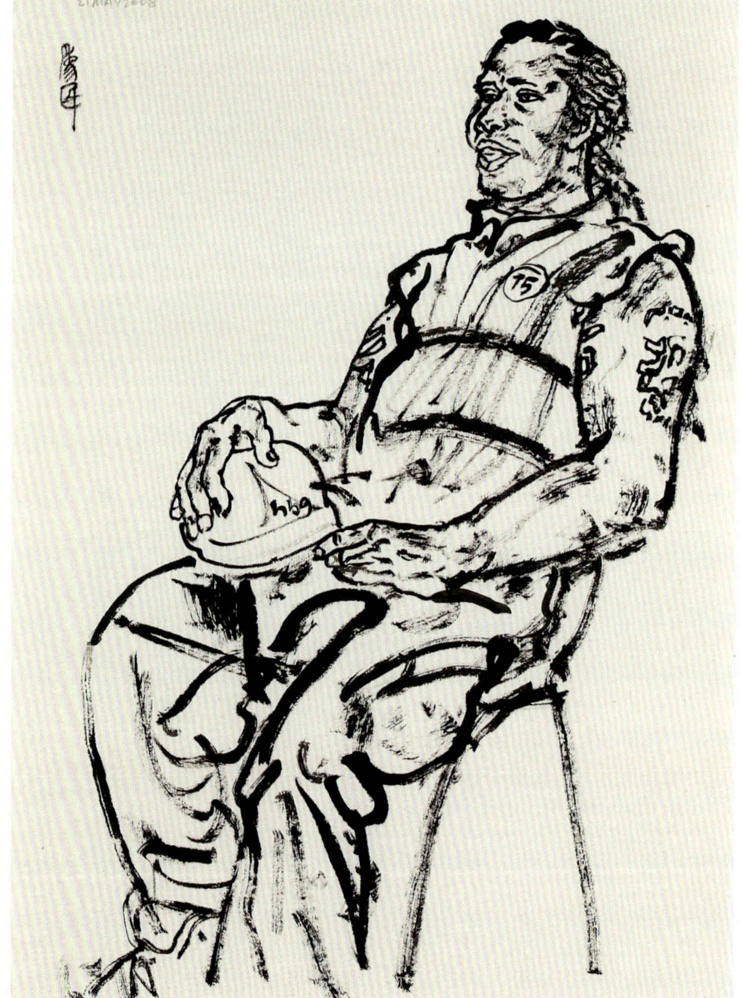

166

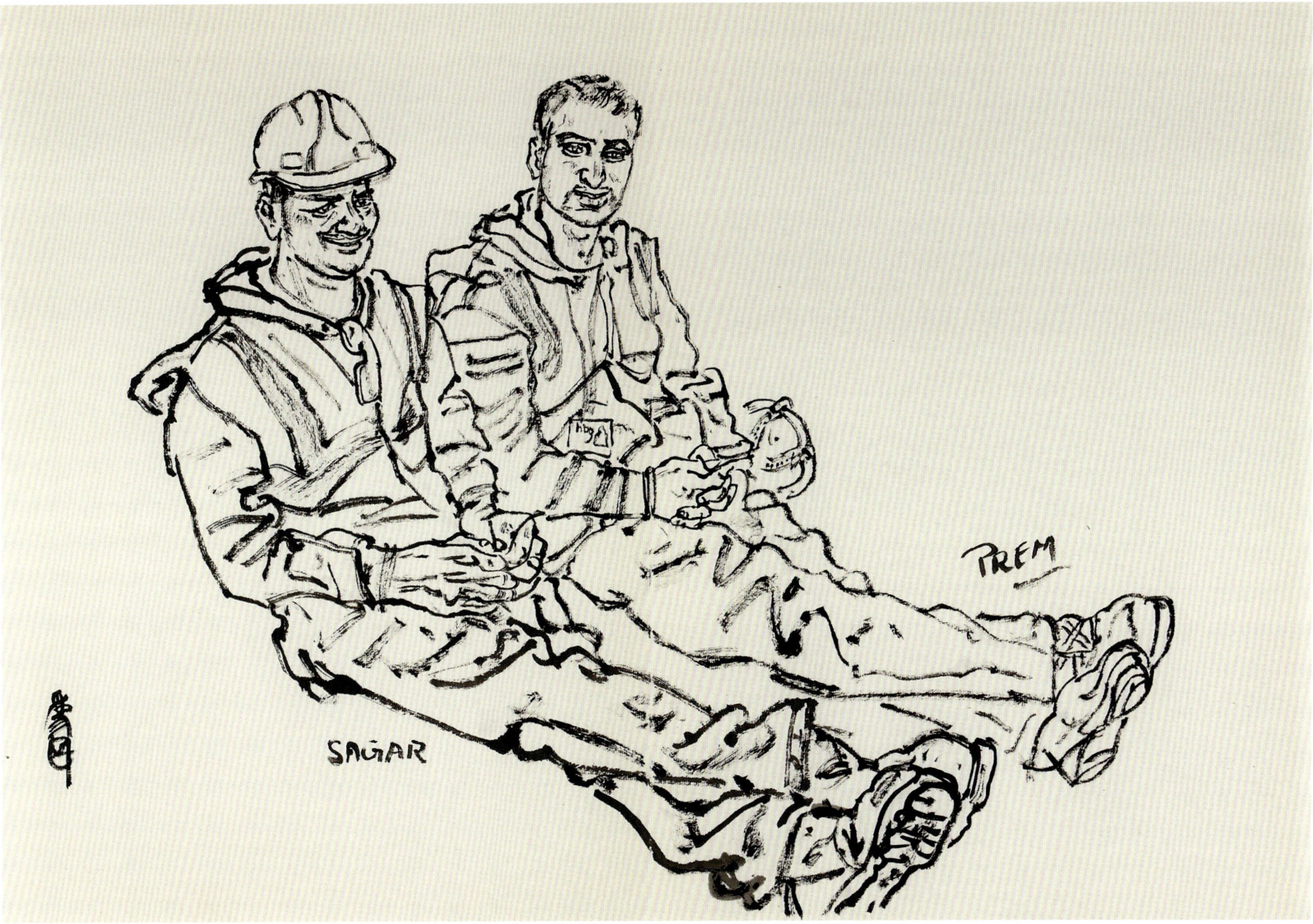

167

167 Sagar and Prem
Ground workers
2008. Brush and ink on album leaves.
Paper size: 44.2 × 64.6 cm

168 Martin
2008. Brush and ink on album leaves.
Paper size: 44.2 × 32.3 cm

169 Dale *Bricklayer*
2008. Brush and ink on album leaves.
Paper size: 44.2 × 32.3 cm

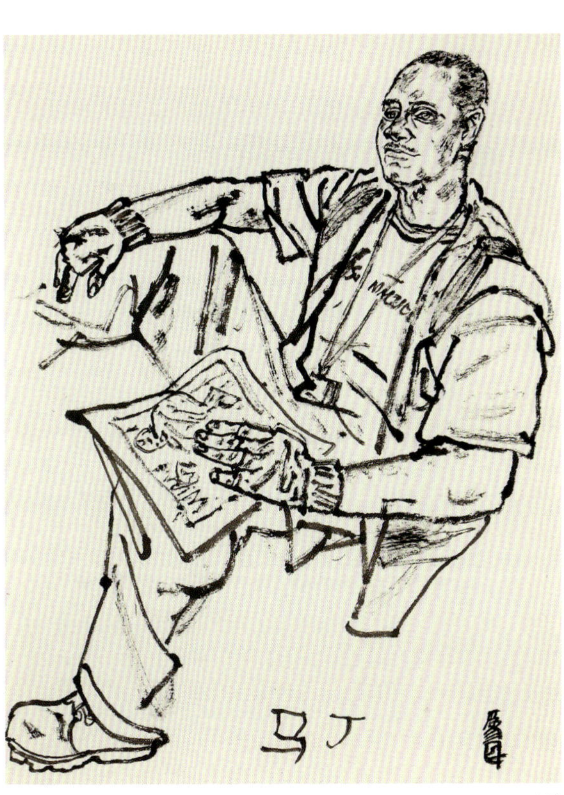

168

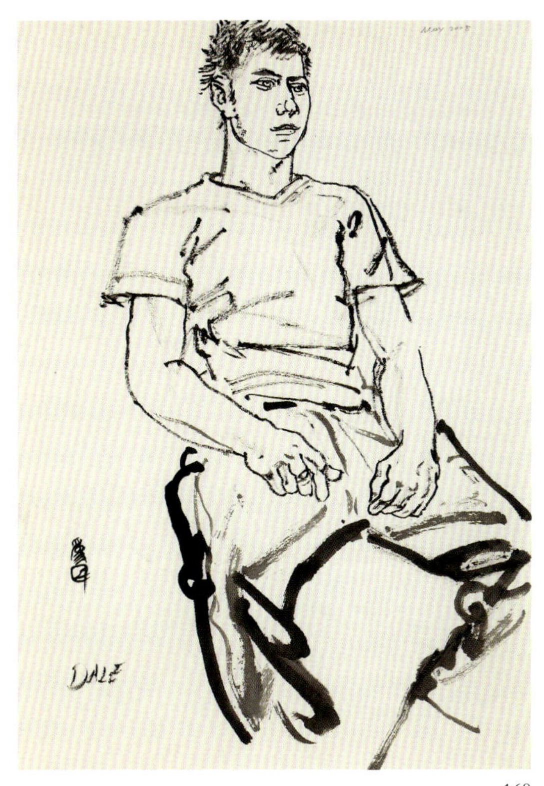

169

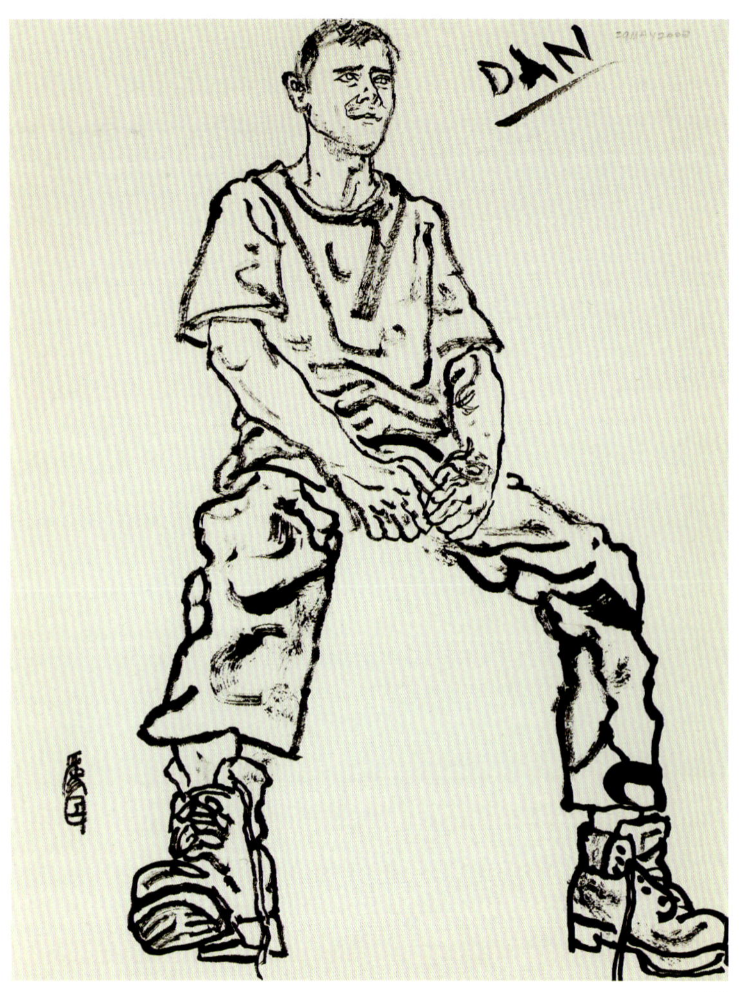

170

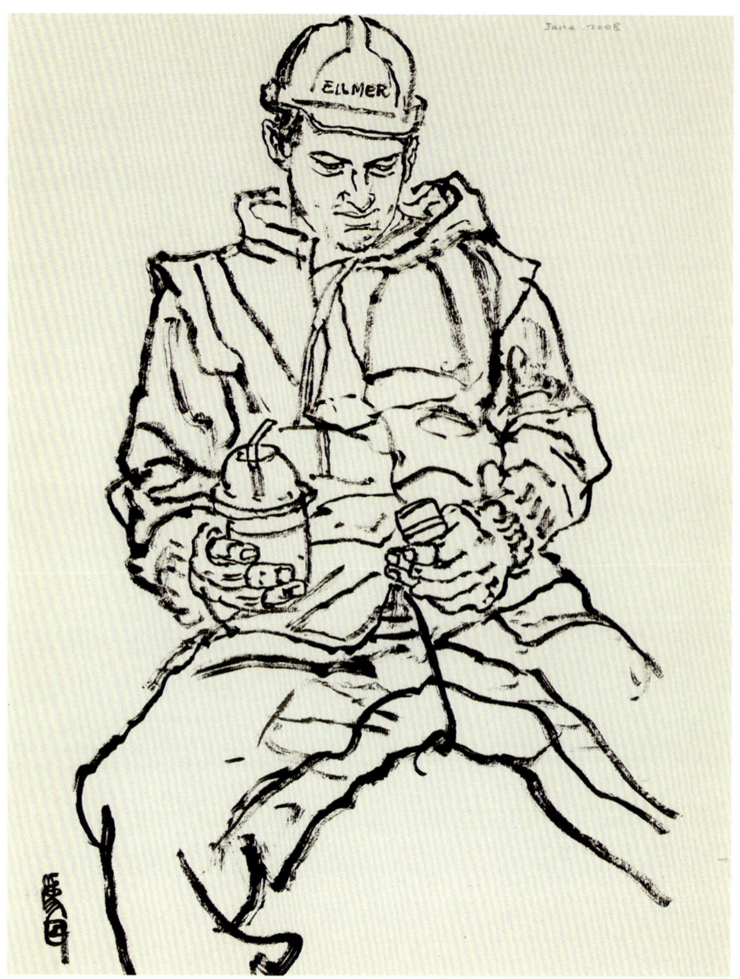

171

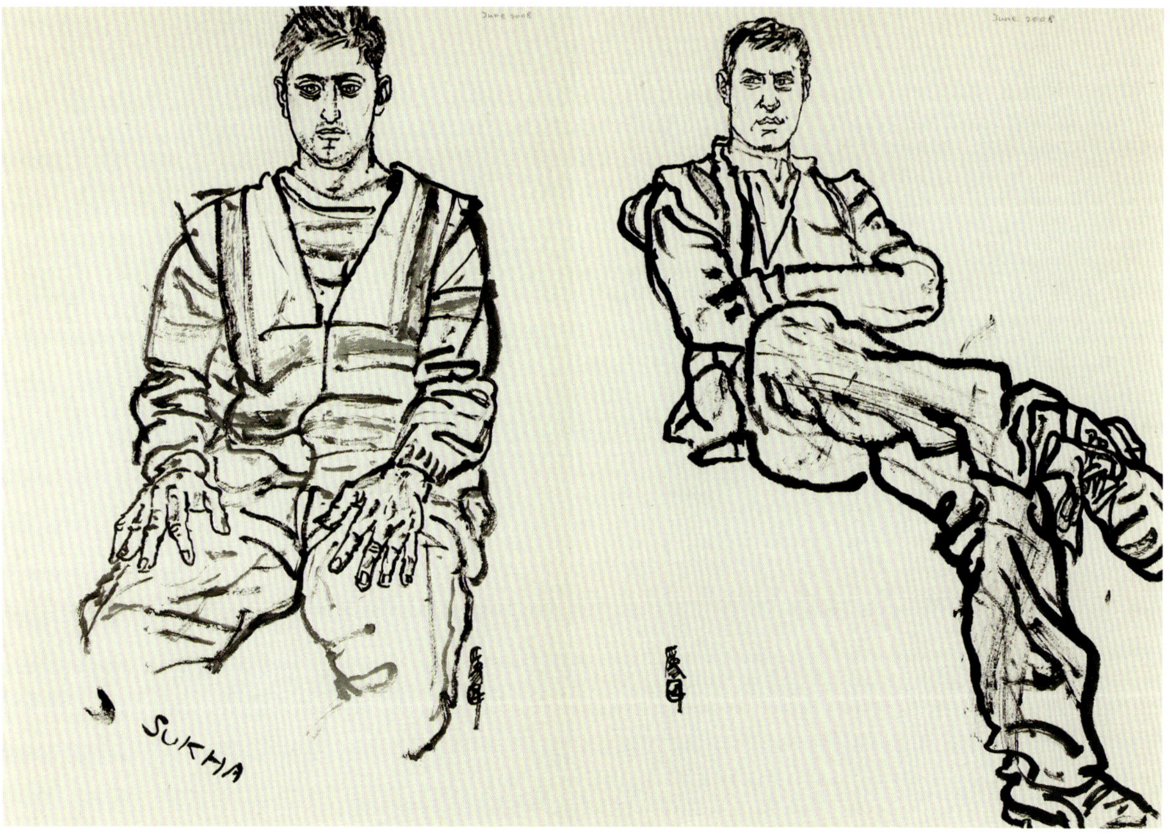

172

170 Dan *Hod carrier*
2008. Brush and ink on album leaves.
Paper size: 44.2 × 32.3 cm

171 *Carpenter*
2008. Brush and ink on album leaves.
Paper size: 44.2 × 32.3 cm

172 *Ground worker and Carpenter*
2008. Brush and ink on album leaves.
Paper size: 44.2 × 64.6 cm

173 Chris *Bricklayer*
2008. Brush and ink on album leaves.
Paper size: 44.2 × 32.3 cm

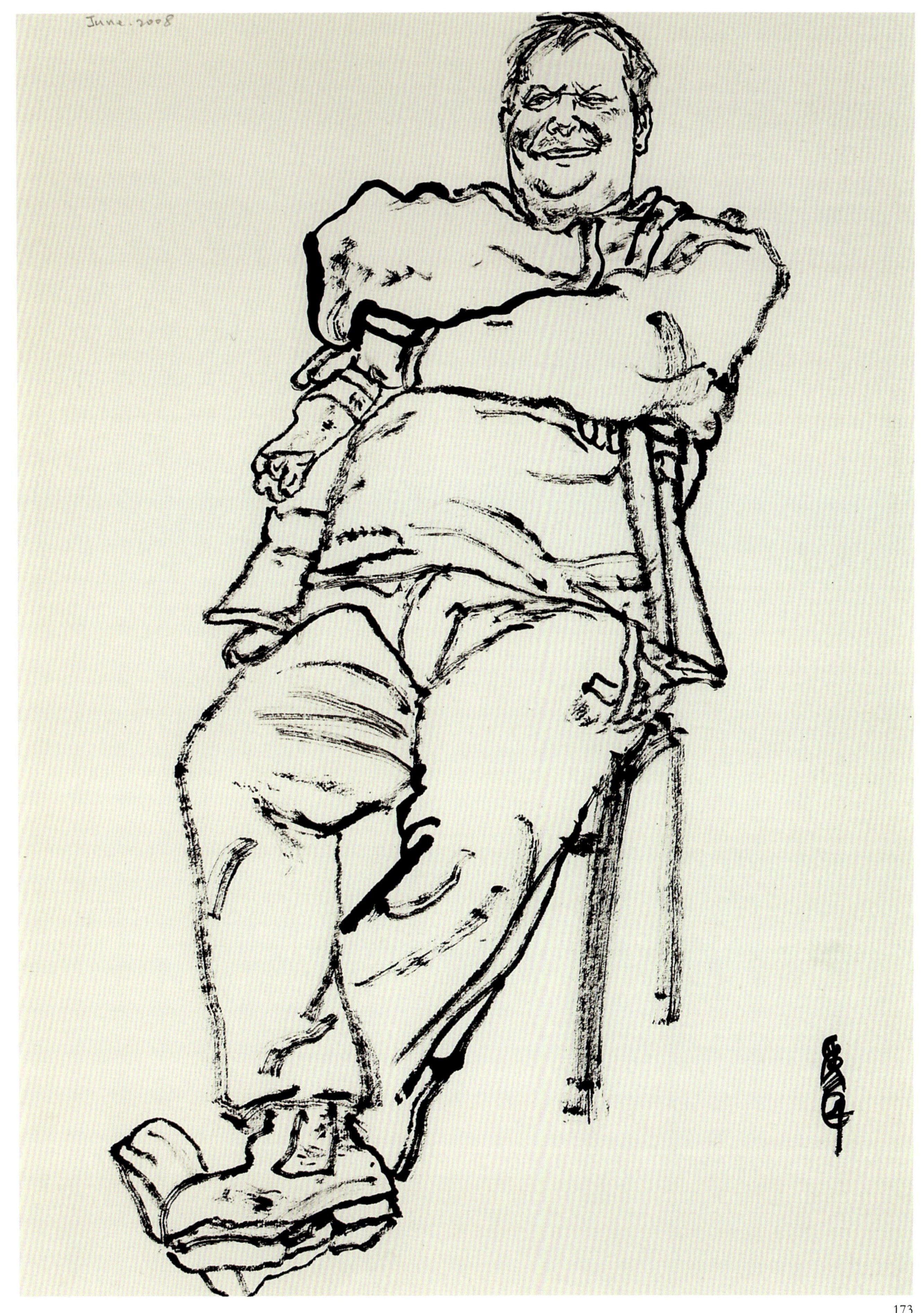

173

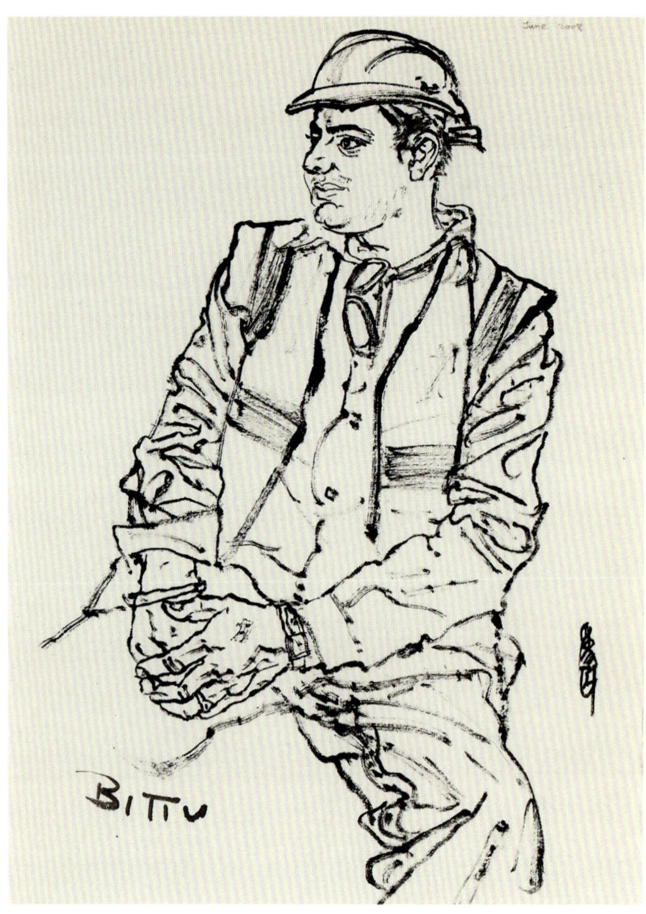

174

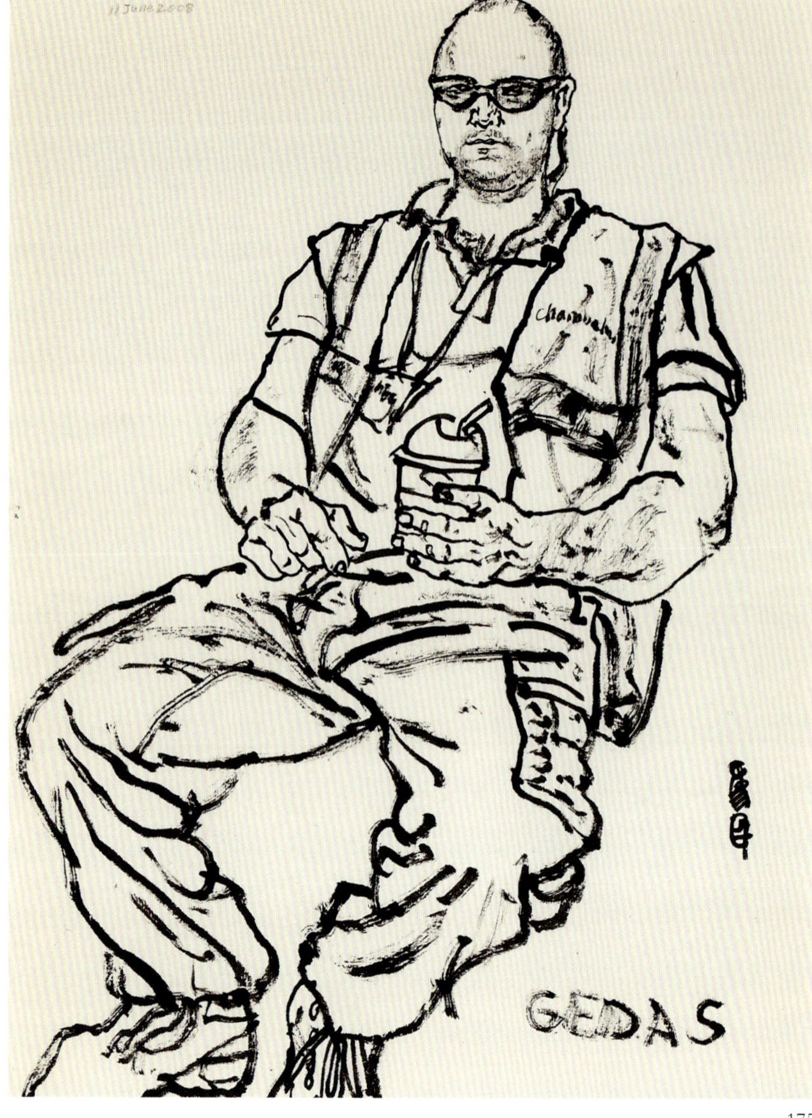

175

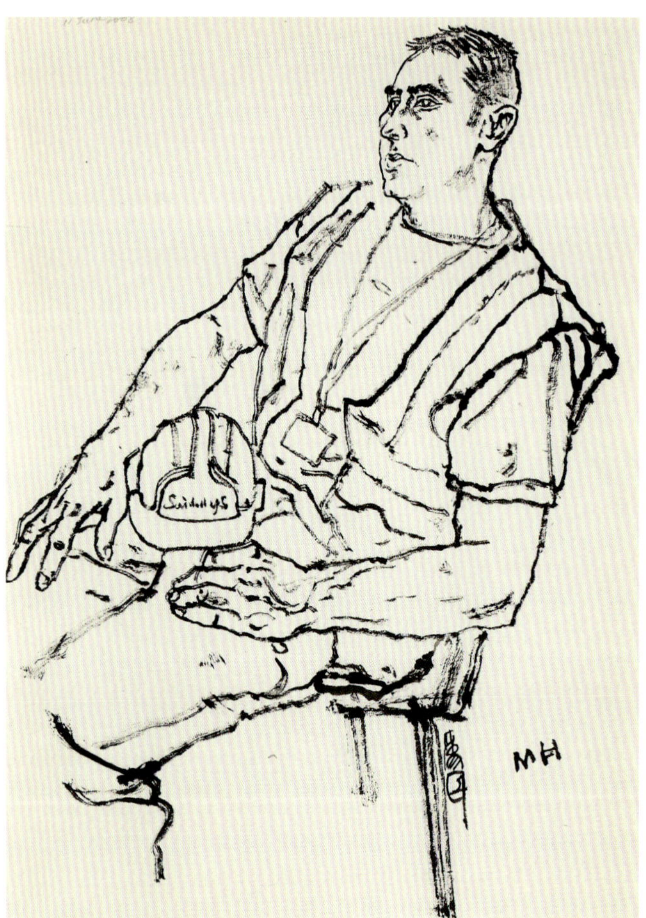

176

174 **Bitiv** *Concrete layer*
2008. Brush and ink on album leaves. Paper size: 44.2 × 32.3 cm

175 **Gedas** *Carpenter*
2008. Brush and ink on album leaves. Paper size: 44.2 × 32.3 cm

176 *Construction worker*
2008. Brush and ink on album leaves. Paper size: 44.2 × 32.3 cm

177 *Construction workers*
2008. Brush and ink on album leaves. Paper size: 44.2 × 64.6 cm

178 **Bobby and Alex** *Demolition workers*
2008. Brush and ink on album leaves. Paper size: 44.2 × 64.6 cm

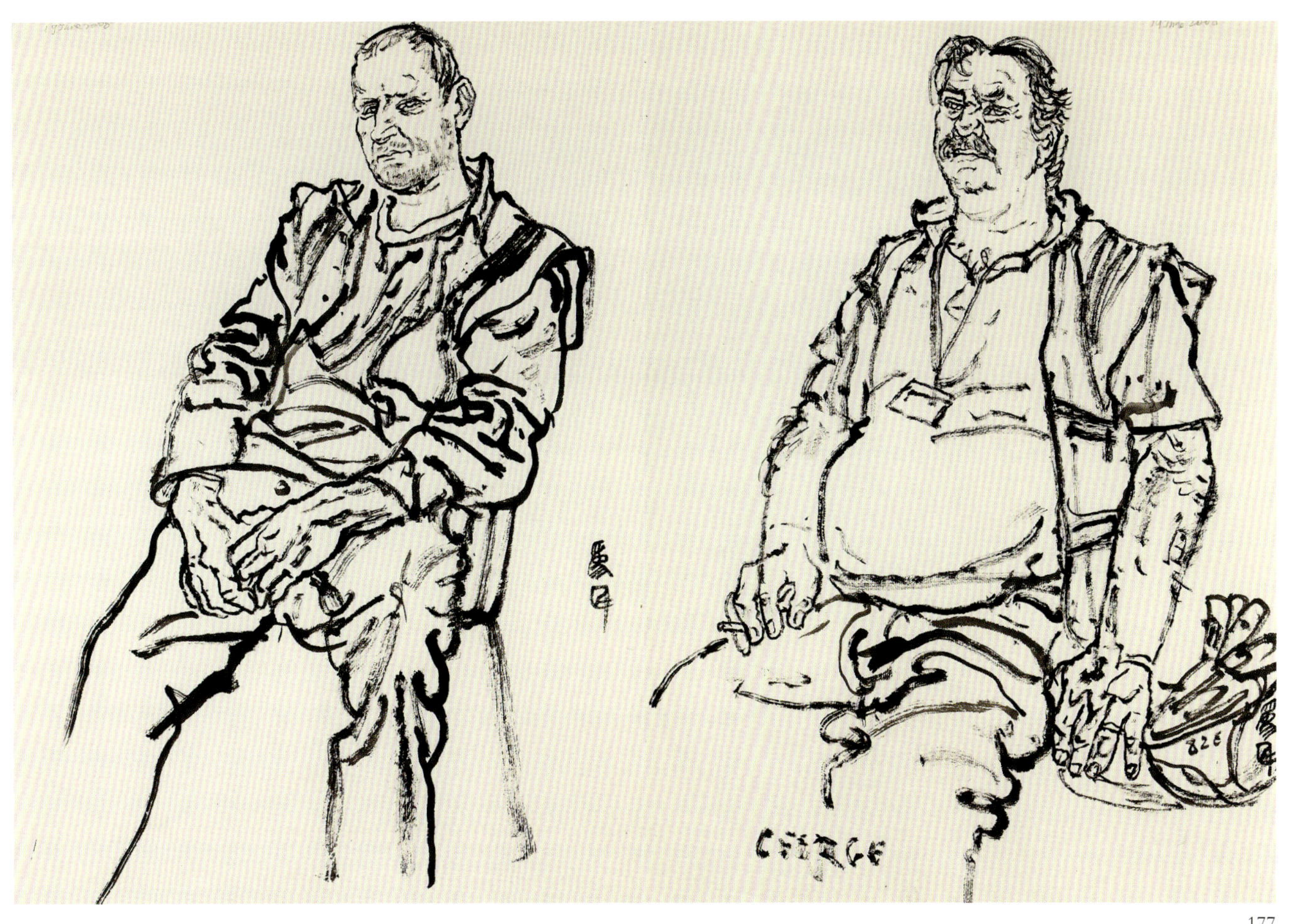

177

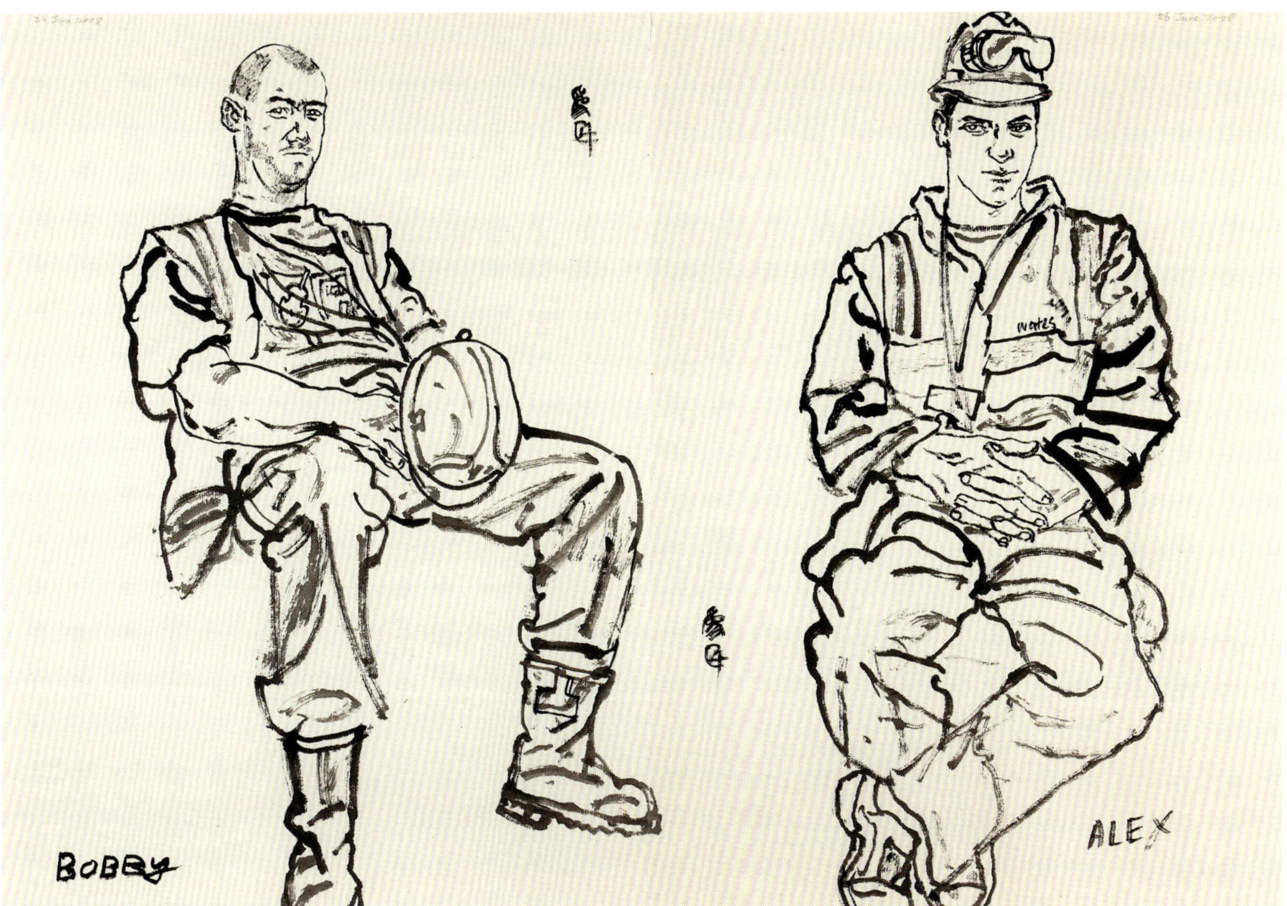

178

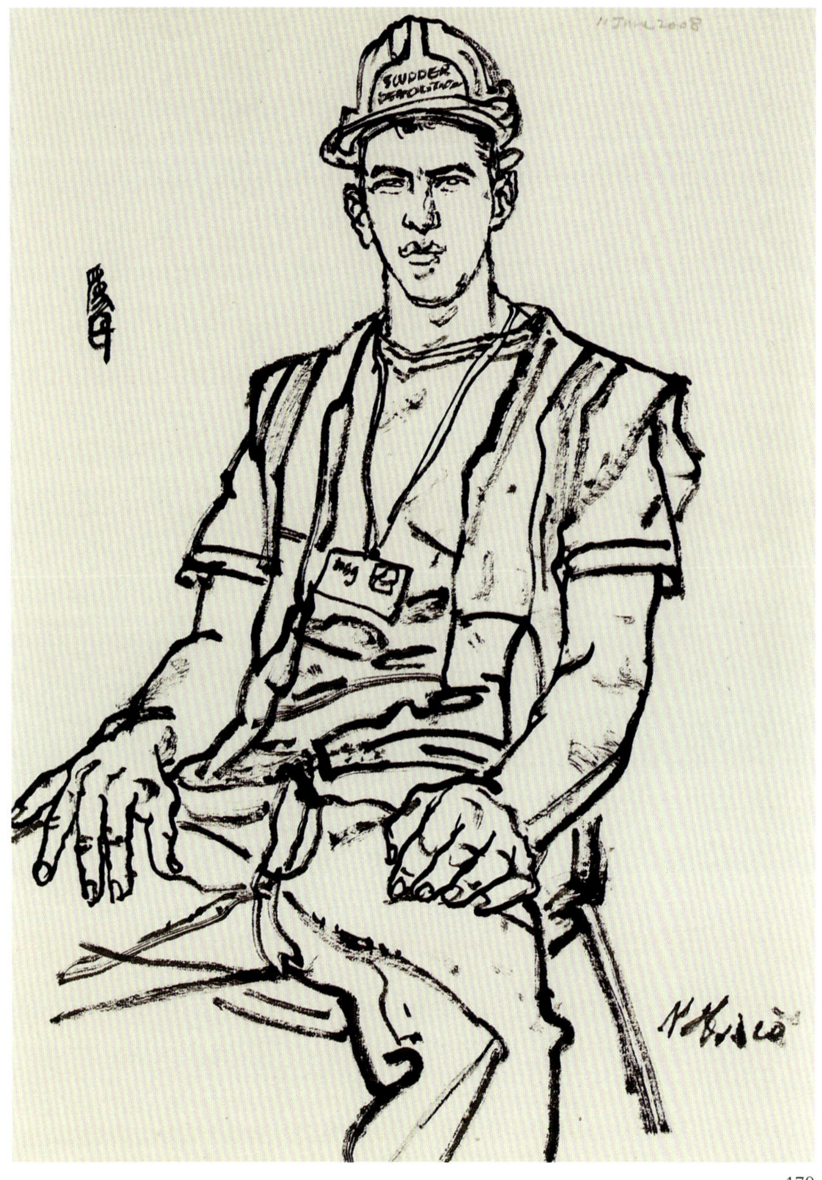

179

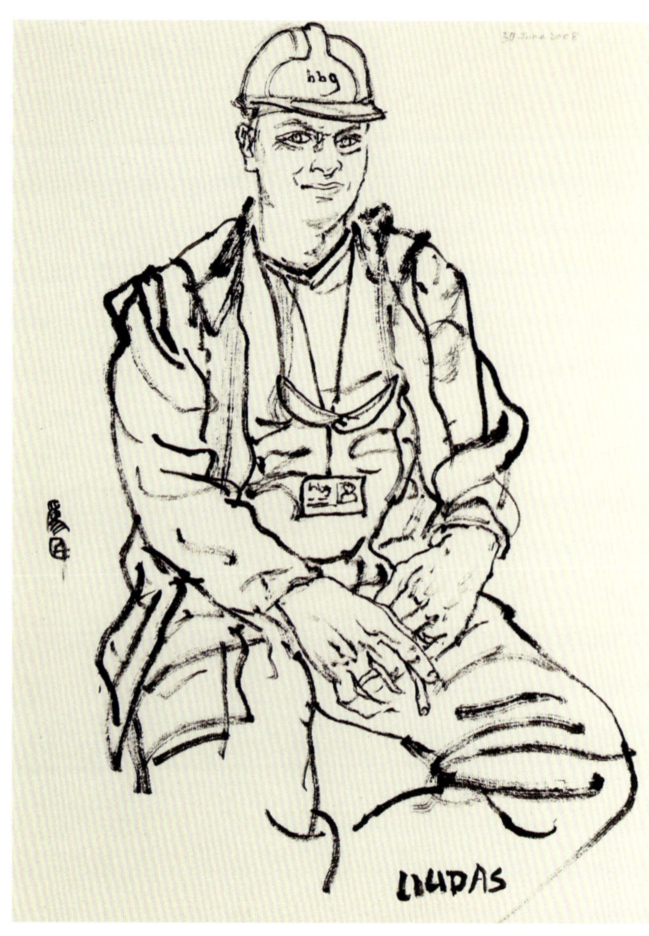

180

181

179 *Demolition worker*
2008. Brush and ink on album leaves. 44.2 × 32.3 cm

180 *Construction worker*
2008. Brush and ink on album leaves. Paper size: 44.2 × 32.3 cm

181 **Martin** *Electrician*
2008. Brush and ink on album leaves. Paper size: 44.2 × 32.3 cm

182 **Dan** *Pipe fitter*
2008. Brush and ink on album leaves. Paper size: 44.2 × 32.3 cm

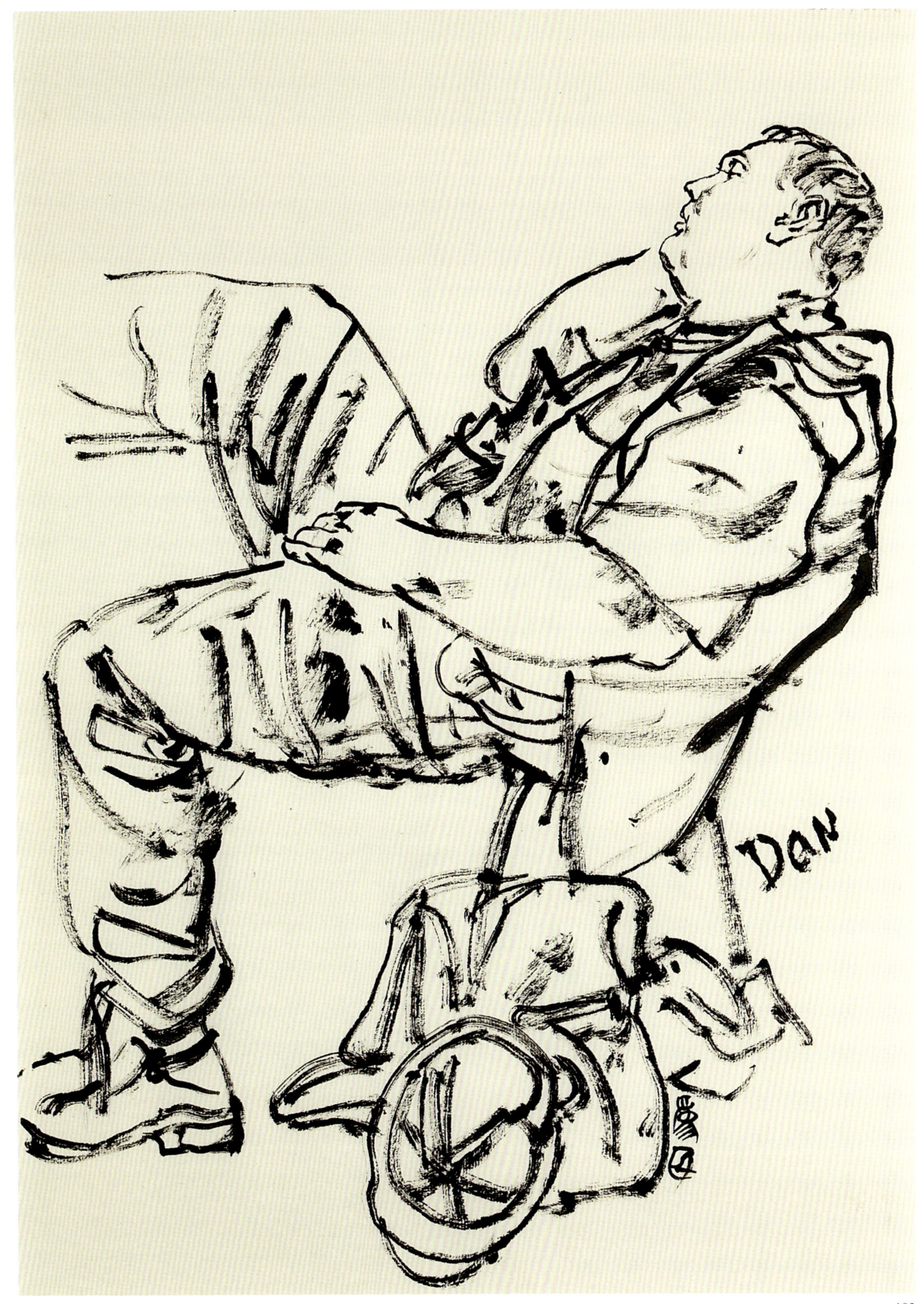

182

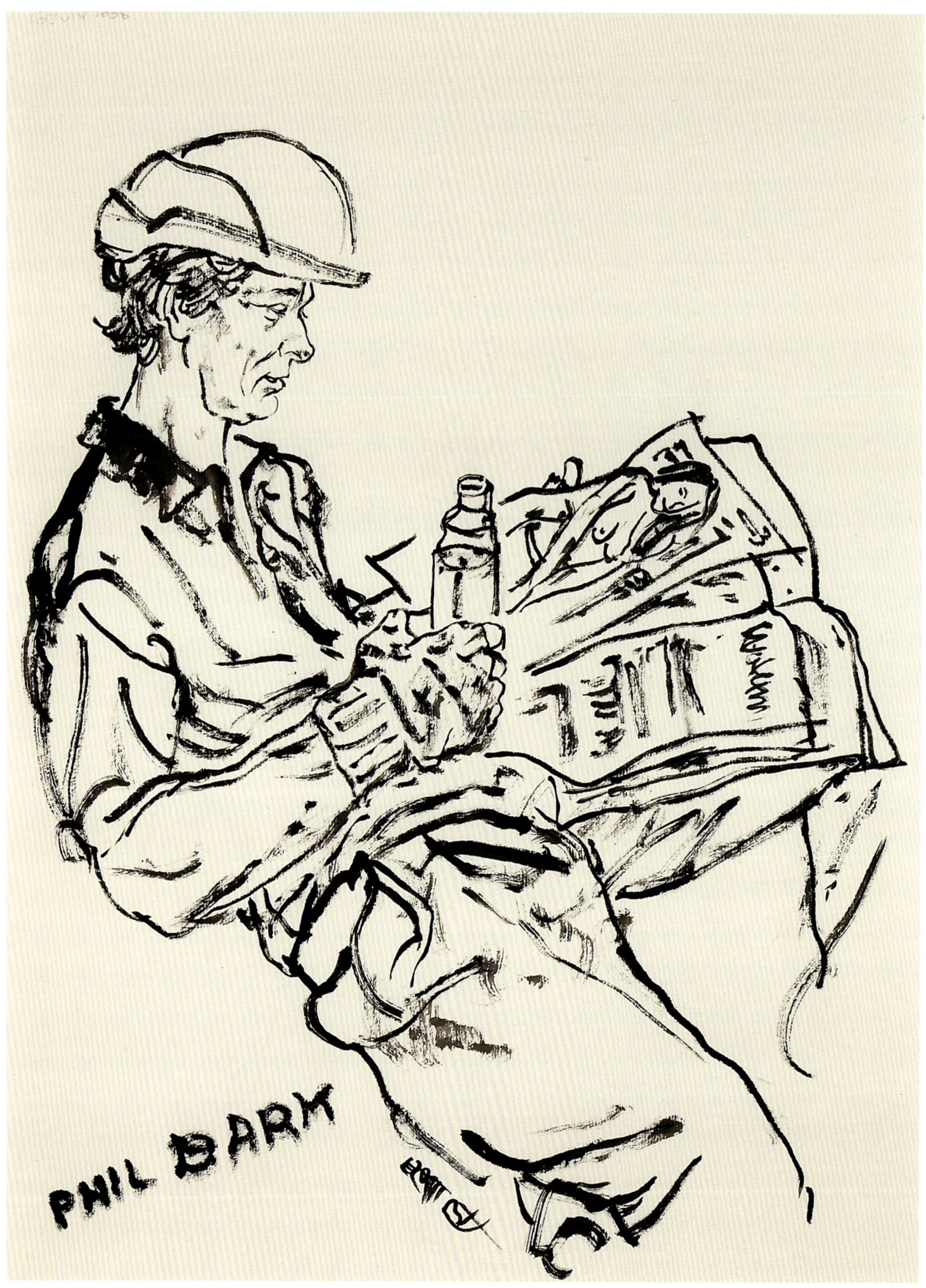

183

183 Phil *Plumber*
2008.
Brush and ink on album leaves.
Paper size: 44.2 × 32.3 cm

184 *Three workers from Romania*
2008.
Brush and ink on album leaves.
Paper size: 44.2 × 64.6 cm

185 Andy *Electrician*
and Tony *Scaffolder*
2008.
Brush and ink on album leaves.
Paper size: 44.2 × 64.6 cm

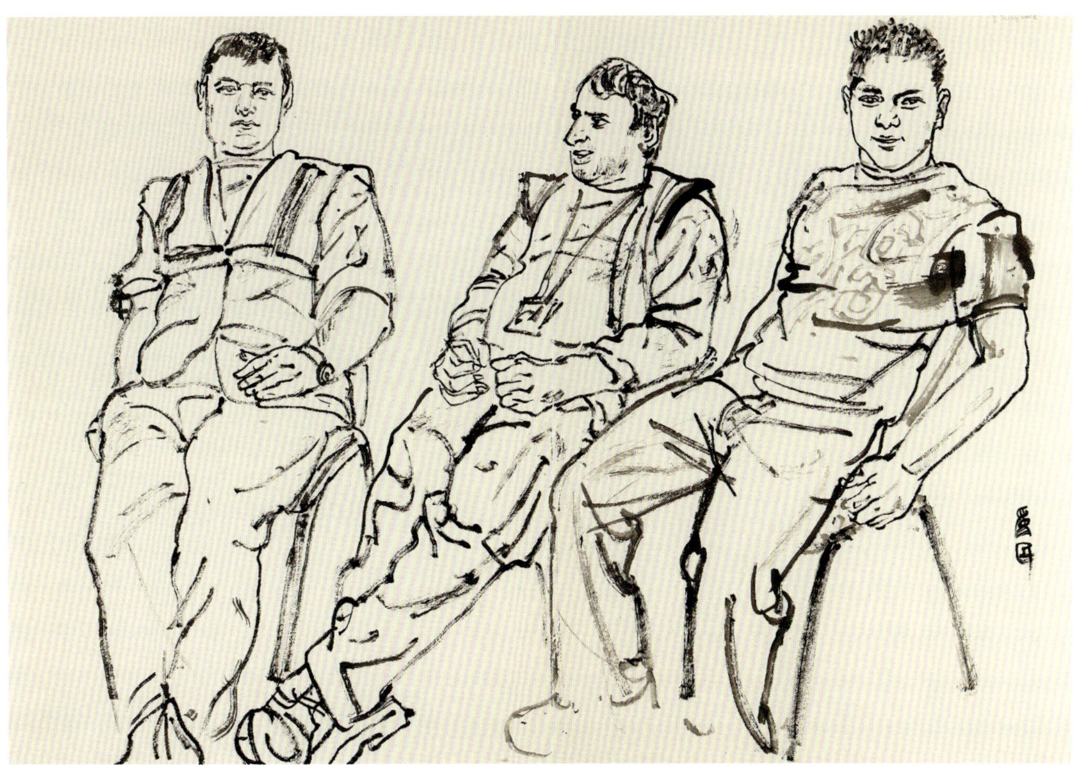

184

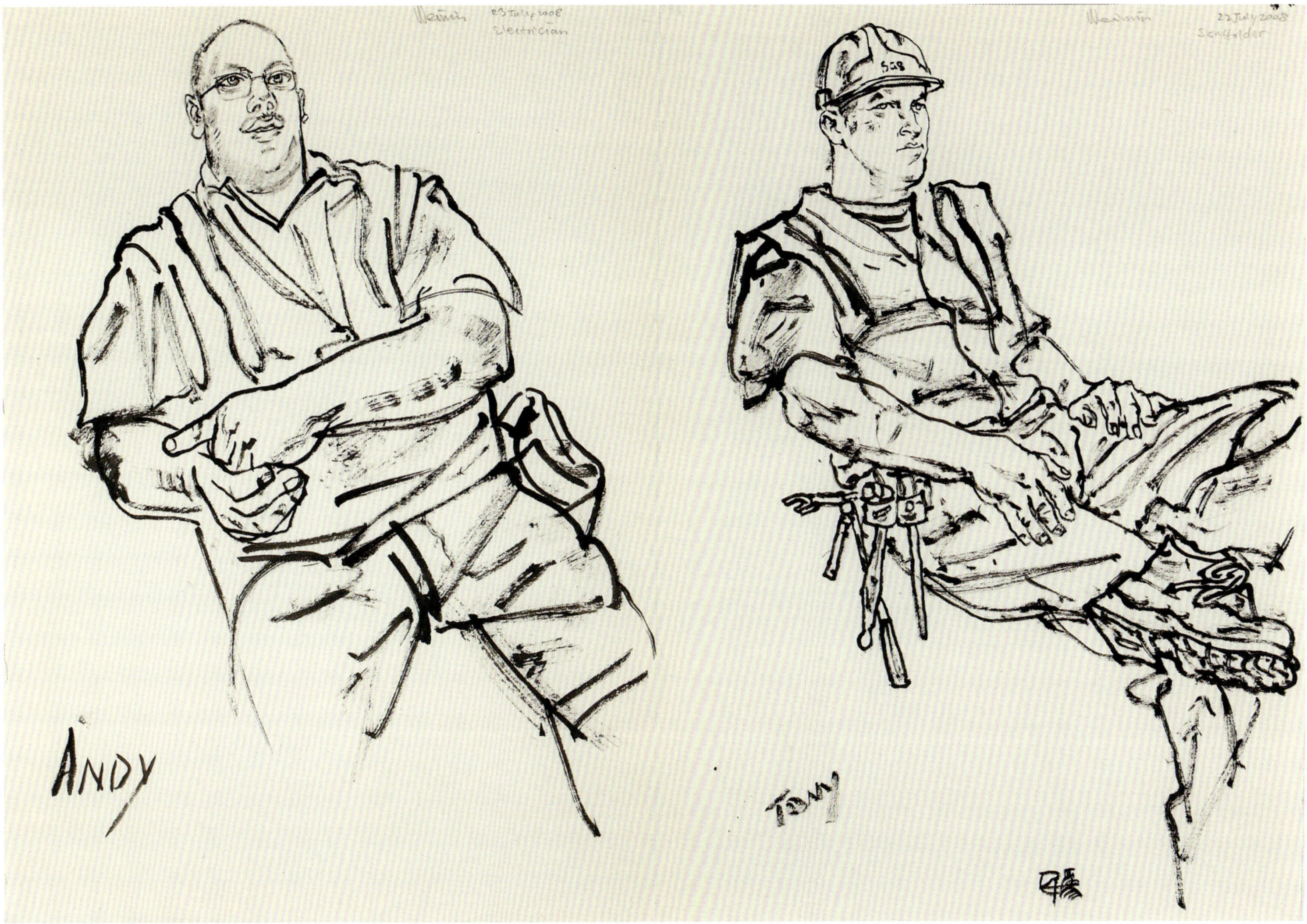

185

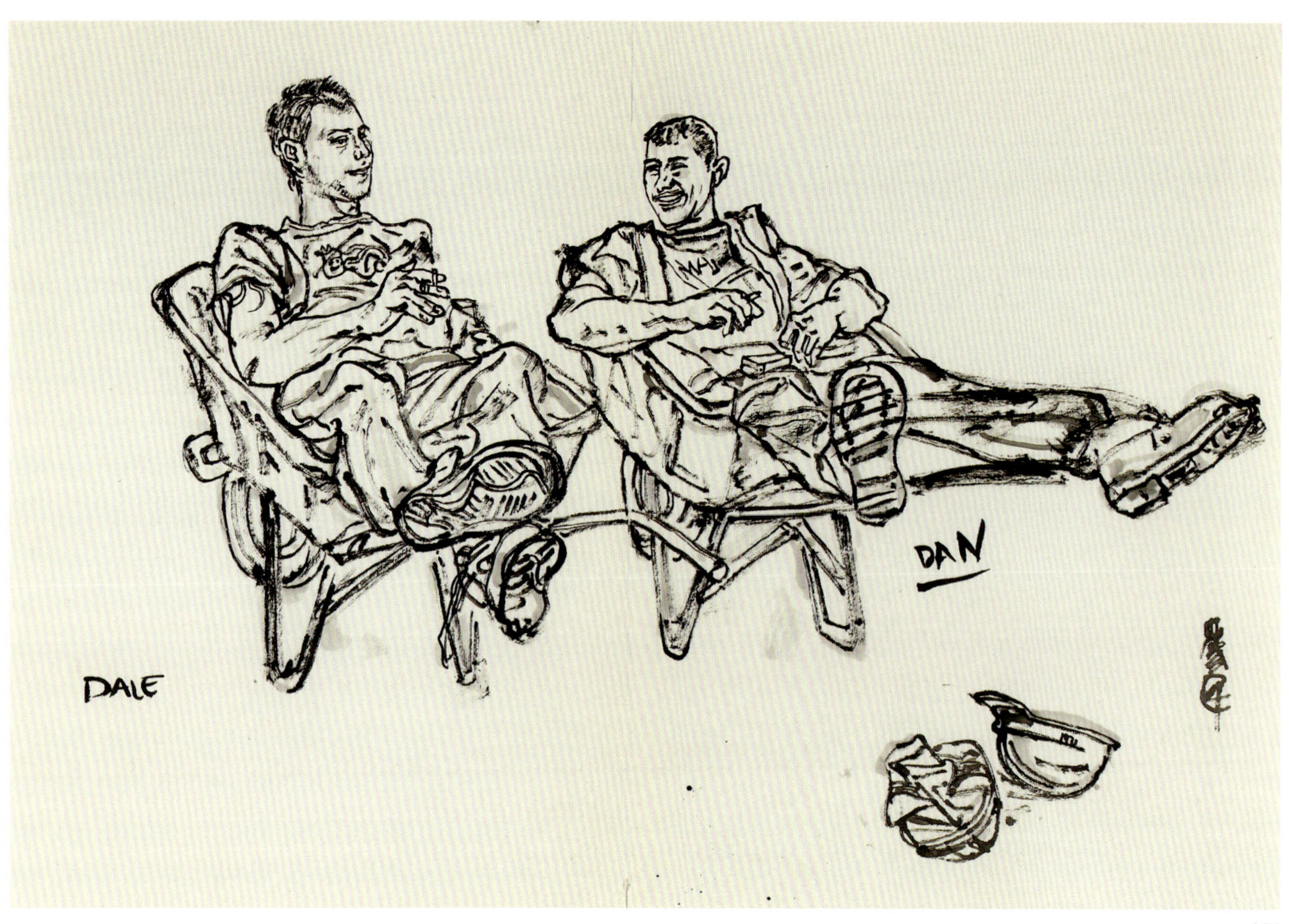

186

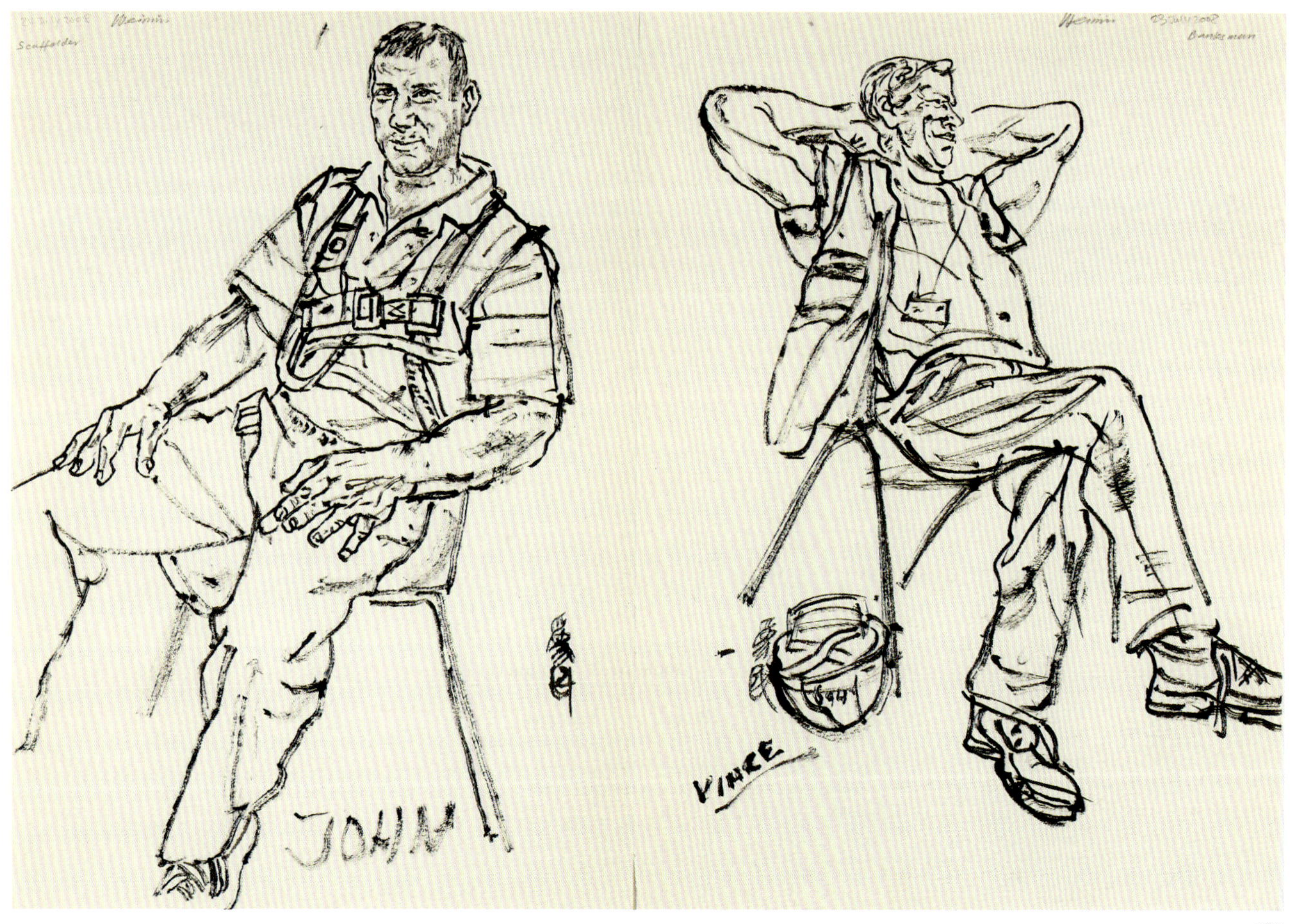

187

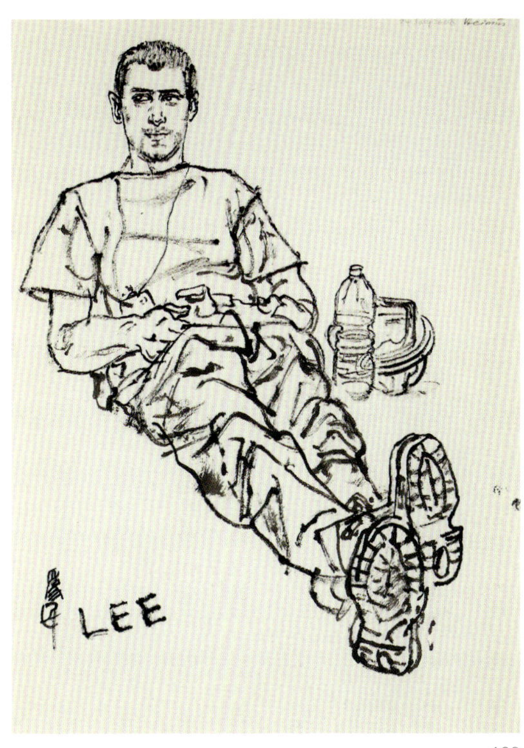

188

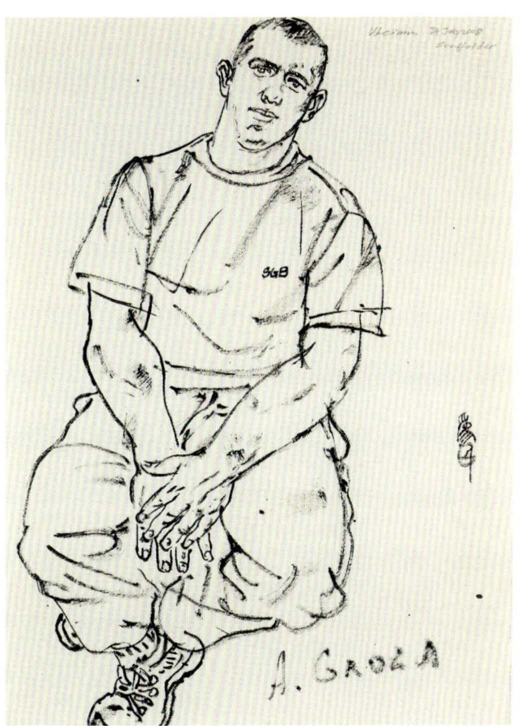

190

189

186 Dale and Dan *Ground workers*
2008. Brush and ink on album leaves. Paper size: 44.2 × 64.6 cm

187 John *Scaffolder* **and Vince** *Gangerman*
2008. Brush and ink on album leaves. Paper size: 44.2 × 64.6 cm

188 Lee *Construction worker*
2008. Brush and ink on album leaves. Paper size: 44.2 × 32.3 cm

189 Paul *Painter*
2008. Brush and ink on album leaves. Paper size: 44.2 × 32.3 cm

190 *Scaffolder*
2008. Brush and ink on album leaves. Paper size: 44.2 × 32.3 cm

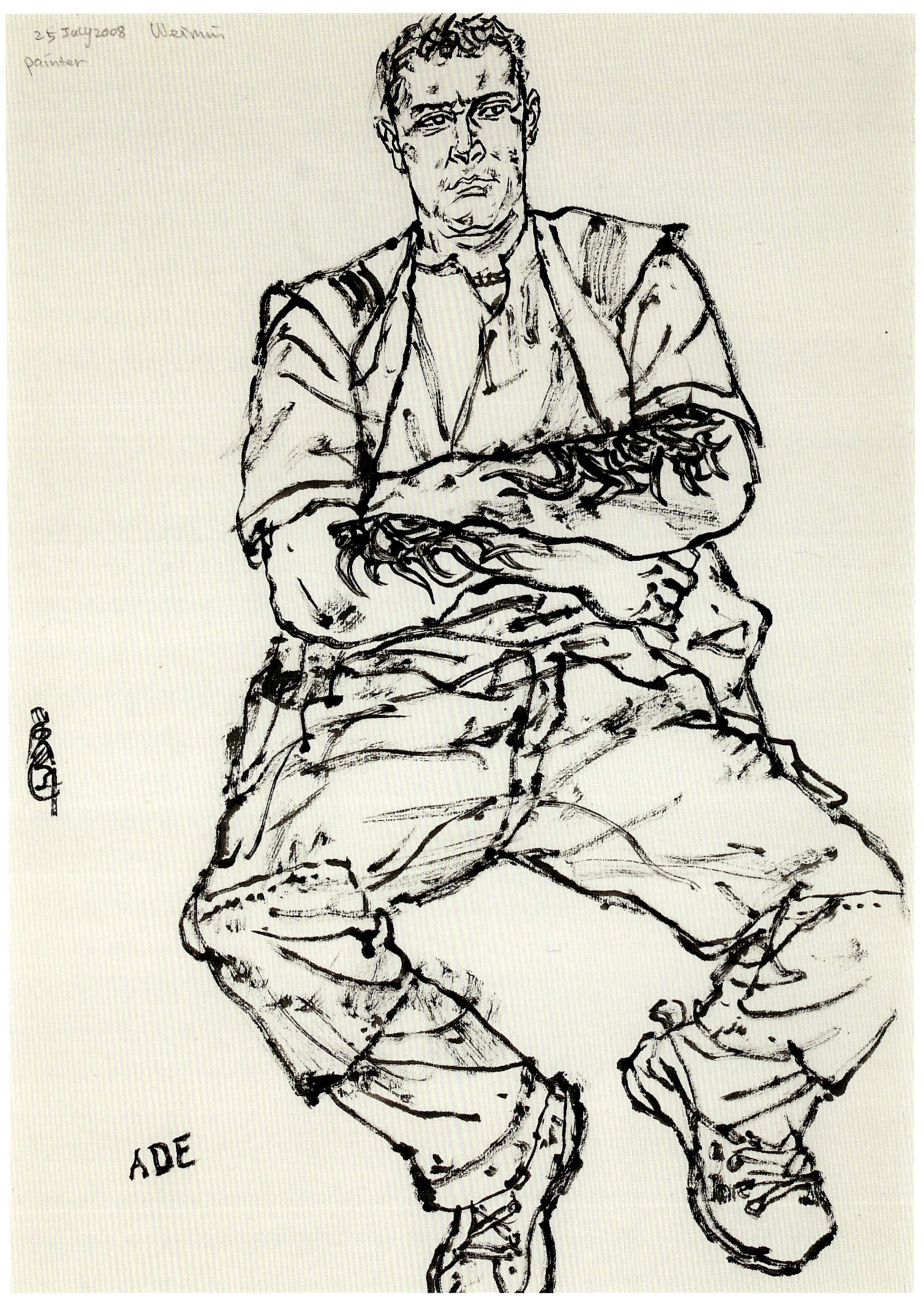

191

191 Ade *Painter*
2008.
Brush and ink on album leaves.
Paper size: 44.2 × 32.3 cm

192 Phil and Jay *Welders*
2008.
Brush and ink on album leaves.
Paper size: 44.2 × 64.6 cm

193 Gemma and Iain *Electricians*
2008.
Brush and ink on album leaves.
Paper size: 44.2 × 64.6 cm

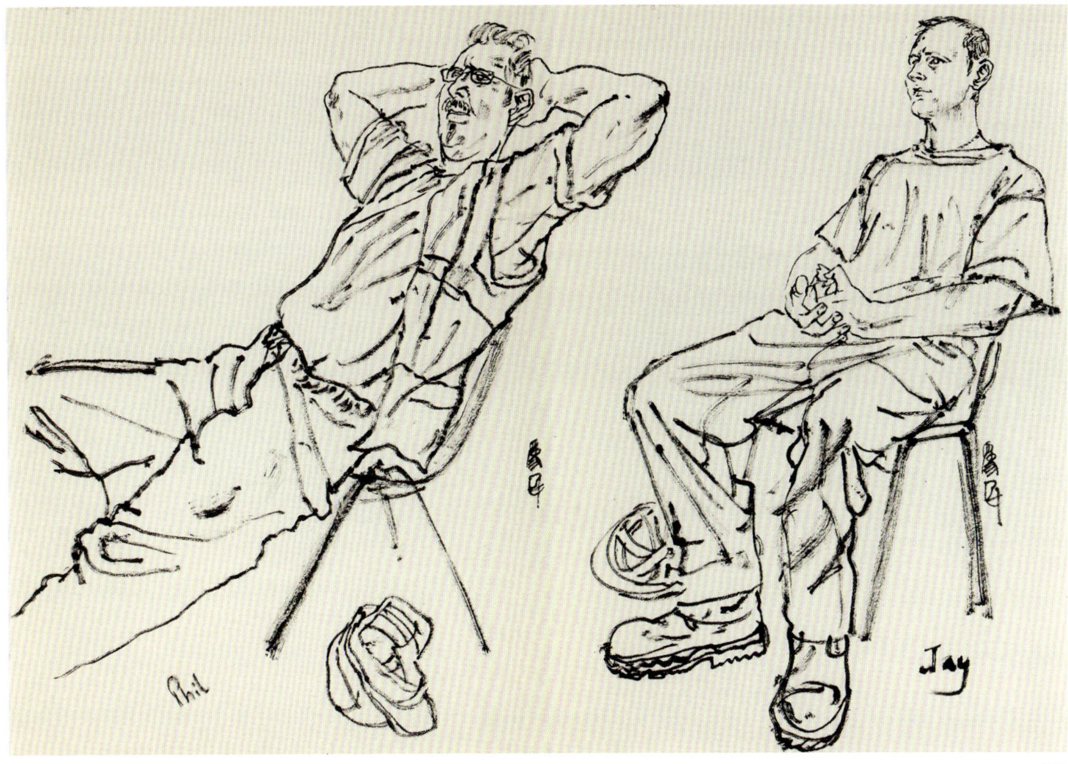

192

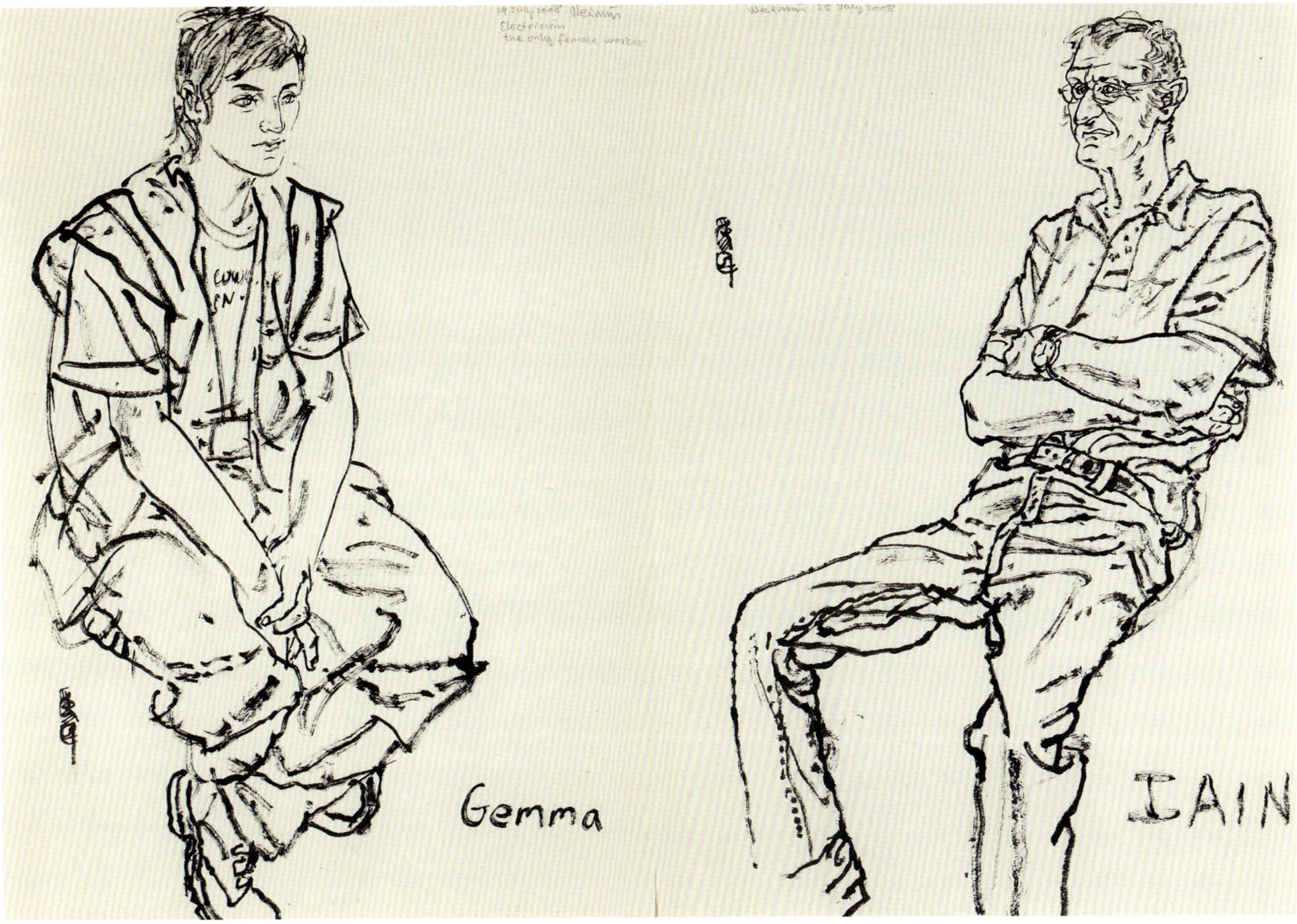

193

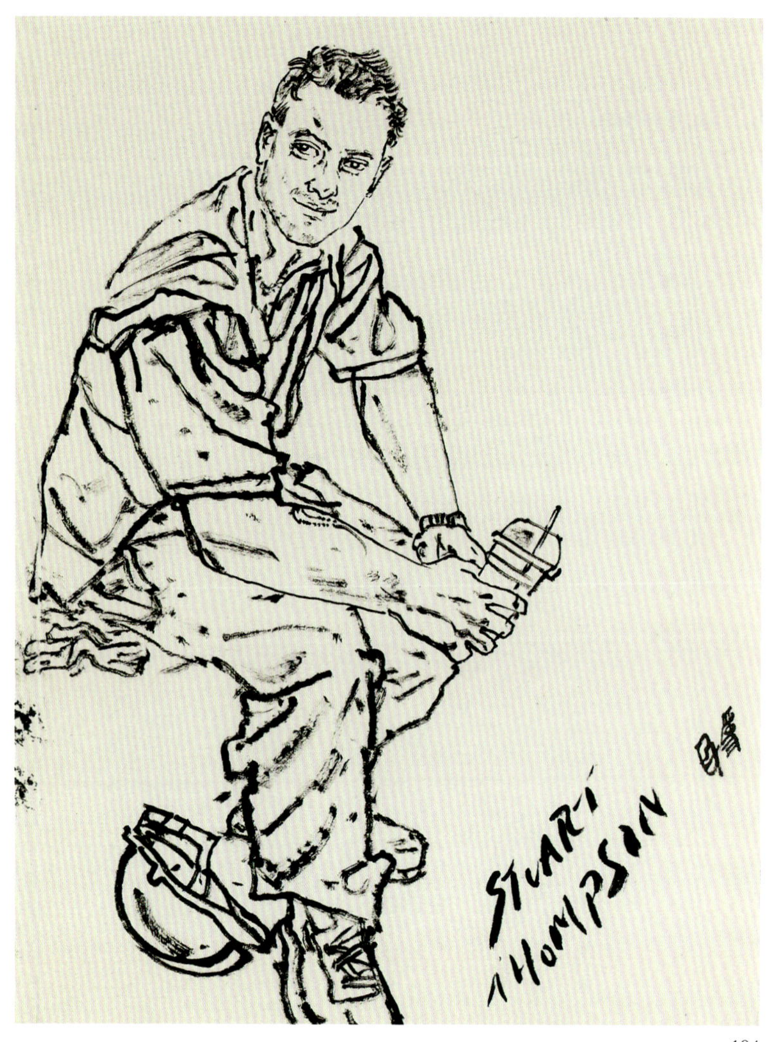

194

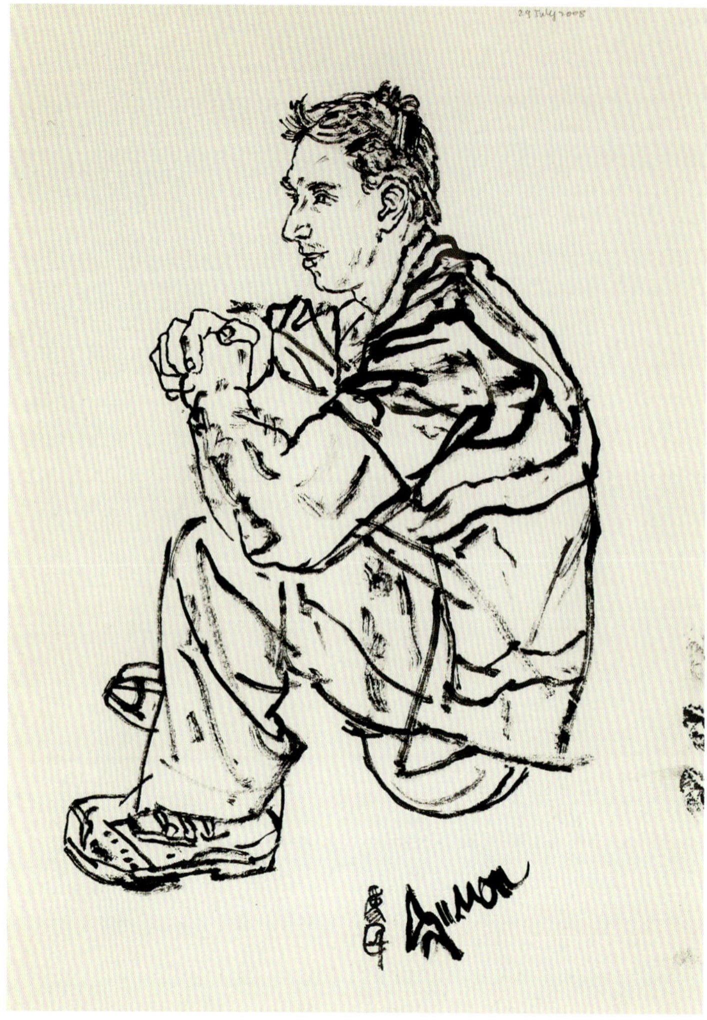

195

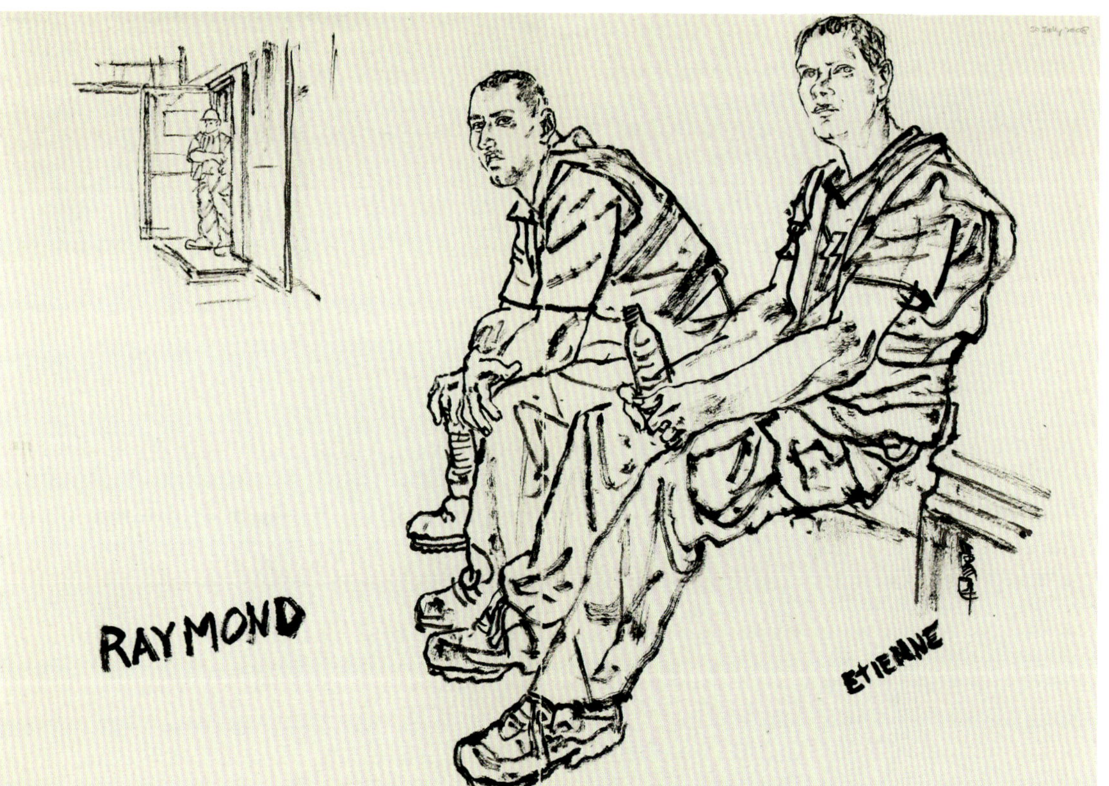

196

194 Stuart *Construction worker*
2008.
Brush and ink on album leaves.
Paper size: 44.2 × 2.3 cm

195 *Construction worker*
2008.
Brush and ink on album leaves.
Paper size: 44.2 × 32.3 cm

196 Raymond and Étienne
Dryliners
2008.
Brush and ink on album leaves.
Paper size: 44.2 × 64.6 cm

197 Nick and Kev *Damp proofers*
2008. Brush and ink on album leaves.
Paper size: 44.2 × 64.6 cm

198 George *Banksman*
2008. Brush and ink on album leaves.
Paper size: 44.2 × 32.3 cm

199 *Framework carpenter*
2008. Brush and ink on album leaves.
Paper size: 44.2 × 32.3 cm

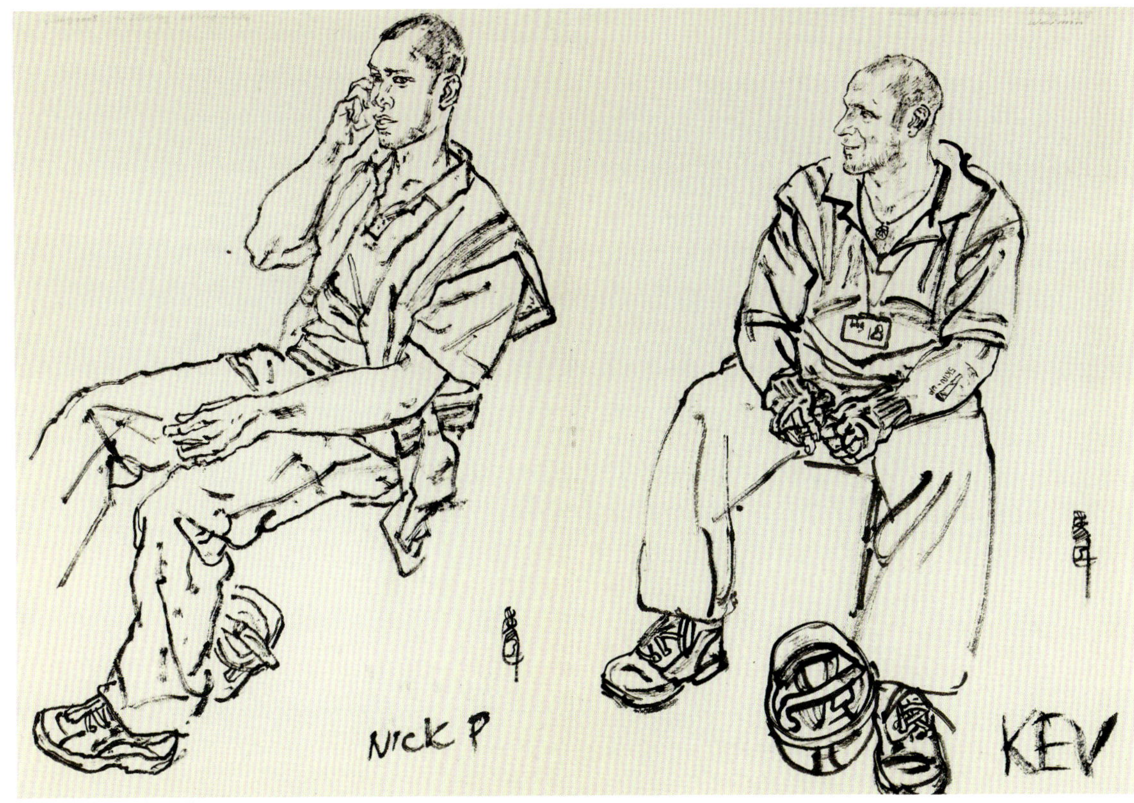

197

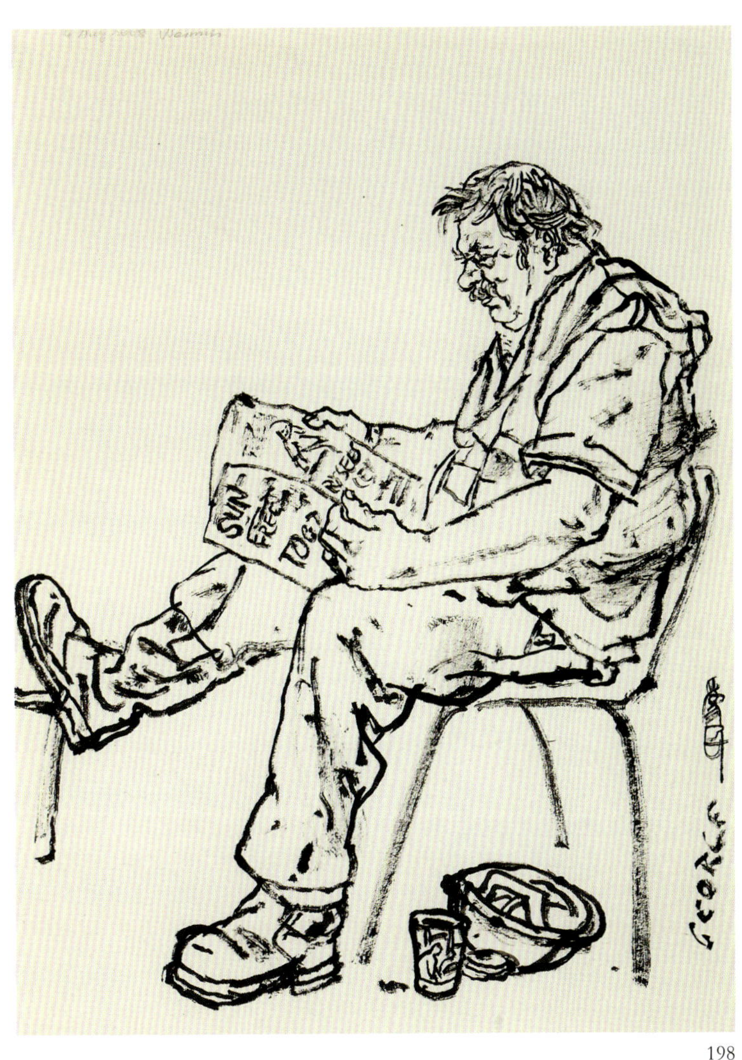

198

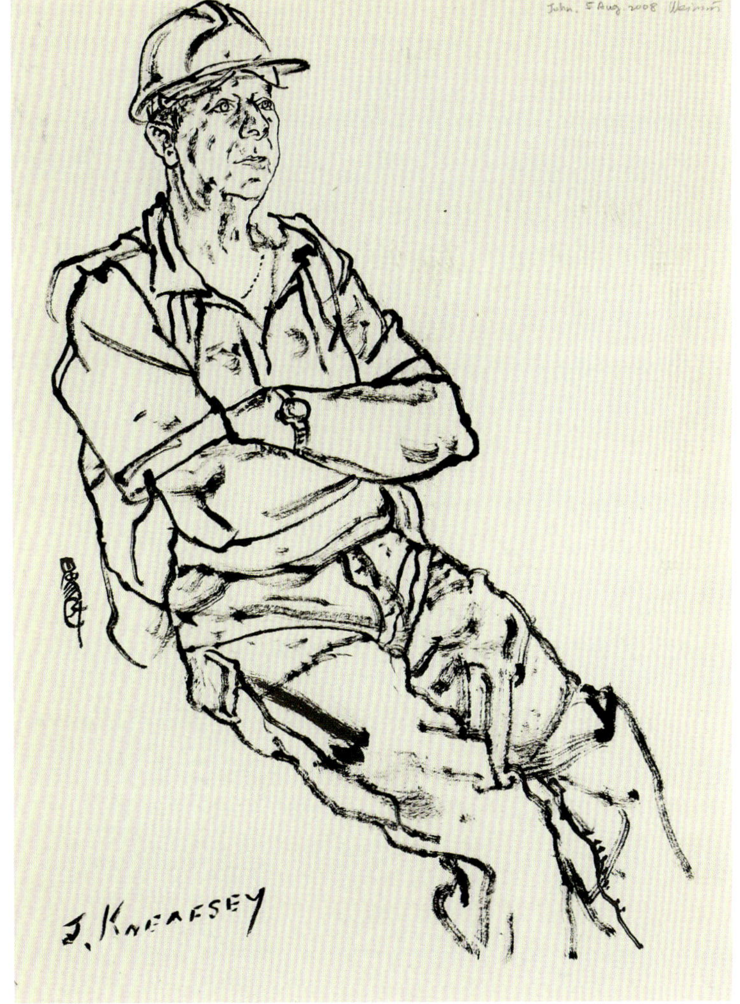

199

200 **Rob** *Construction worker*
2008. Brush and ink on album leaves.
Paper size: 44.2 × 64.6 cm

201 **Alan and Chris** *Bricklayers*
2008. Brush and ink on album leaves.
Paper size: 44.2 × 64.6 cm

202 **Stuart**
2008. Brush and ink on album leaves.
Paper size: 44.2 × 32.3 cm

203 **Gary** *Bricklayer*
2008. Brush and ink on album leaves.
Paper size: 44.2 × 32.3 cm

204 **Jarek**
2008. Brush and ink on album leaves.
Paper size: 44.2 × 32.3 cm

205 **Cristian** *Painter*
2009. Brush and ink on album leaves.
Paper size: 44.2 × 32.3 cm

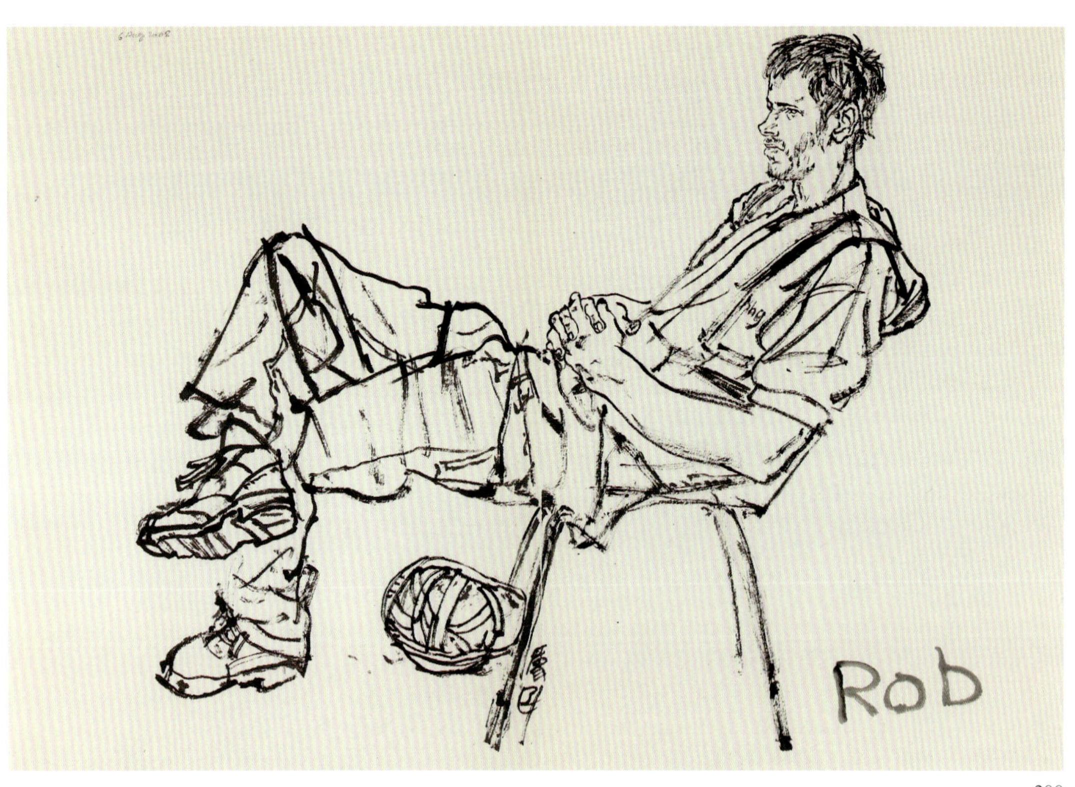

200

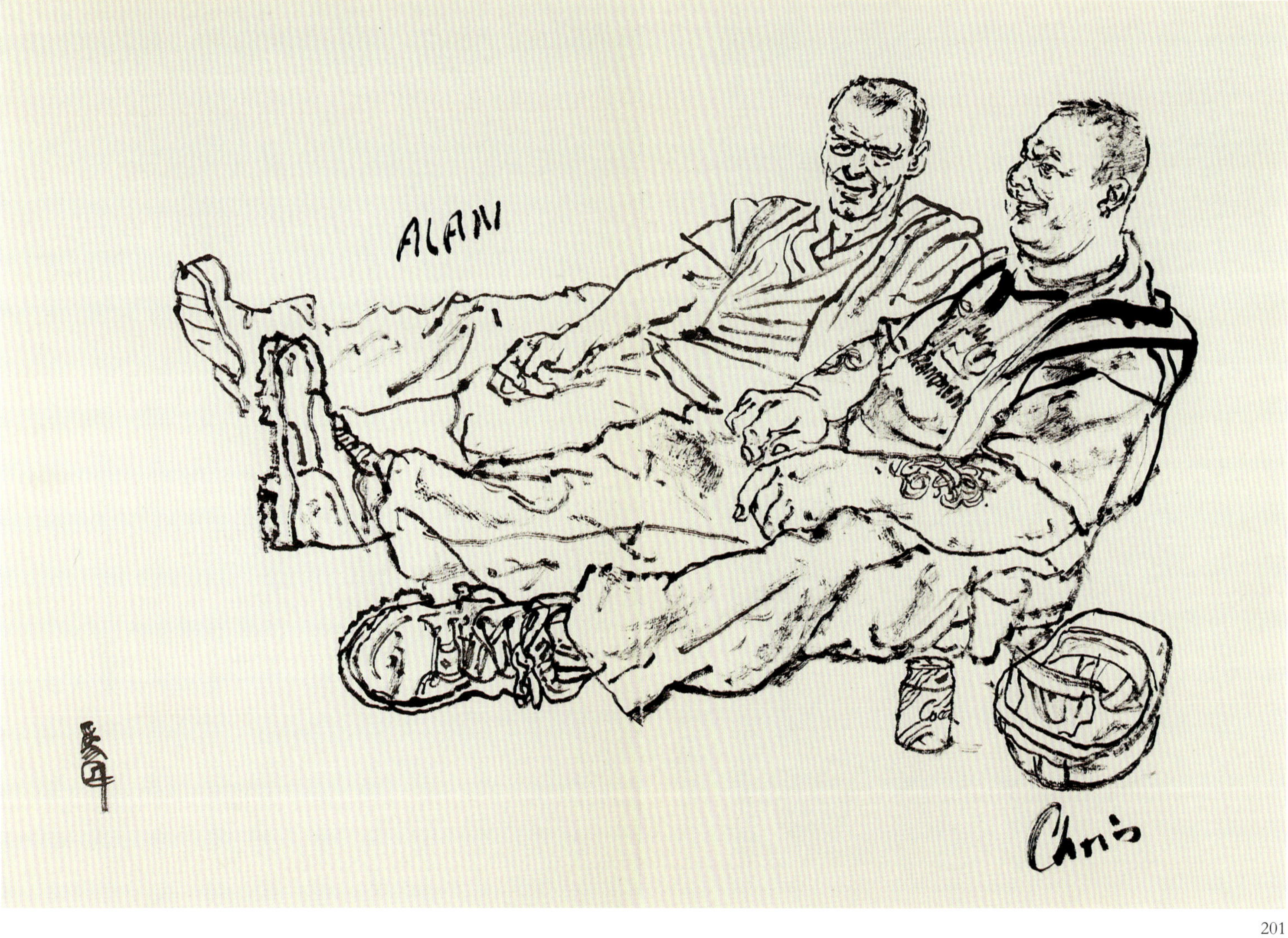

201

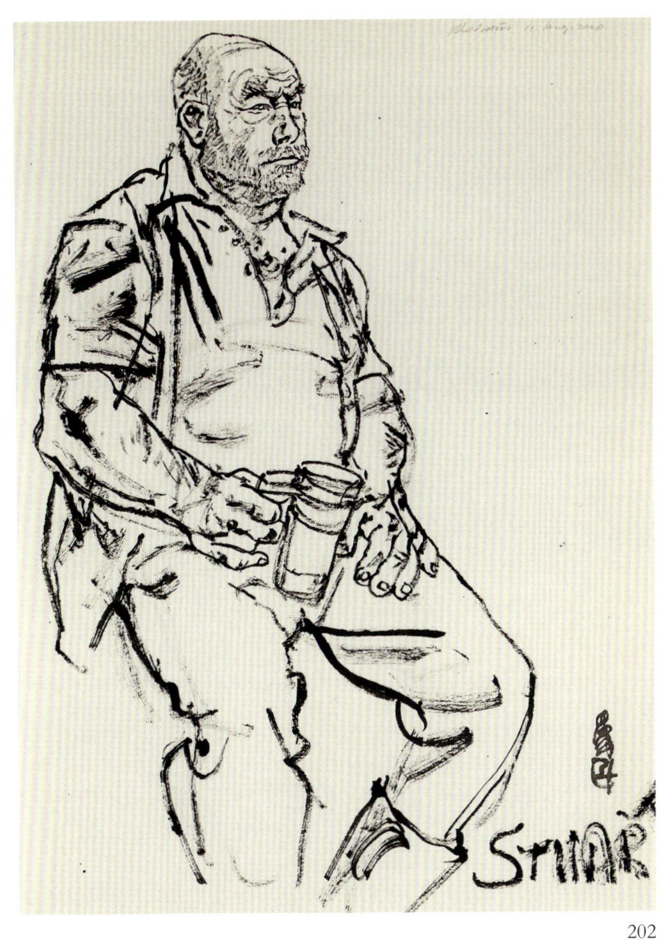

202

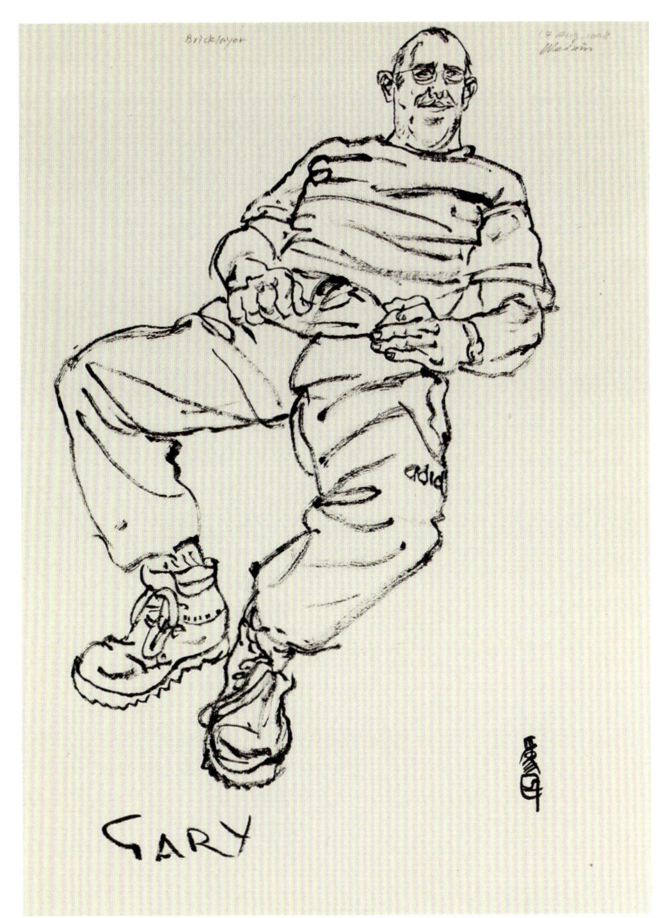

203

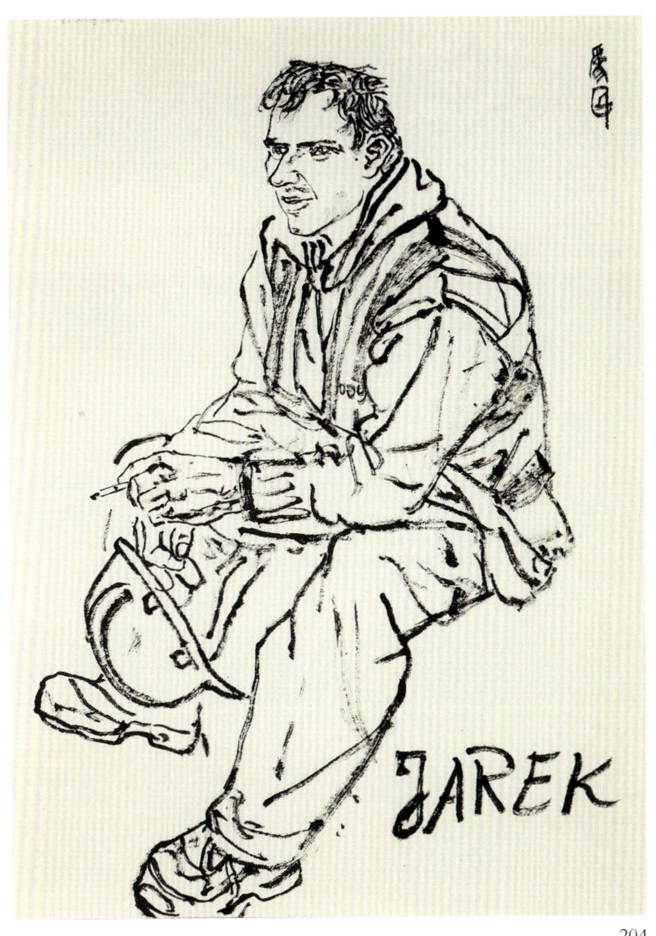

204

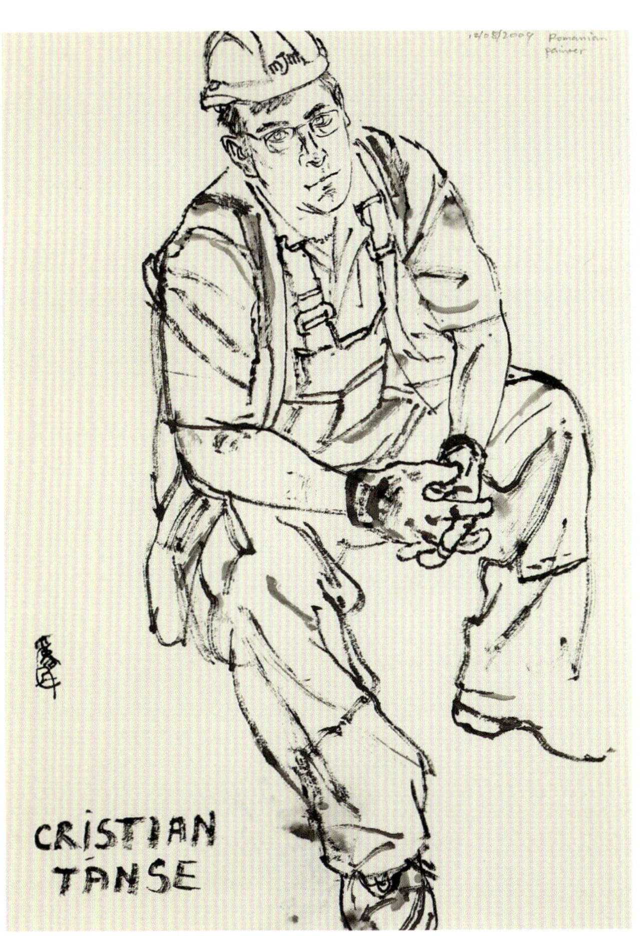

205

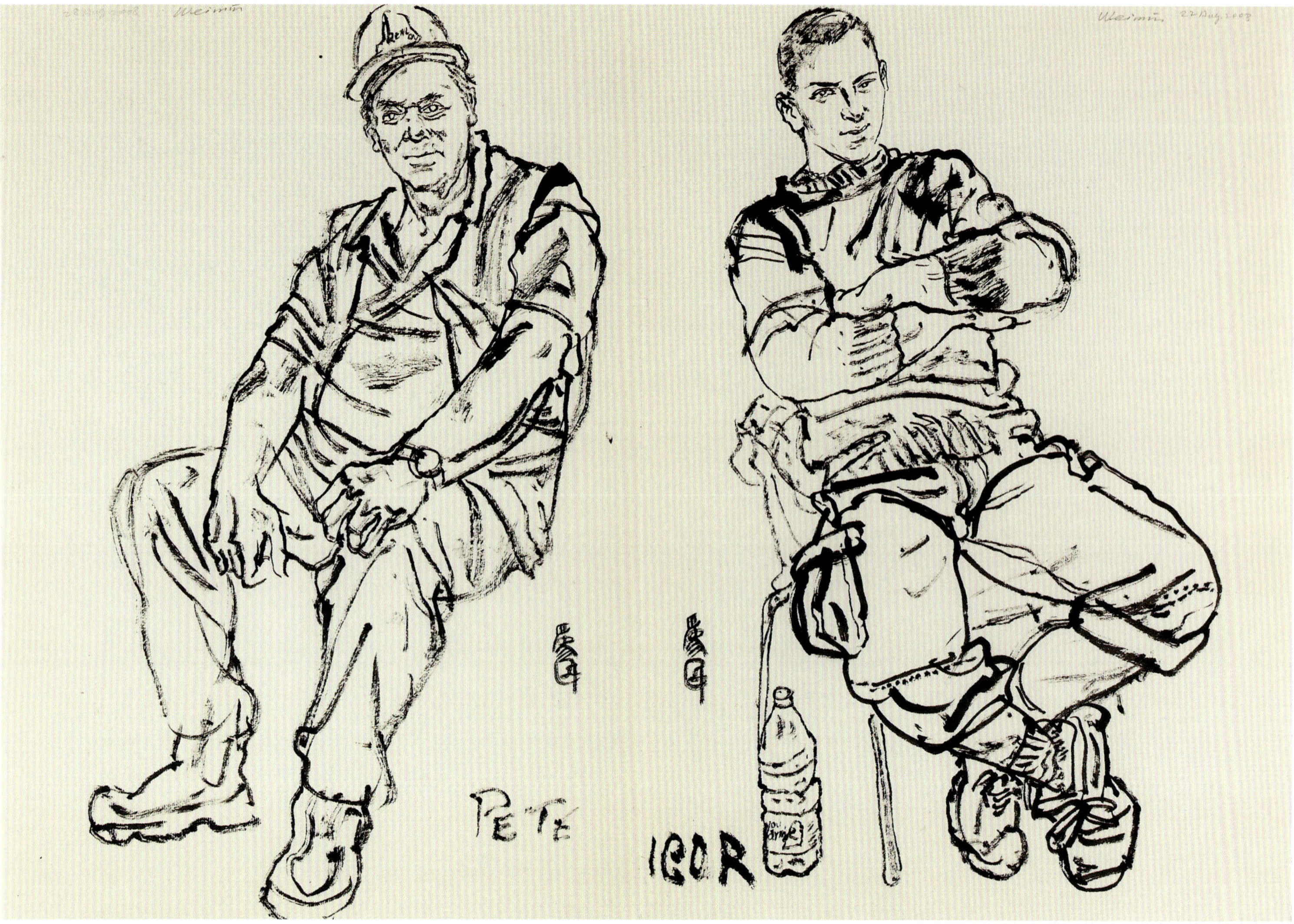

206

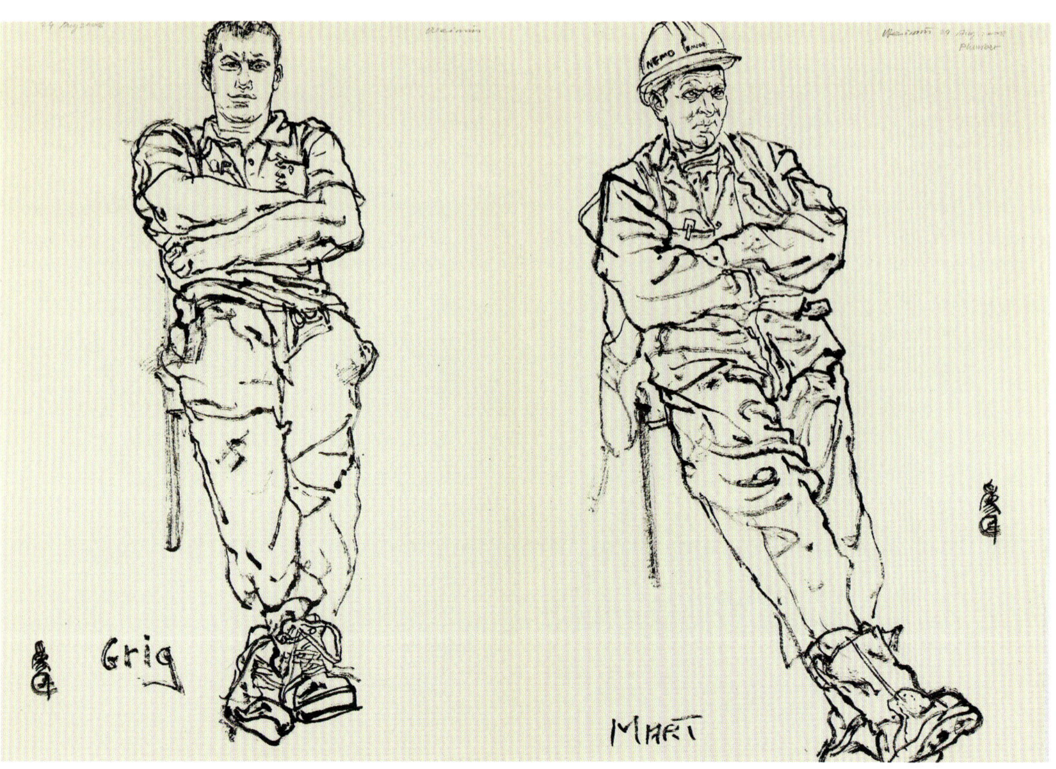

207

206 Pete and Igor
2008. Brush and ink on album leaves.
Paper size: 44.2 × 64.6 cm

207 Grig and Mart *Welders*
2008. Brush and ink on album leaves.
Paper size: 44.2 × 64.6 cm

208 Leigh and Dan *Electricians*
2008. Brush and ink on album leaves.
Paper size: 44.2 × 64.6 cm

209 Richie and Steve *Drillers*
2008. Brush and ink on album leaves.
Paper size: 44.2 × 64.6 cm

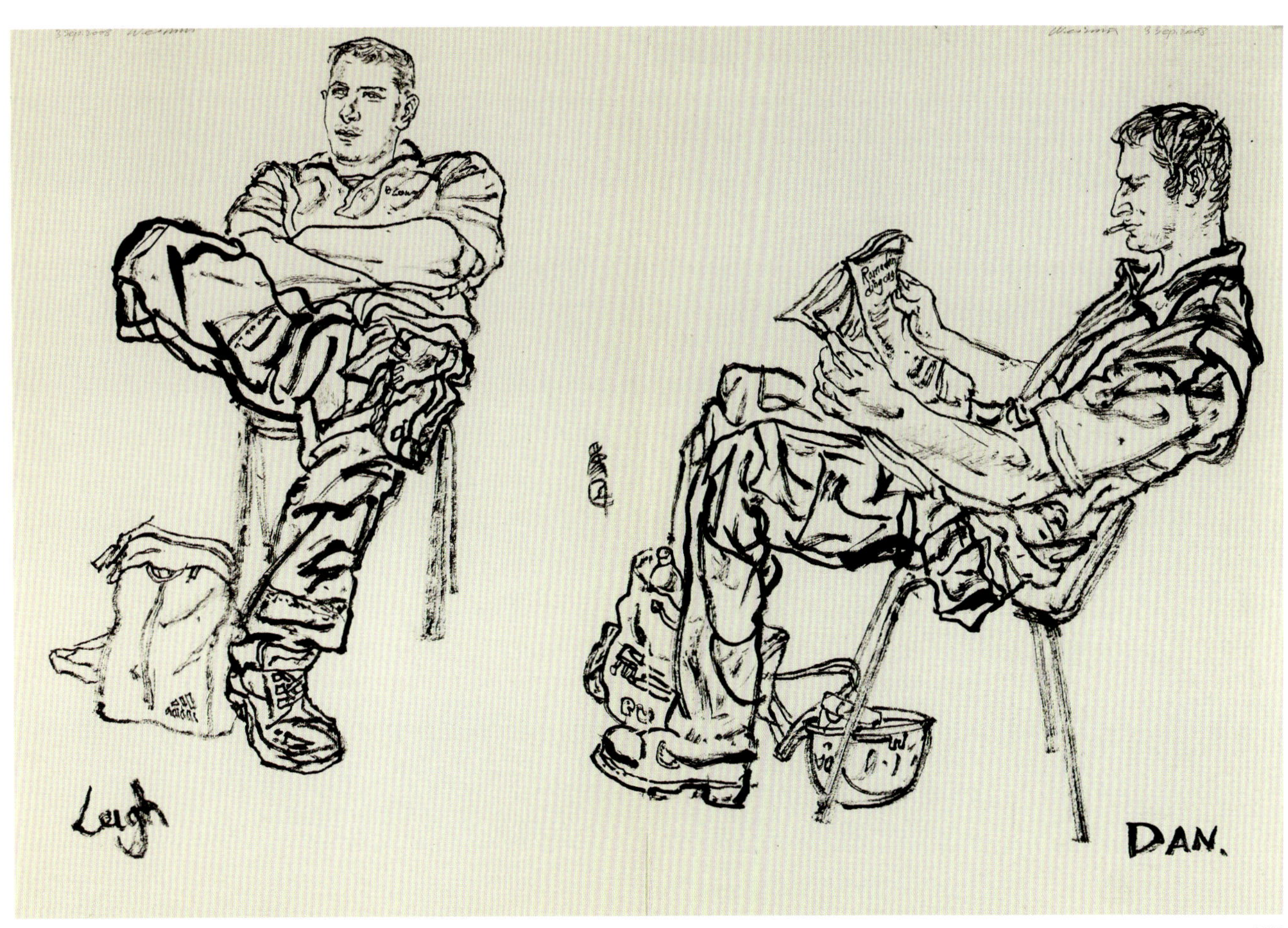

208

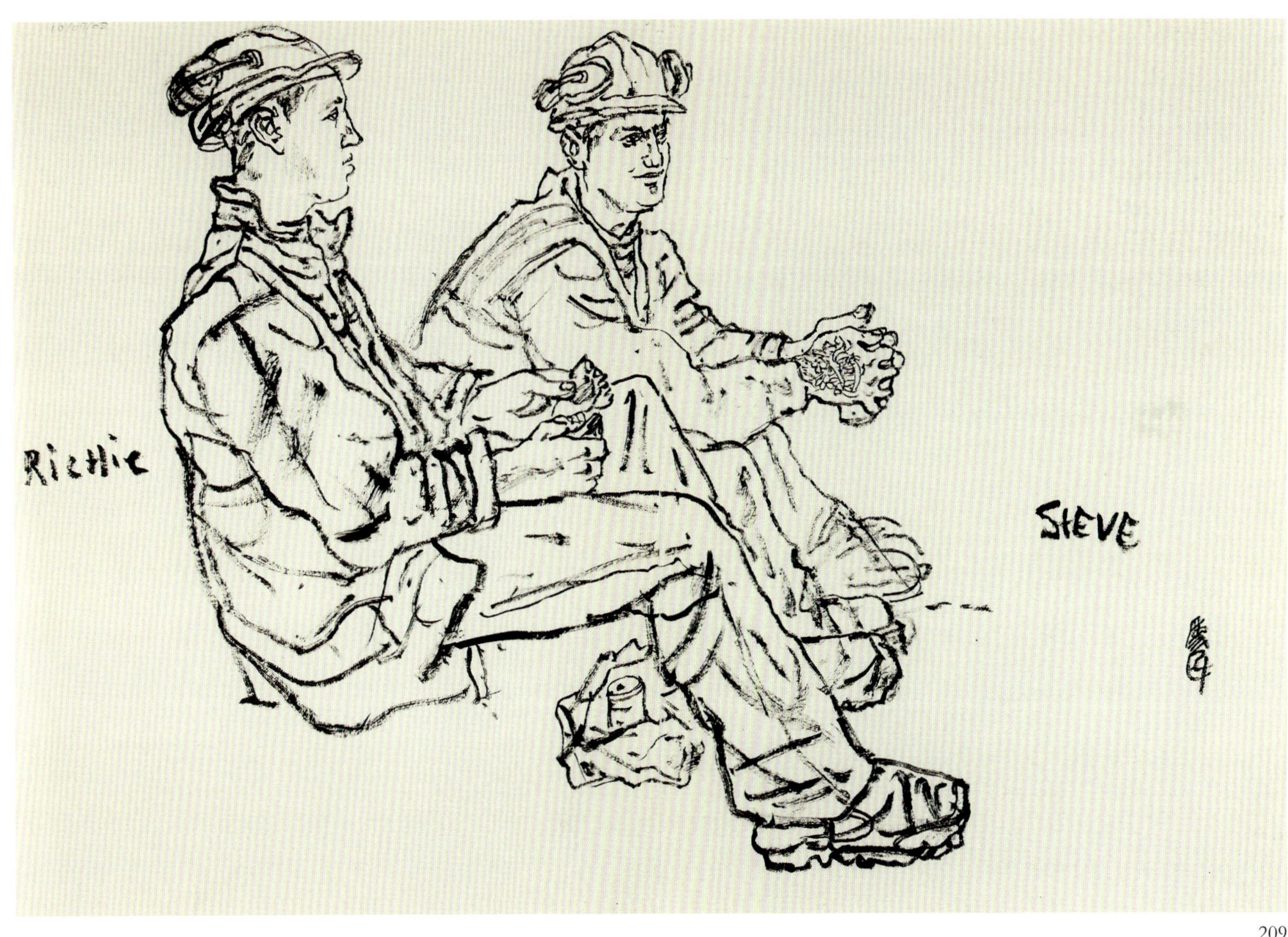

209

210 Saulius and John
2008. Brush and ink on album leaves.
Paper size: 44.2 × 64.6 cm

211 Andrius *Carpenter*
2008. Brush and ink on album leaves.
Paper size: 44.2 × 32.3 cm

212 Tom *Crane driver*
2008. Brush and ink on album leaves.
Paper size: 44.2 × 32.3 cm

213 Peter and Soxy
Steel/fabricates workers
2008. Brush and ink on album leaves.
Paper size: 64.6 × 44.2 cm

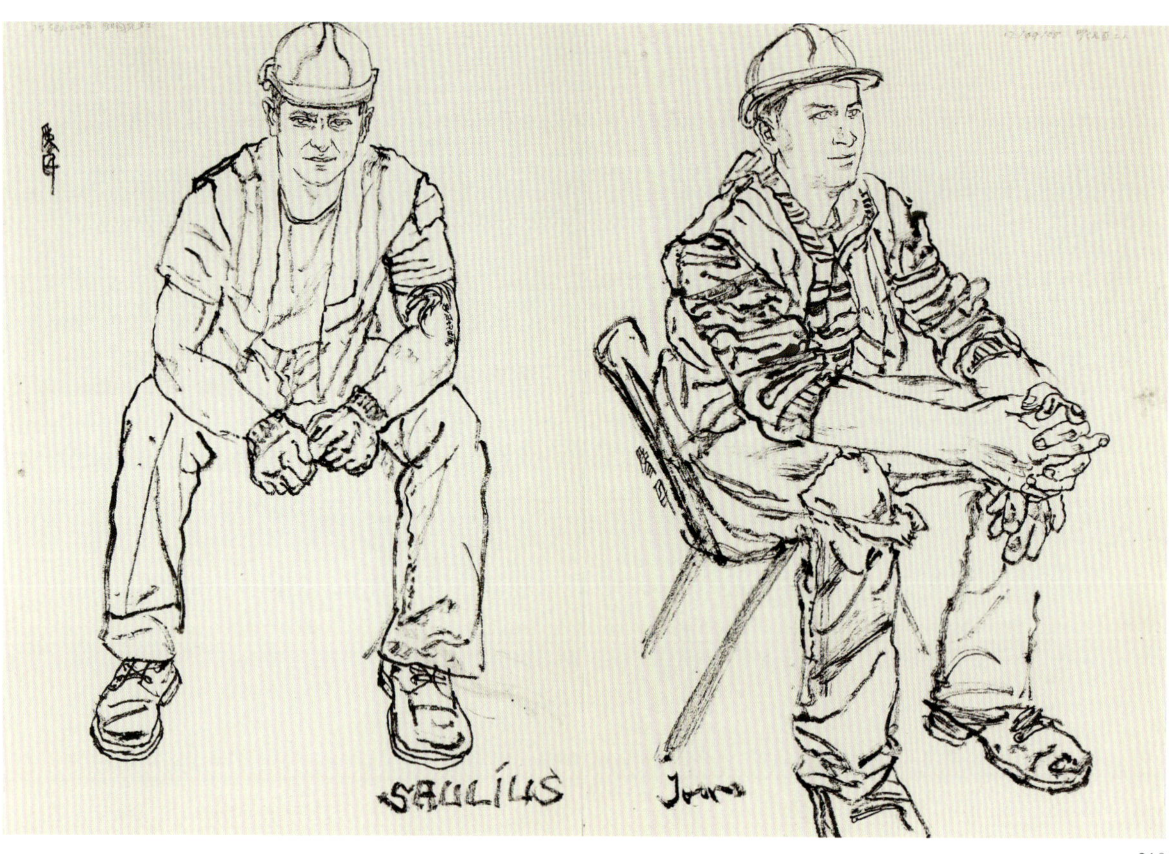

210

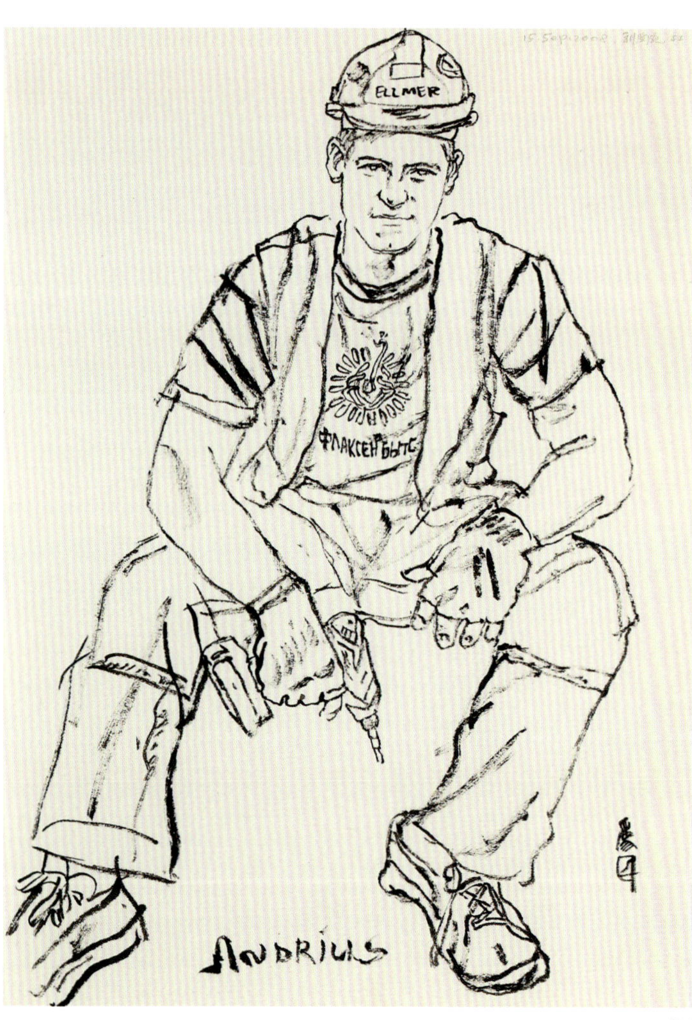

211

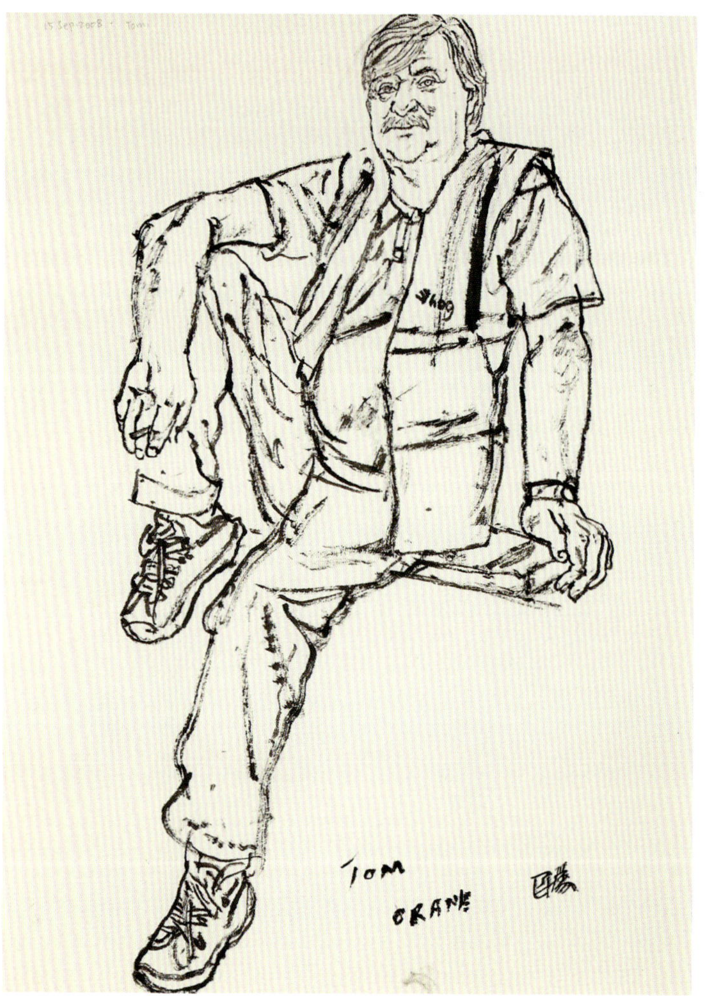

212

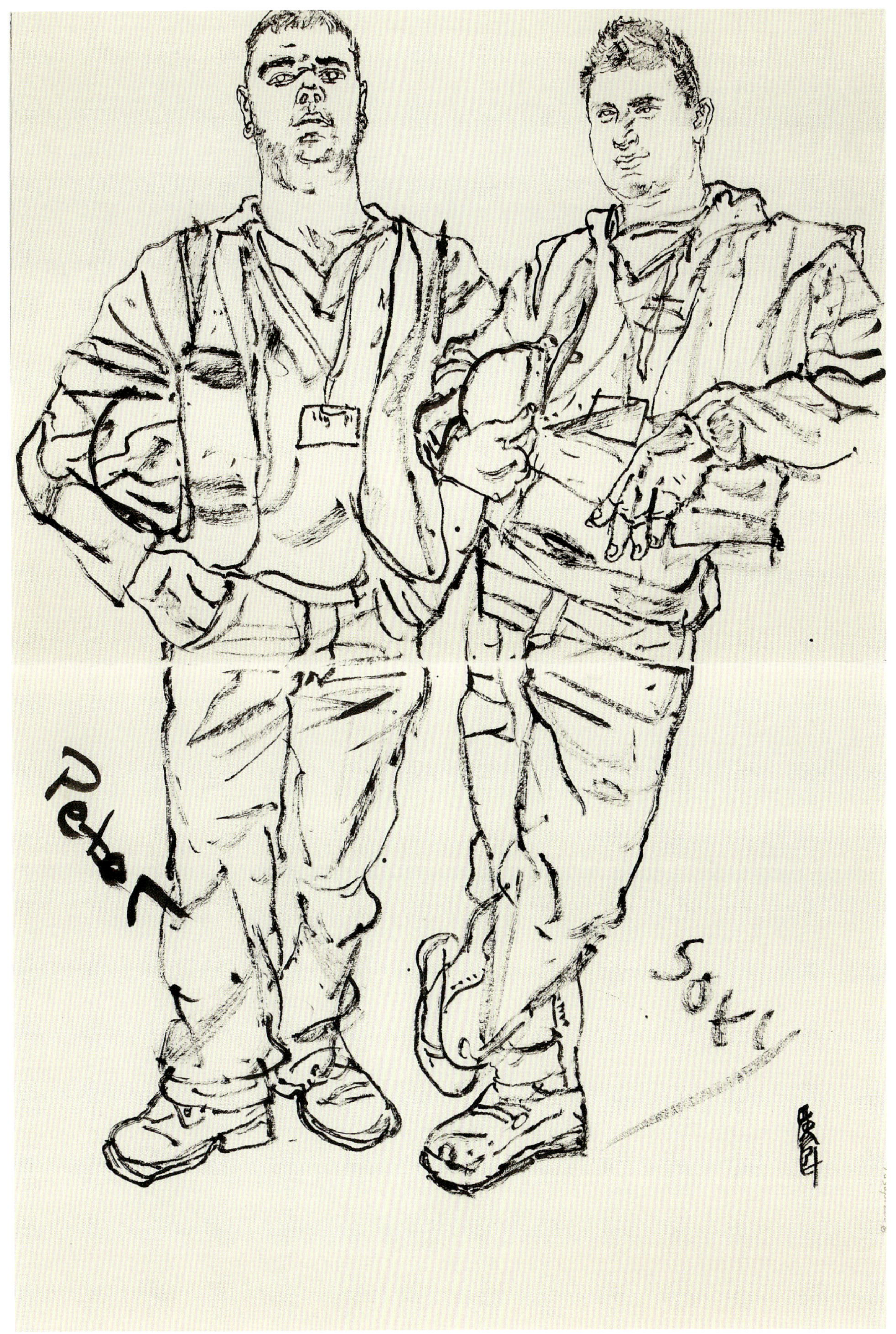

213

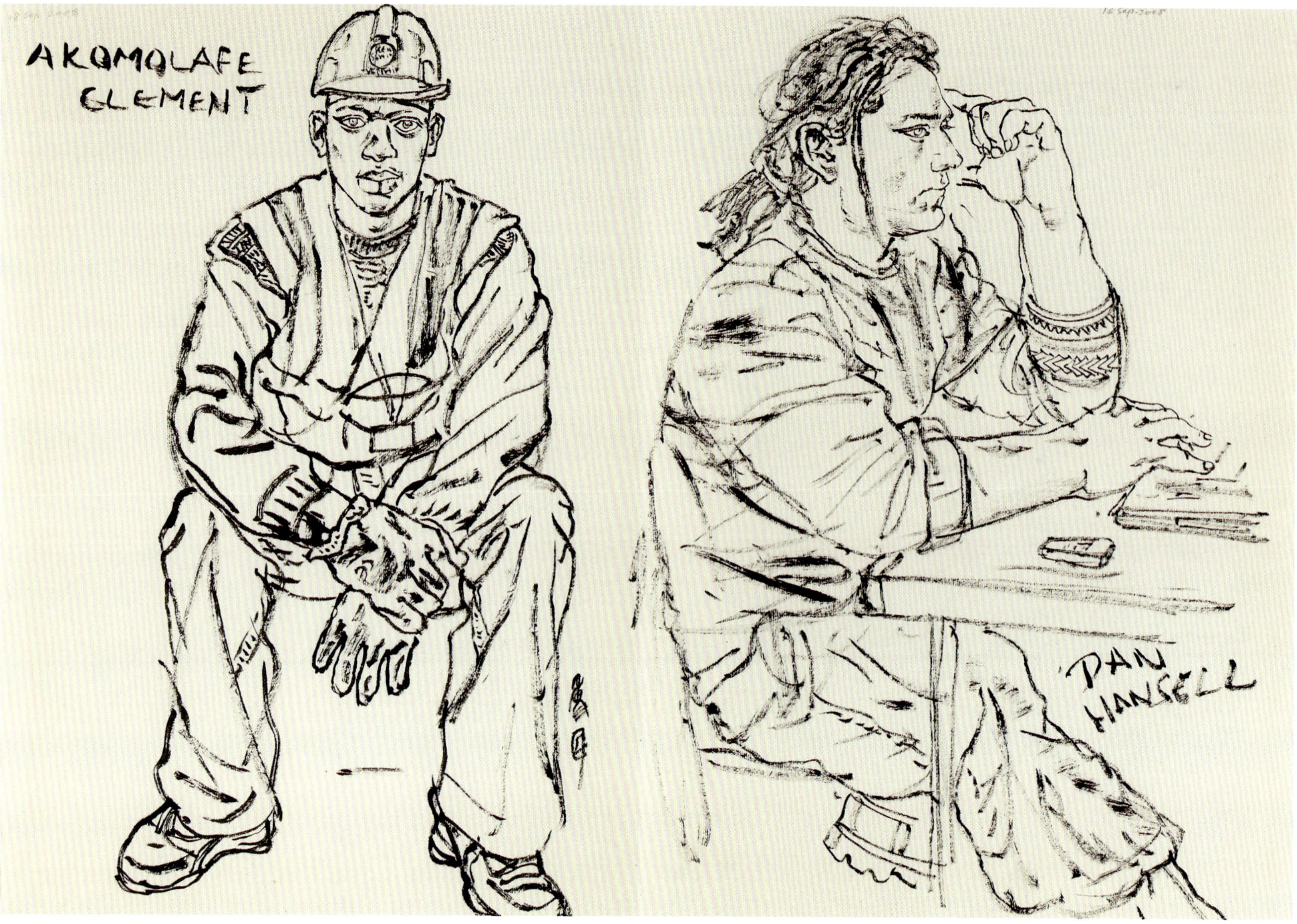

214

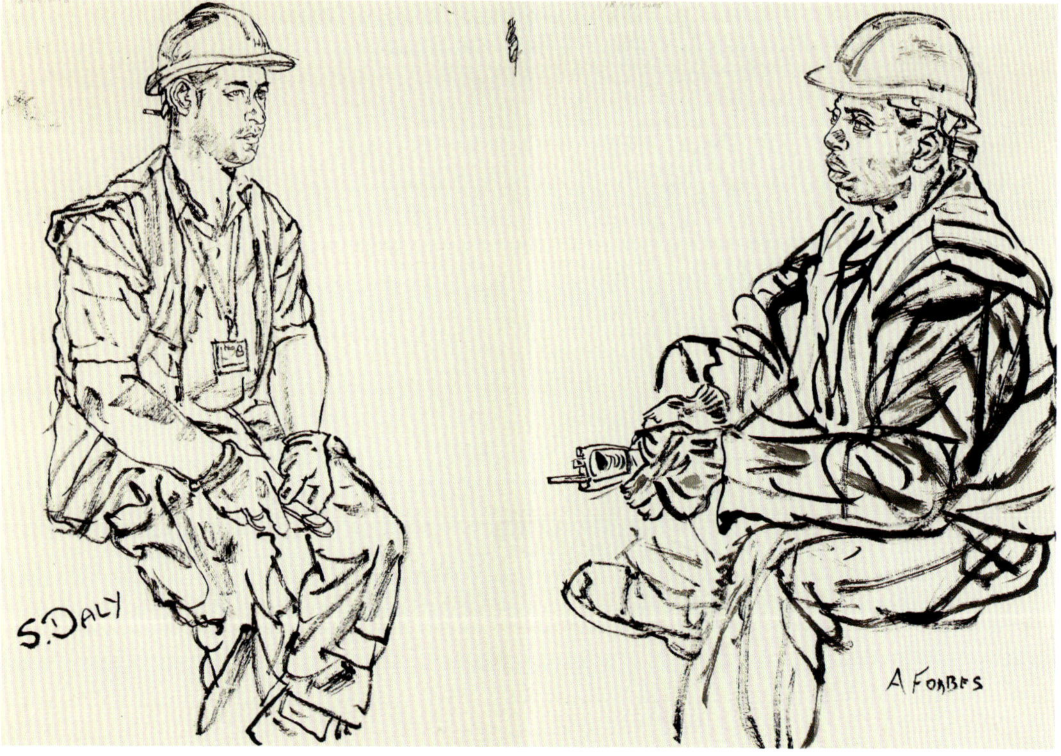

215

214 Akomolafe and Dan
Window fitters
2008.
Brush and ink on album leaves.
Paper size: 44.2 × 64.6 cm

215 Adrian
Hoist driver and electrician
2008.
Brush and ink on album leaves.
Paper size: 44.2 × 64.6 cm

216 Gray and Doug *Roofers*
2008.
Brush and ink on album leaves.
Paper size: 44.2 × 64.6 cm

217 Kevin and John
2008.
Brush and ink on album leaves.
Paper size: 44.2 × 64.6 cm

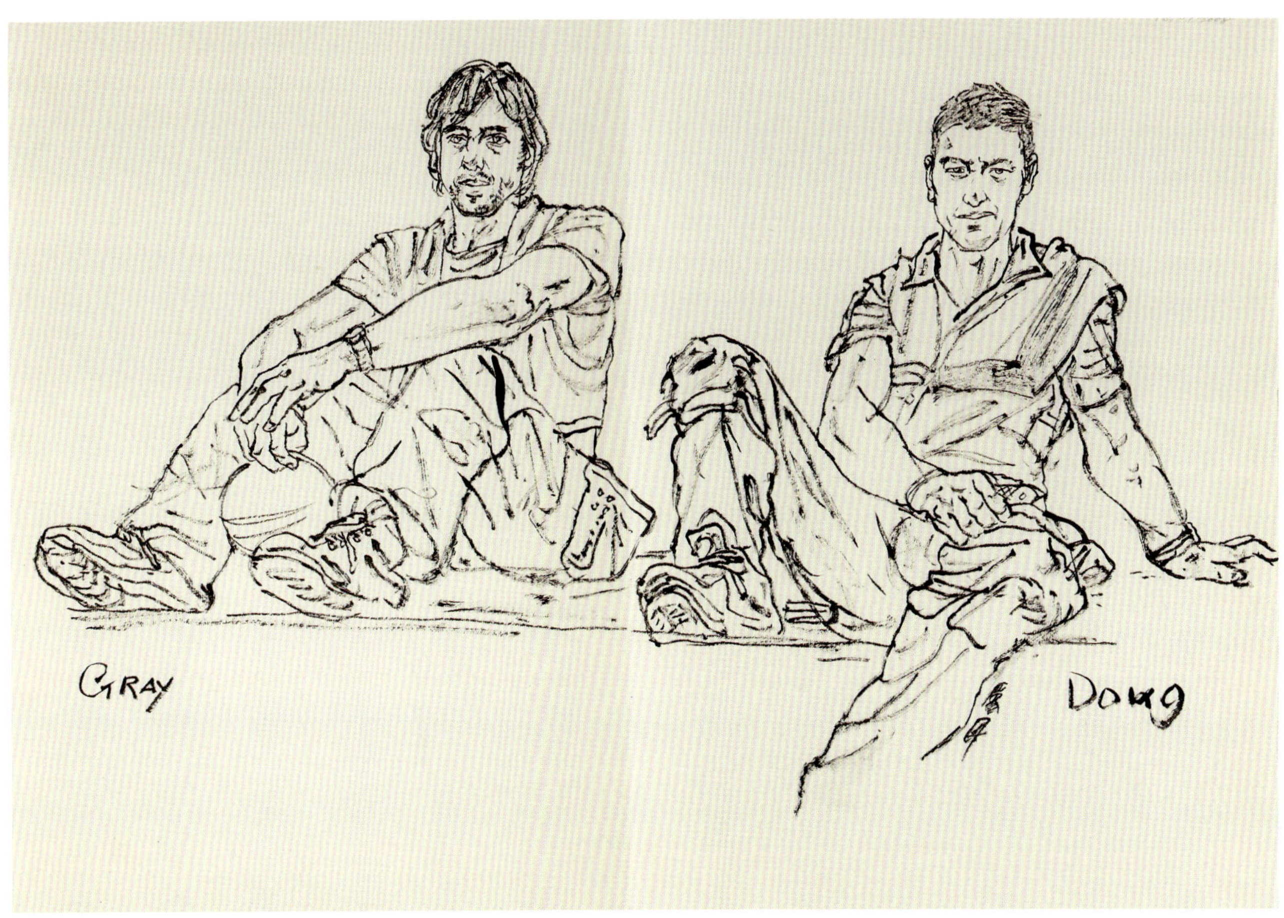

216

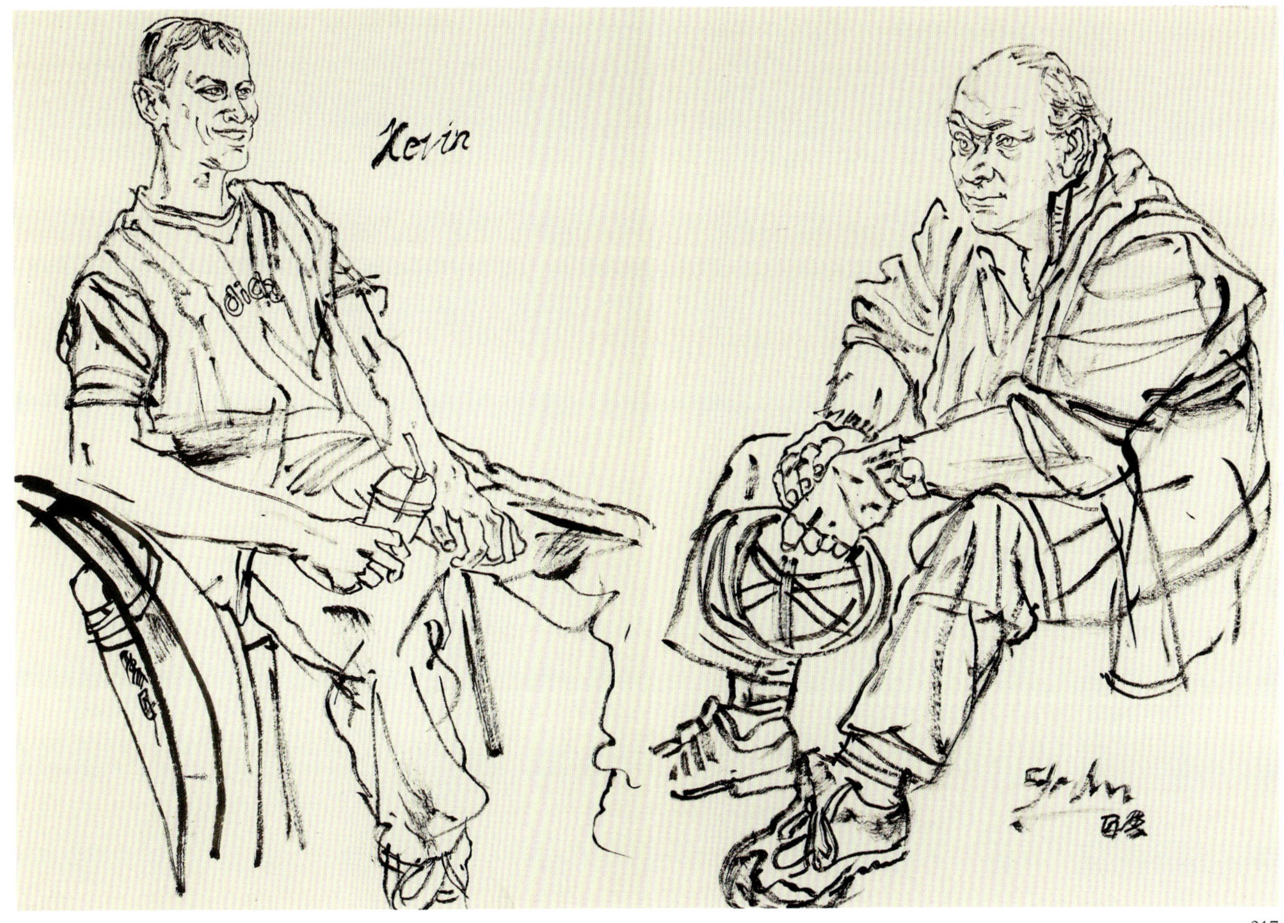

217

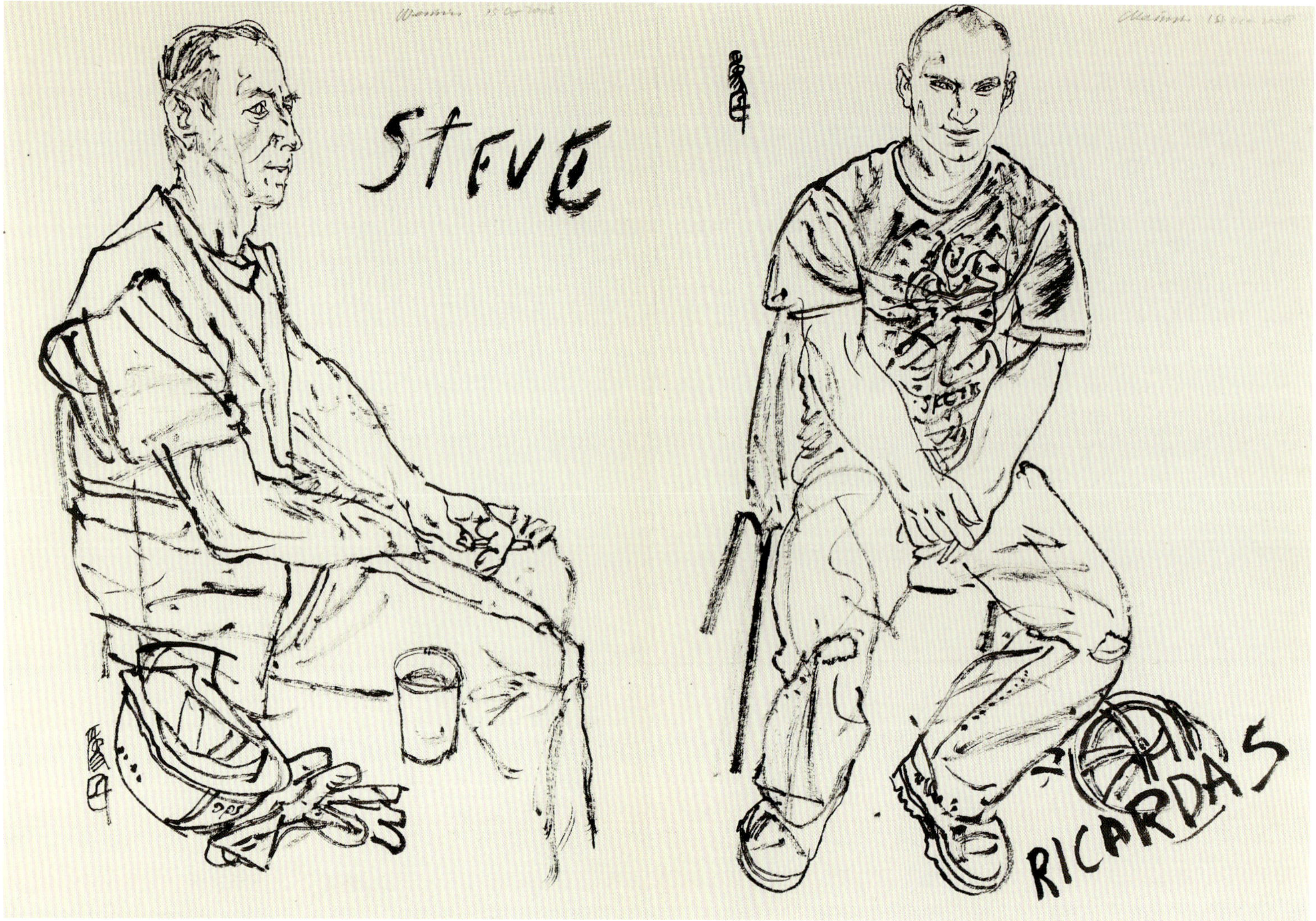

218

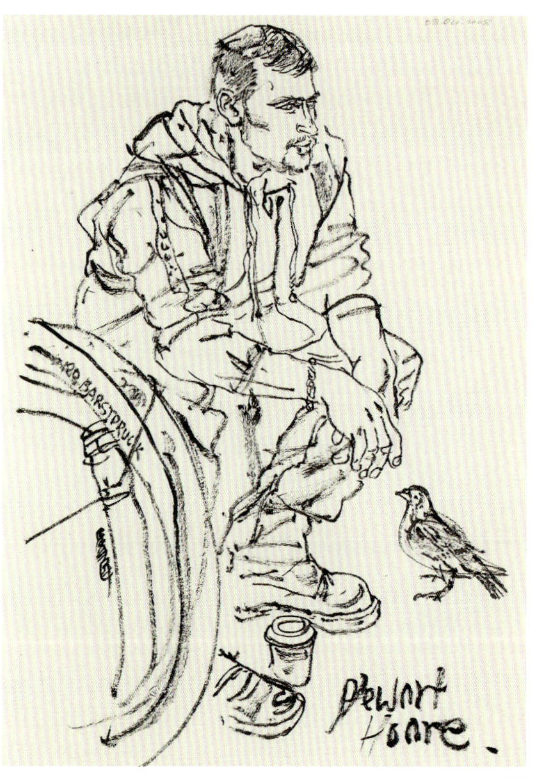

219

218 Steve and Ricardas
2008. Brush and ink on album leaves. Paper size: 44.2 × 64.6 cm

219 Stewart
2008. Brush and ink on album leaves. Paper size: 44.2 × 32.3 cm

220 Freddie and Martin *Scaffolders*
2008. Brush and ink on album leaves. Paper size: 44.2 × 64.6 cm

221 Matthew and Joshua *Construction workers*
2008. Brush and ink on album leaves. Paper size: 44.2 × 64.6 cm

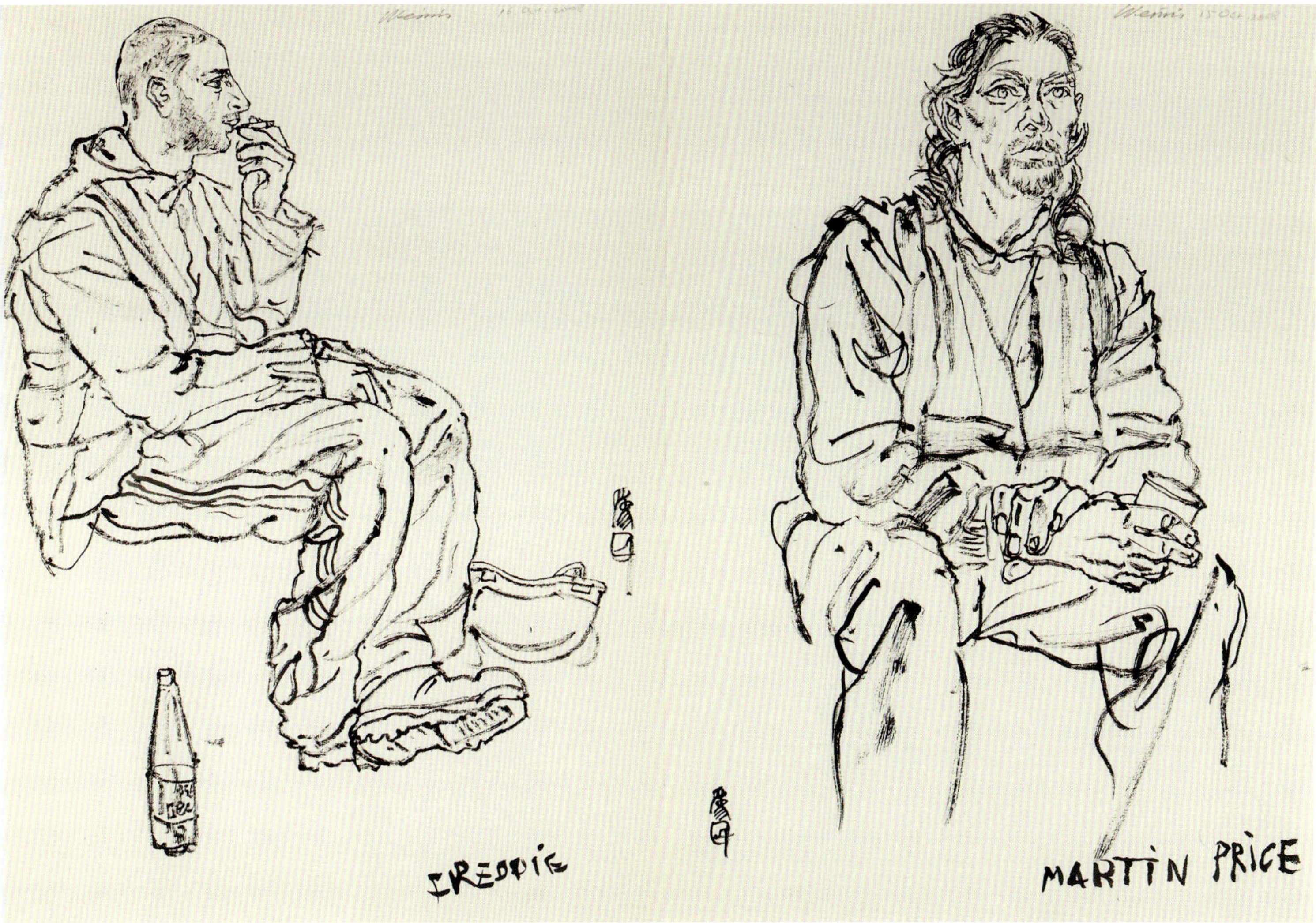

FREDDIE

MARTIN PRICE

220

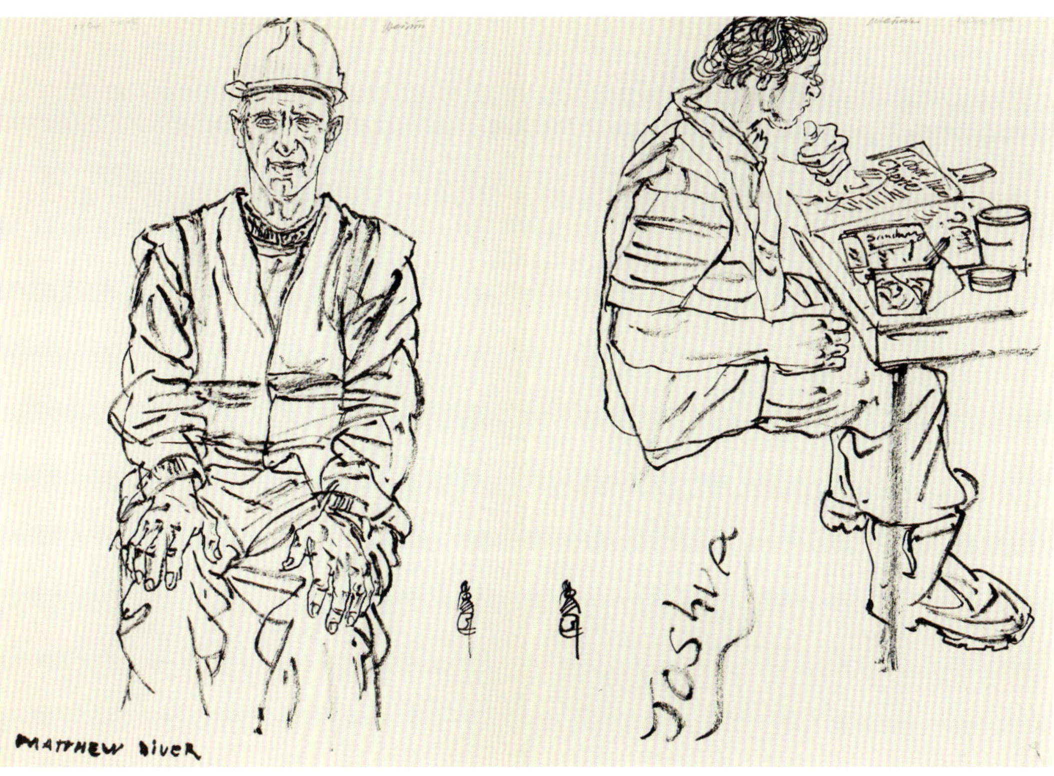

221

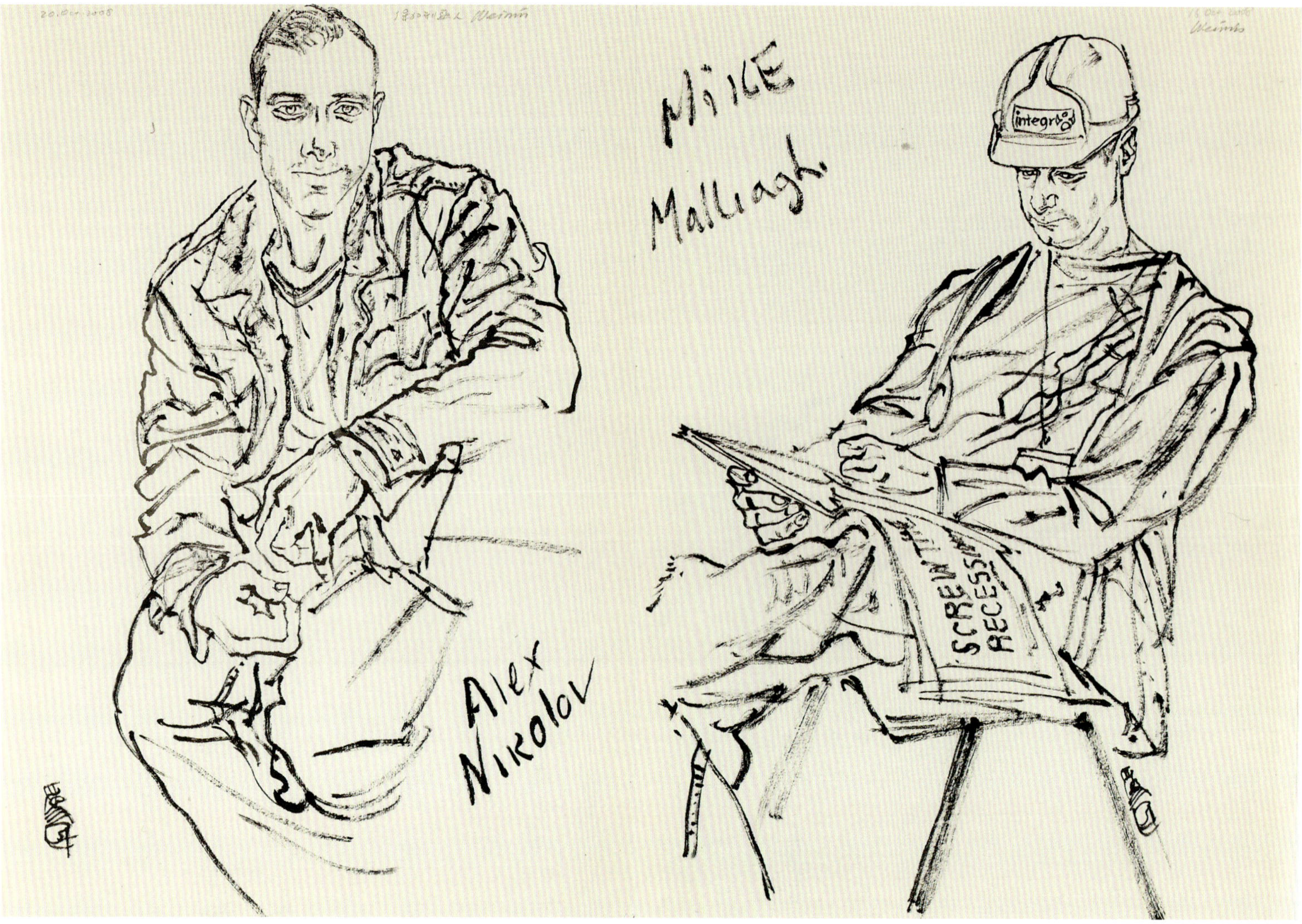

222

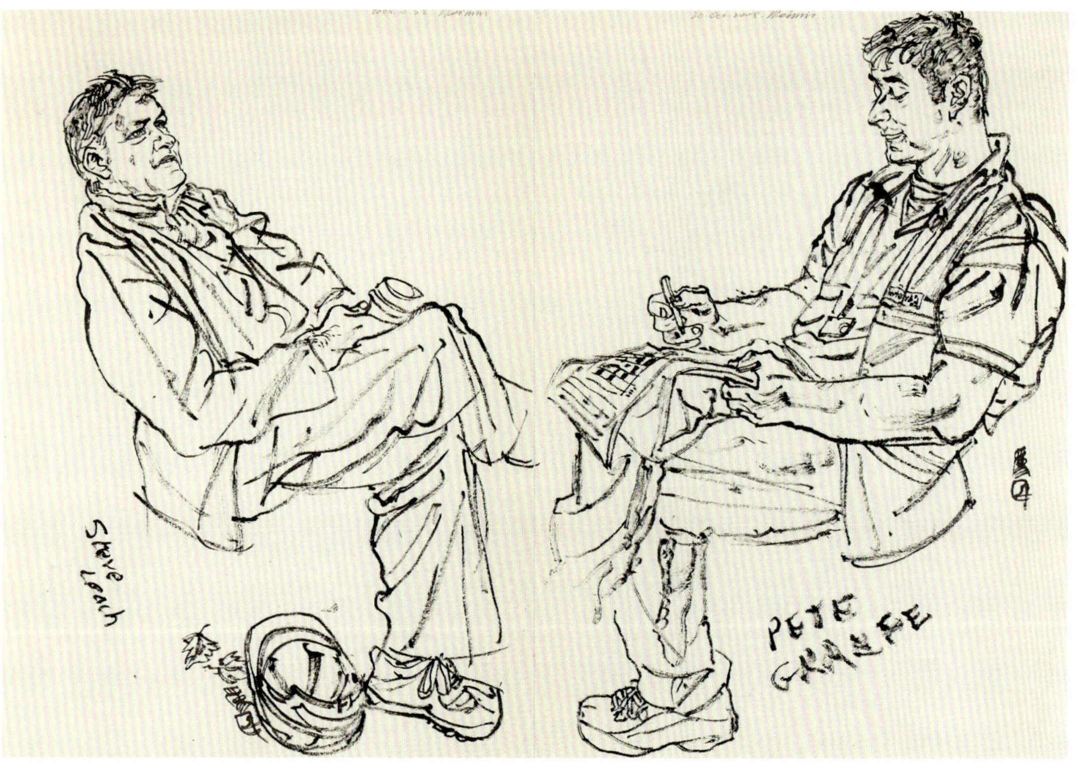

223

222 Alex and Mike *Dryliners*
2008.
Brush and ink on album leaves.
Paper size: 44.2 × 64.6 cm

223 Steve *Electrician*
and Pete *Dryliner*
2008.
Brush and ink on album leaves.
Paper size: 44.2 × 64.6 cm

224 Antony and Ben
Construction workers
2008.
Brush and ink on album leaves.
Paper size: 44.2 × 64.6 cm

225 Dany *Dryliner*
and Dan *Steel worker*
2008.
Brush and ink on album leaves.
Paper size: 44.2 × 64.6 cm

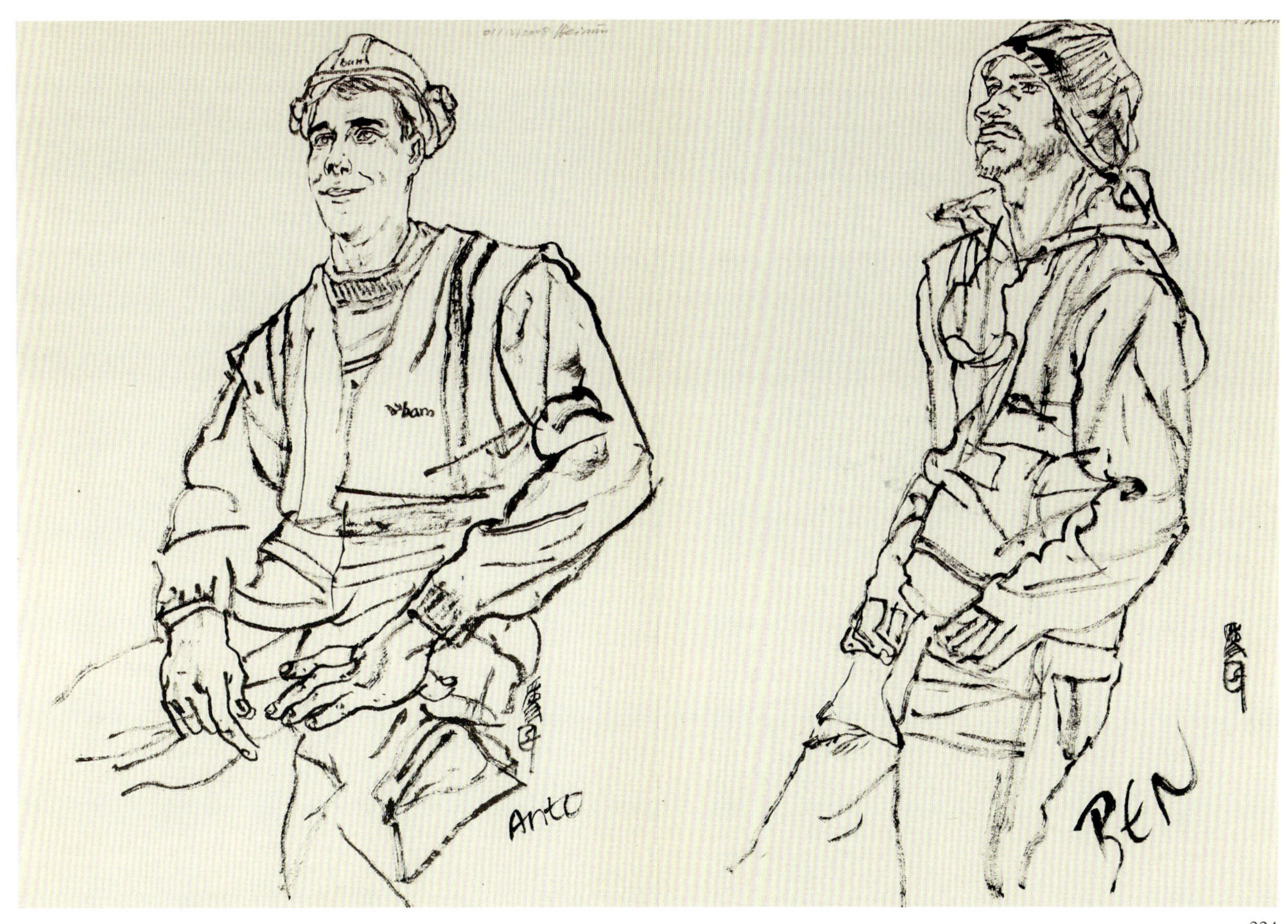

224

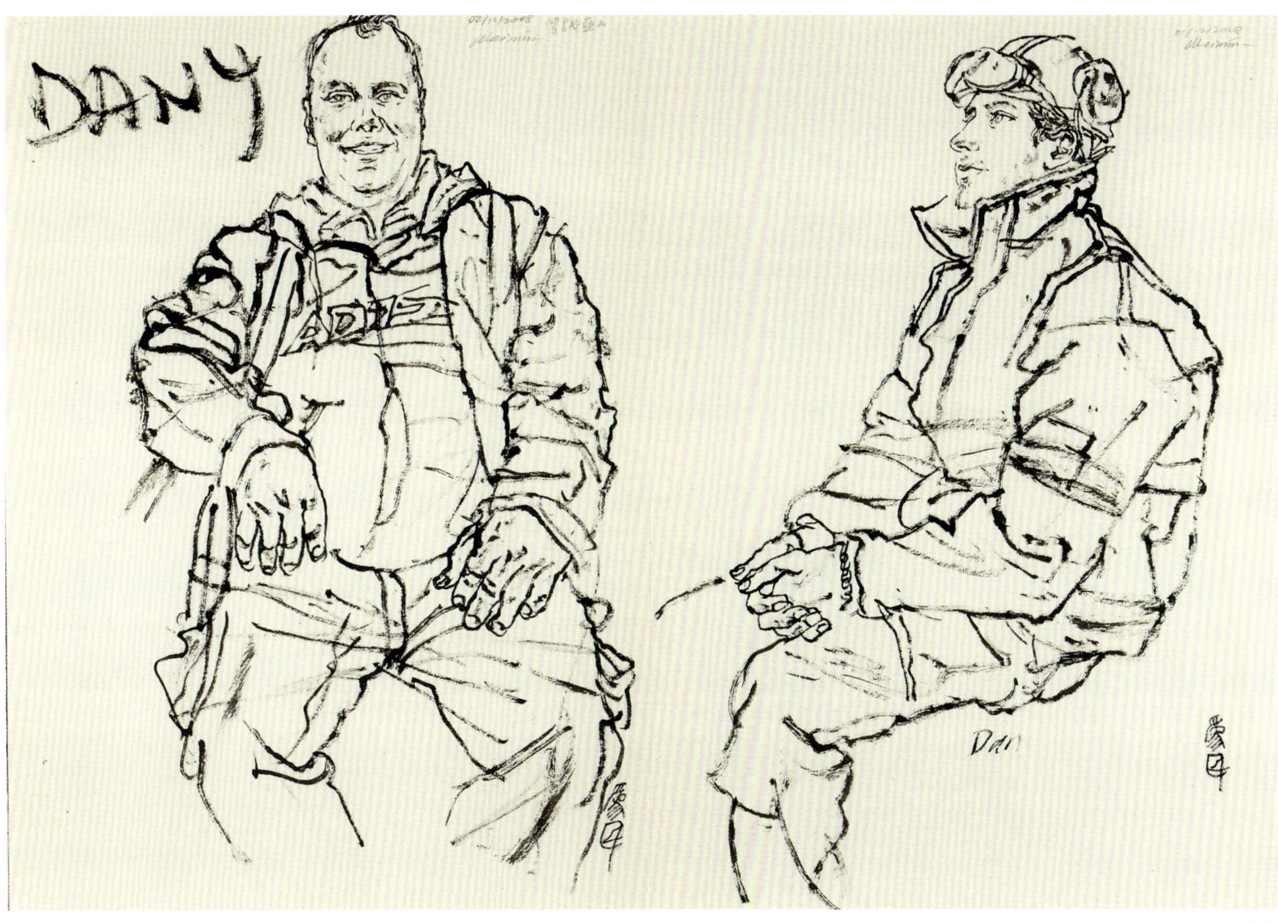

225

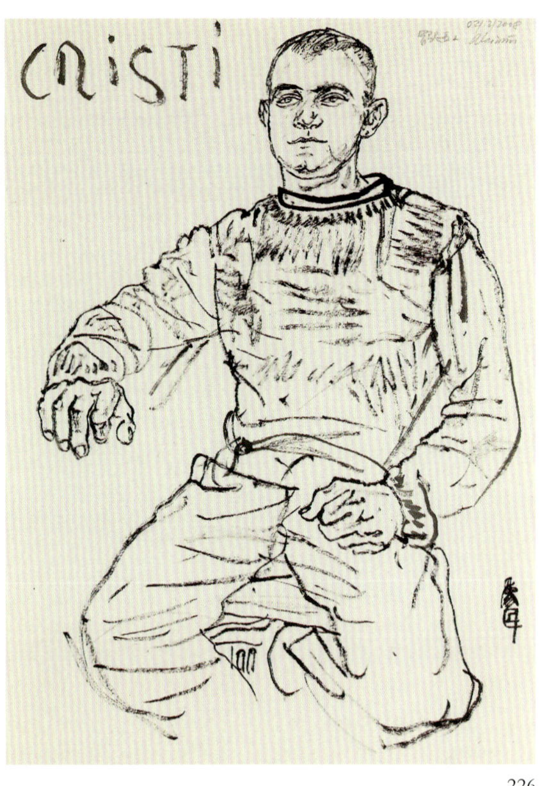

226

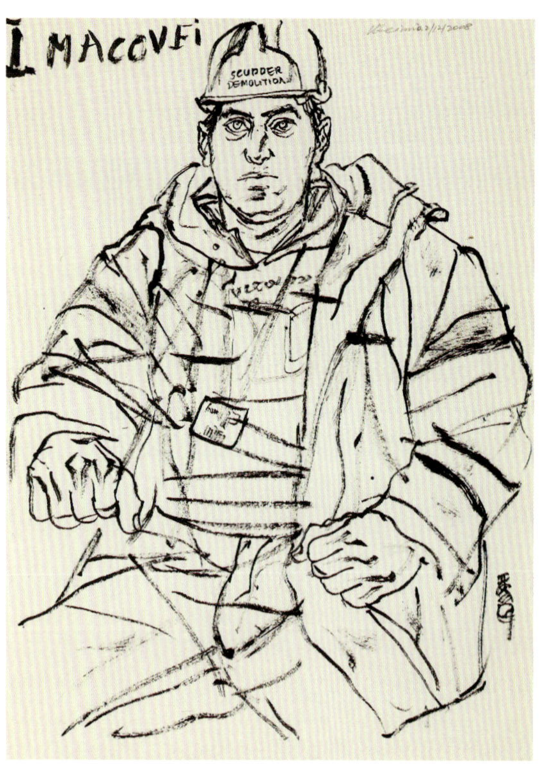

227

226 Cristi
2008.
Brush and ink on album leaves.
Paper size: 44.2 × 32.3 cm

227 *Ground worker*
2008.
Brush and ink on album leaves.
Paper size: 44.2 × 32.3 cm

228 Dummru and Lucian
2009.
Brush and ink on album leaves.
Paper size: 44.2 × 64.6 cm

229 Reece *Ground worker*
2009.
Brush and ink on album leaves.
Paper size: 44.2 × 32.3 cm

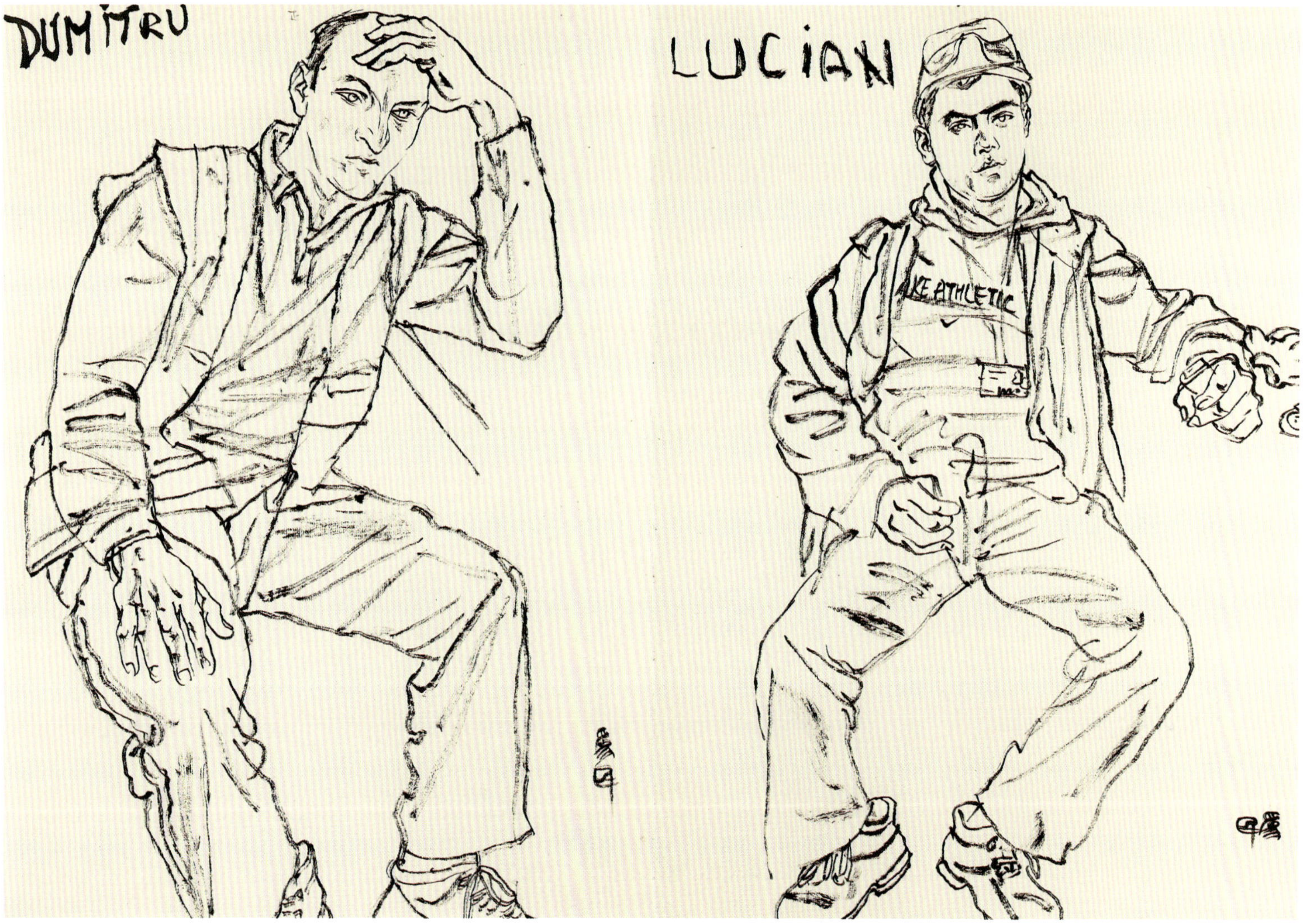

228

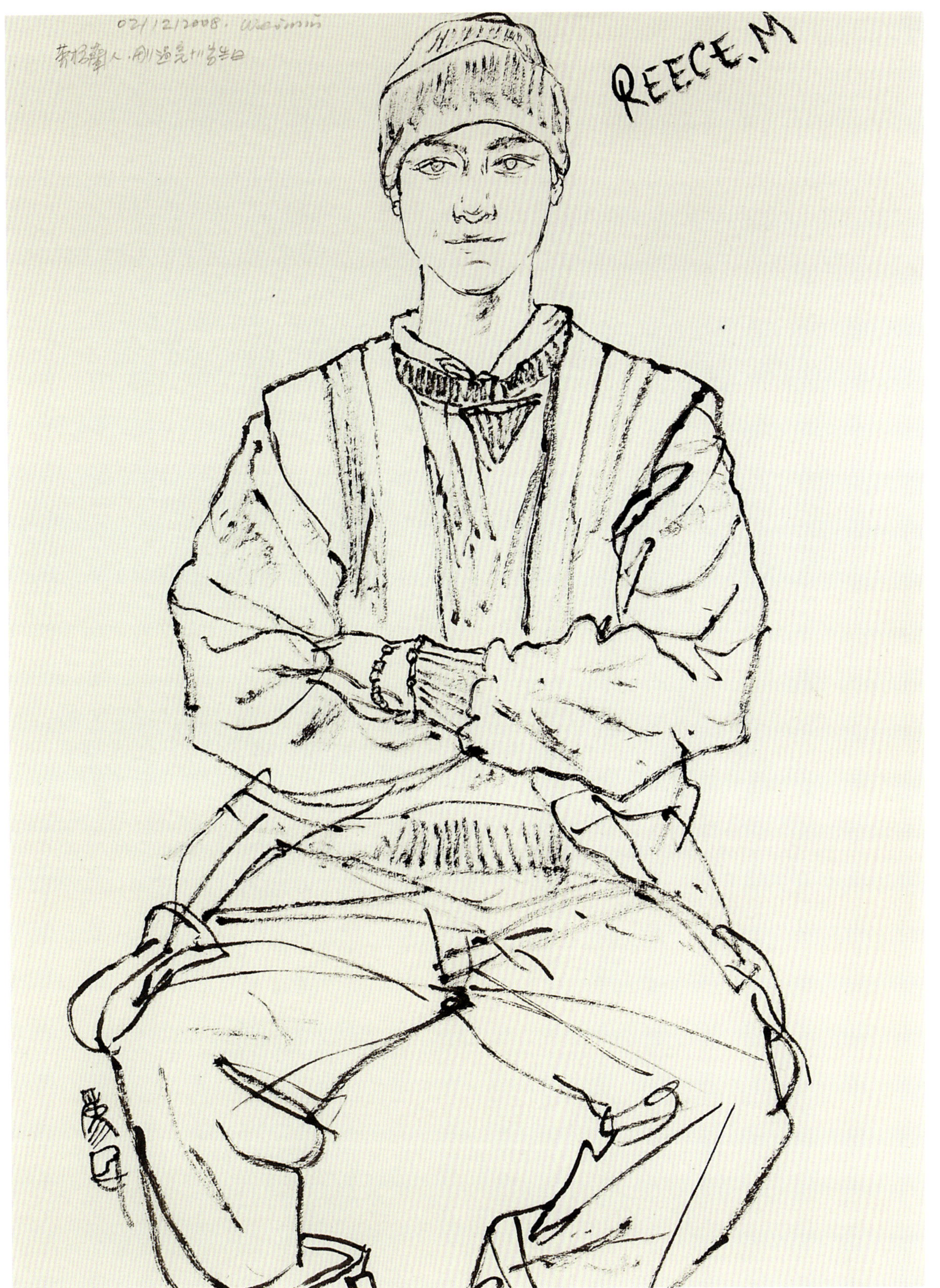

229

230 Yvliyan and Biggy
2009.
Brush and ink on album leaves.
Paper size: 44.2 × 64.6 cm

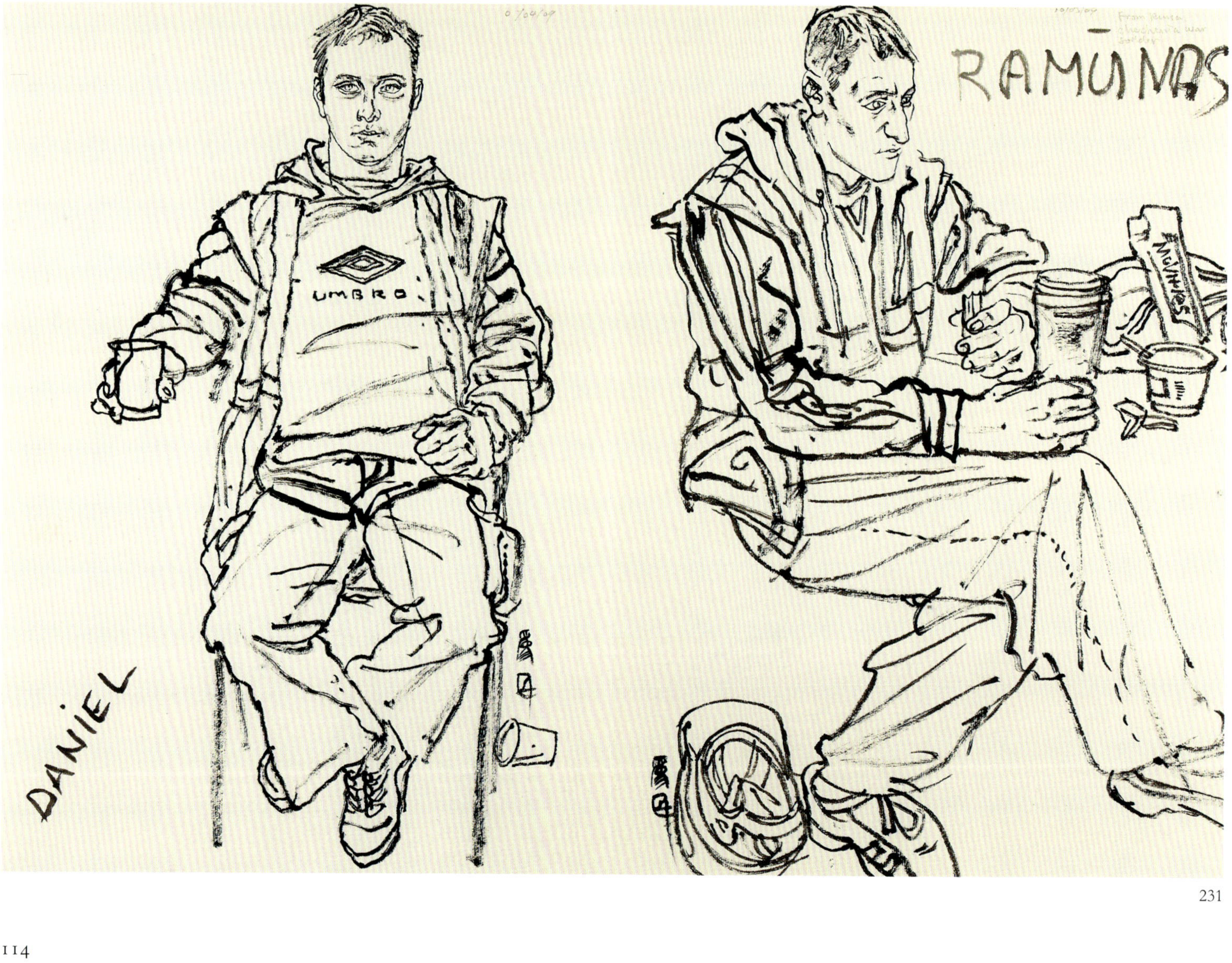

231 Daniel and Ramunas
2009.
Brush and ink on album leaves.
Paper size: 44.2 × 64.6 cm

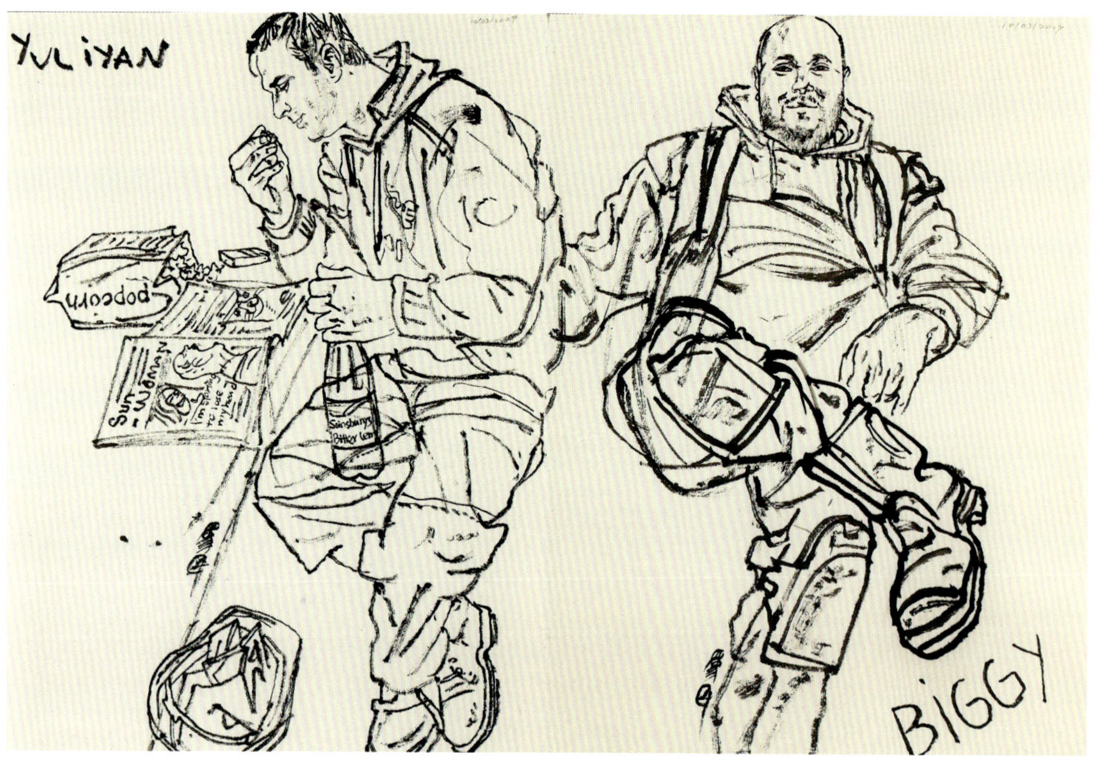

230

231

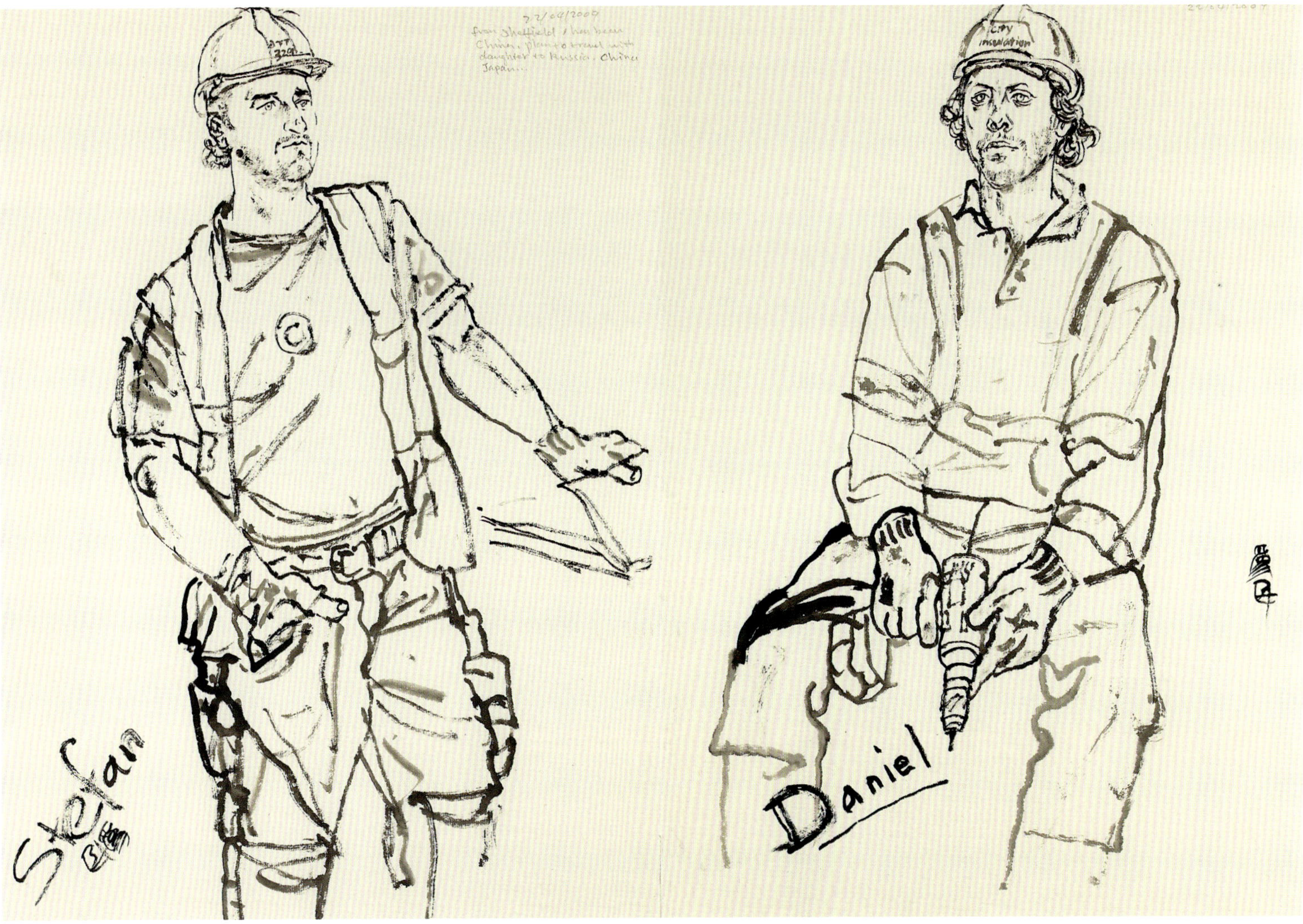

232

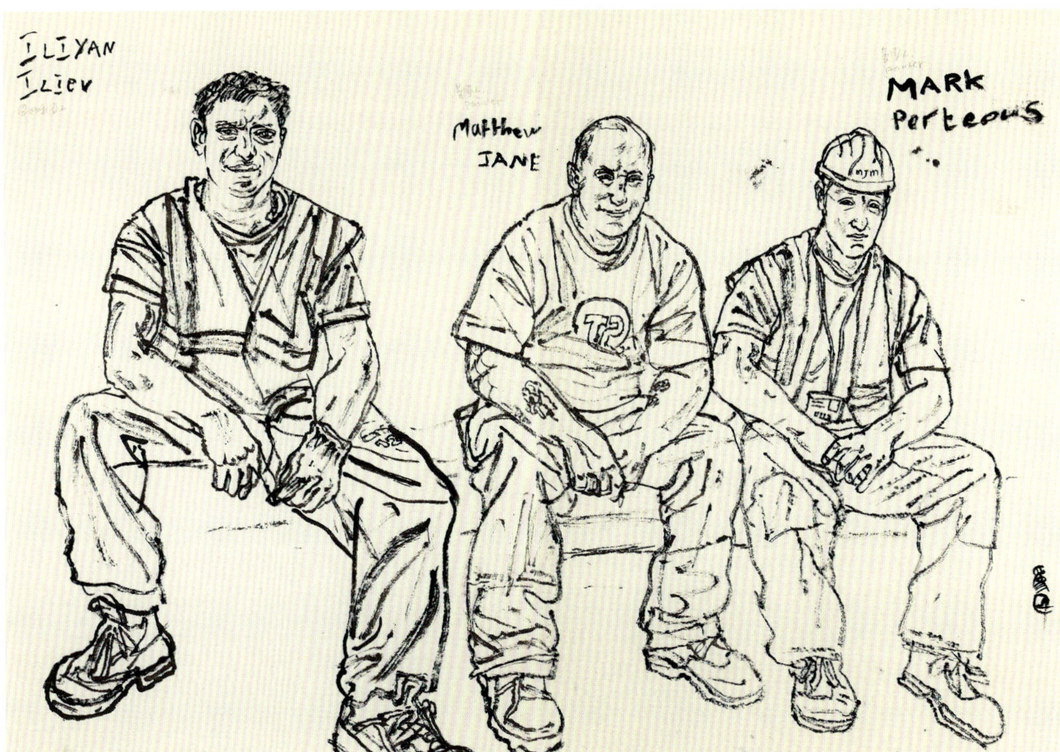

233

232 **Stefan and Daniel** *Installers*
2009.
Brush and ink on album leaves.
Paper size: 44.2 × 64.6 cm

233 **Iliyan** *Dryliner*
and Matthew and Mark *Painters*
2009.
Brush and ink on album leaves.
Paper size: 44.2 × 64.6 cm

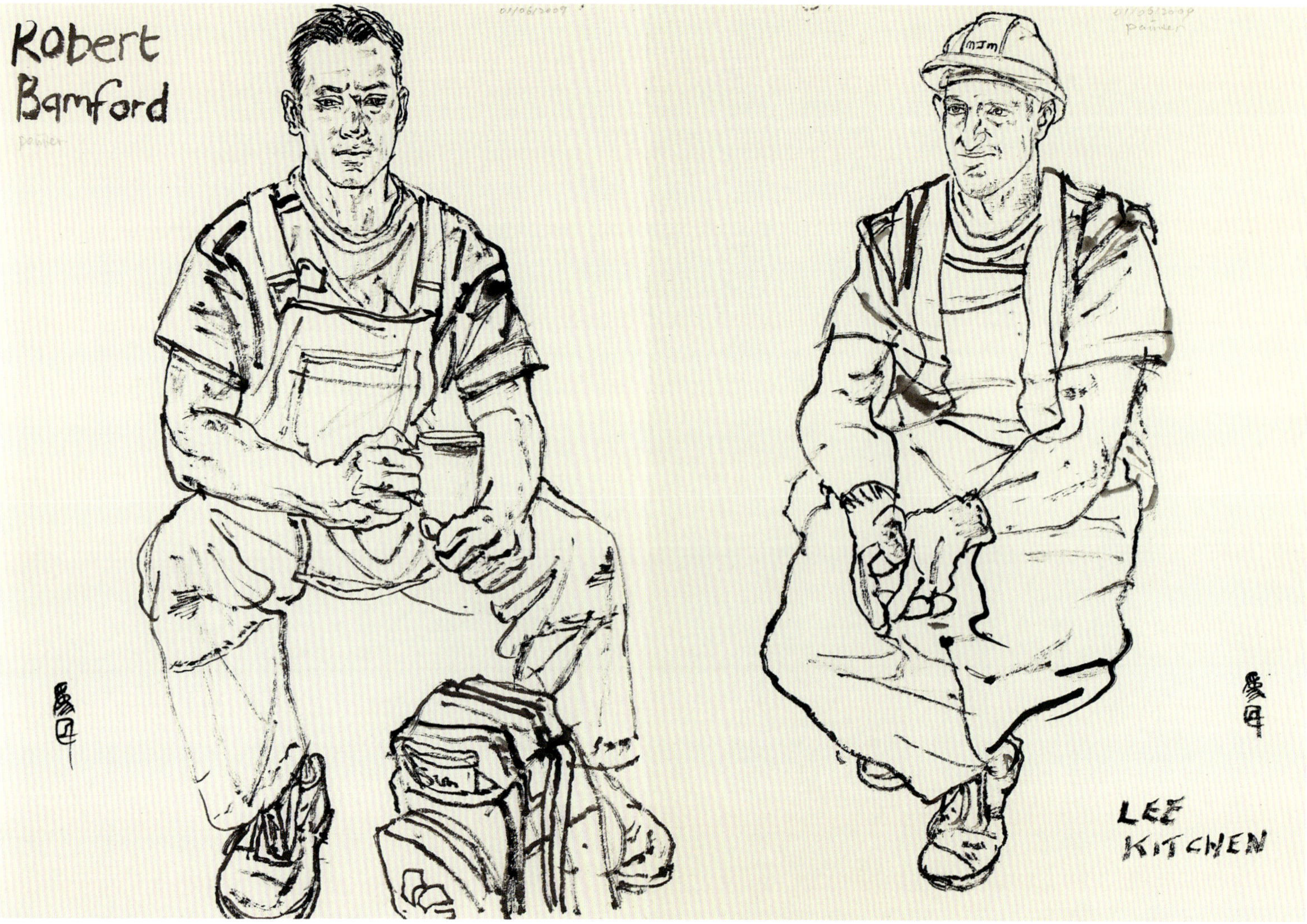

234

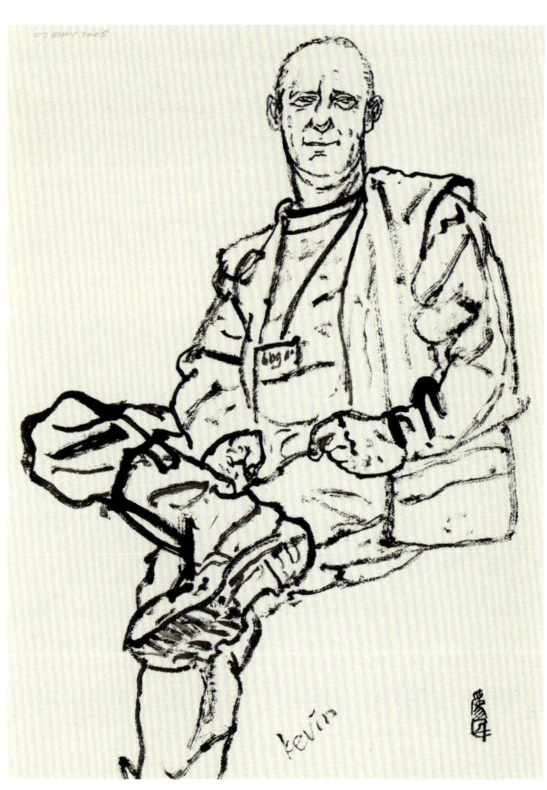

235

234 Robert and Lee *Painters*
2009. Brush and ink on album leaves. Paper size: 44.2 × 64.6 cm

235 Kevin *Construction worker*
2008. Brush and ink on album leaves. Paper size: 44.2 × 32.3 cm

236 Chris *Electrician*
2008. Brush and ink on *pi* paper. Paper size: 46.1 × 33.3 cm

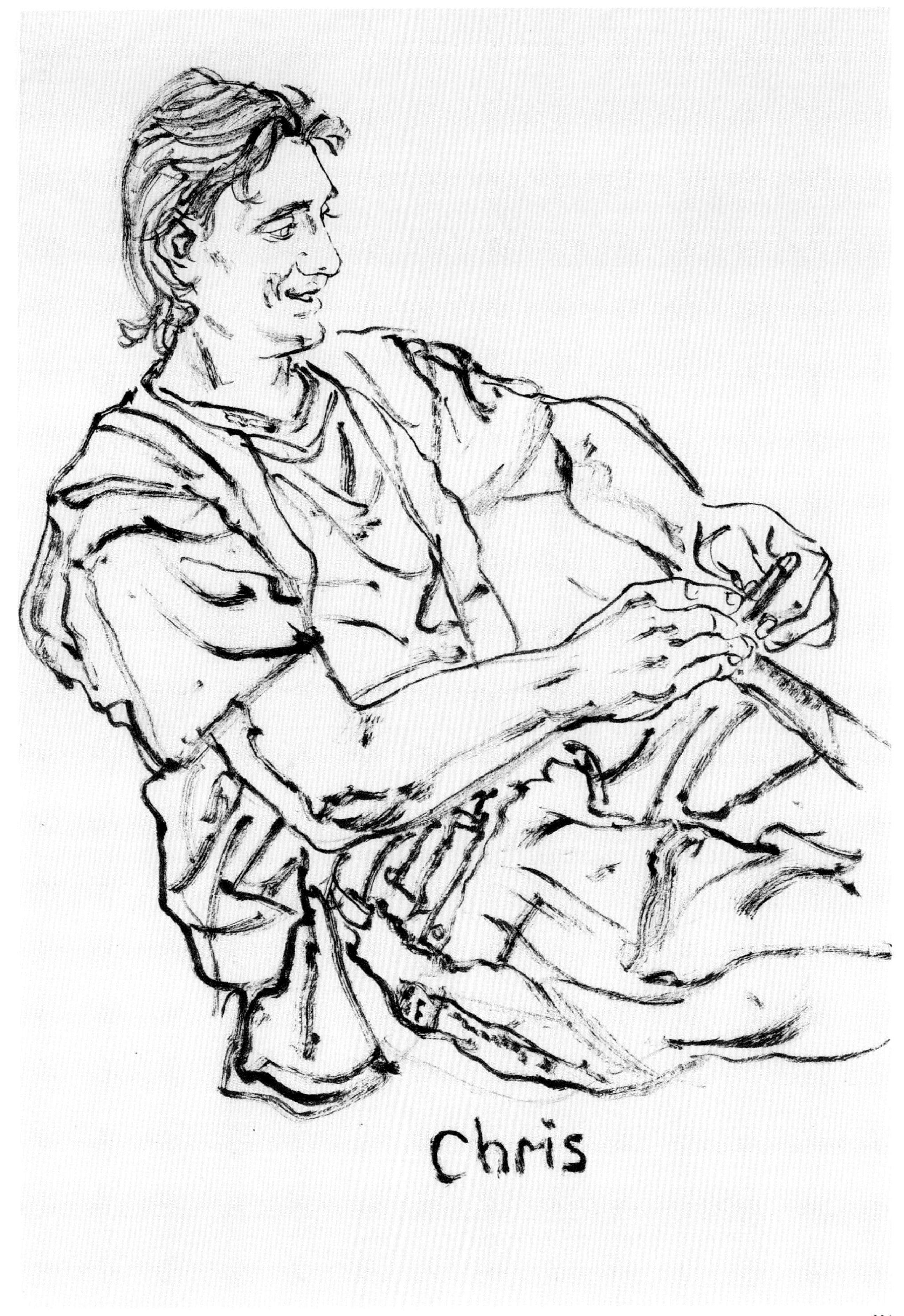

236

Sketches

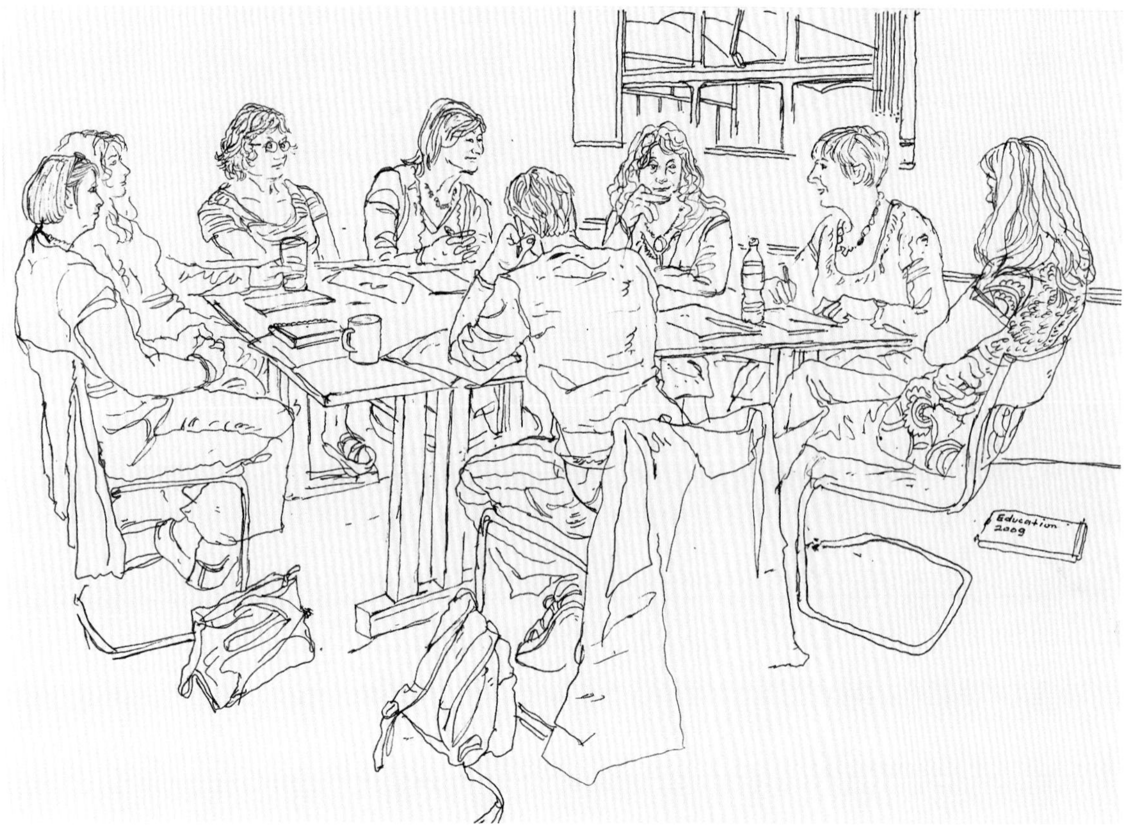

237

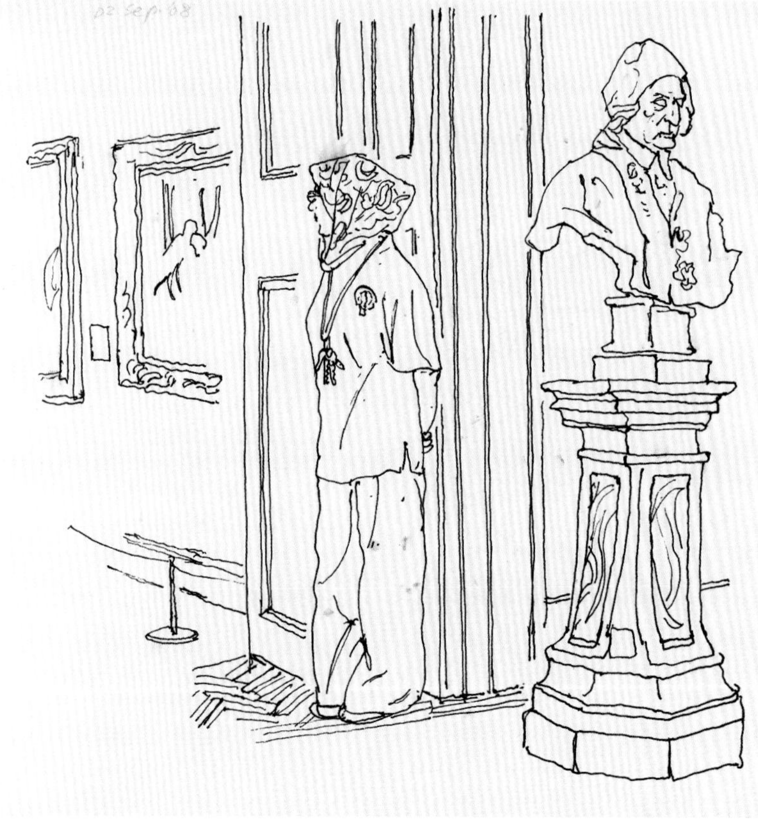

238

237 Education Department meeting
26 March 2009.
Pen and ink on paper.
Paper size: 29.7 × 42 cm

238 Ruth invigilating the Renaissance Gallery
2 September 2008.
Pen and ink on sketch book.
Paper size: 19.3 × 19.3 cm

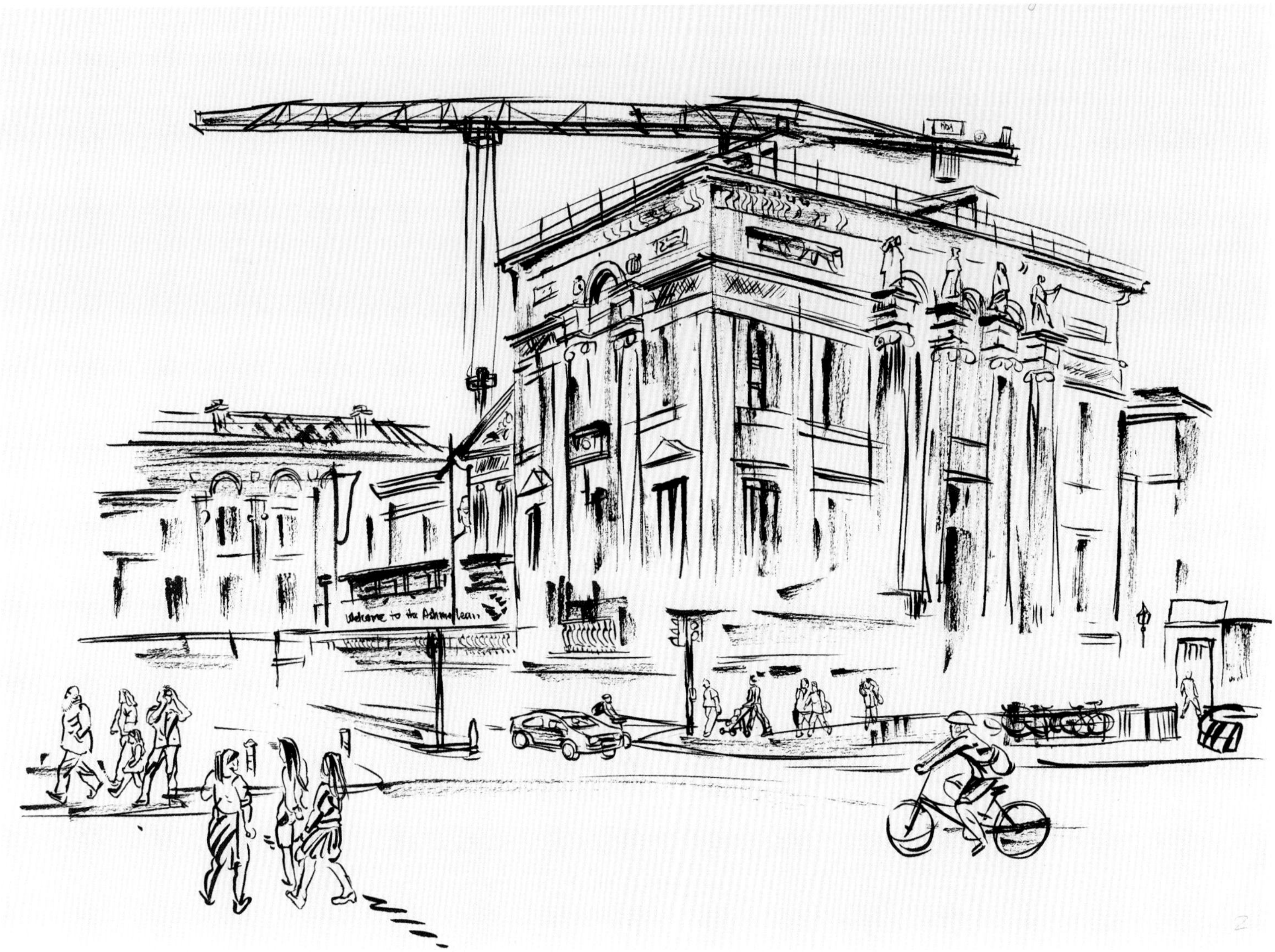

239

239 Crane over the Ashmolean
26 August 2008.
Pen and ink on paper.
Paper size: 29.7 × 42 cm

240 Site entrance
2 May 2008.
Pen and ink on sketch book.
Paper size: 19.3 × 38.6 cm

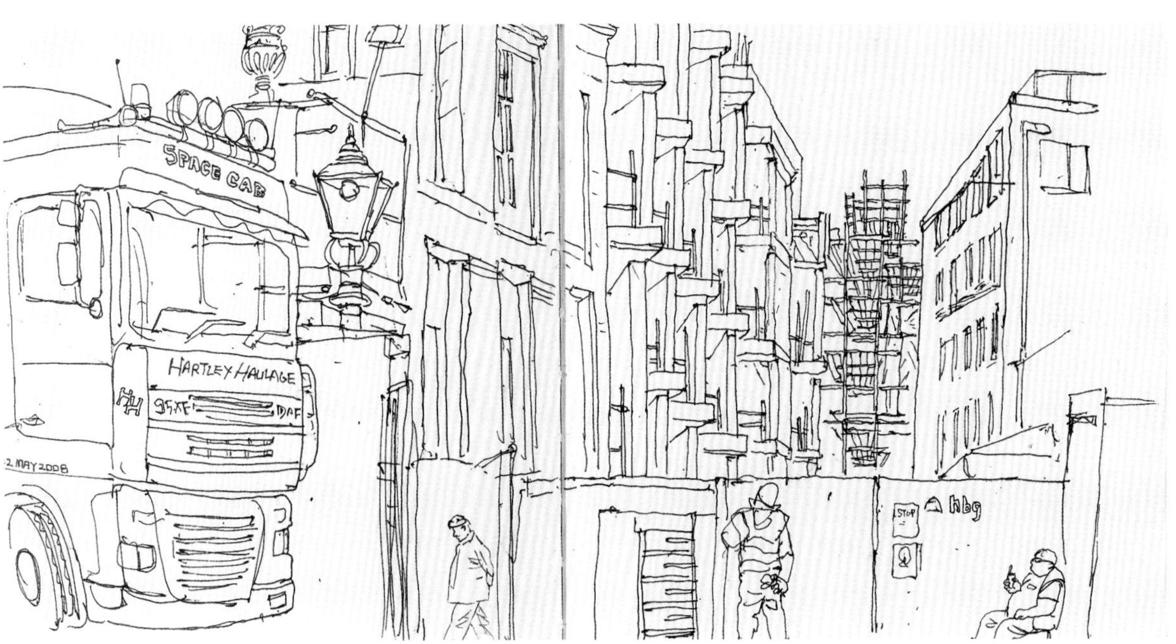

240

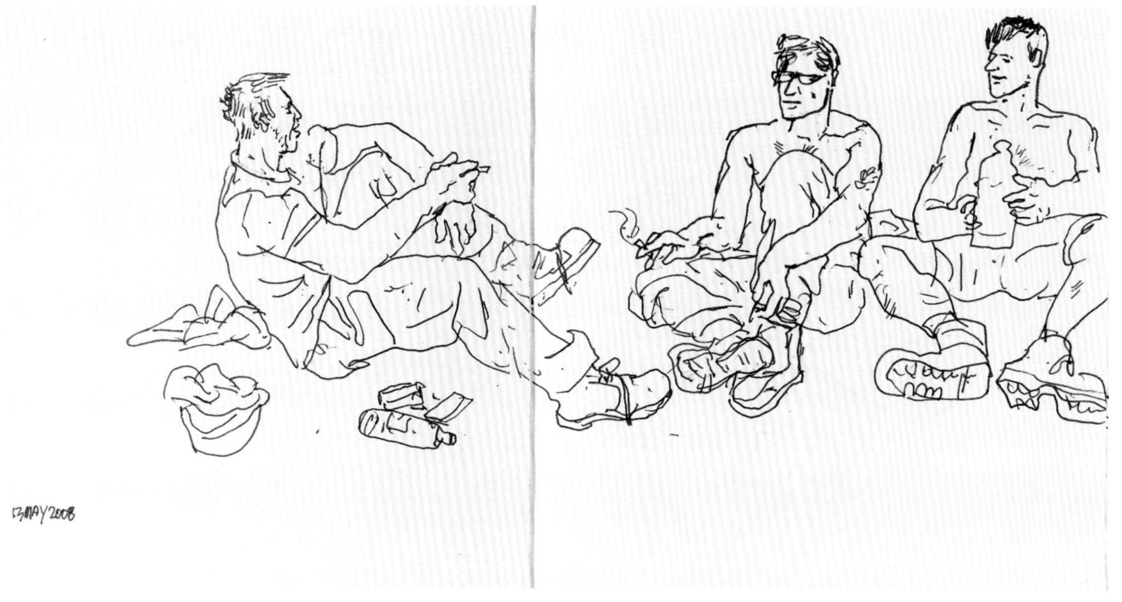

241

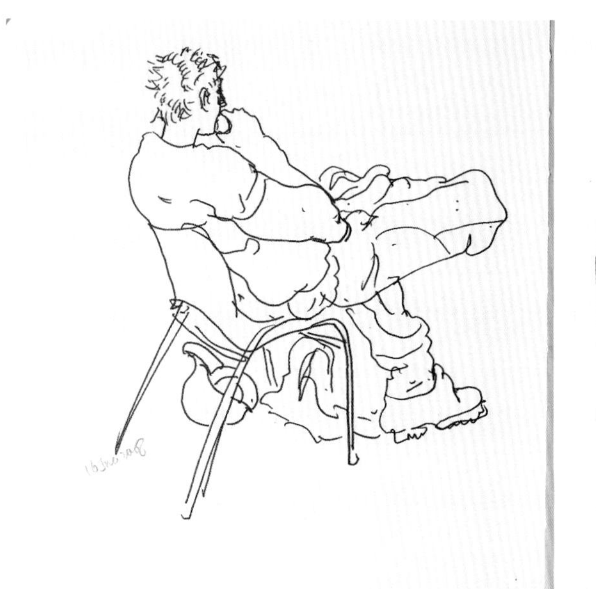

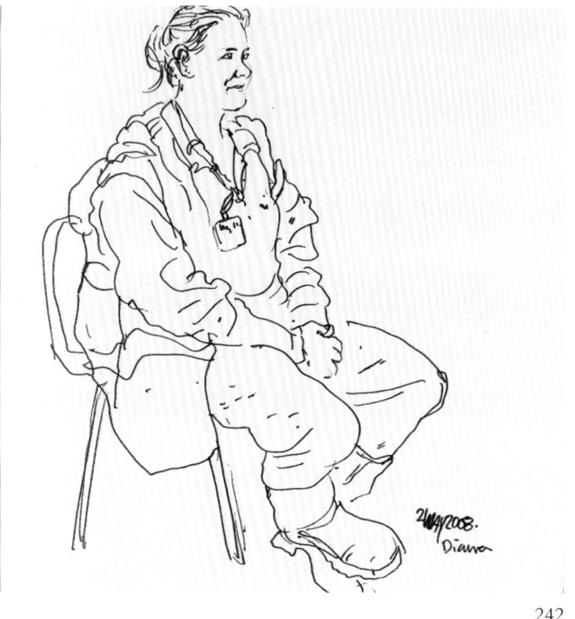

242

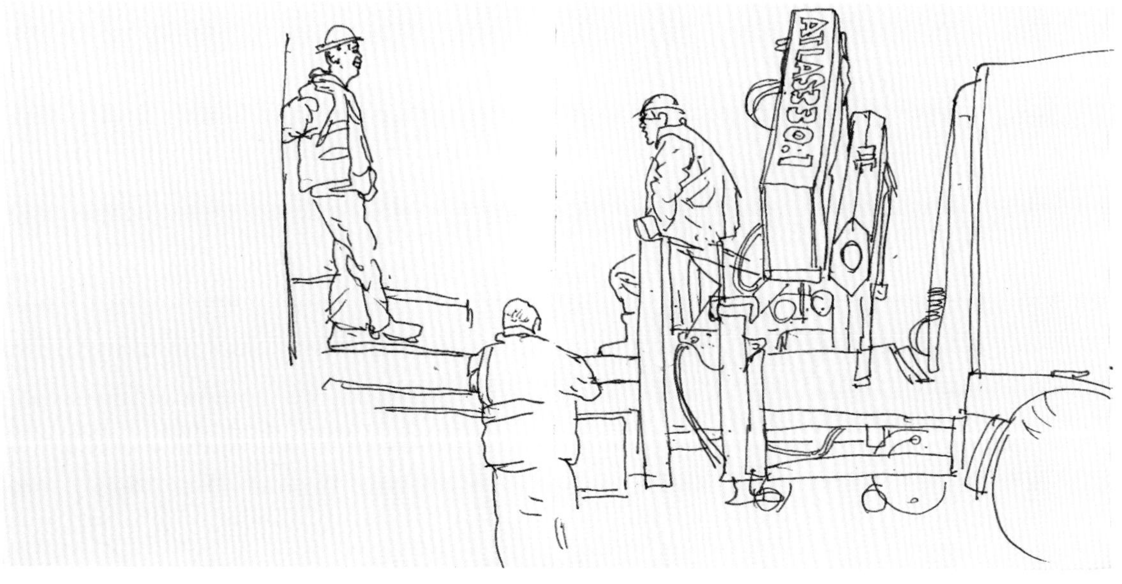

243

241 Lunch-break chatting
13 May 2008.
Pen and ink on sketch book.
Paper size: 19.3 × 38.6 cm

242 Dale
16 June 2008.
Pen and ink on sketch book.
Paper size: 19.3 × 19.3 cm

Diane
21 May 2008.
Pen and ink on sketch book.
Paper size: 19.3 × 19.3 cm

243 By the site entrance
May 2008.
Pen and ink on sketch book.
Paper size: 19.3 × 38.6 cm

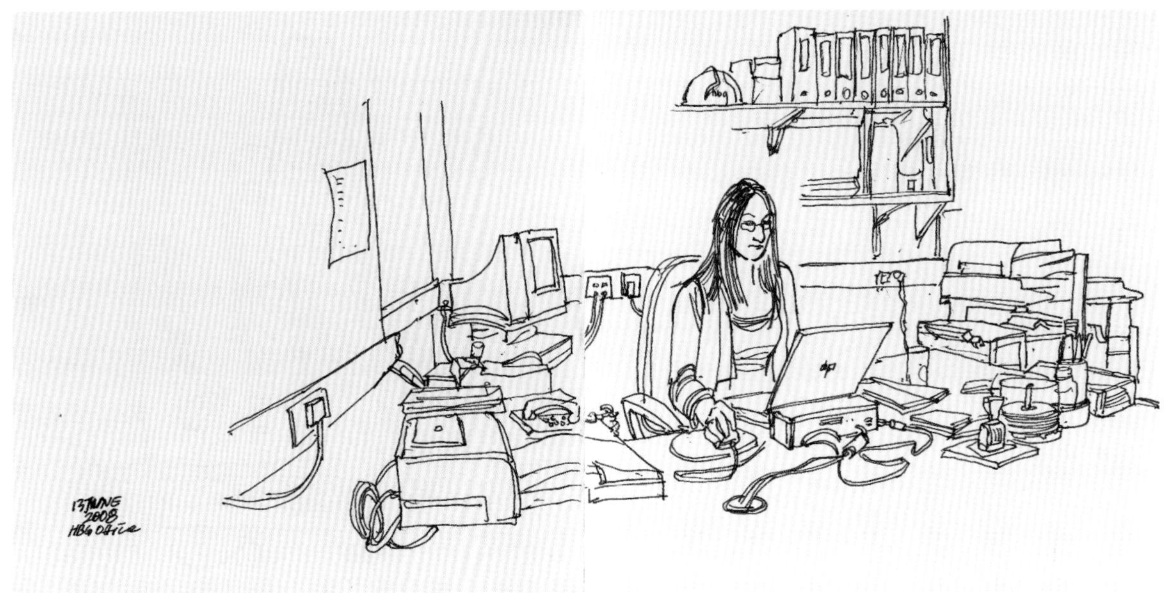

244

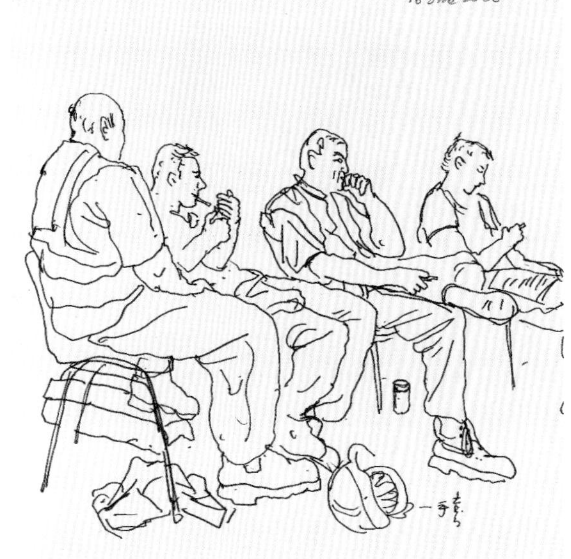

245

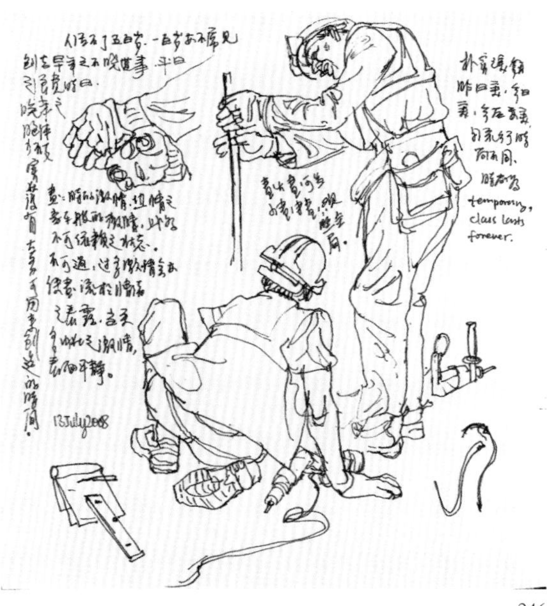

246

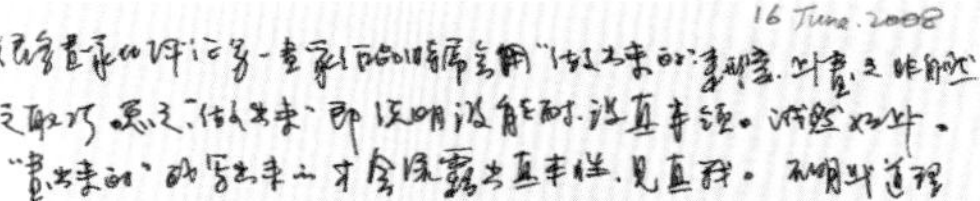

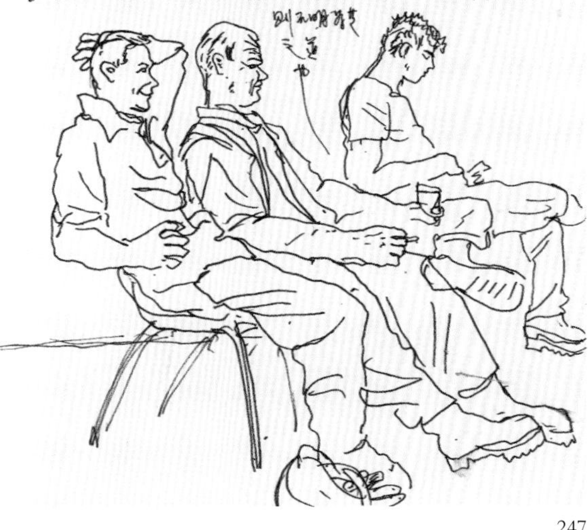

247

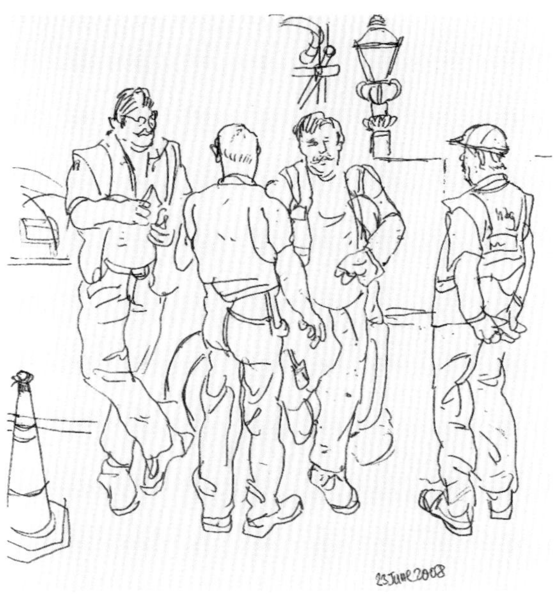

248

244 Amy *Site administrator*
13 June 2008.
Pen and ink on sketch book.
Paper size: 19.3 × 38.6 cm

245 Break time
16 June 2008.
Pen and ink on sketch book.
Paper size: 19.3 × 19.3 cm

246 Study of electricians
13 July 2008.
Pen and ink on sketch book.
Paper size: 19.3 × 19.3 cm

247 Dan and his mates
16 June 2008.
Pen and ink on sketch book.
Paper size: 19.3 × 19.3 cm

248 George and mates chatting
23 June 2008.
Pen and ink on sketch book.
Paper size: 19.3 × 19.3 cm

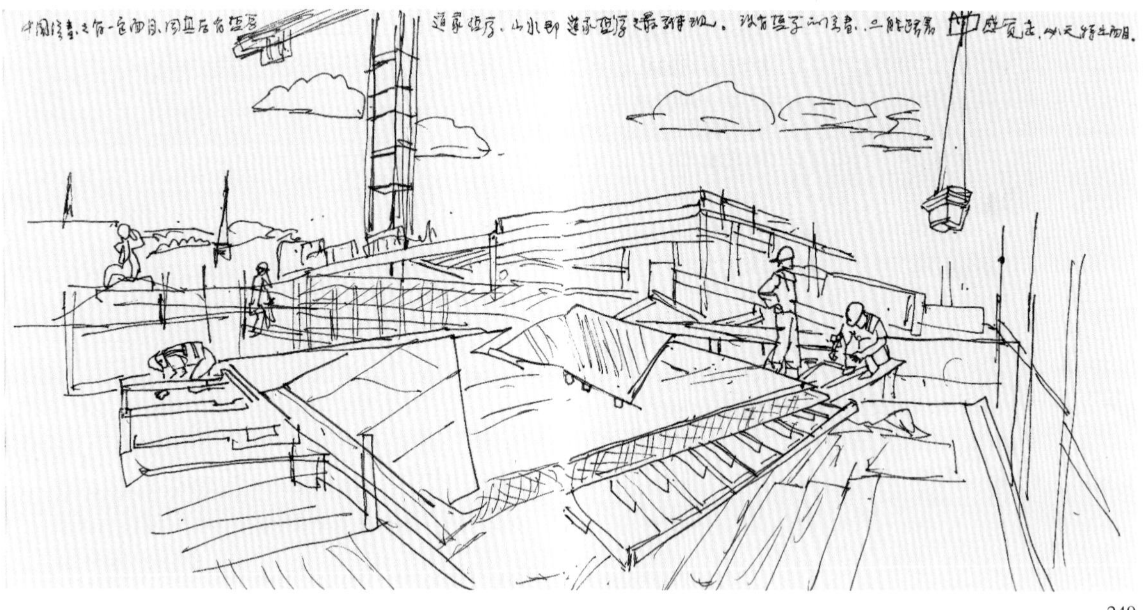

249

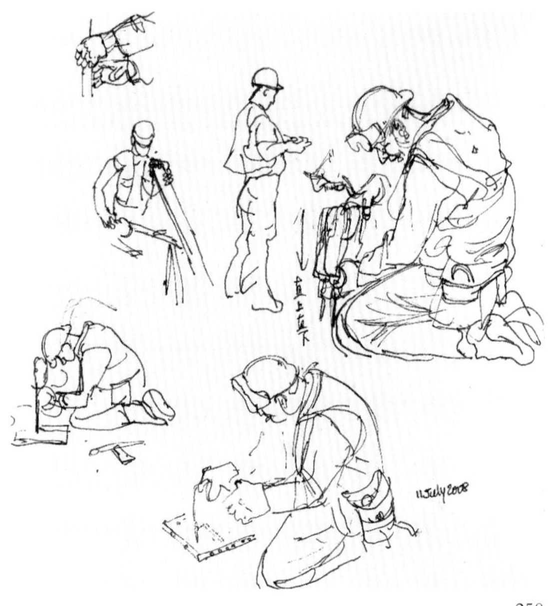

250

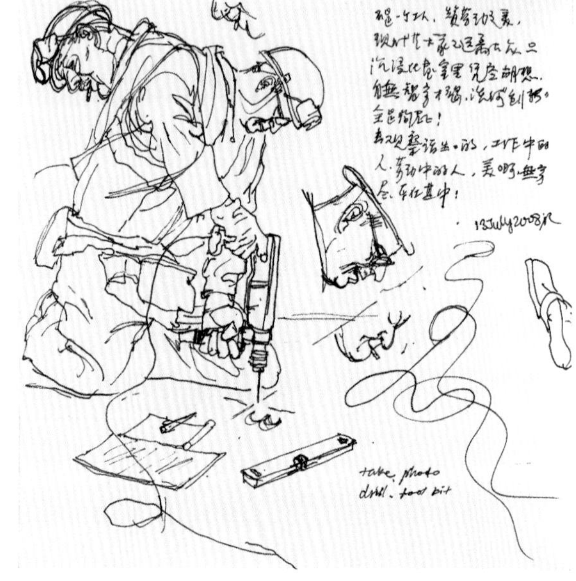

251

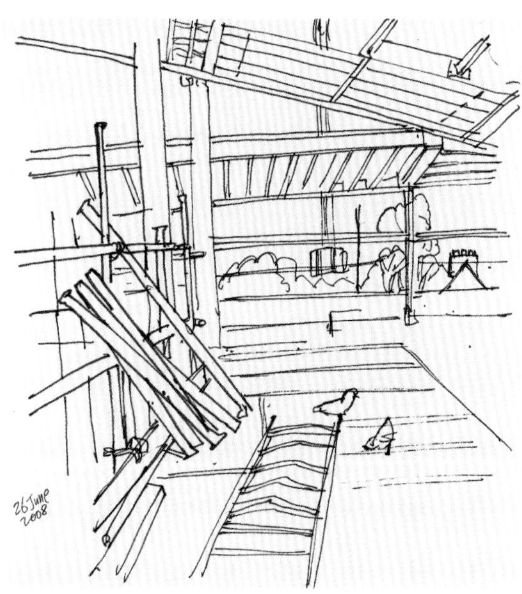

252

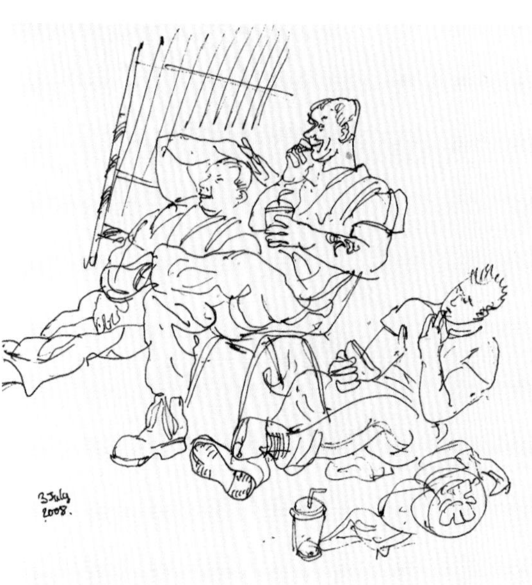

253

249 Carpenters on the roof
June 2008.
Pen and ink on sketch book.
Paper size: 19.3 × 38.6 cm

250 Study of workmen
11 July 2008.
Pen and ink on sketch book.
Paper size: 19.3 × 19.3 cm

251 Study of electrician drilling
13 July 2008.
Pen and ink on sketch book.
Paper size: 19.3 × 19.3 cm

252 Top floor of the new building
26 June 2008.
Pen and ink on sketch book.
Paper size: 19.3 × 19.3 cm

253 Lunch break
3 July 2008.
Pen and ink on sketch book.
Paper size: 19.3 × 19.3 cm

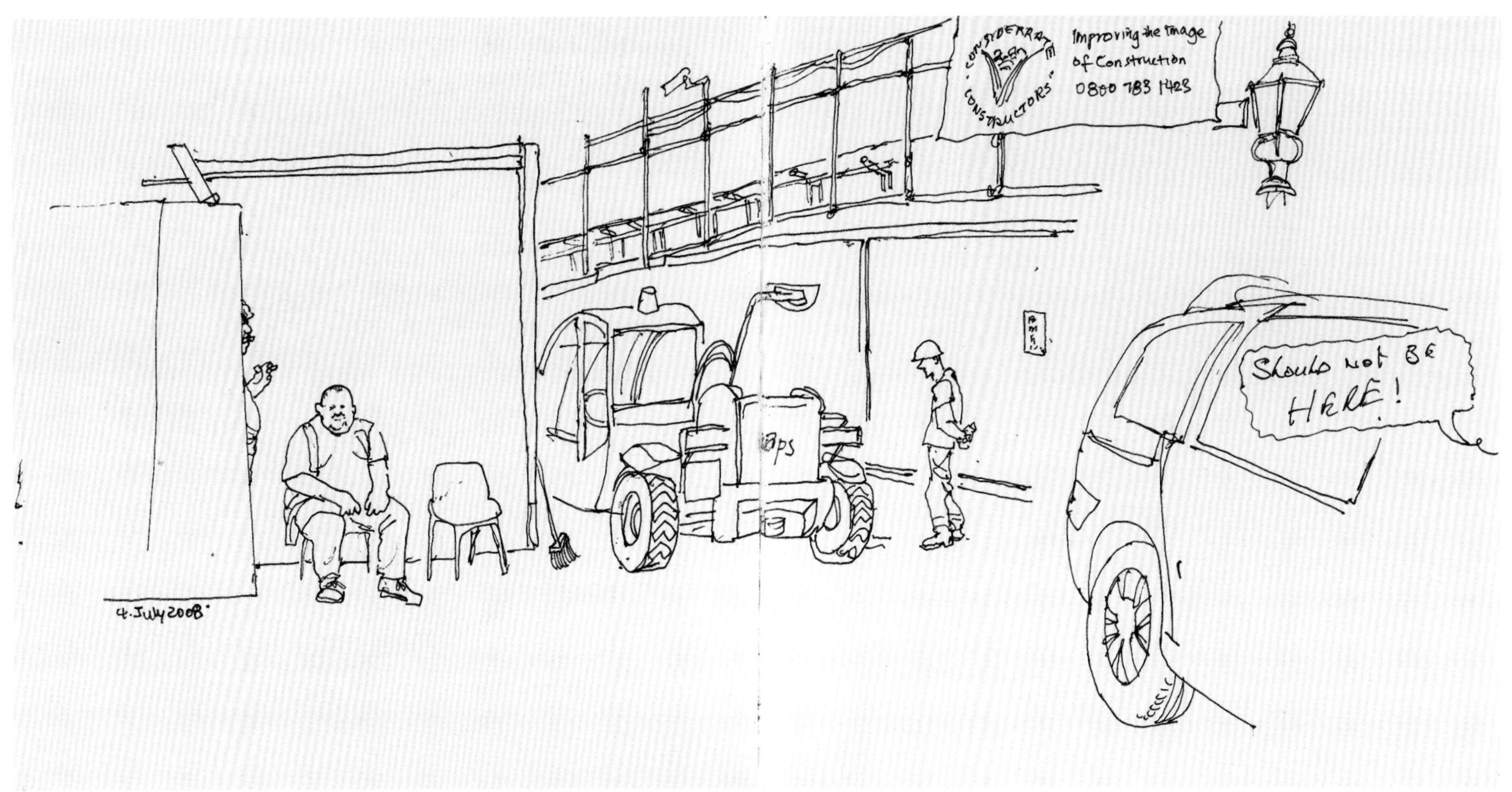

254

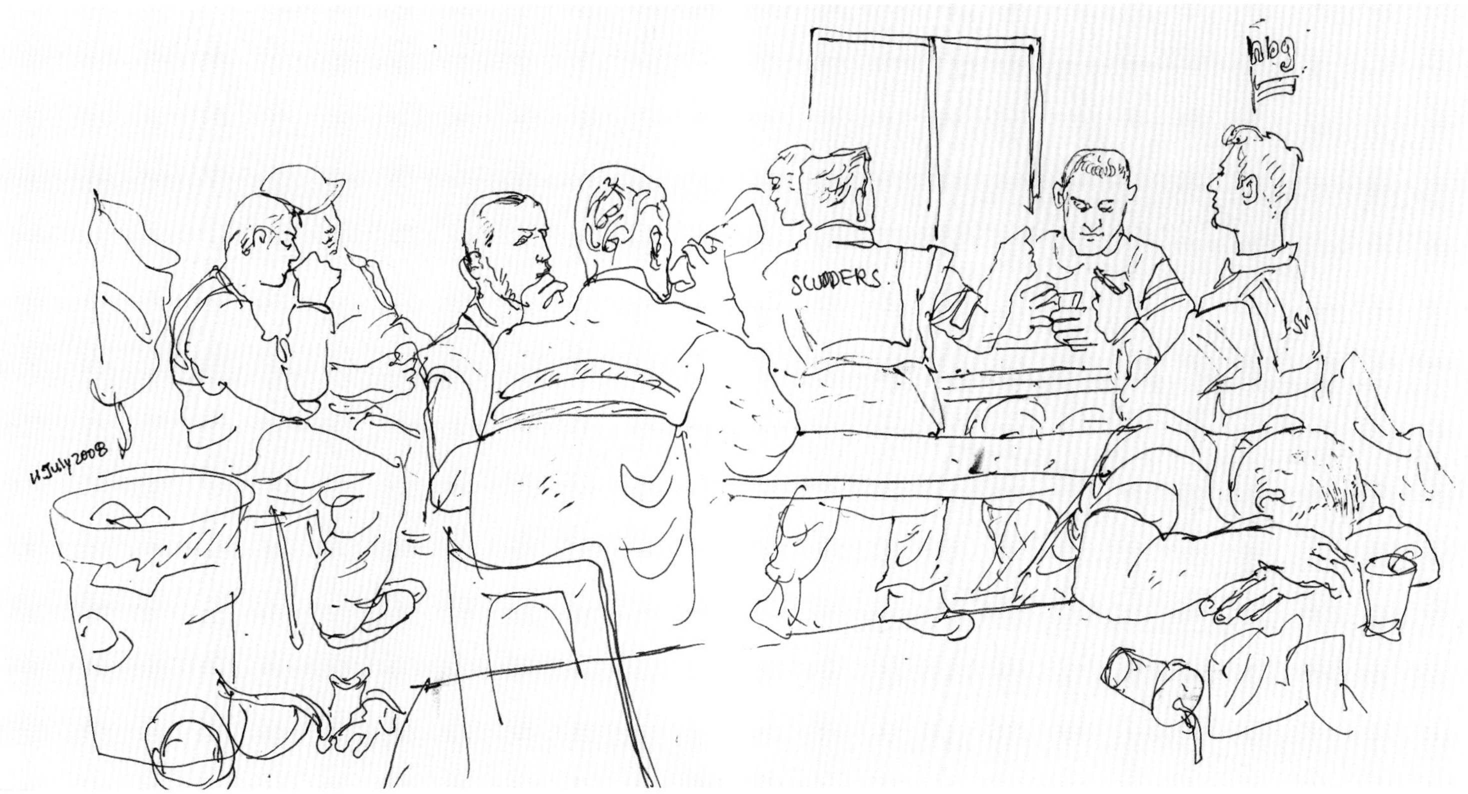

255

254 Nick on duty
4 July 2008. Pen and ink on sketch book. Paper size: 19.3 × 38.6 cm

255 In the canteen
11 July 2008. Pen and ink on sketch book. Paper size: 19.3 × 19.3 cm

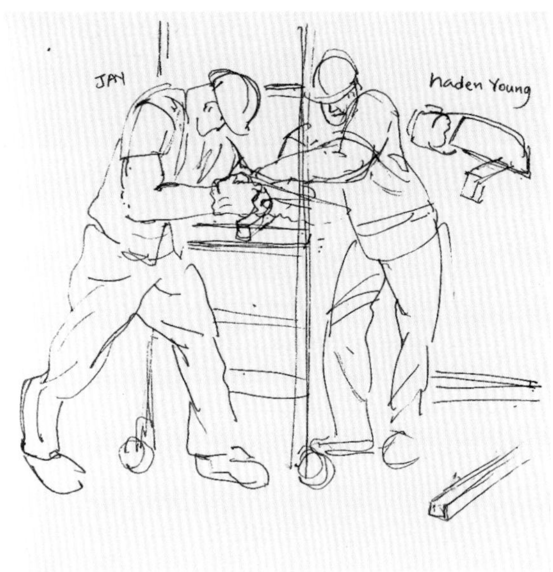

256

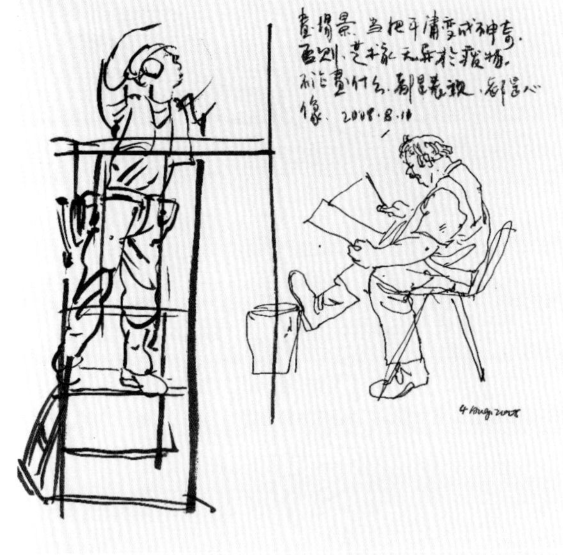

257

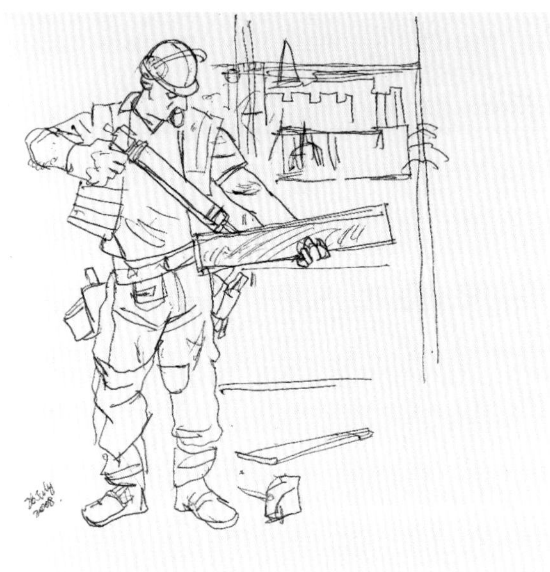

258

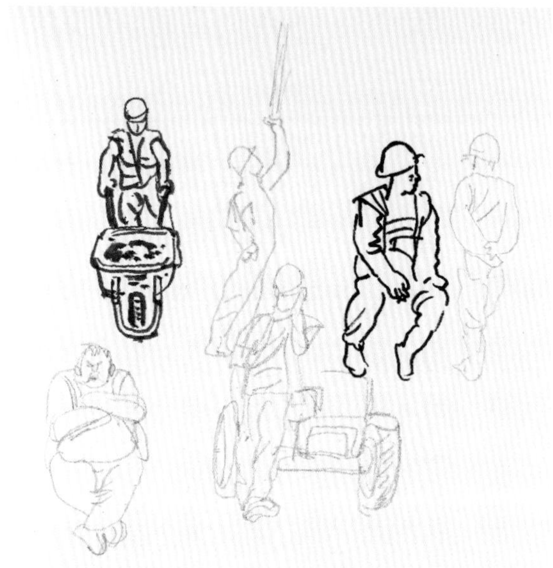

259

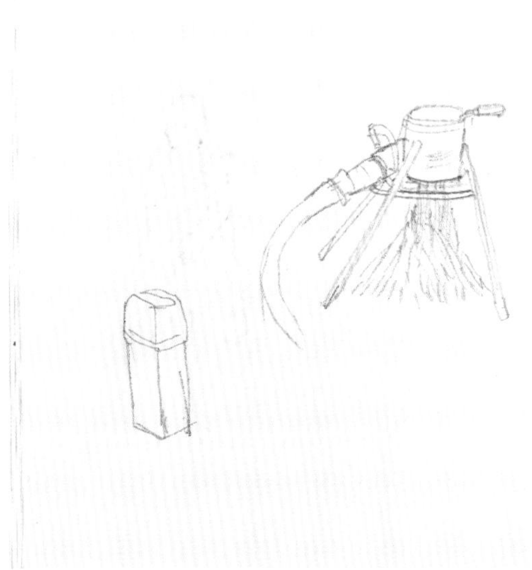

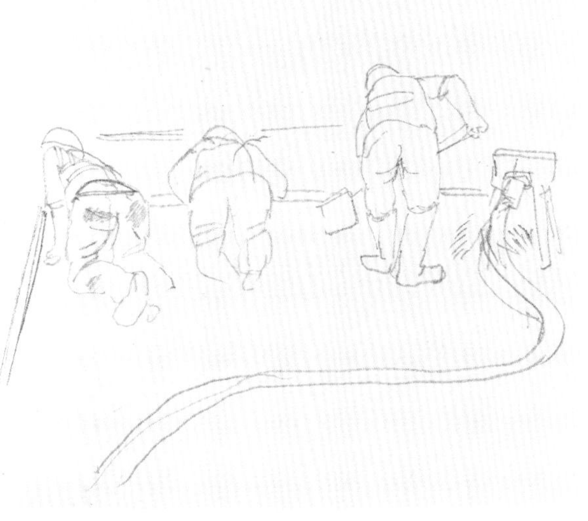

260

256 Cutting metal
July 2008.
Pen and ink on sketch book.
Paper size: 19.3 × 19.3 cm

257 George reading newspaper
4 August 2008.
Pen and ink on sketch book.
Paper size: 19.3 × 19.3 cm

258 Raymond with glue-gun
26 July 2008.
Pen and ink on sketch book.
Paper size: 19.3 × 19.3 cm

259 Sketches of workers
August 2008.
Pencil, pen and ink on sketch book.
Paper size: 19.3 × 19.3 cm

260 Floor screeding
August 2008.
Pencil on sketch book.
Paper size: 19.3 × 38.6 cm

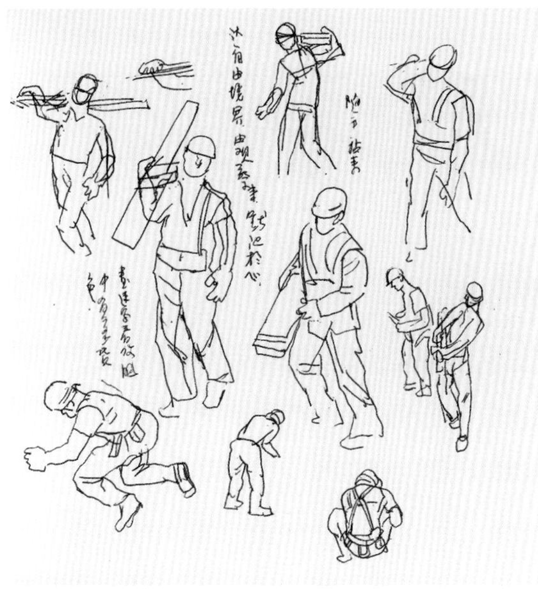

261

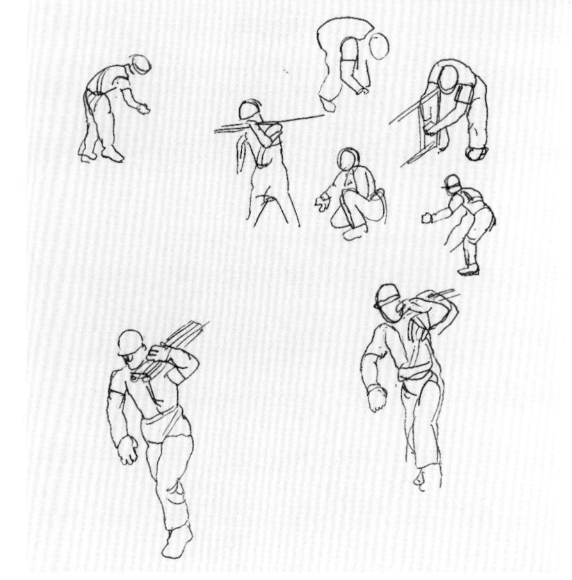

262

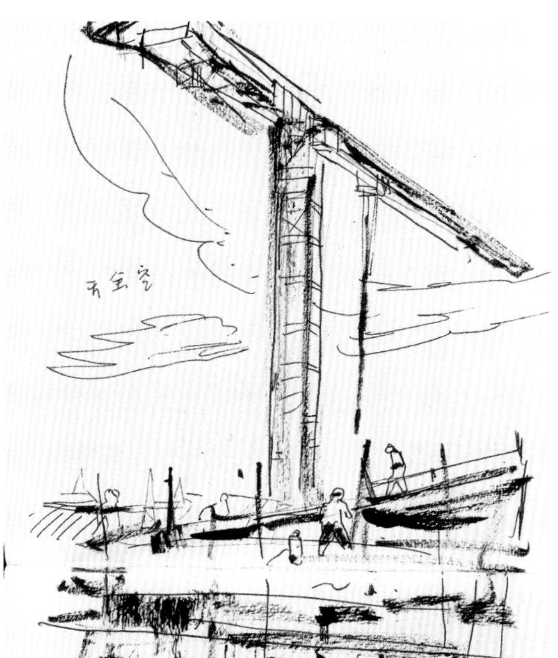

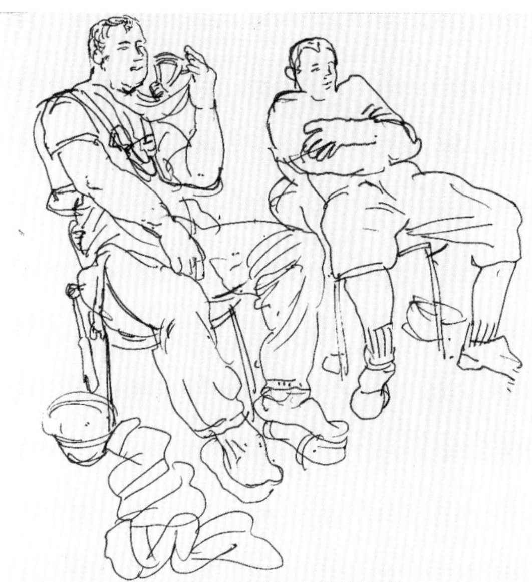

264

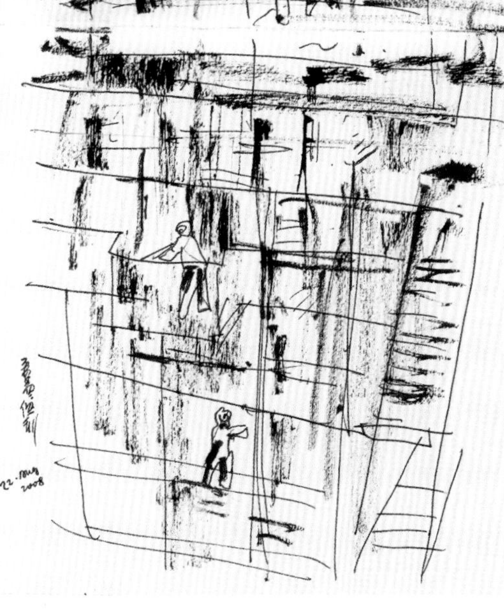

263

265

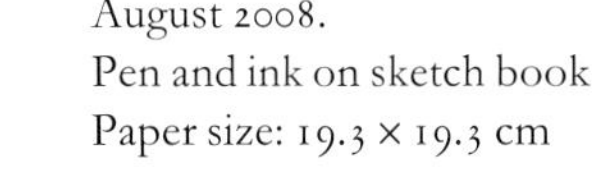

261 Sketches of workmen
August 2008.
Pen and ink on sketch book.
Paper size: 19.3 × 19.3 cm

262 Sketches of workmen
August 2008.
Pen and ink on sketch book.
Paper size: 19.3 × 19.3 cm

263 Scaffolding and crane
22 August 2008.
Pen, brush and ink on sketch book.
Paper size: 38.6 × 19.3 cm

264 Listening to Romanian songs
August 2008.
Pen and ink on sketch book.
Paper size: 19.3 × 19.3 cm

265 Sketches of scaffolders
2 September 2008.
Pen and ink on sketch book.
Paper size: 19.3 × 19.3 cm

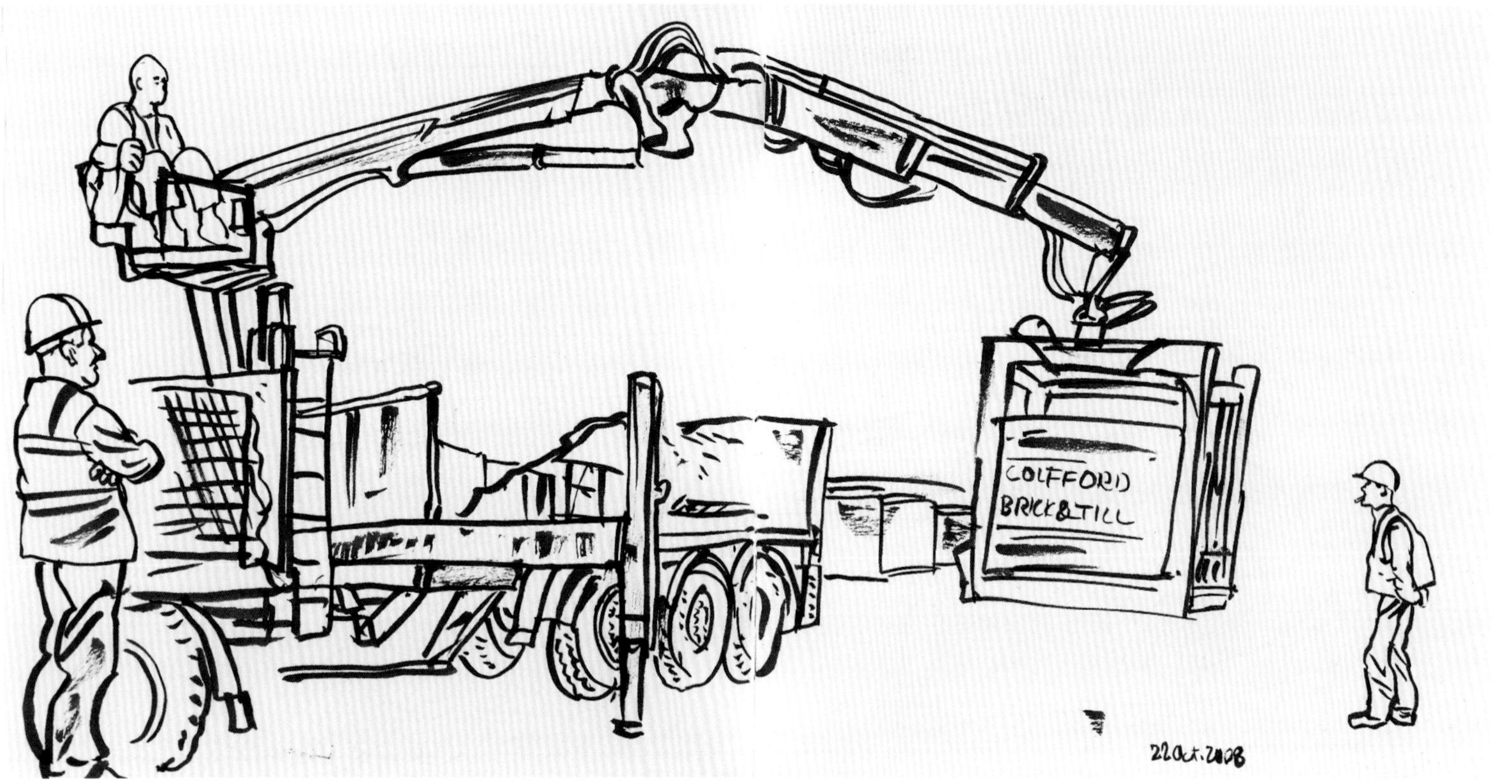

266

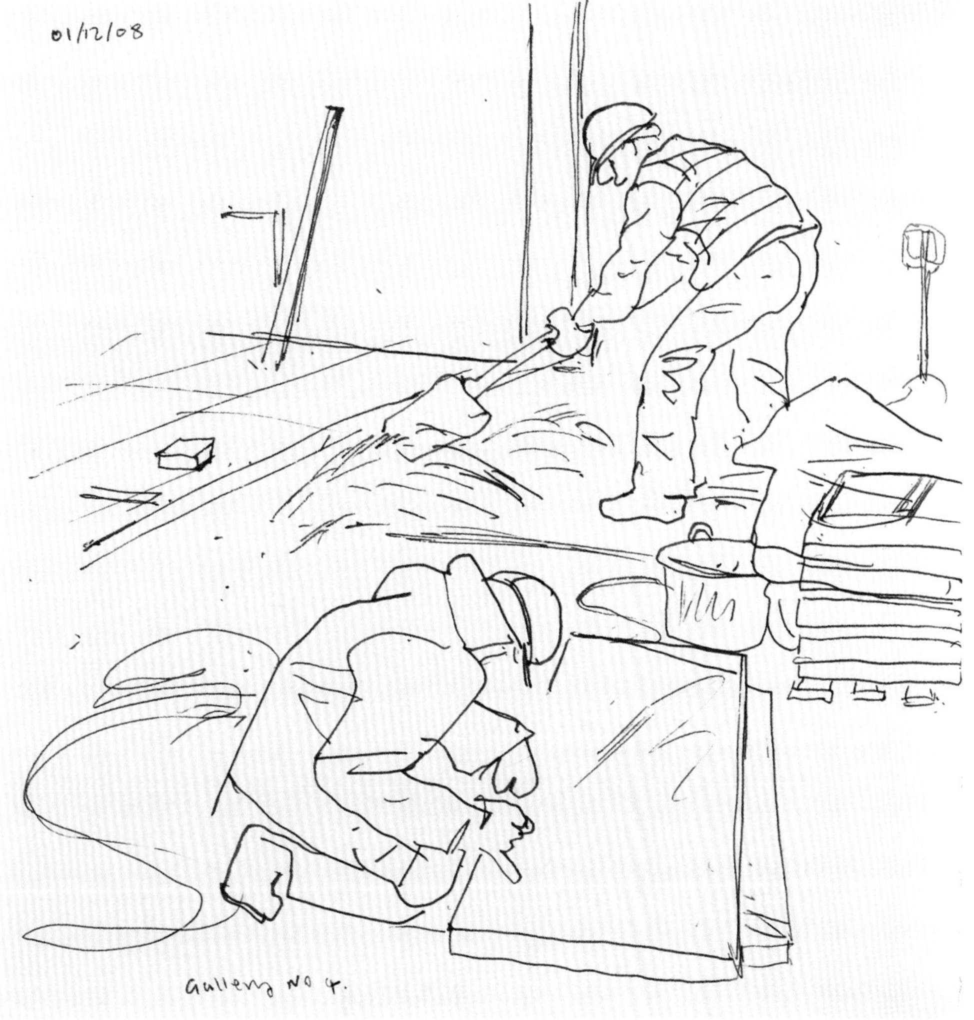

267

266 Unloading bricks
22 October 2008. Pen and ink on sketch book. Paper size: 19.3 × 38.6 cm

267 Laying floor slabs
1 December 2008. Pen and ink on sketch book. Paper size: 19.3 × 19.3 cm

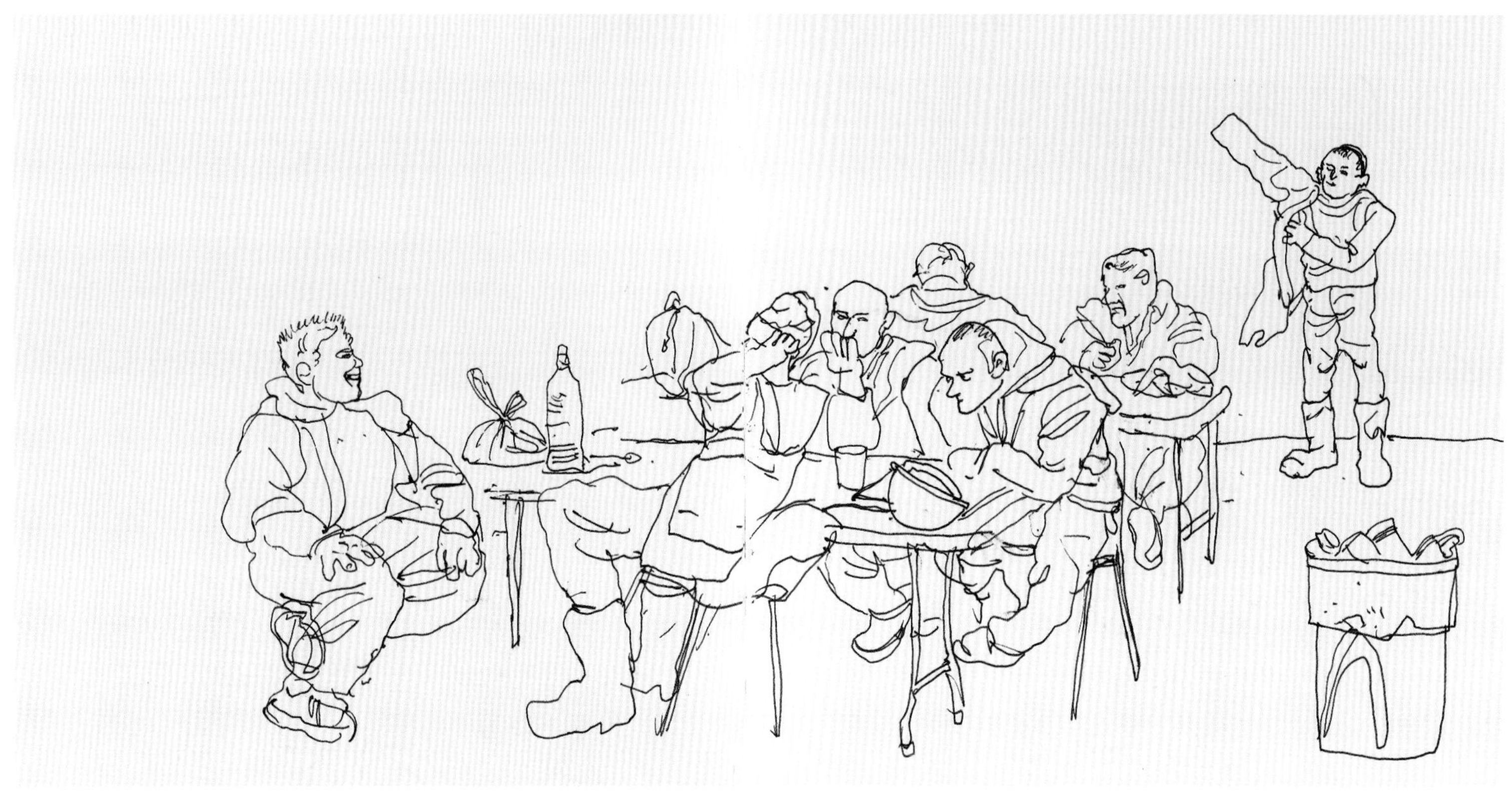
268

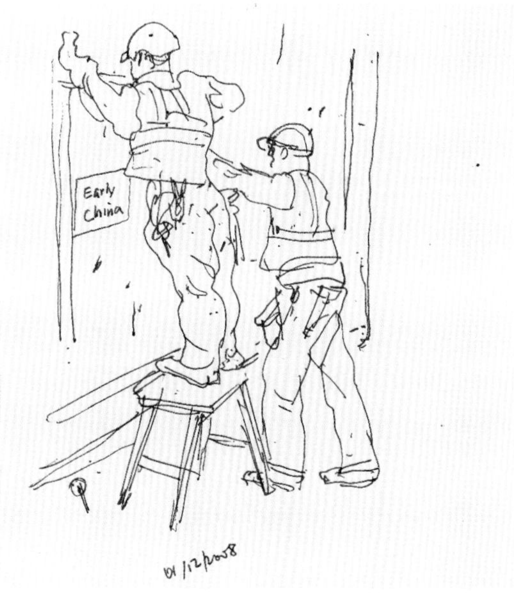

269

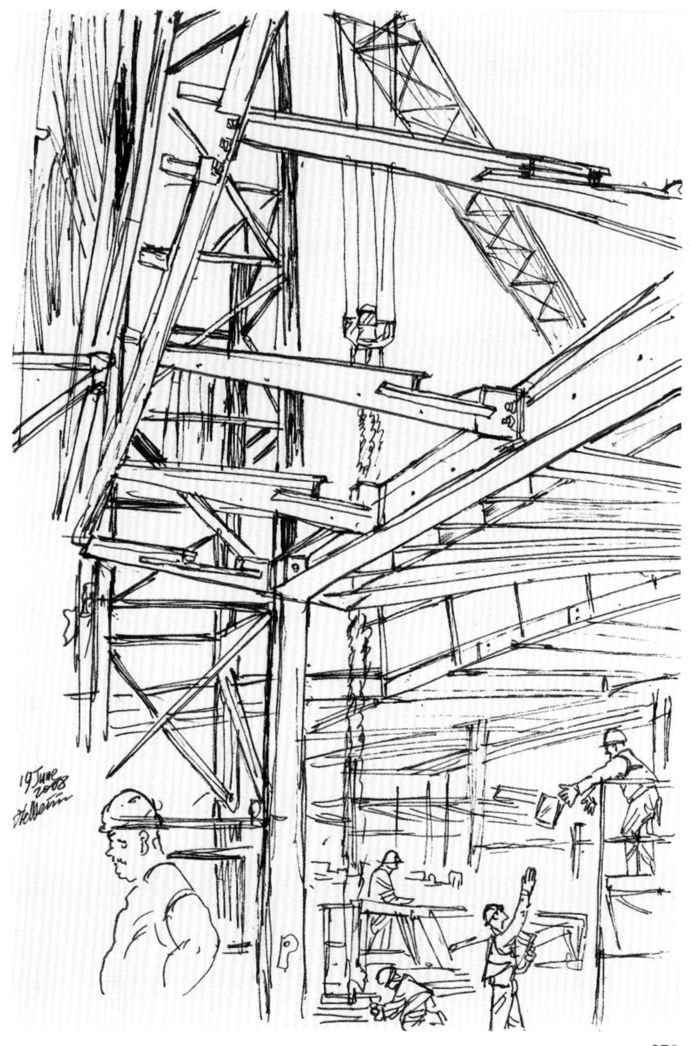

270

268 Site canteen
26 July 2008. Pen and ink on sketch book. Paper size: 19.3 × 19.3 cm

269 Drilling in Early China Gallery
1 December 2008. Pen and ink on sketch book. Paper size: 19.3 × 19.3 cm

270 Roof construction on the top floor
19 June 2008. Pen and ink on paper. Paper size: 29.7 × 21 cm

271 Delicious lunch
December 2008. Pen and ink on sketch book. Paper size: 19.3 × 38.6 cm

272 Clearing the screed pipe
December 2008. Pen and ink on paper. Paper size: 21 × 29.7 cm

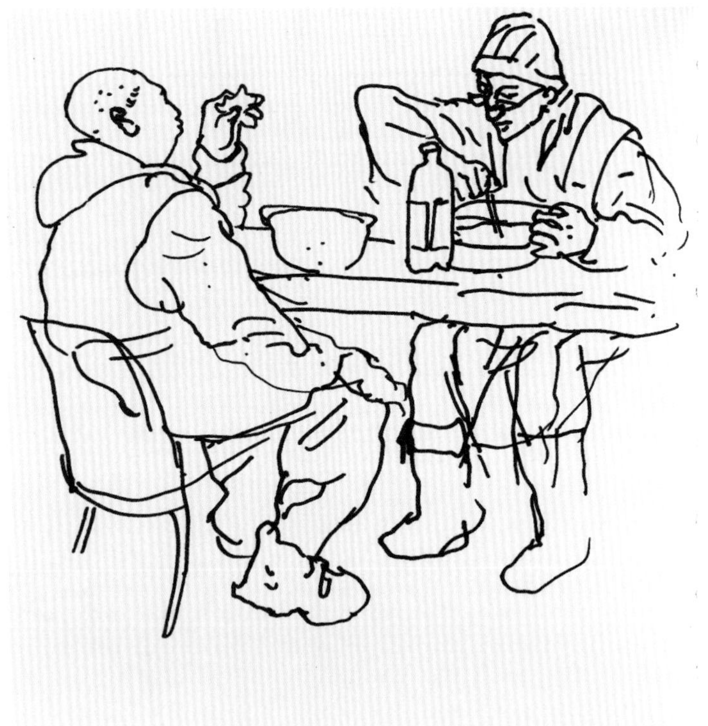

271

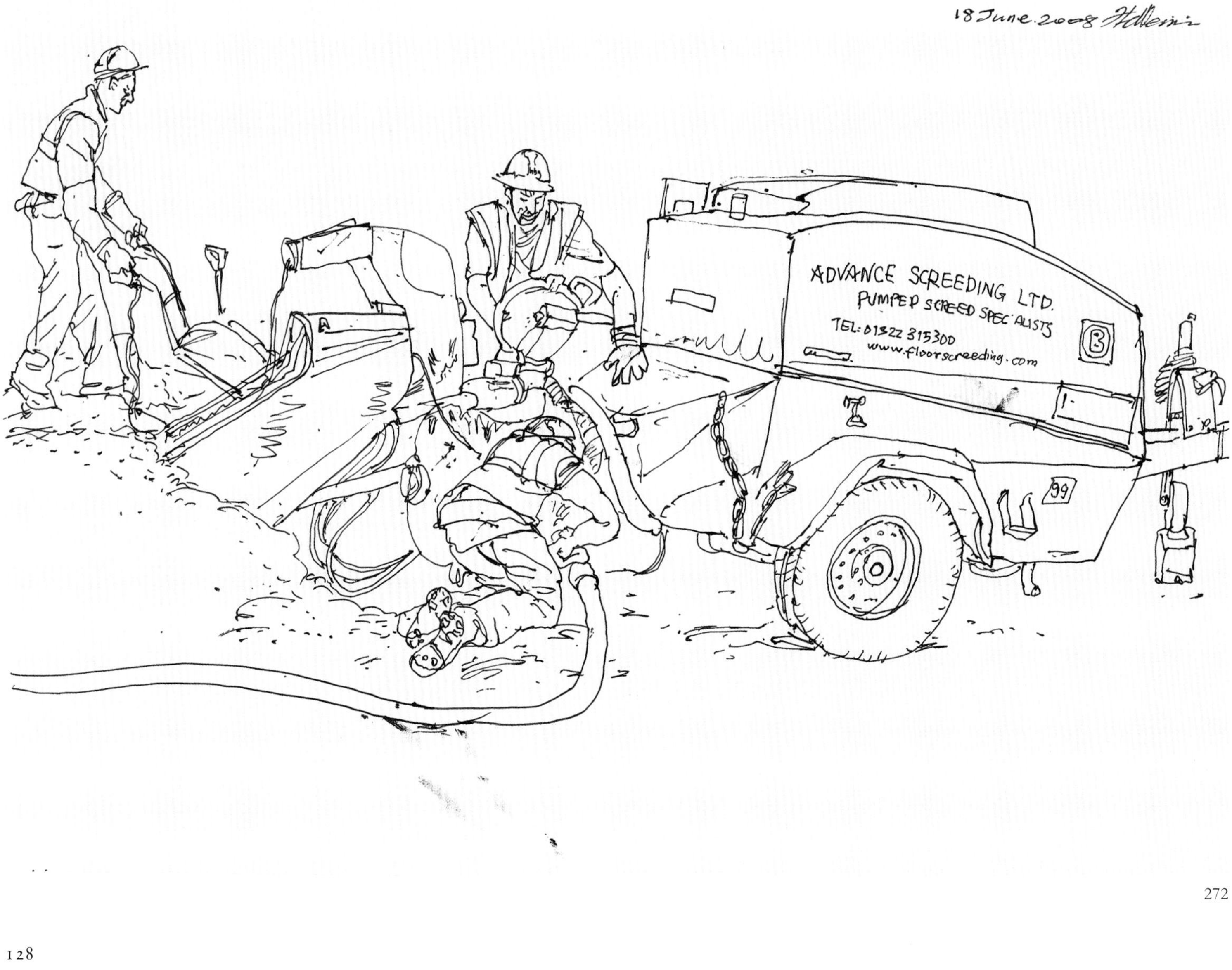

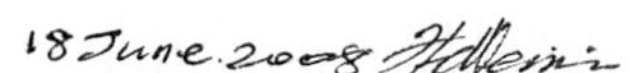

272

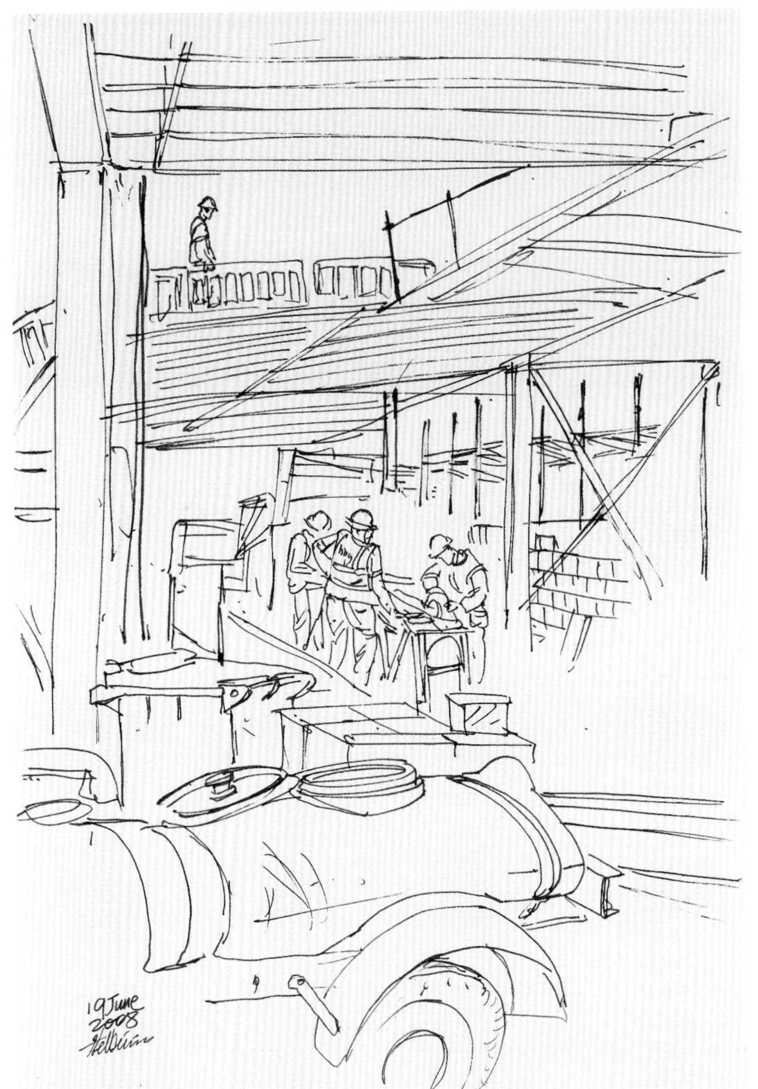

273

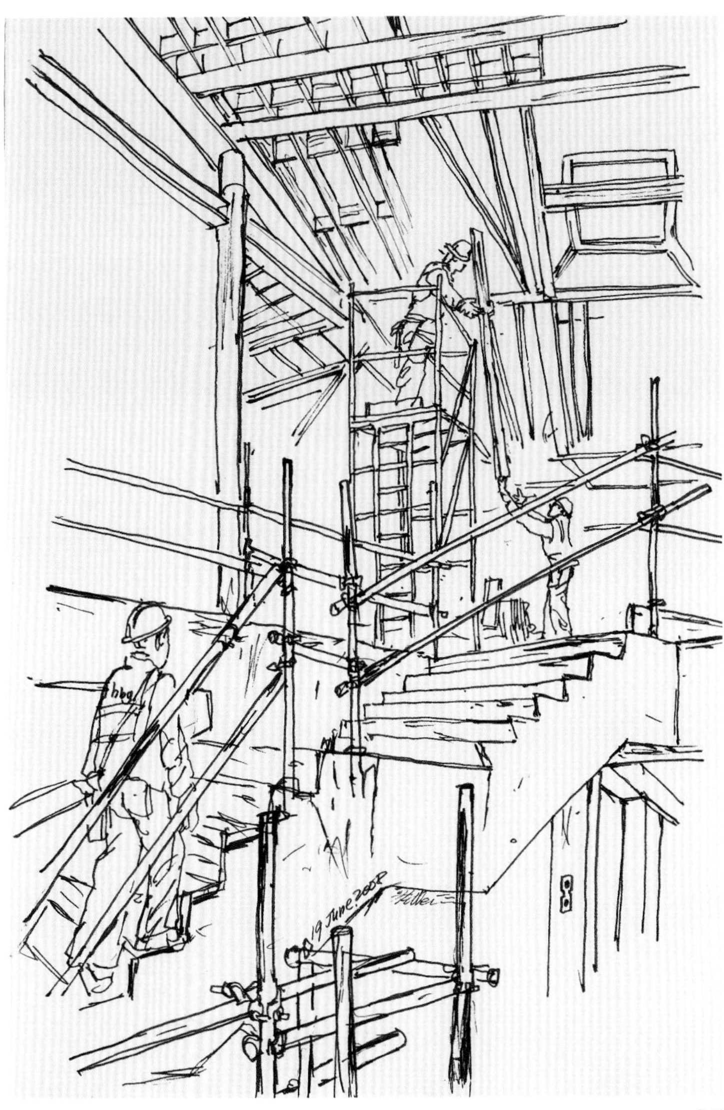

274

273 Carpenters on the top floor
19 June 2008. Pen and ink on paper. Paper size: 29.7 × 21 cm

274 Passing up a beam
19 June 2008. Pen and ink on paper. Paper size: 29.7 × 21 cm

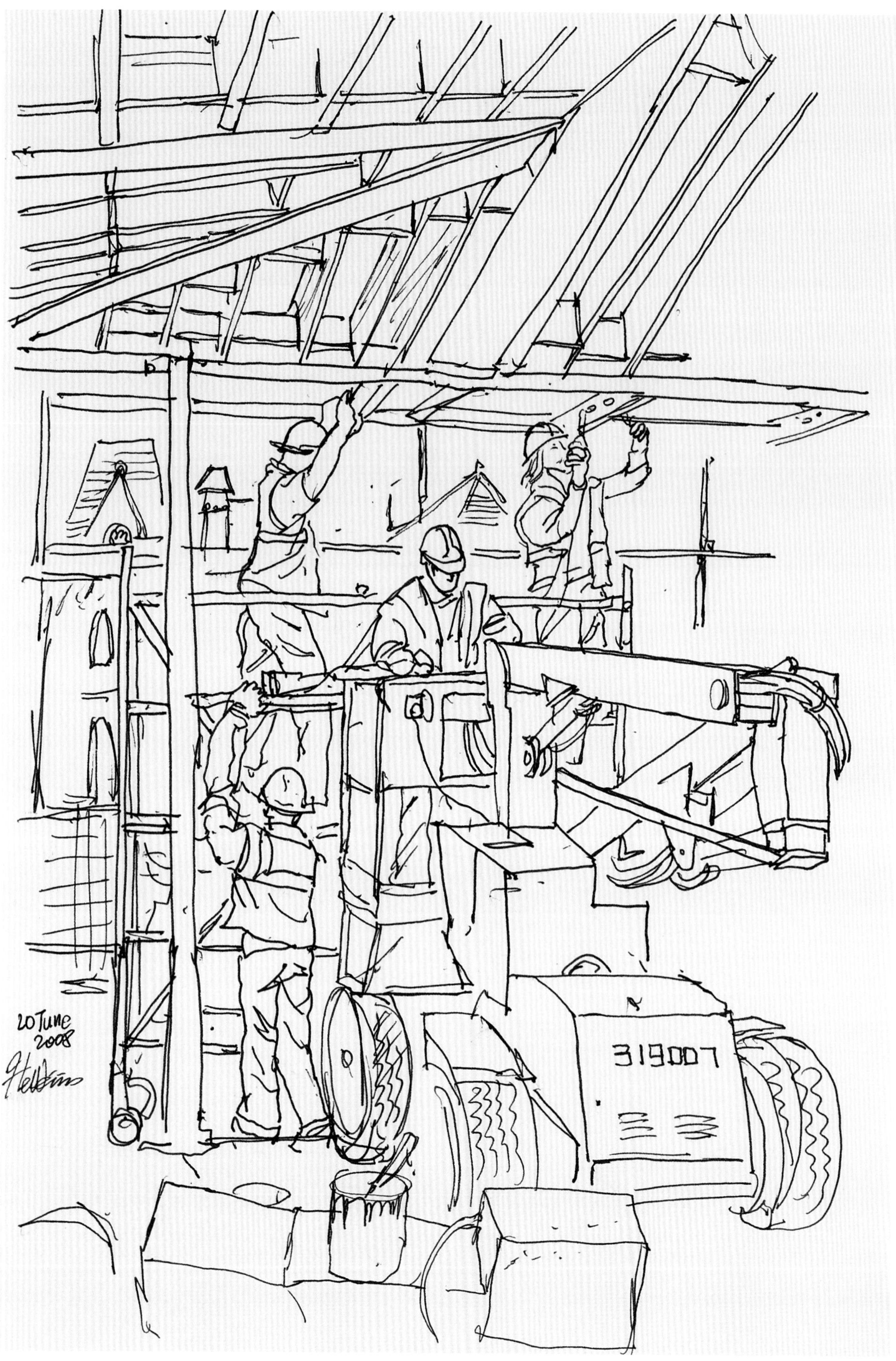

275

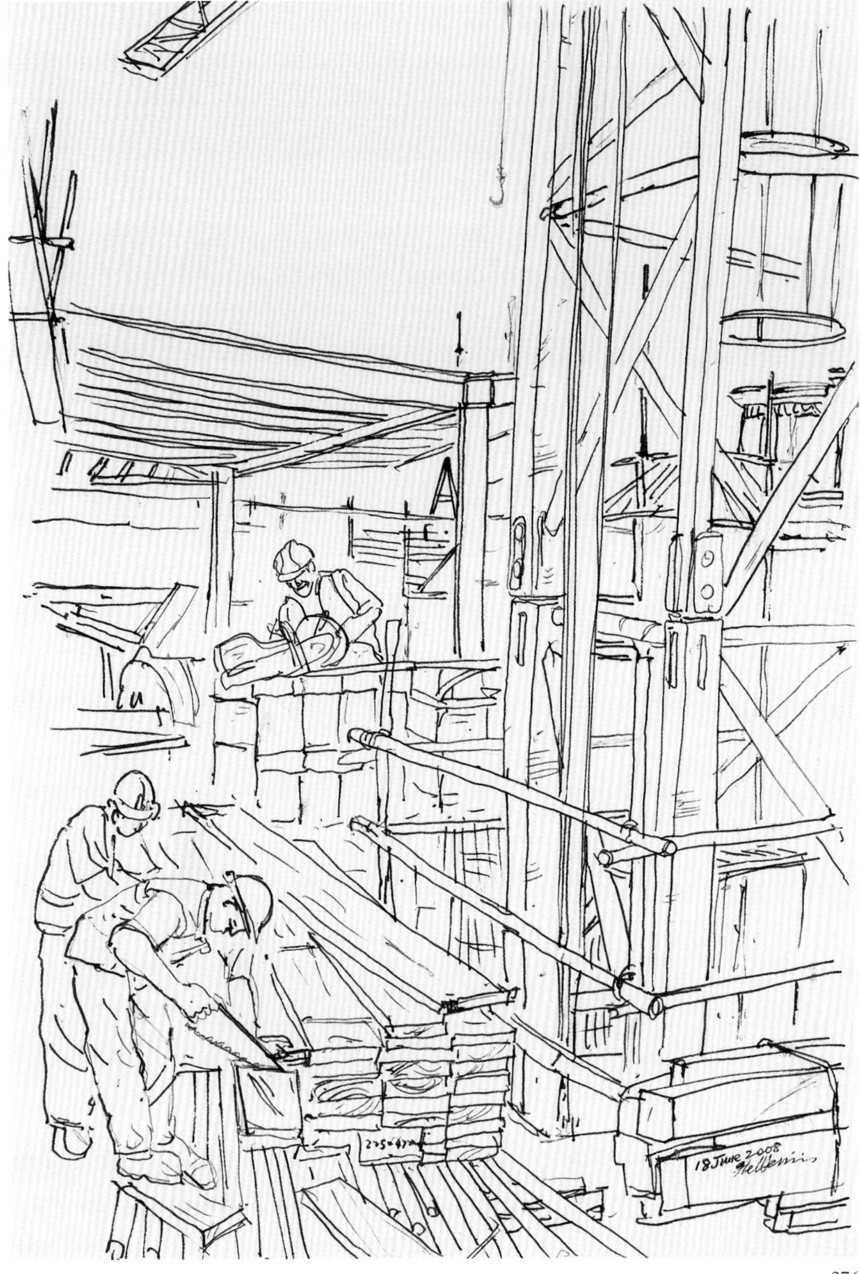

276

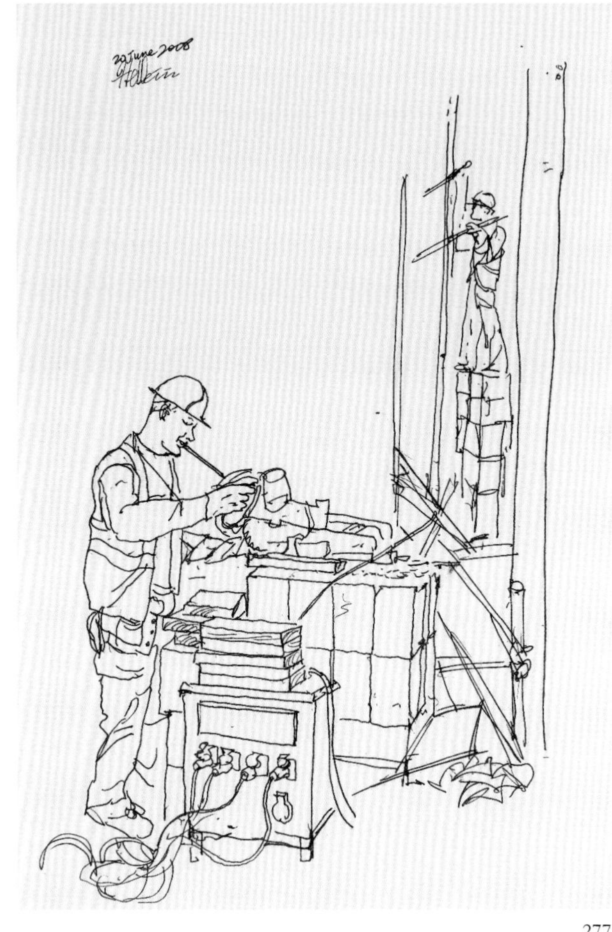

277

278

275 Ceiling construction
20 June 2008. Pen and ink on paper. Paper size: 29.7 × 21 cm

276 Carpenters at work
18 June 2008. Pen and ink on paper. Paper size: 29.7 × 21 cm

277 Carpenter cutting wood
20 June 2008. Pen and ink on paper. Paper size: 29.7 × 21 cm

278 On a corner of the roof
23 June 2008. Pen and ink on paper. Paper size: 29.7 × 21 cm

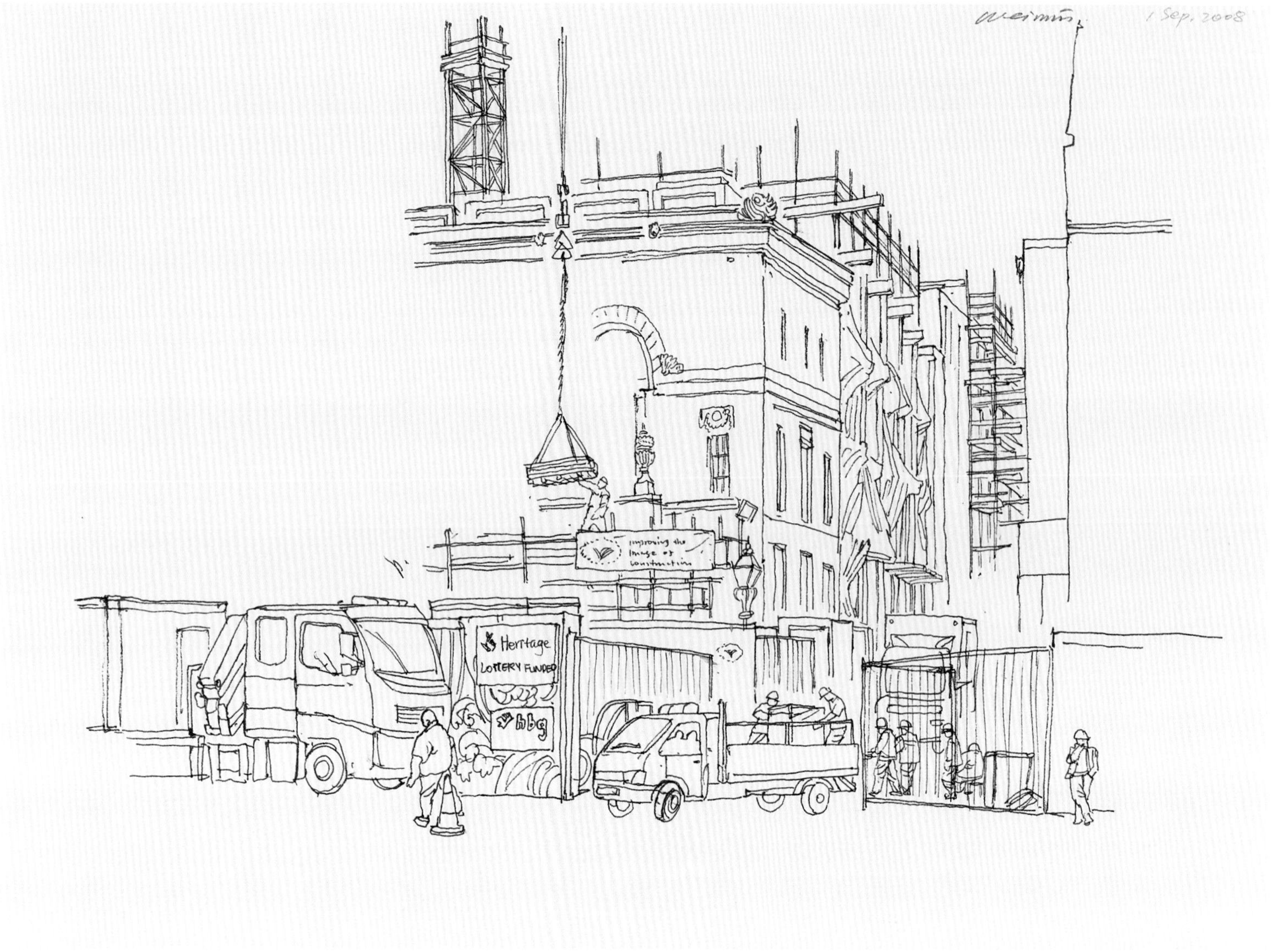

279

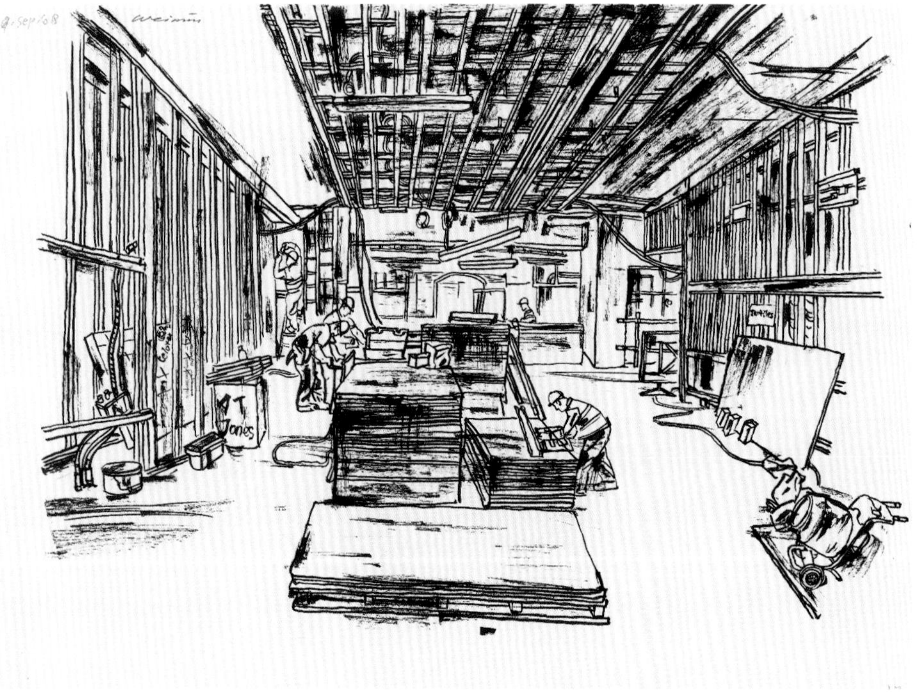

280

279 View from St Giles
1 September 2008. Pen and ink on paper.
Paper size: 29.7 × 42 cm

280 The Textile Gallery
9 September 2008. Brush and ink on paper.
Paper size: 29.7 × 42 cm

281 **Clearing cement drums**
8 October 2008. Brush and ink on paper. Paper size: 42 × 29.7 cm

282 **Welder in the basement**
16 September 2008. Brush and ink on paper. Paper size: 42 × 29.7 cm

283 **Dismantling the tower crane**
17 October 2008. Brush and ink on paper. Paper size: 42 × 29.7 cm

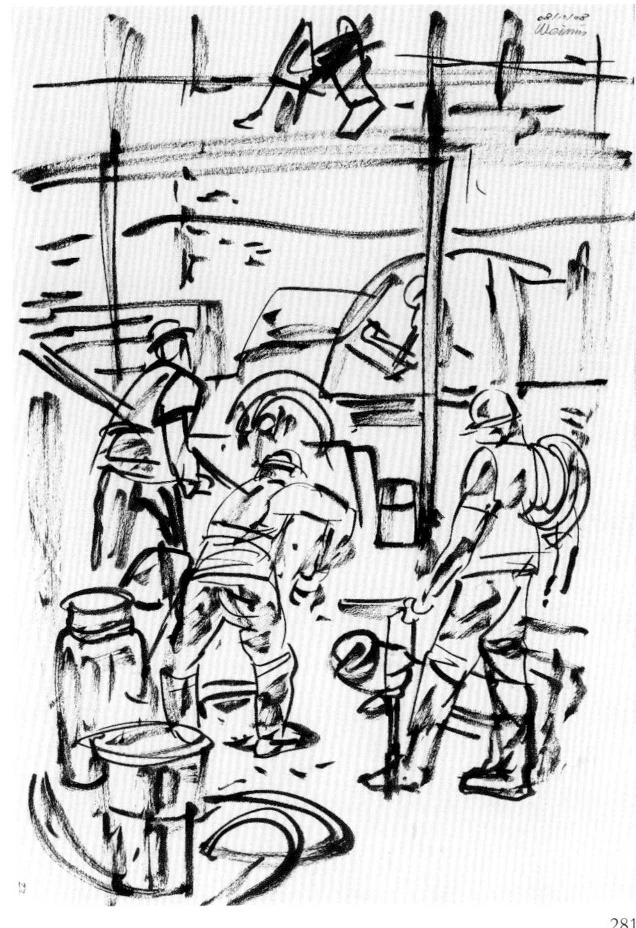

281

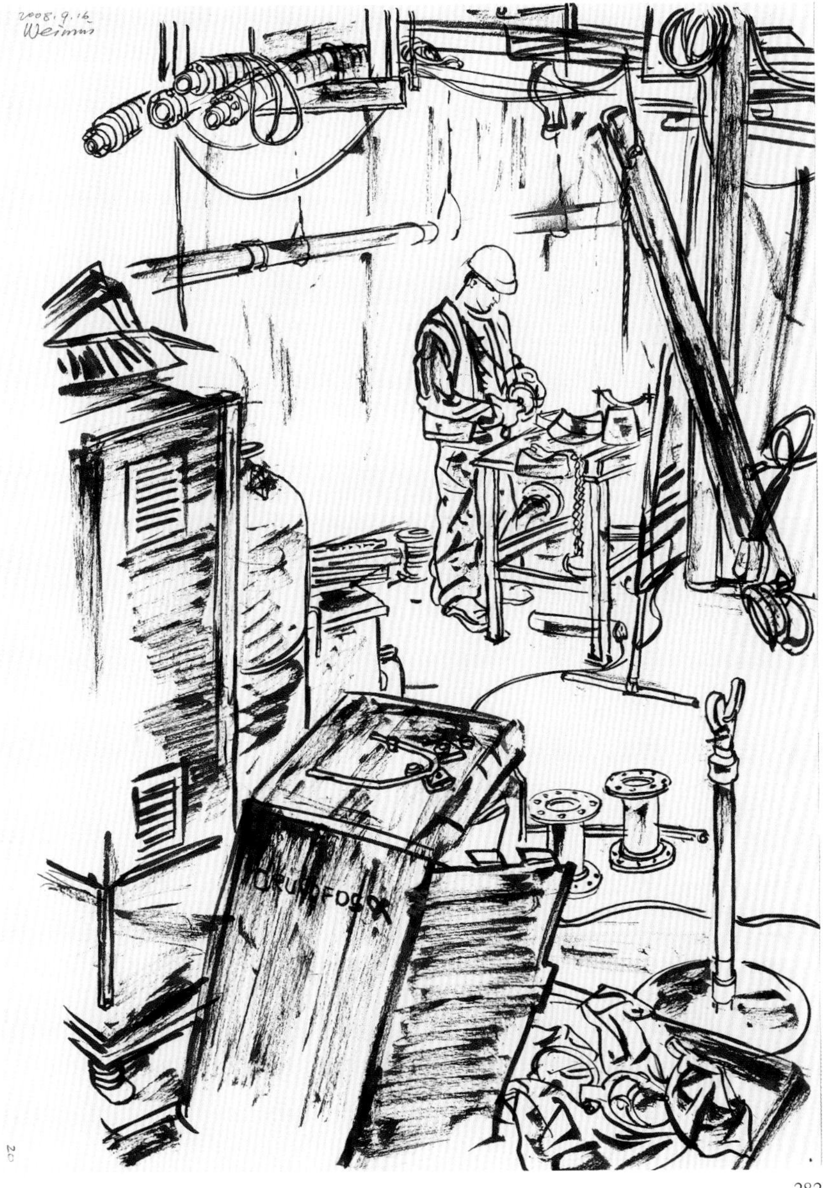

282

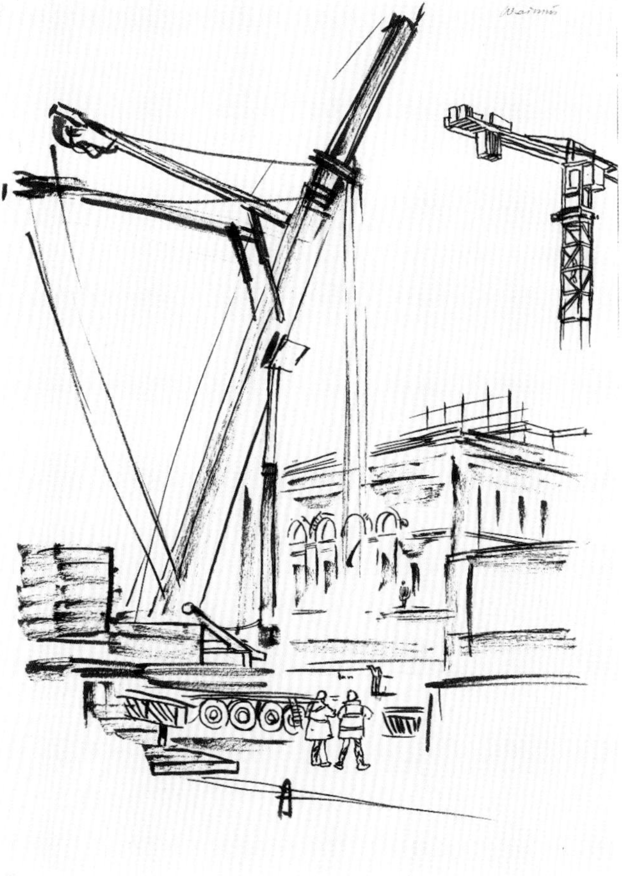

283

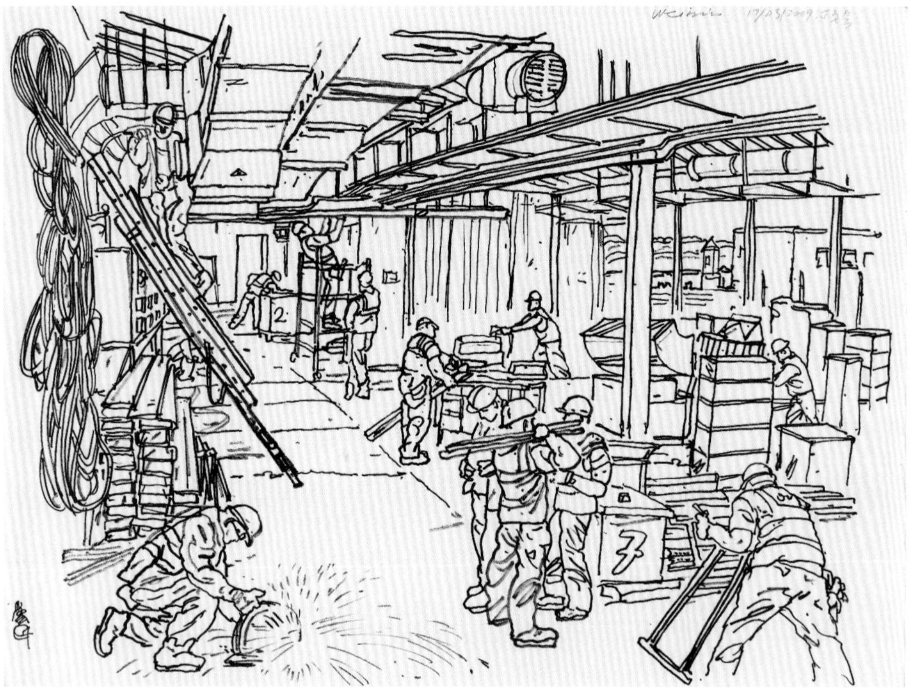

284

284 Constructing the conservation lab
17 March 2009. Marker on paper.
Paper size: 29.7 × 42 cm

285 Working on the cafeteria
27 March 2009. Marker on paper.
Paper size: 29.7 × 42 cm

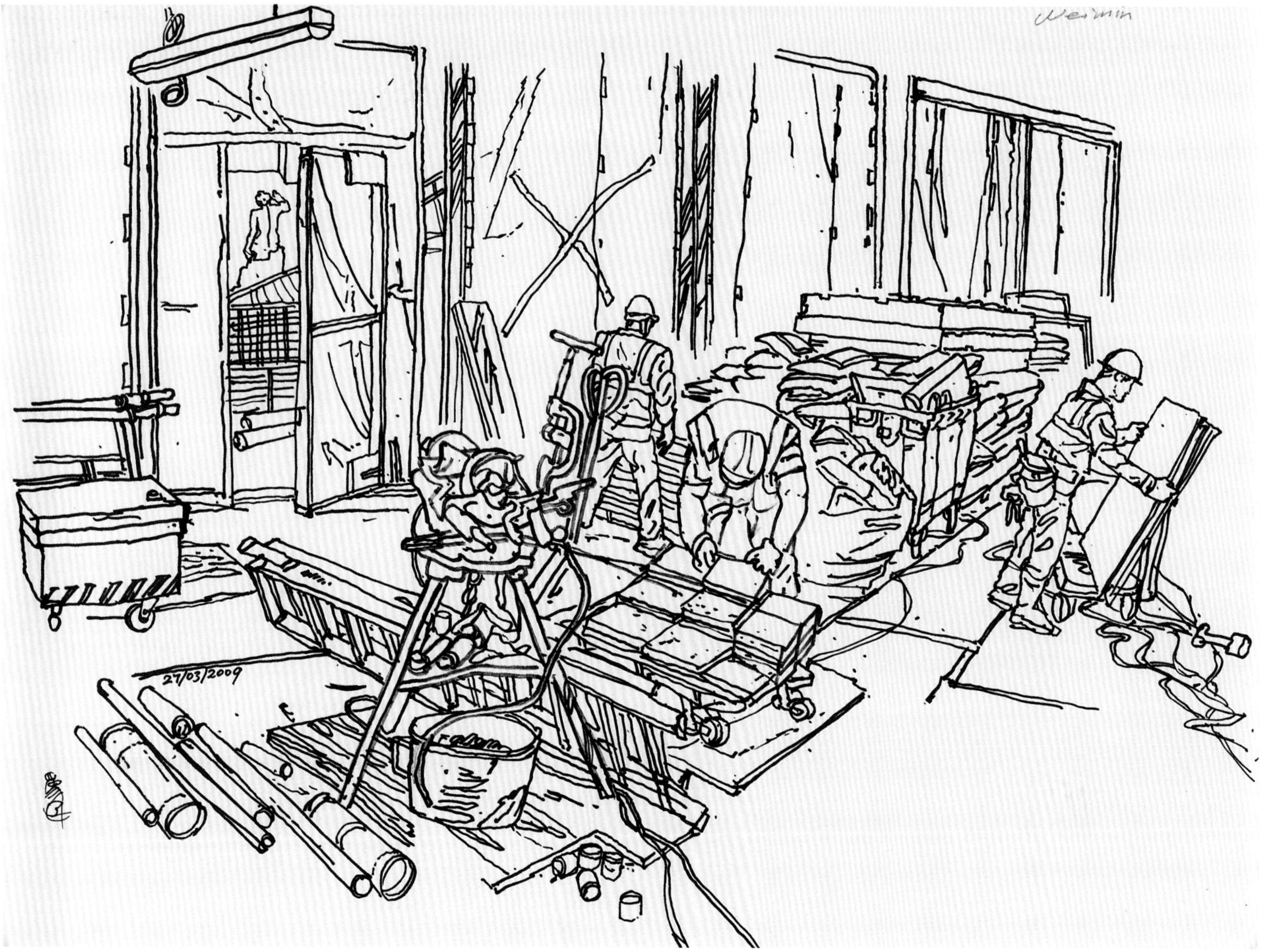

285

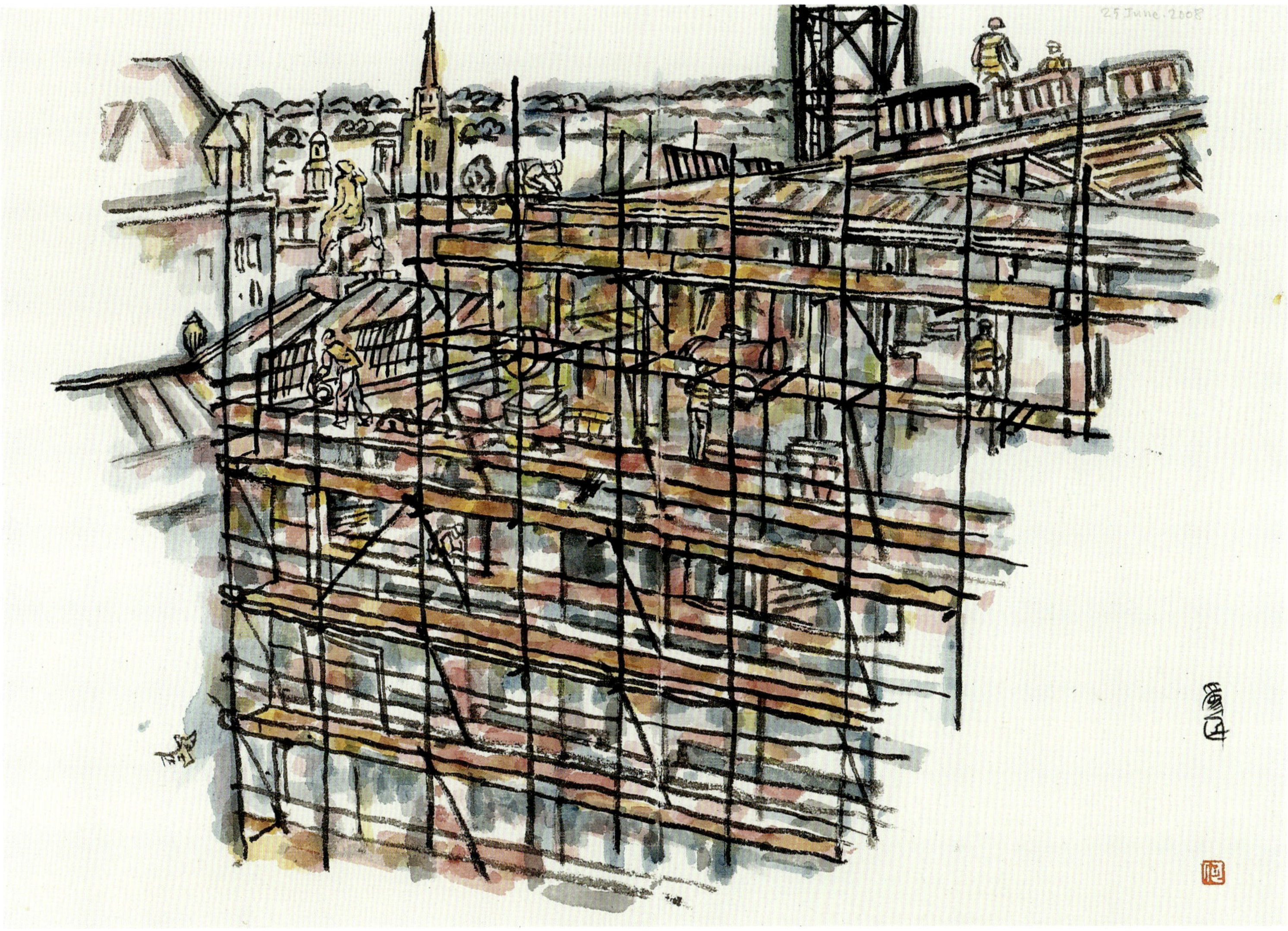

286

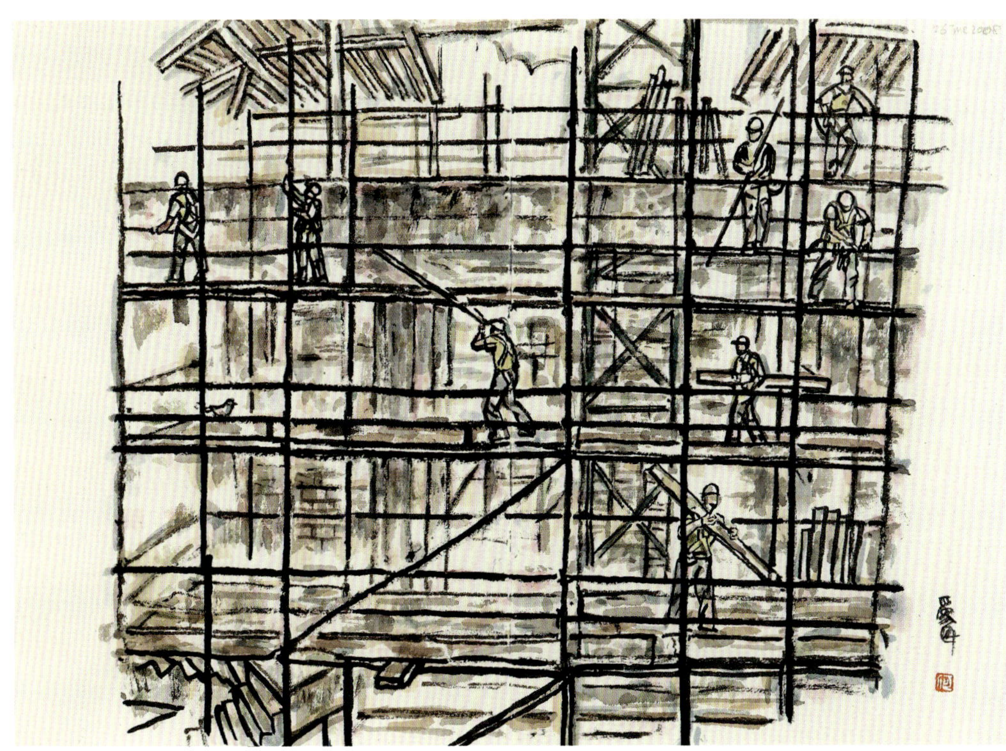

287

286 View with scaffolding
25 June 2008.
Brush and ink on album leaves.
Paper size: 27.9 × 39.8 cm

287 Scaffolders at work
26 June 2008.
Ink and colour on album leaves.
Paper size: 27.9 × 39.8 cm

288 Carpenters on the roof
29 June 2008.
Brush and ink on album leaves.
Paper size: 27.9 × 39.8 cm

289 Roof view
2 July 2008.
Brush and ink on album leaves.
Paper size: 27.9 × 39.8 cm

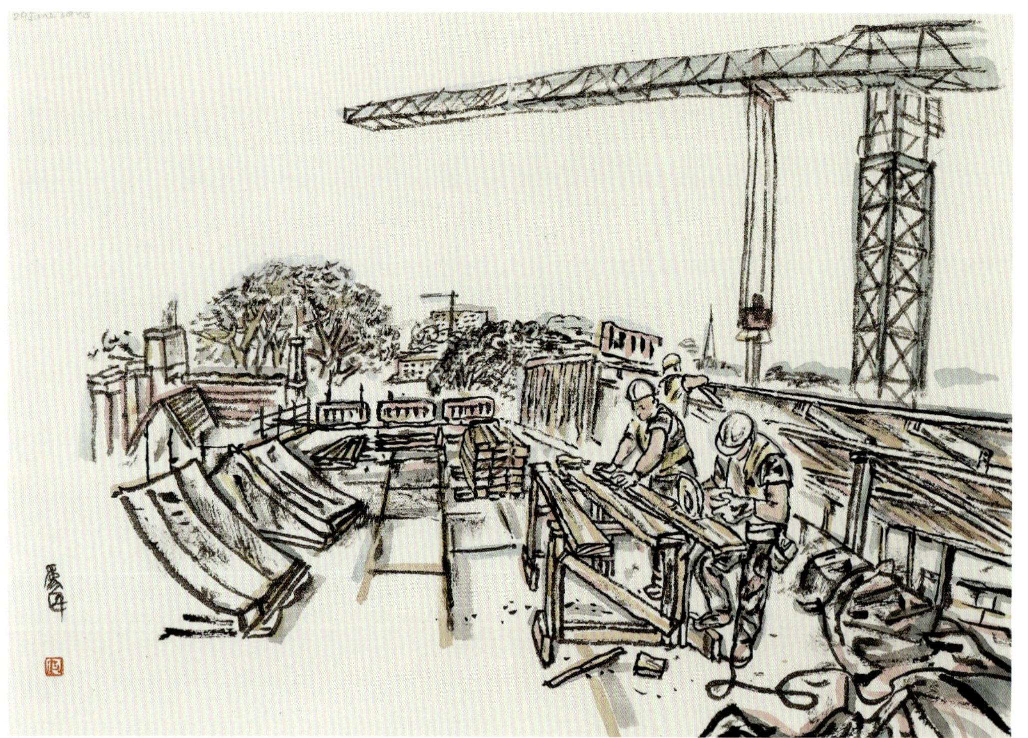

288

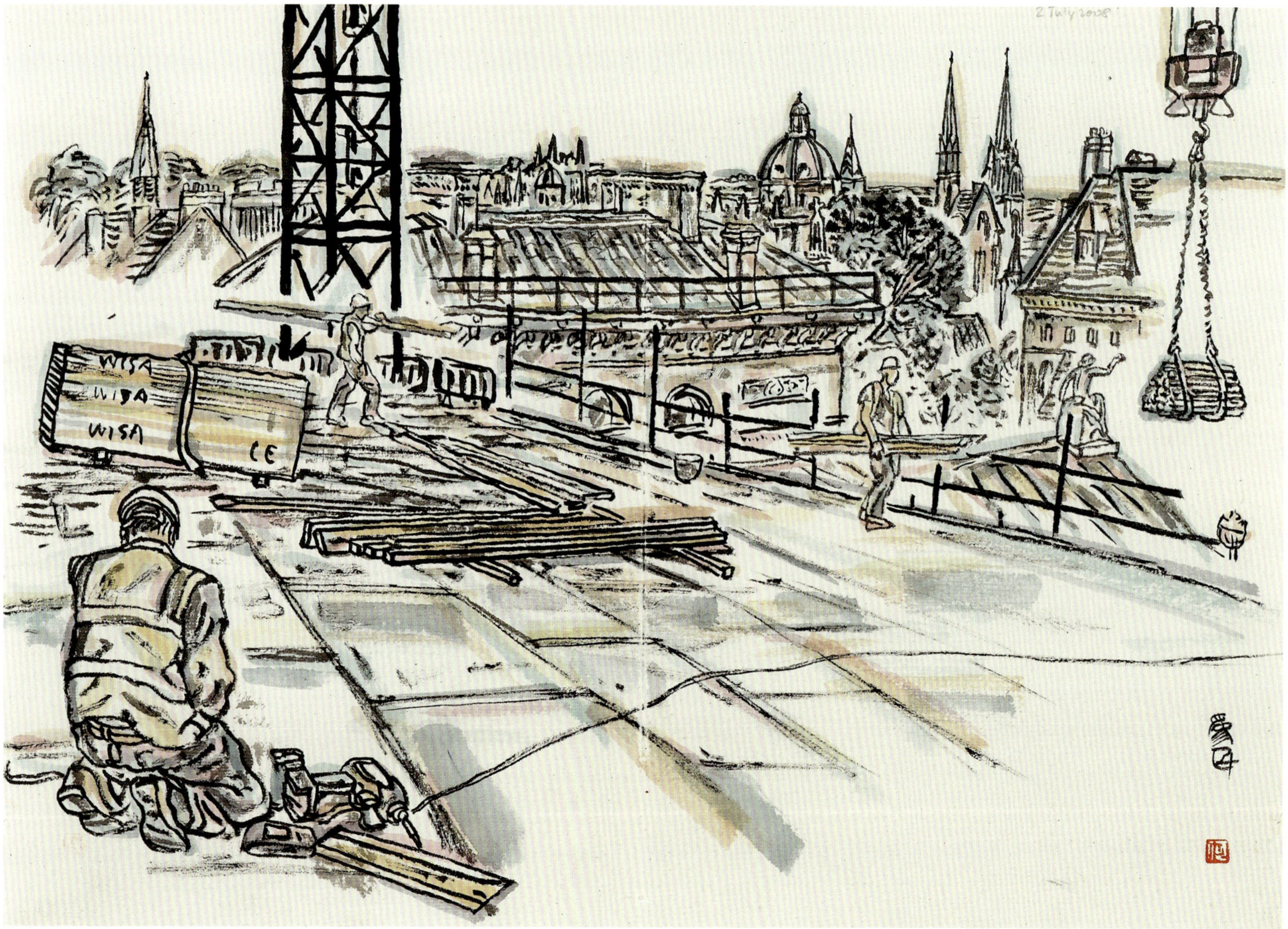

289

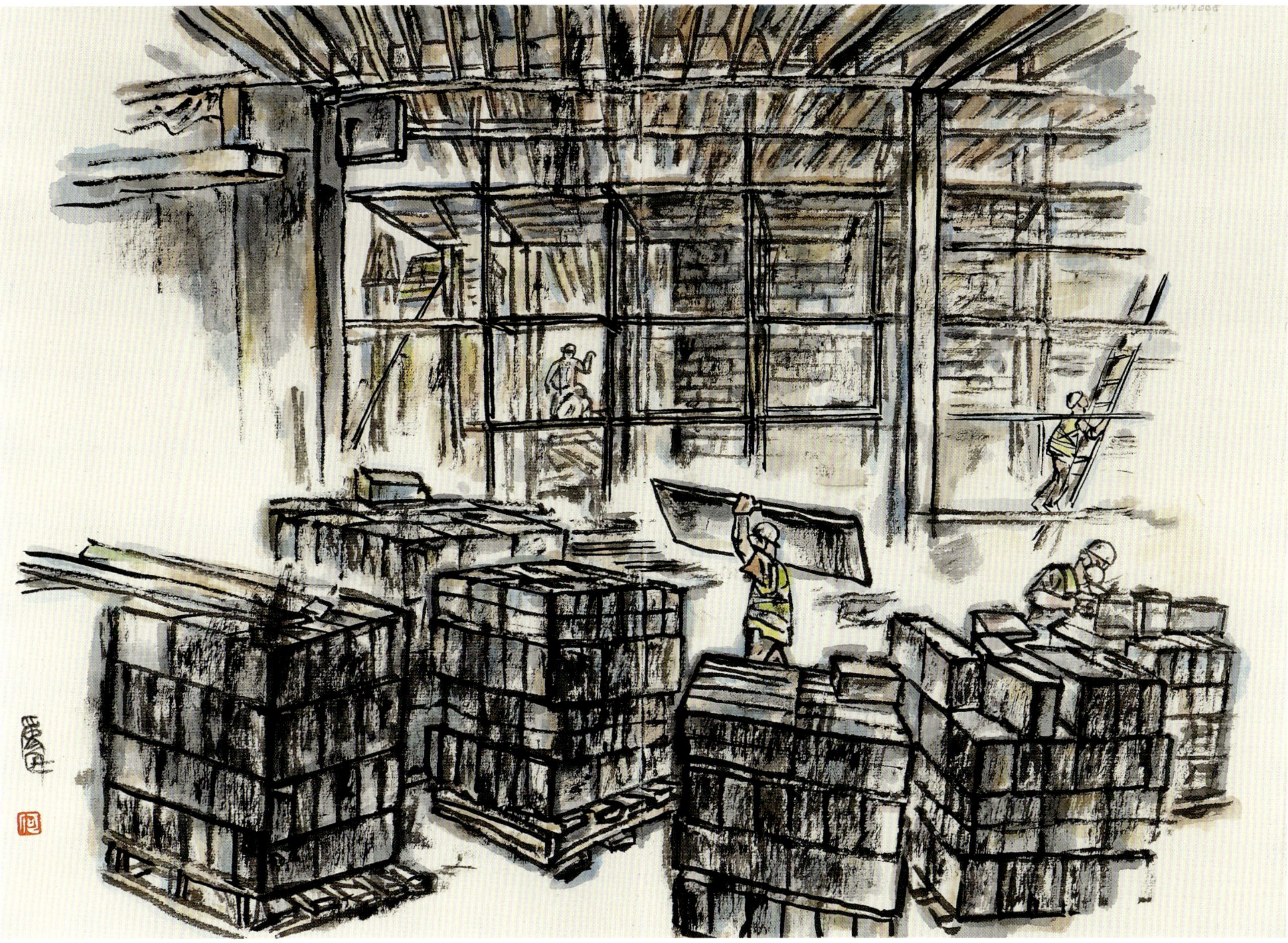

290

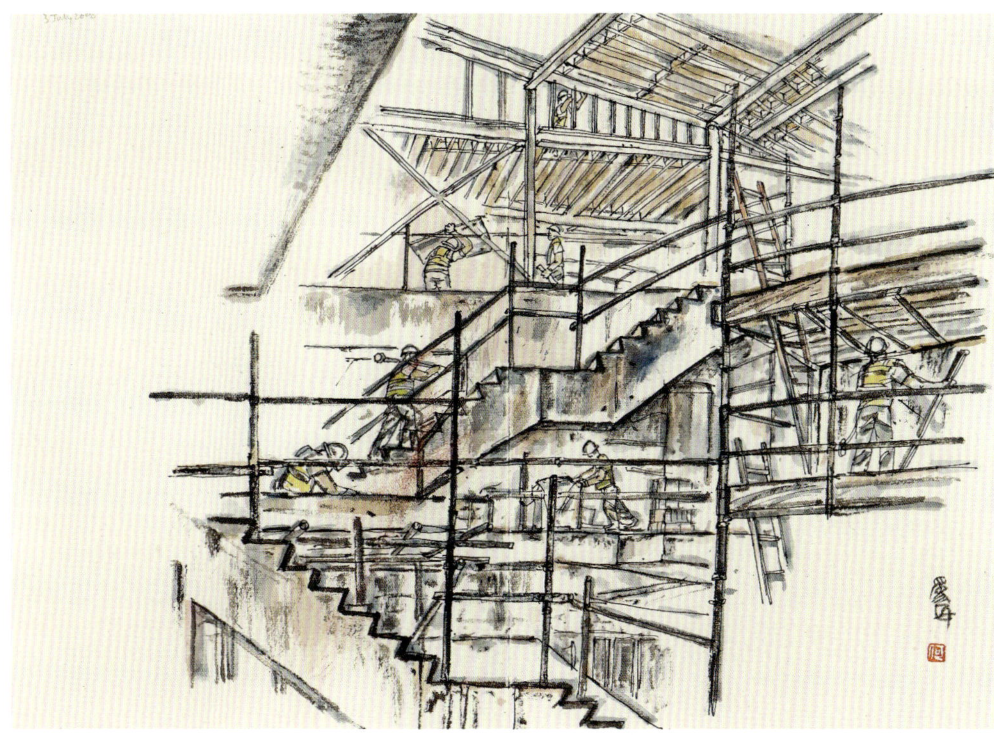

291

290 Pallets of bricks in the conservation lab
3 July 2008.
Ink and colour on album leaves.
Paper size: 27.9 × 39.8 cm

291 Staircase from Japan Gallery
3 July 2008.
Ink and colour on album leaves.
Paper size: 27.9 × 39.8 cm

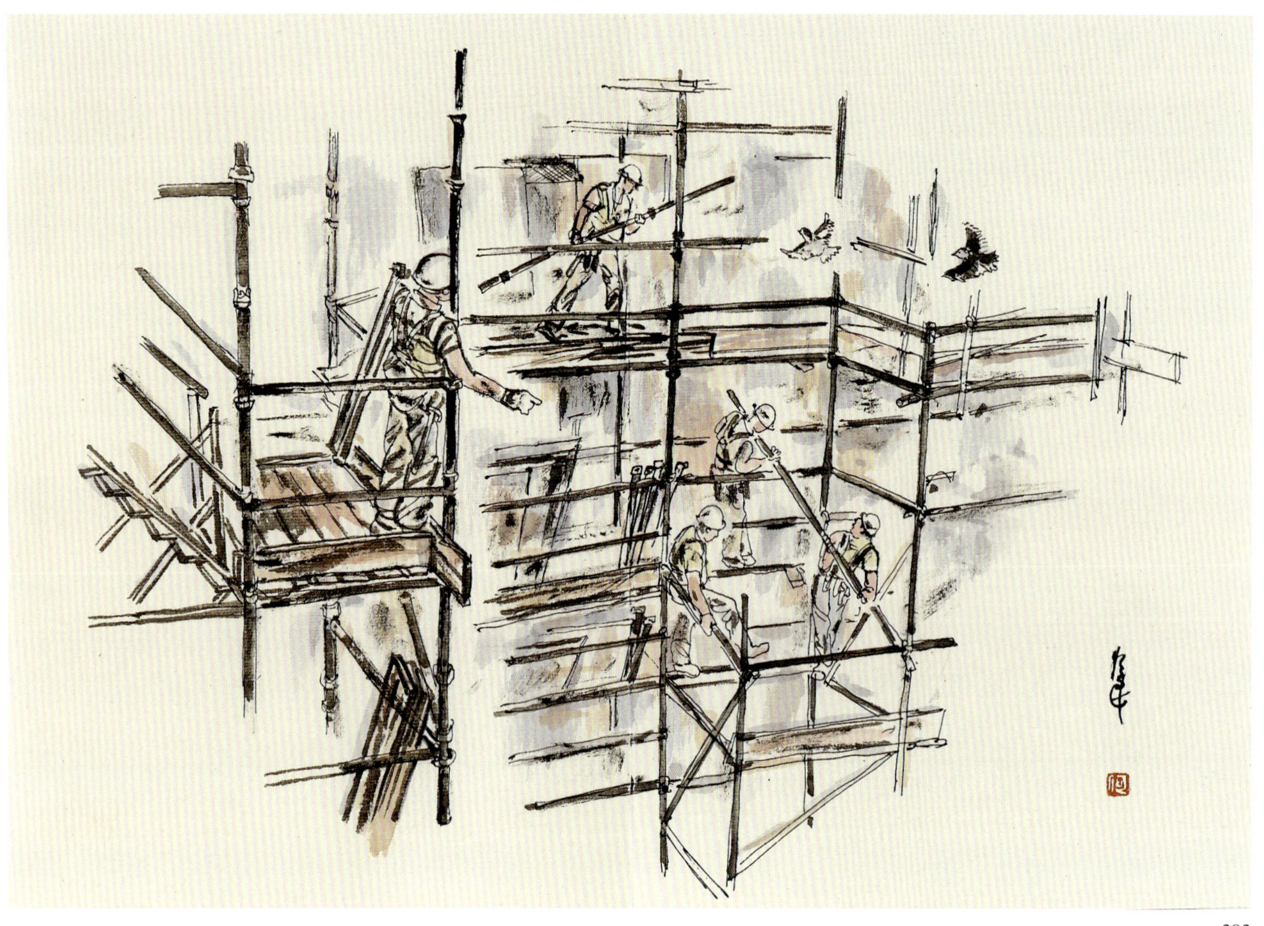

292

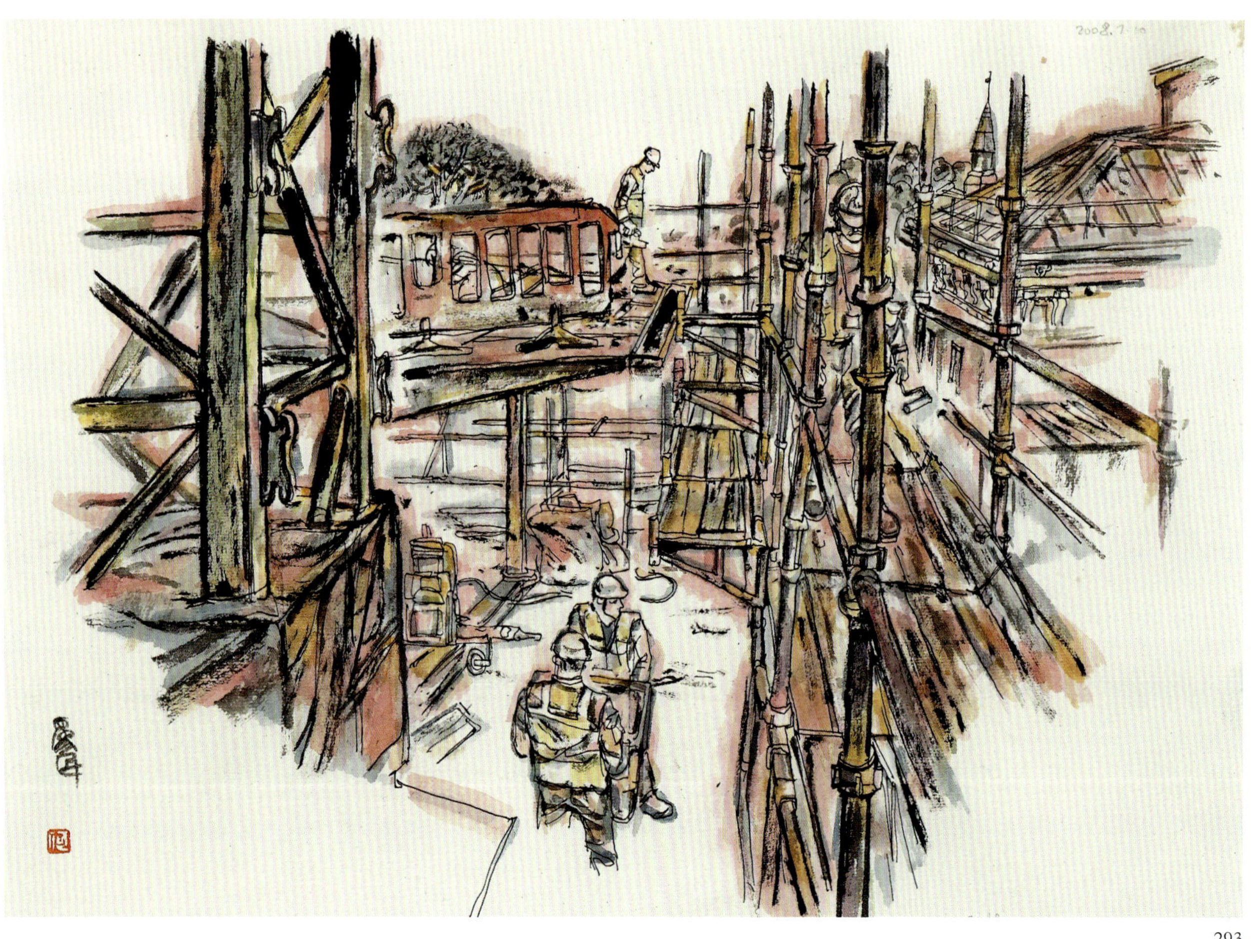

293

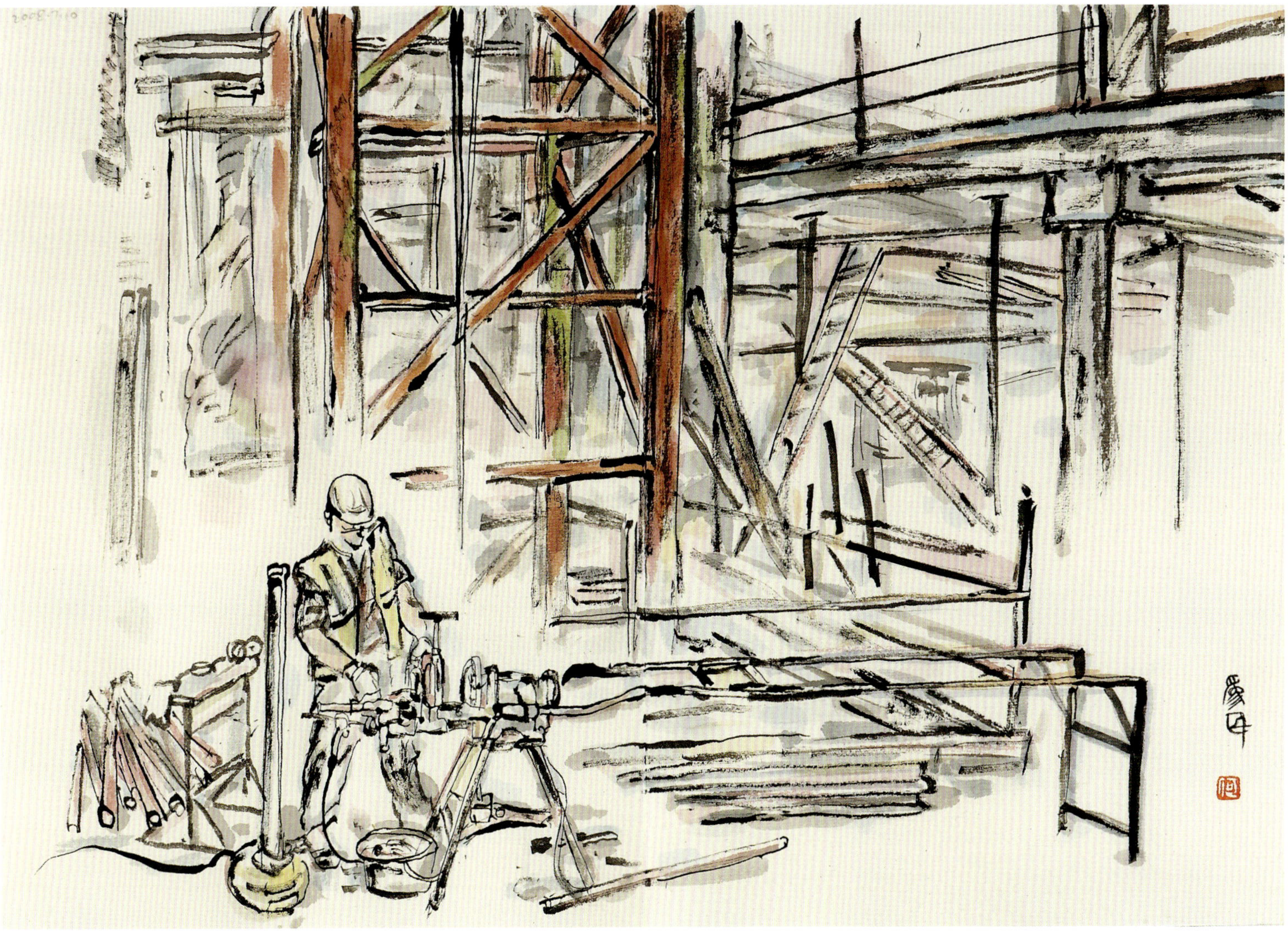

294

292 Erecting scaffolding
July 2008.
Ink and colour on album leaves.
Paper size: 27.9 × 39.8 cm

293 At work on the roof
10 July 2008.
Brush and ink on album leaves.
Paper size: 27.9 × 39.8 cm

294 Metalworker in the Ancient World Gallery
10 July 2008.
Ink and colour on album leaves.
Paper size: 27.9 × 39.8 cm

295 In the new Aegean World Gallery
11 July 2008.
Brush and ink on album leaves.
Paper size: 27.9 × 39.8 cm

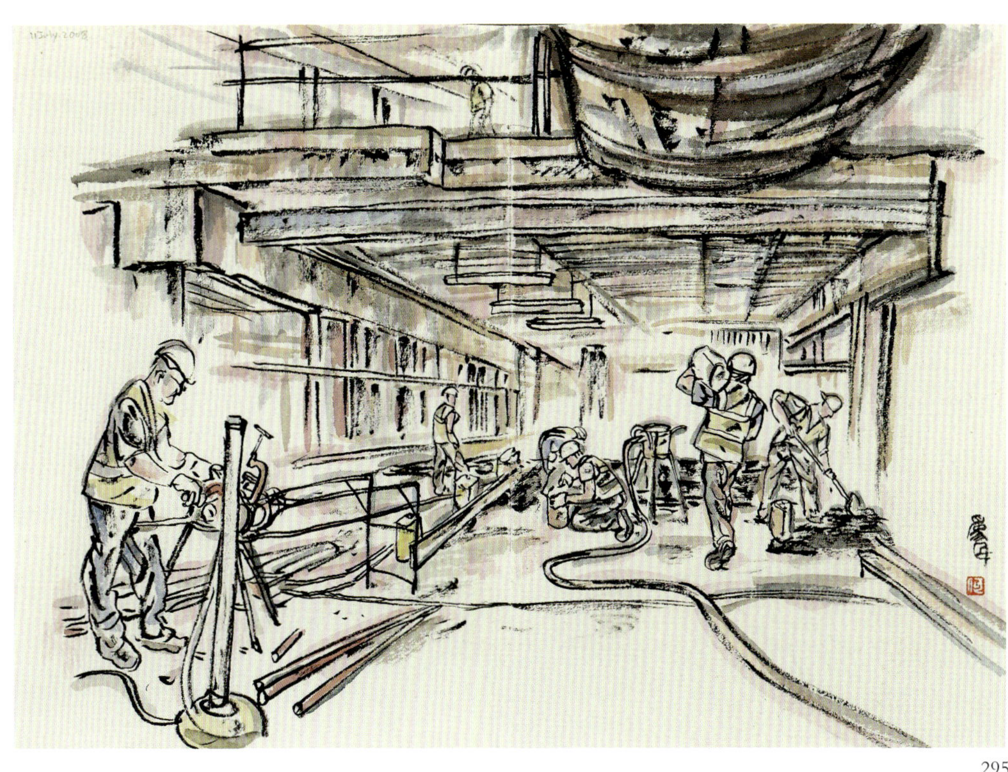

295

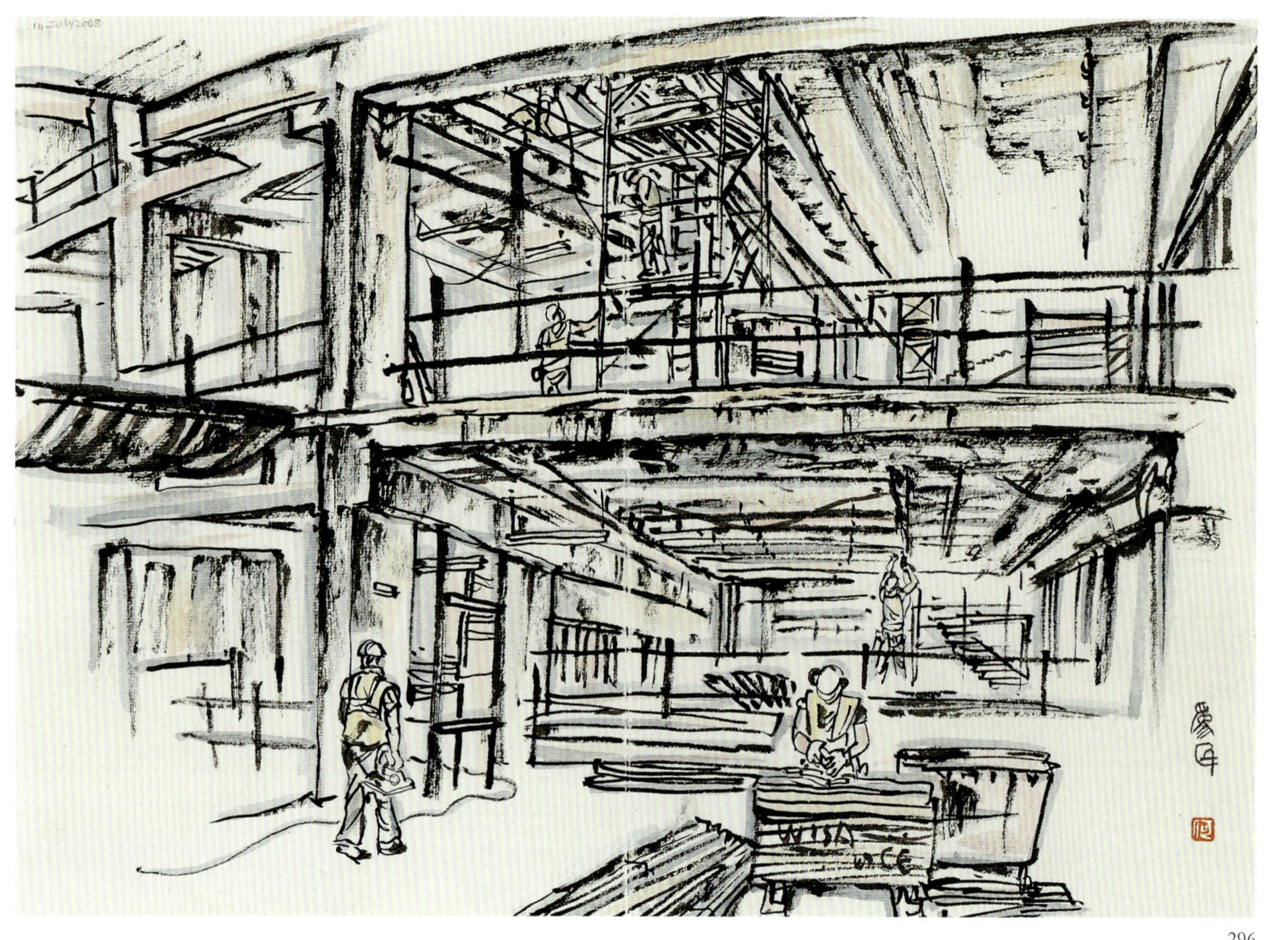

296

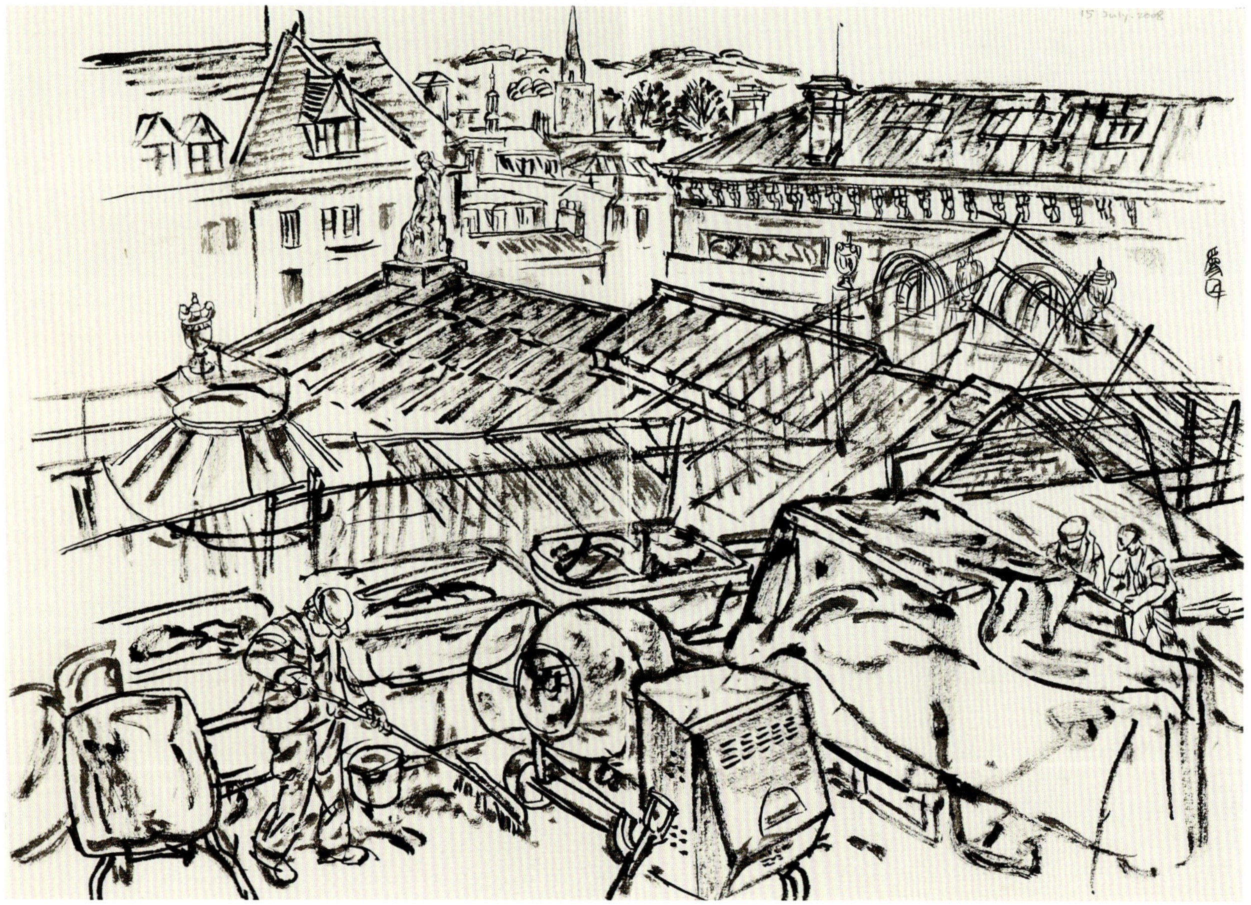

297

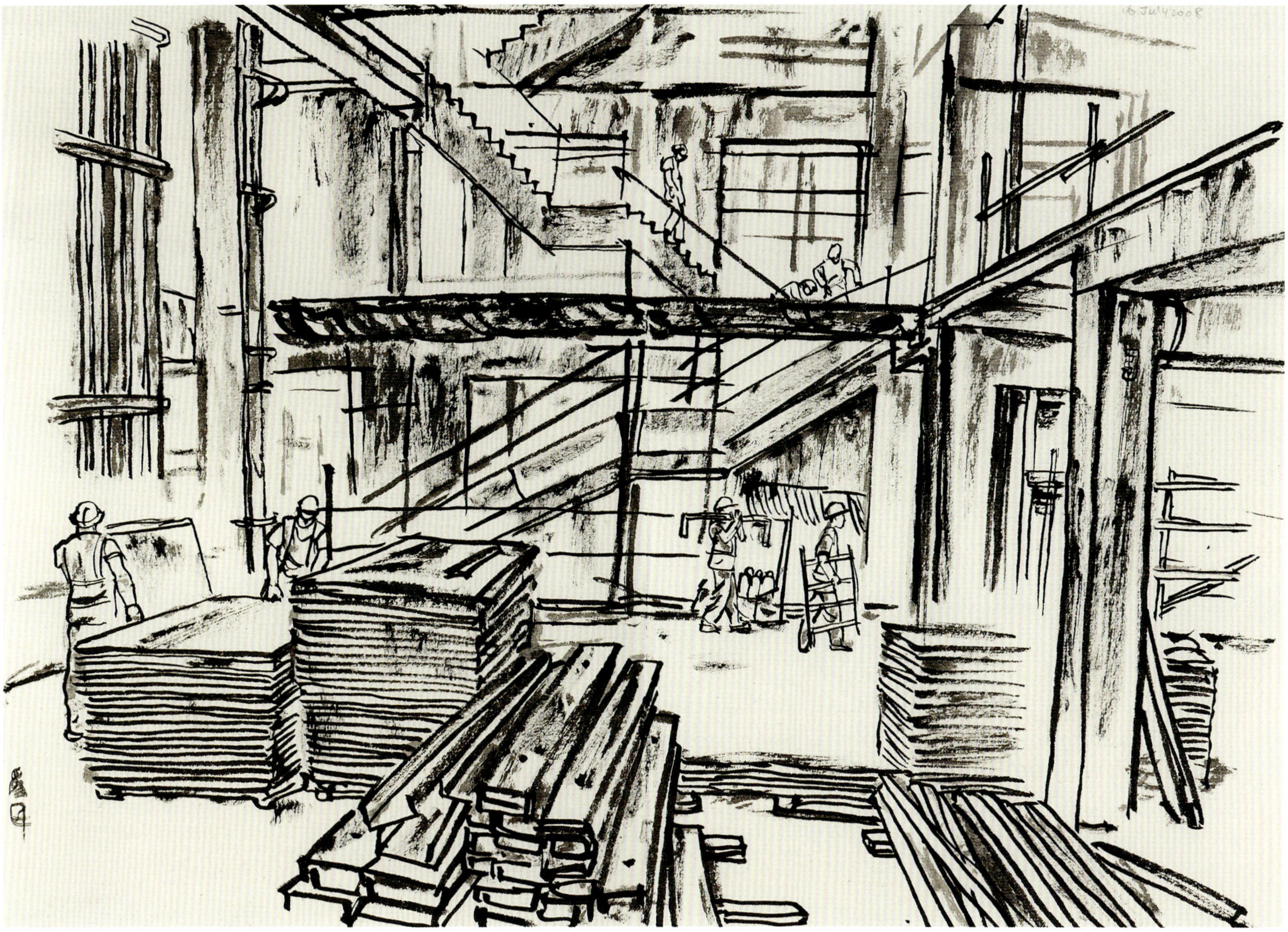

298

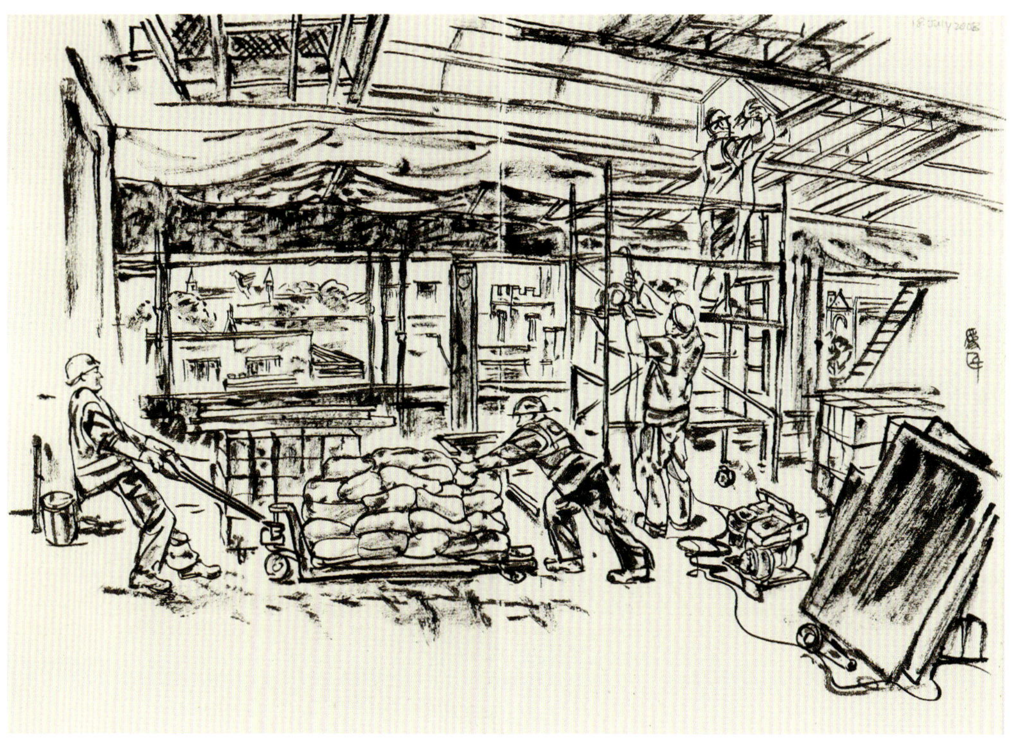

299

296 New Islamic Gallery and Rome Gallery
14 July 2008.
Brush and ink on album leaves.
Paper size: 27.9 × 39.8 cm

297 New and old roofs
15 July 2008.
Brush and ink on album leaves.
Paper size: 27.9 × 39.8 cm

298 View from the Cyprus Gallery
16 July 2008.
Brush and ink on album leaves.
Paper size: 27.9 × 39.8 cm

299 Conservation lab under construction
18 July 2008.
Brush and ink on album leaves.
Paper size: 27.9 × 39.8 cm

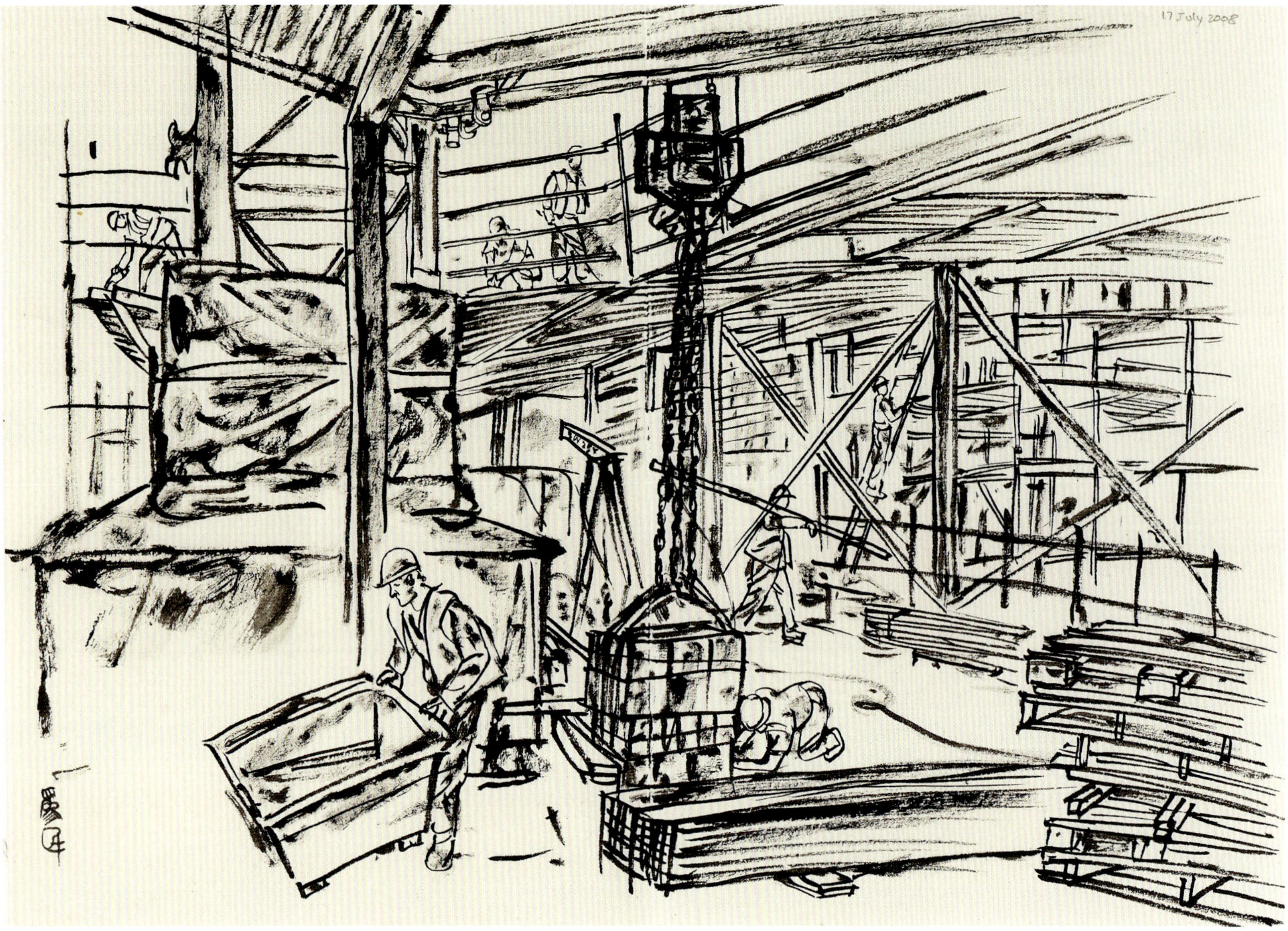

300

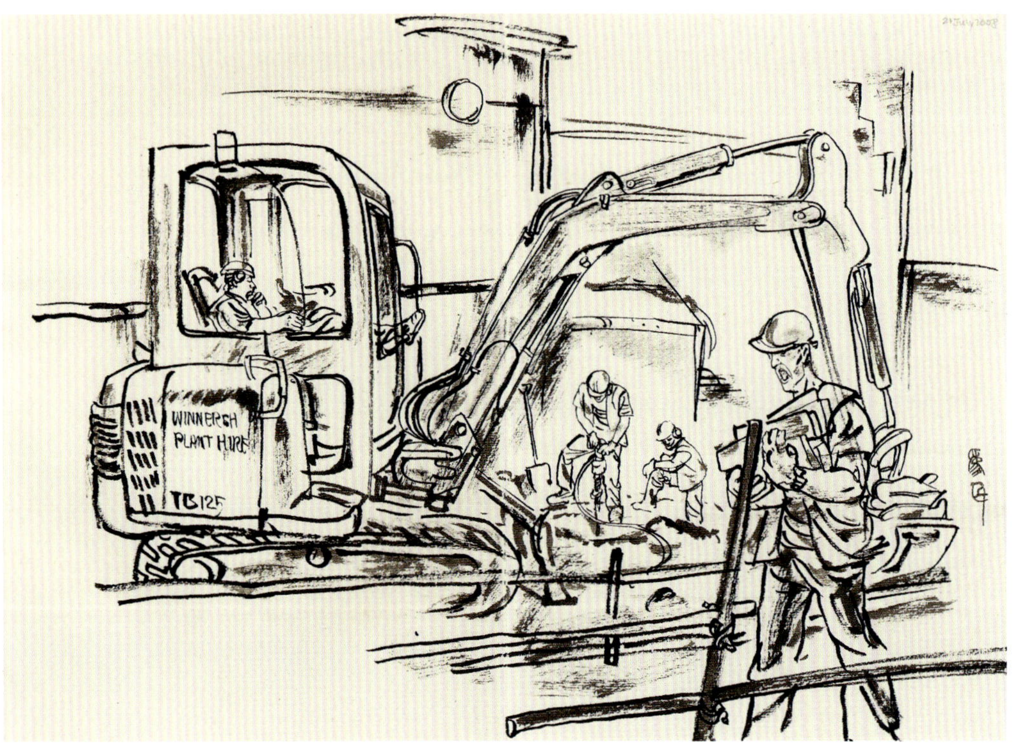

301

300 Unloading bricks
17 July 2008.
Brush and ink on album leaves.
Paper size: 27.9 × 39.8 cm

301 Digging at the site entrance
21 July 2008.
Brush and ink on album leaves.
Paper size: 27.9 × 39.8 cm

302 Inside and outside the new building
21 July 2008.
Brush and ink on album leaves.
Paper size: 27.9 × 39.8 cm

303 The Japan Gallery
22 July 2008.
Brush and ink on album leaves.
Paper size: 27.9 × 39.8 cm

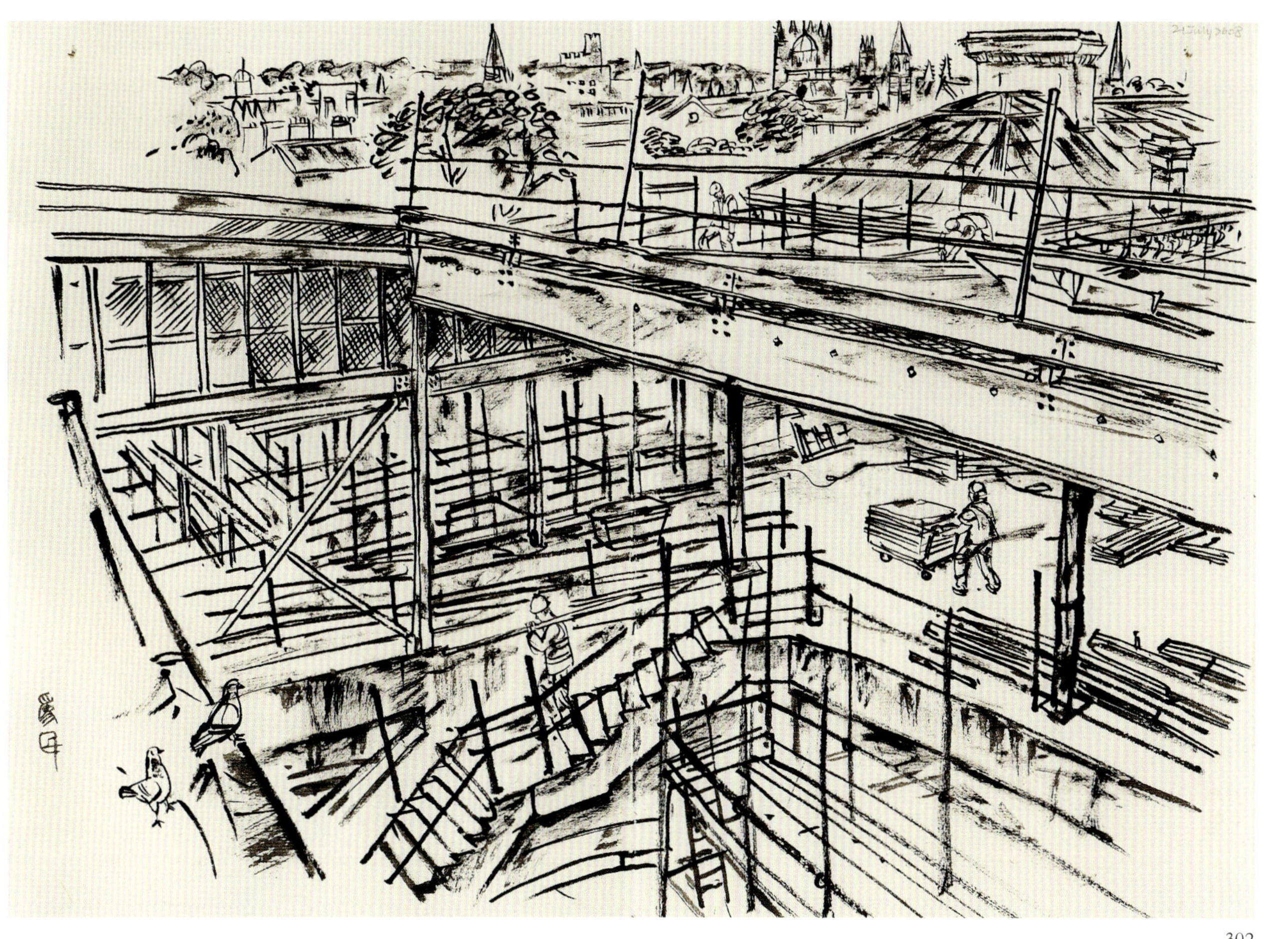

302

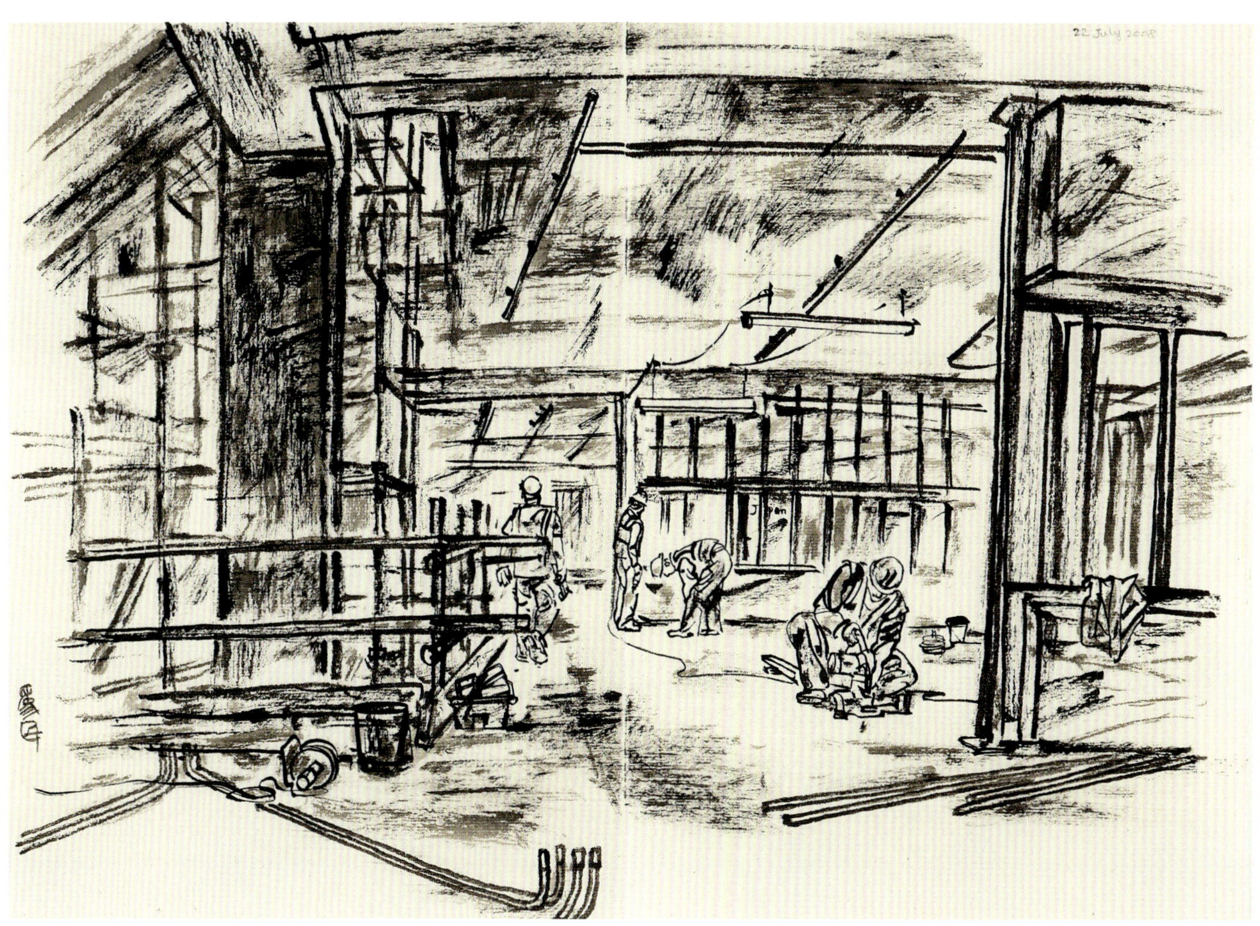

303

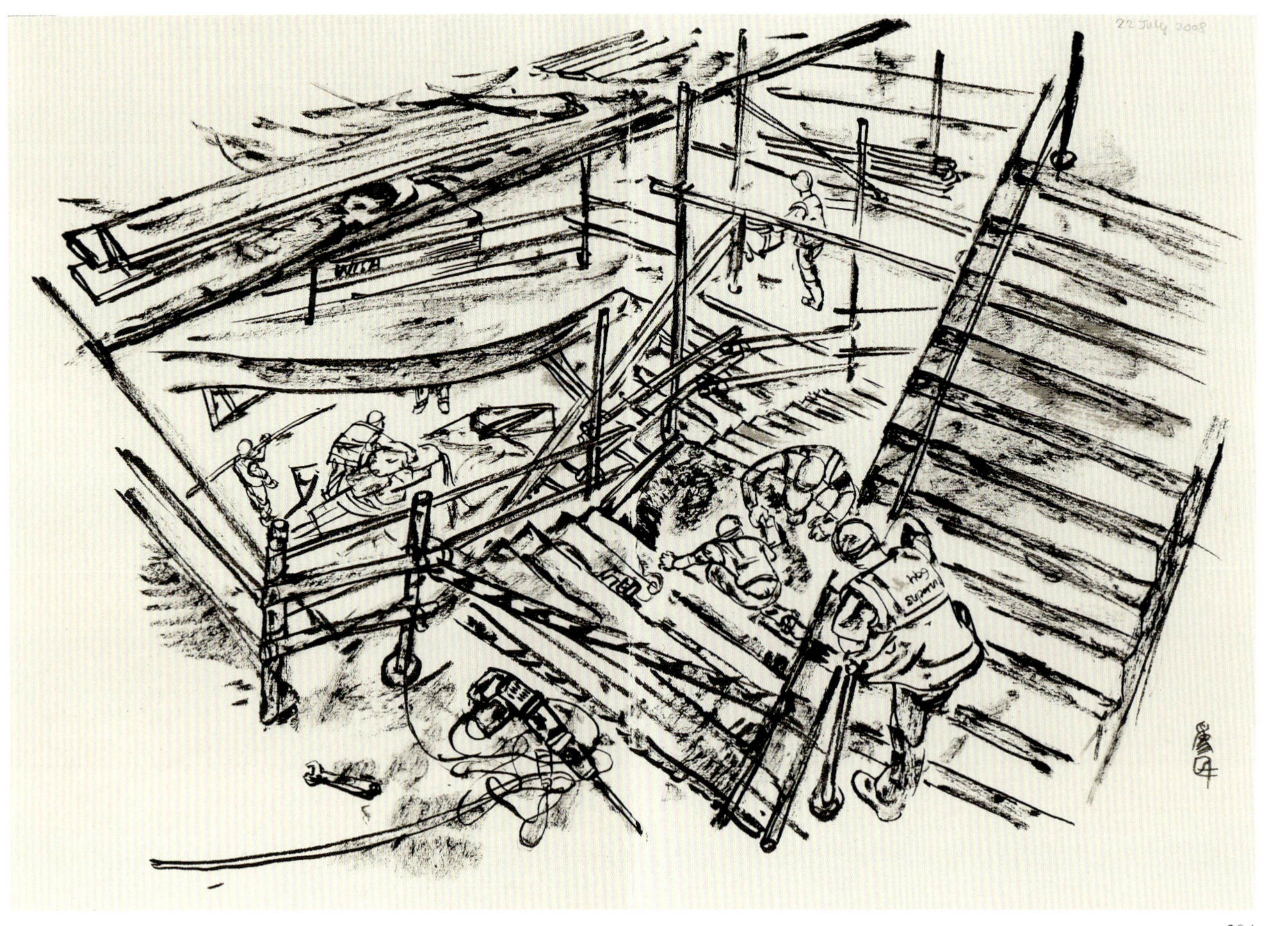

304

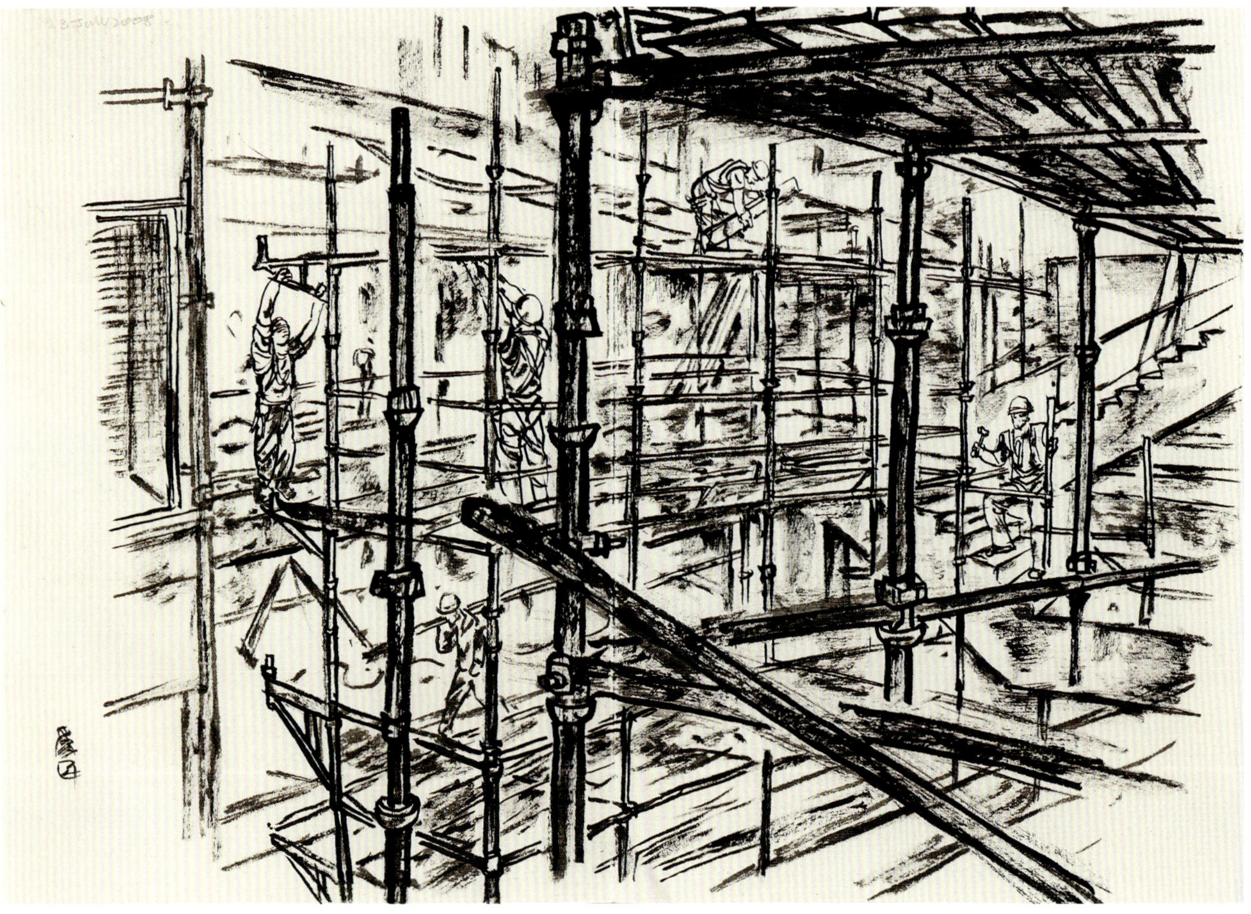

305

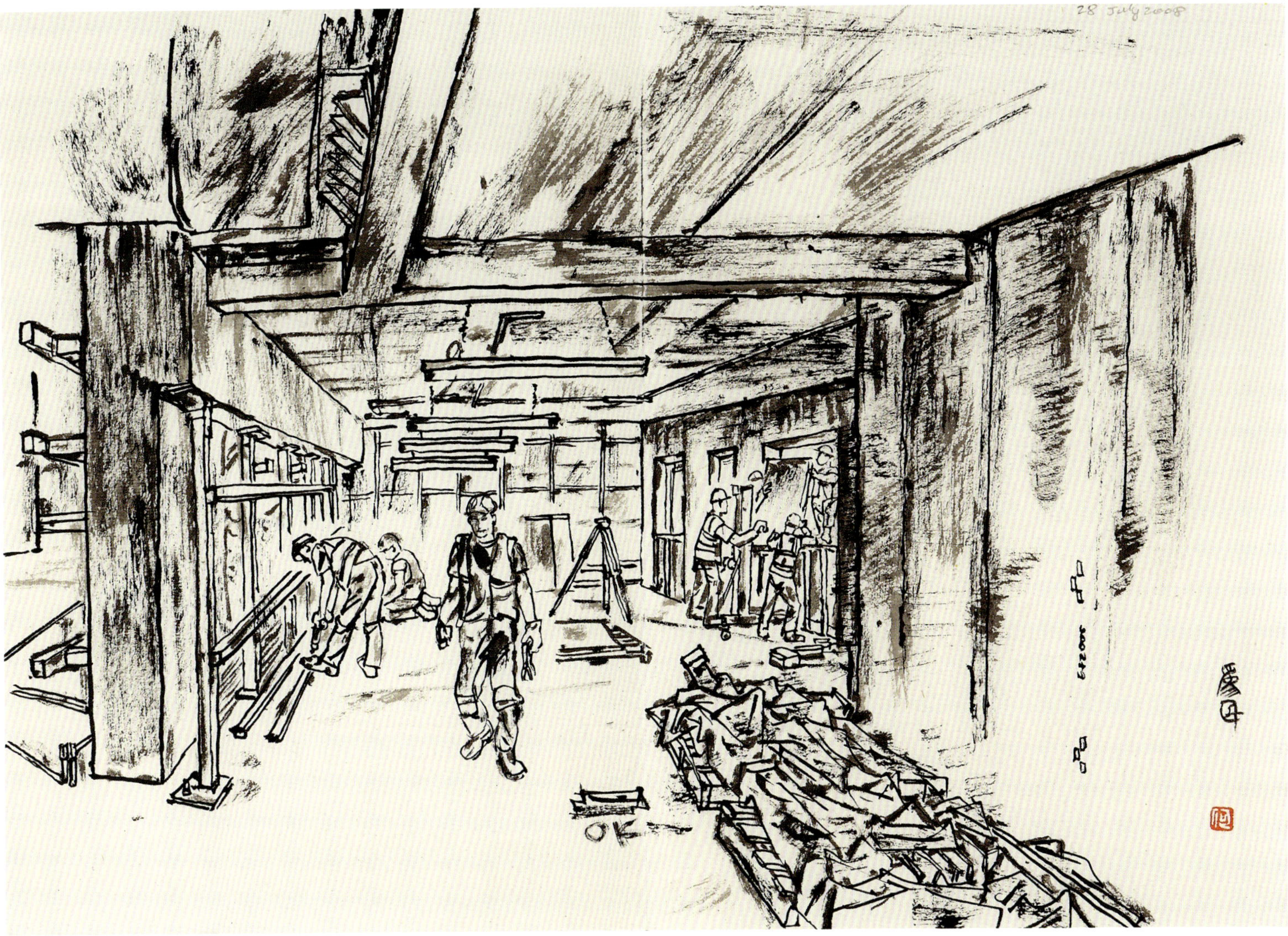

306

304 **Adjusting the stairs**
22 July 2008.
Brush and ink on album leaves.
Paper size: 27.9 × 39.8 cm

305 **Setting up scaffolding**
23 July 2008.
Brush and ink on album leaves.
Paper size: 27.9 × 39.8 cm

306 **The new seminar room**
28 July 2008.
Brush and ink on album leaves.
Paper size: 27.9 × 39.8 cm

307 **Gemma in front of the Early Italy Gallery**
July 2008.
Brush and ink on album leaves.
Paper size: 27.9 × 39.8 cm

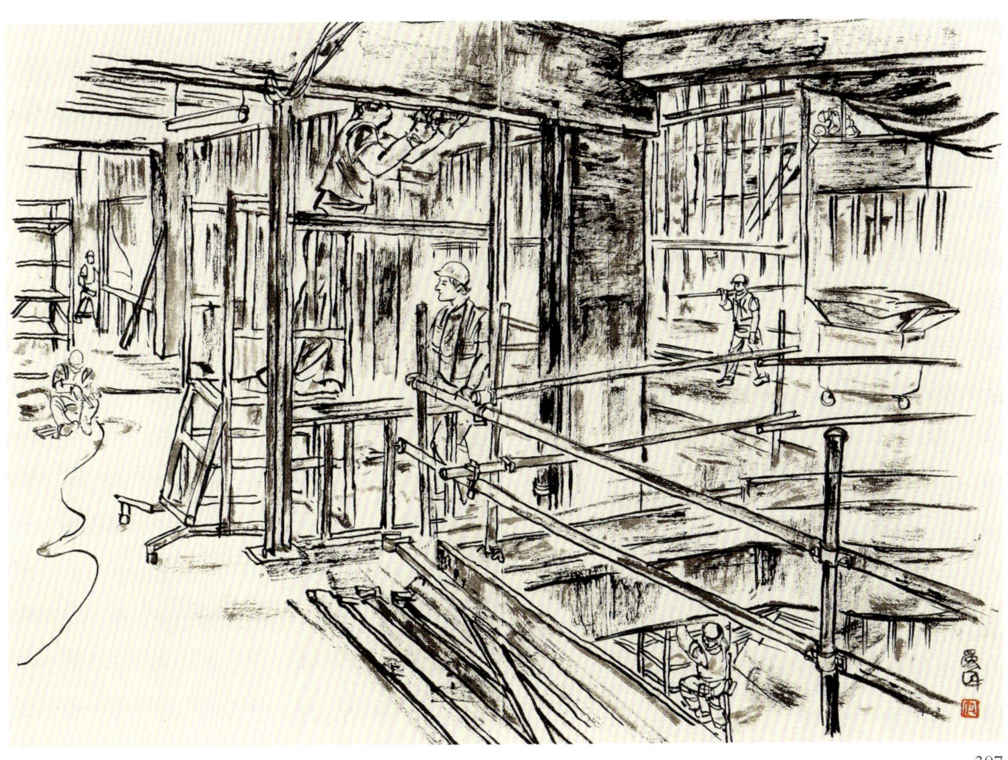

307

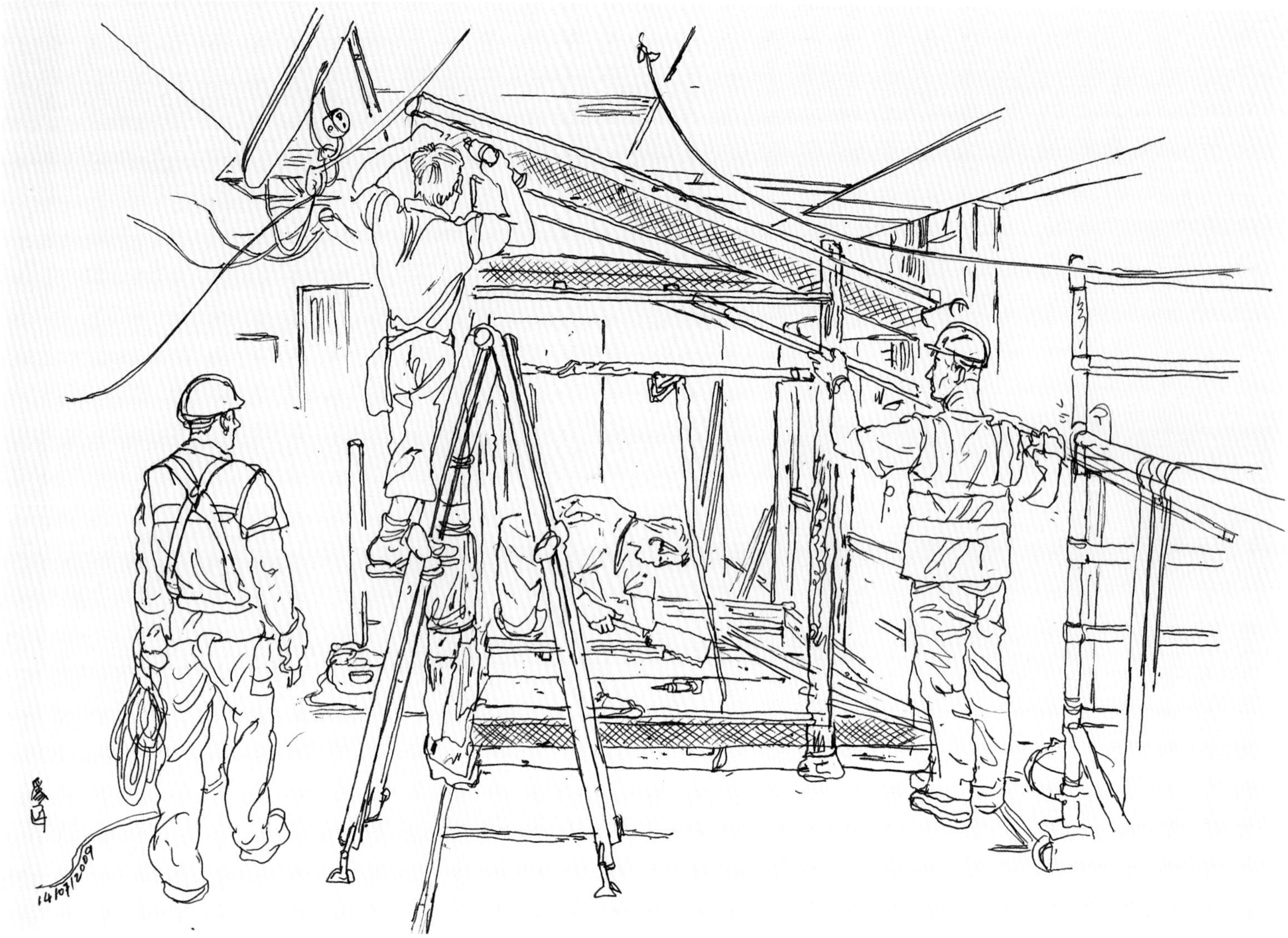

308

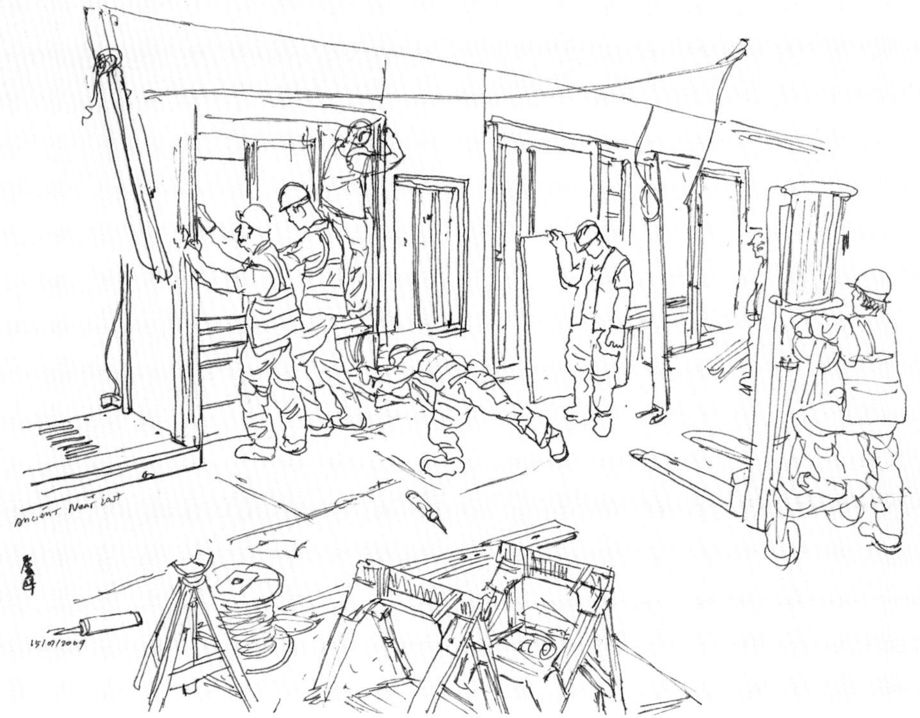

309

308 Building the Japanese tea house
14 July 2009. Pen on paper.
Paper size: 29.7 × 42 cm

309 Installing cases in the Ancient Near East Gallery
15 July 2009. Pen on paper.
Paper size: 29.7 × 42 cm

310 Installing cases in the China Gallery
15 July 2009. Pen on paper.
Paper size: 29.7 × 42 cm

311 Three Bulgarian plasterers working in the India Gallery
15 July 2009. Pen on paper.
Paper size: 29.7 × 42 cm

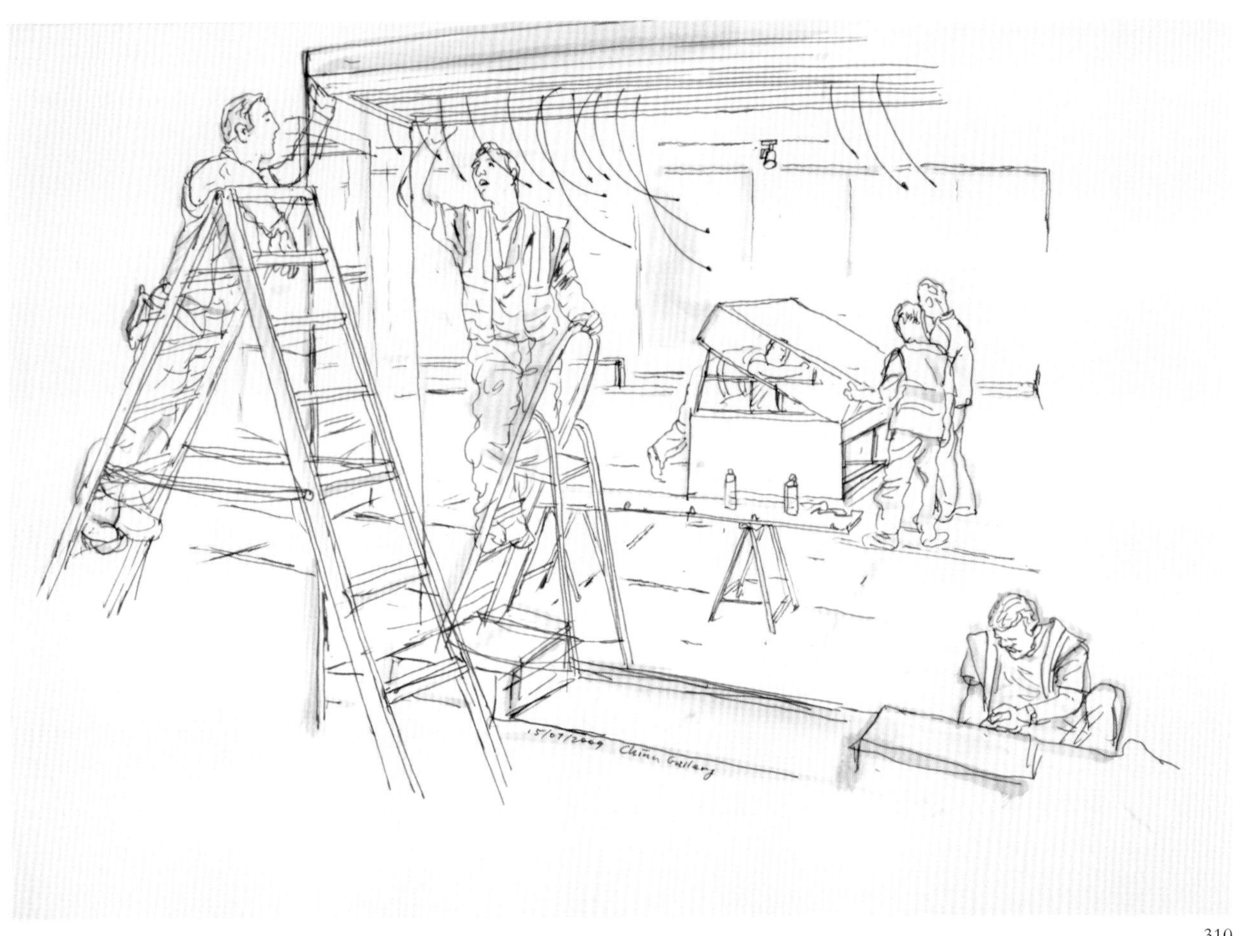

15/07/2009 China Gallery

ANYEL ILIEV
NIKOLAY MULAROV
15/07/2009
IVELIN IVANOV
Indian Gallery

310

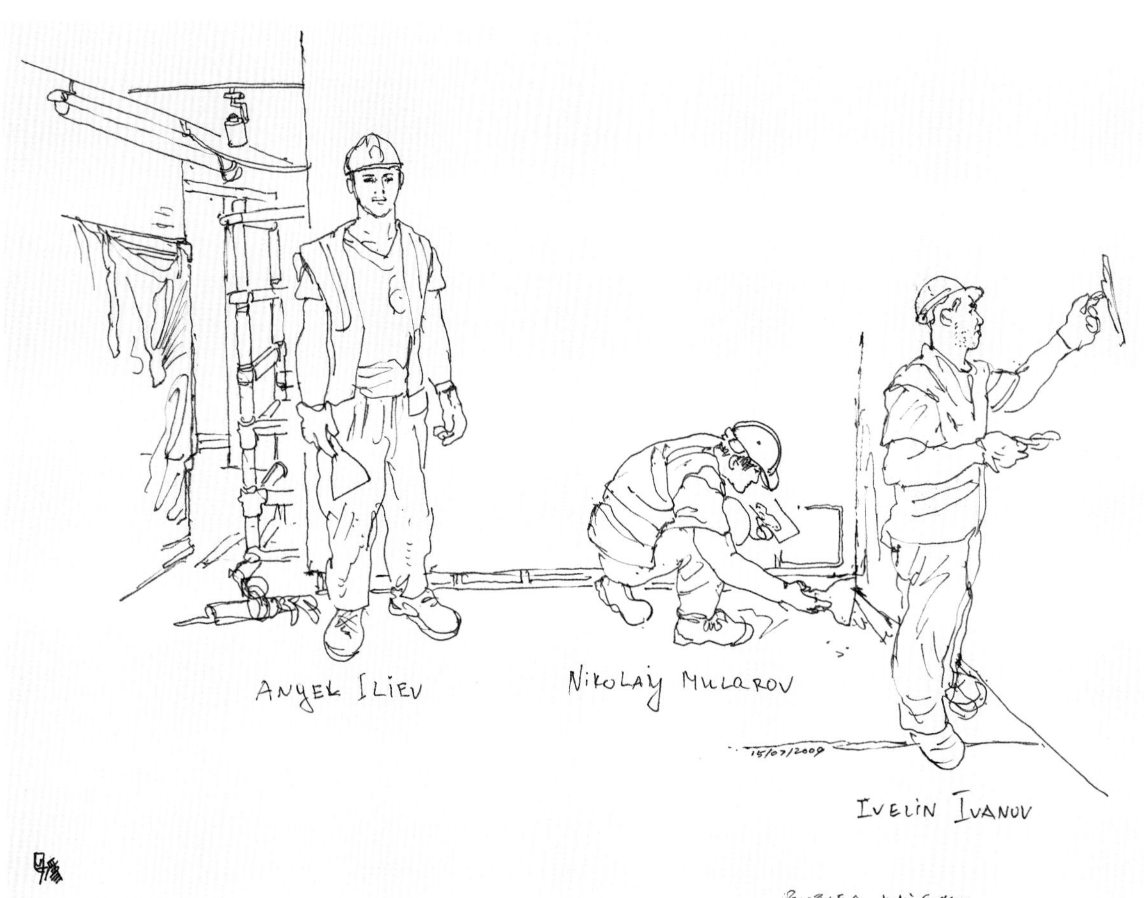

311

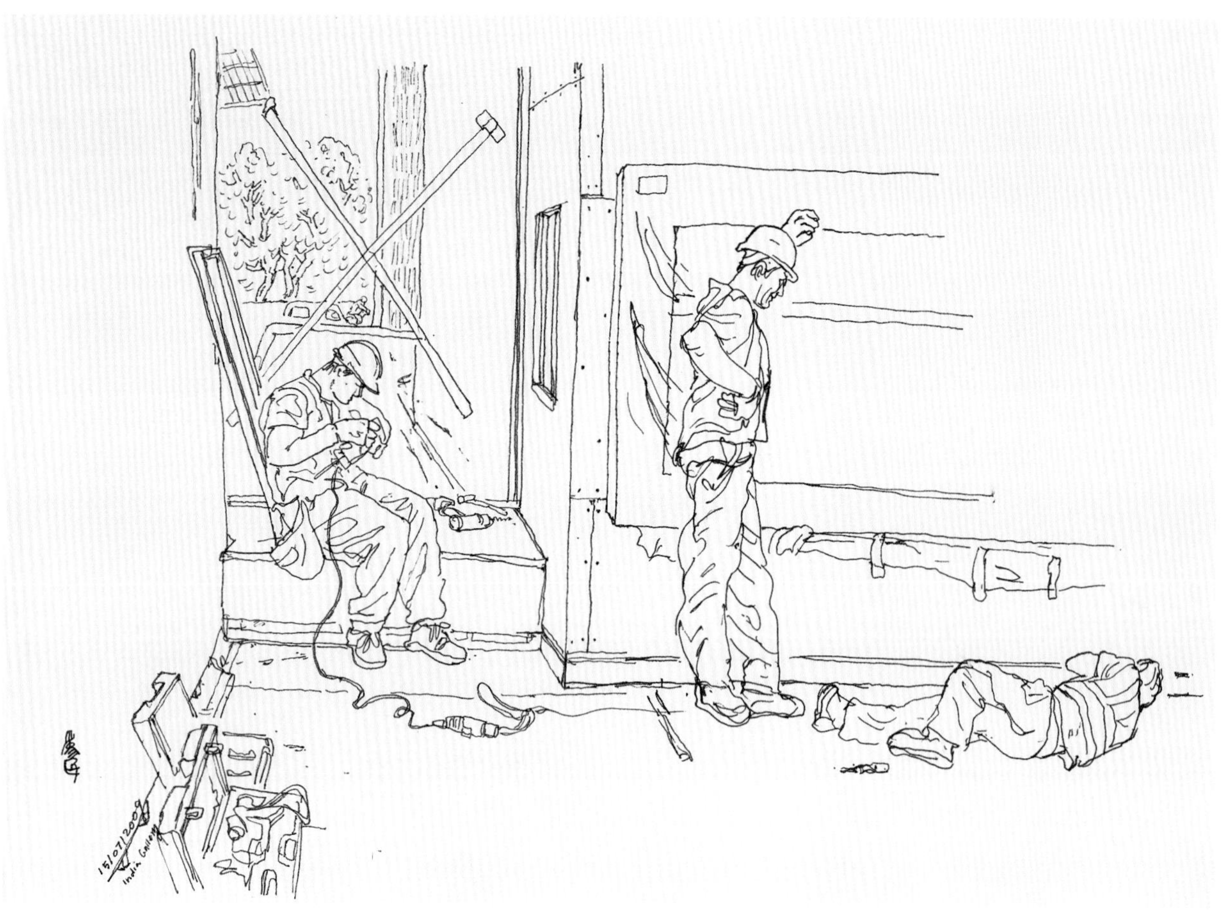

312

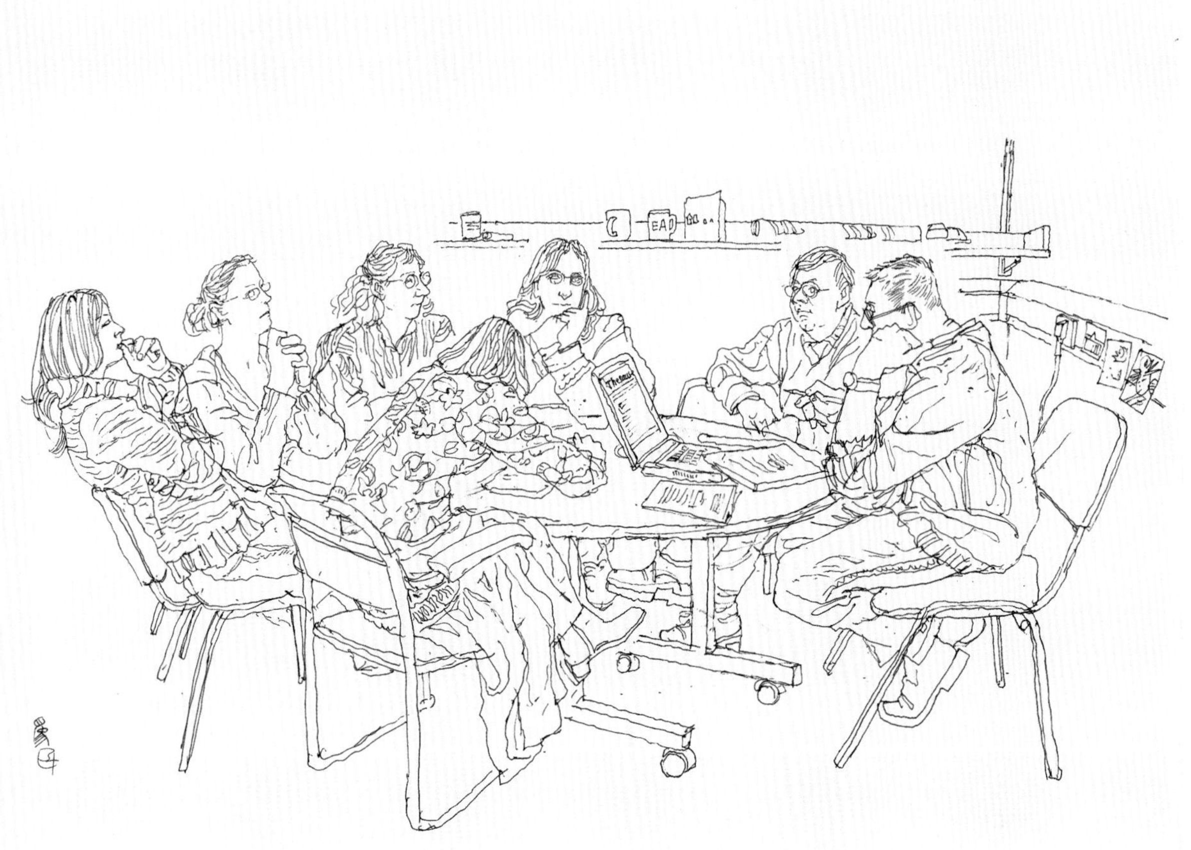

313

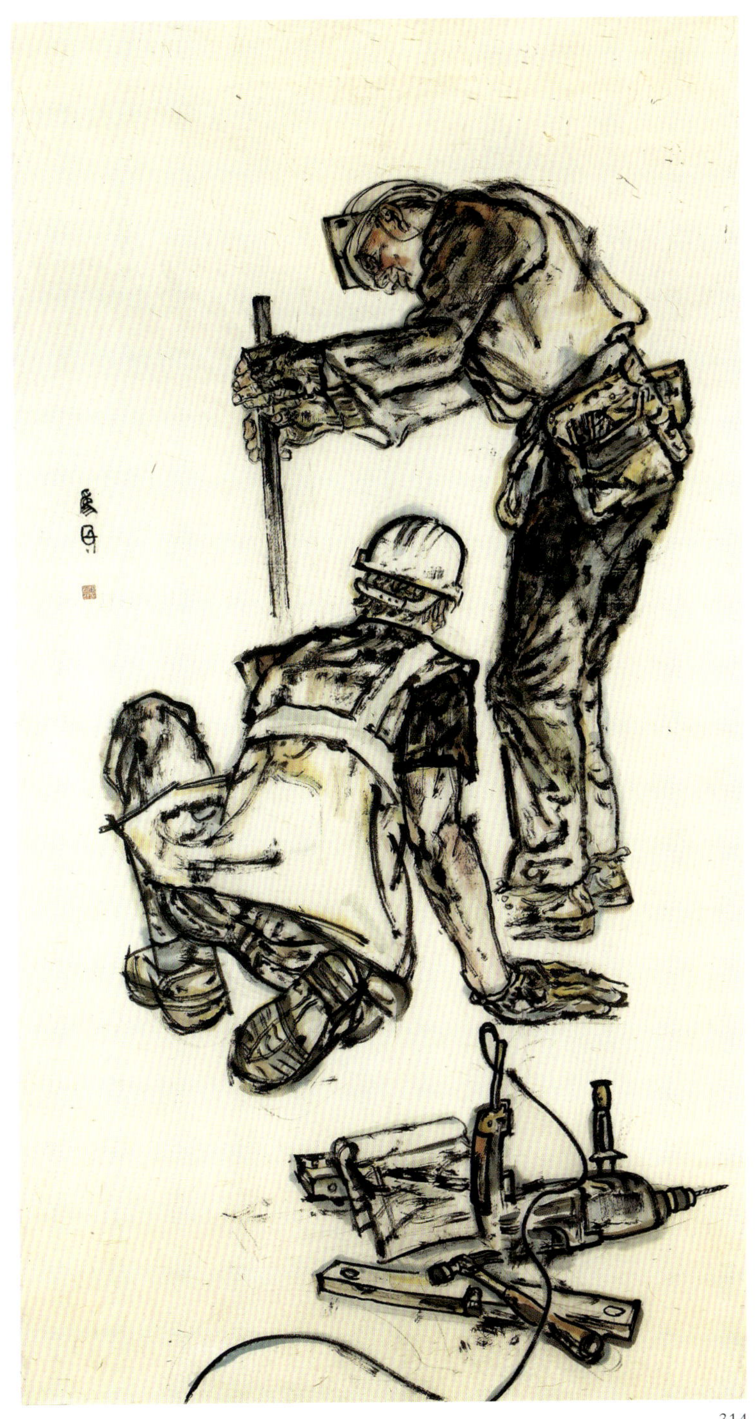

314

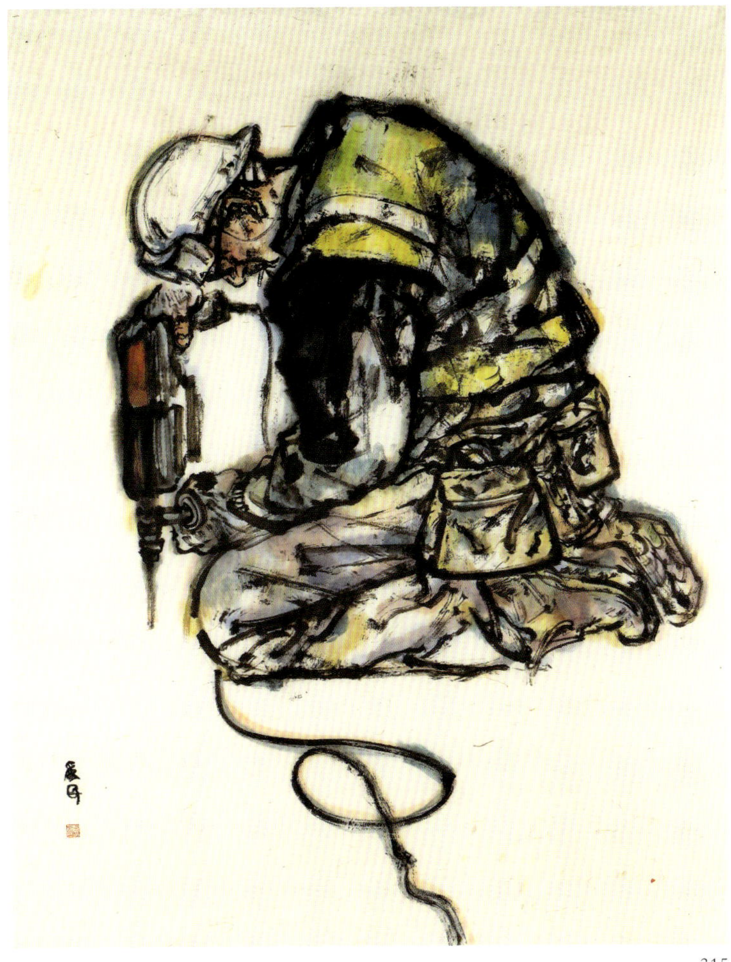

315

312 The India Gallery
15 July 2009. Pen on paper. Paper size: 29.7 × 42 cm

313 Eastern Art Department meeting
14 January 2009. Pen on paper. Paper size: 29.7 × 42 cm

314 Electricians
July 2008. Brush and ink on *xuan* paper. Paper size: 178.8 × 96 cm

315 Drilling
12 July 2008. Brush and ink on *xuan* paper. Paper size: 121.4 × 96 cm

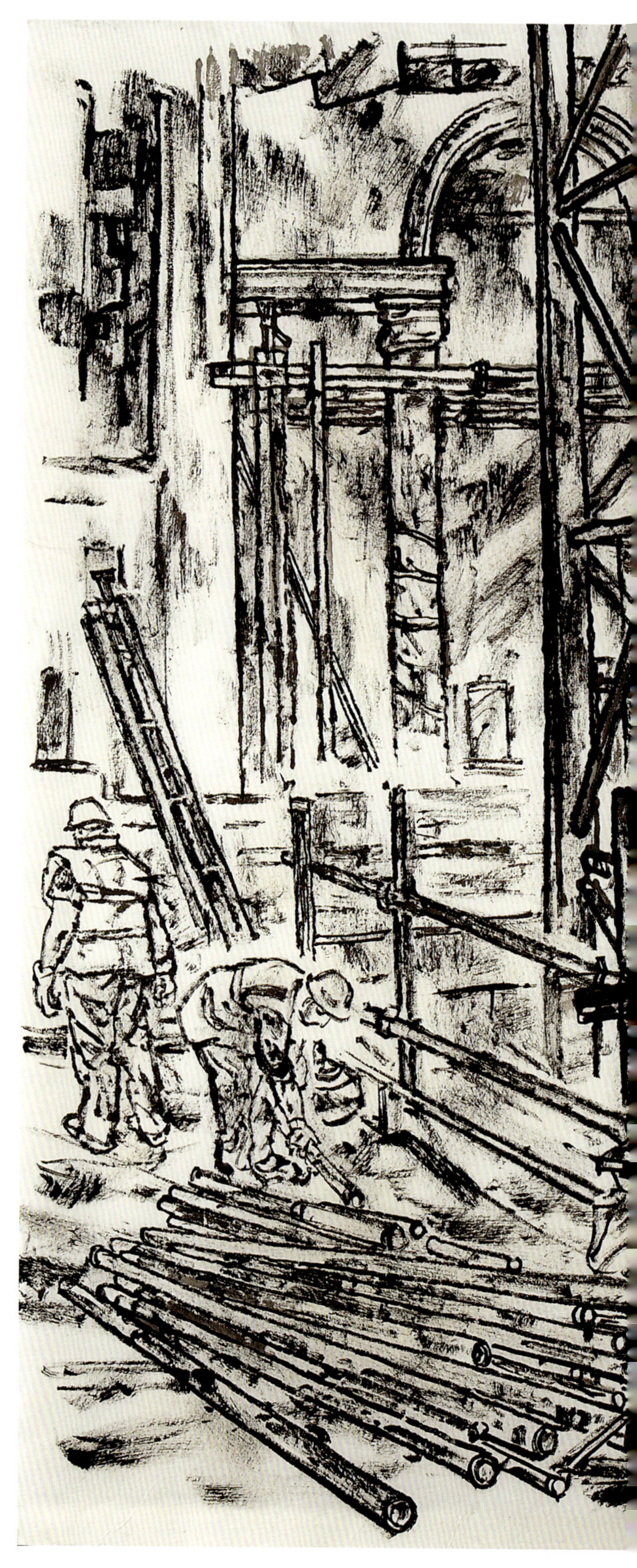

316 Under the crane
August 2008. Brush and ink on album leaves.
Paper size: 68.3x 92 cm

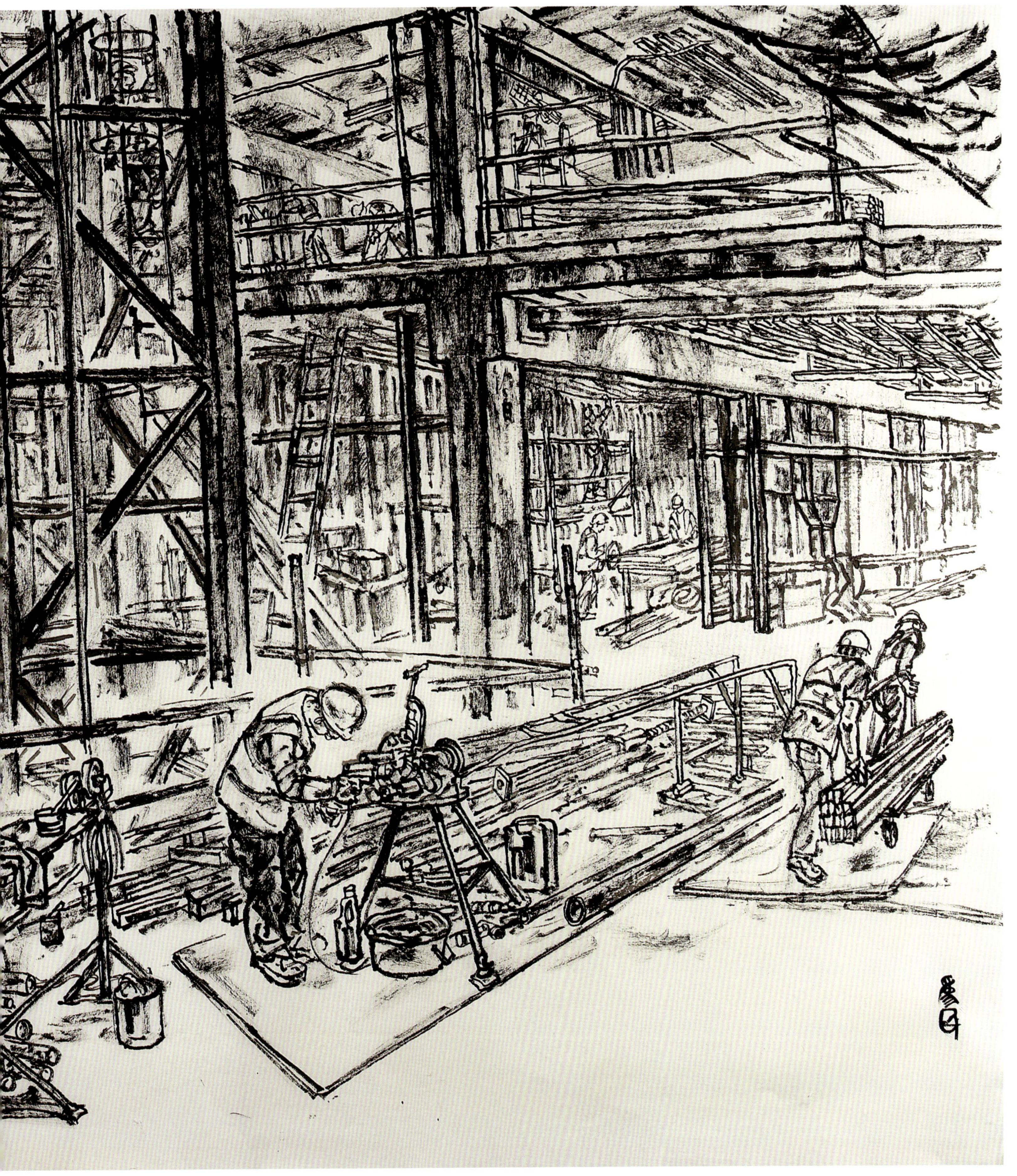

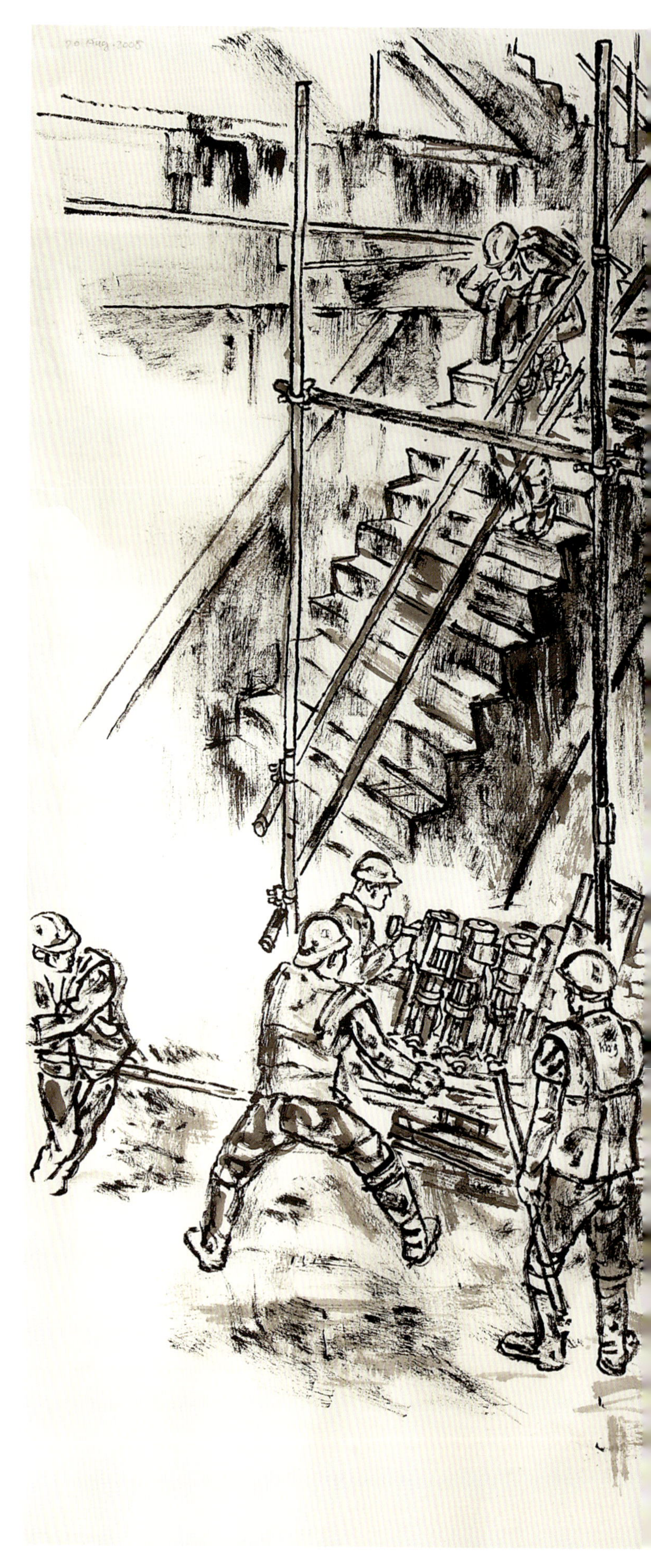

317 **The noise of construction**
August 2008. Brush and ink on album leaves.
Paper size: 69.5 × 93 cm

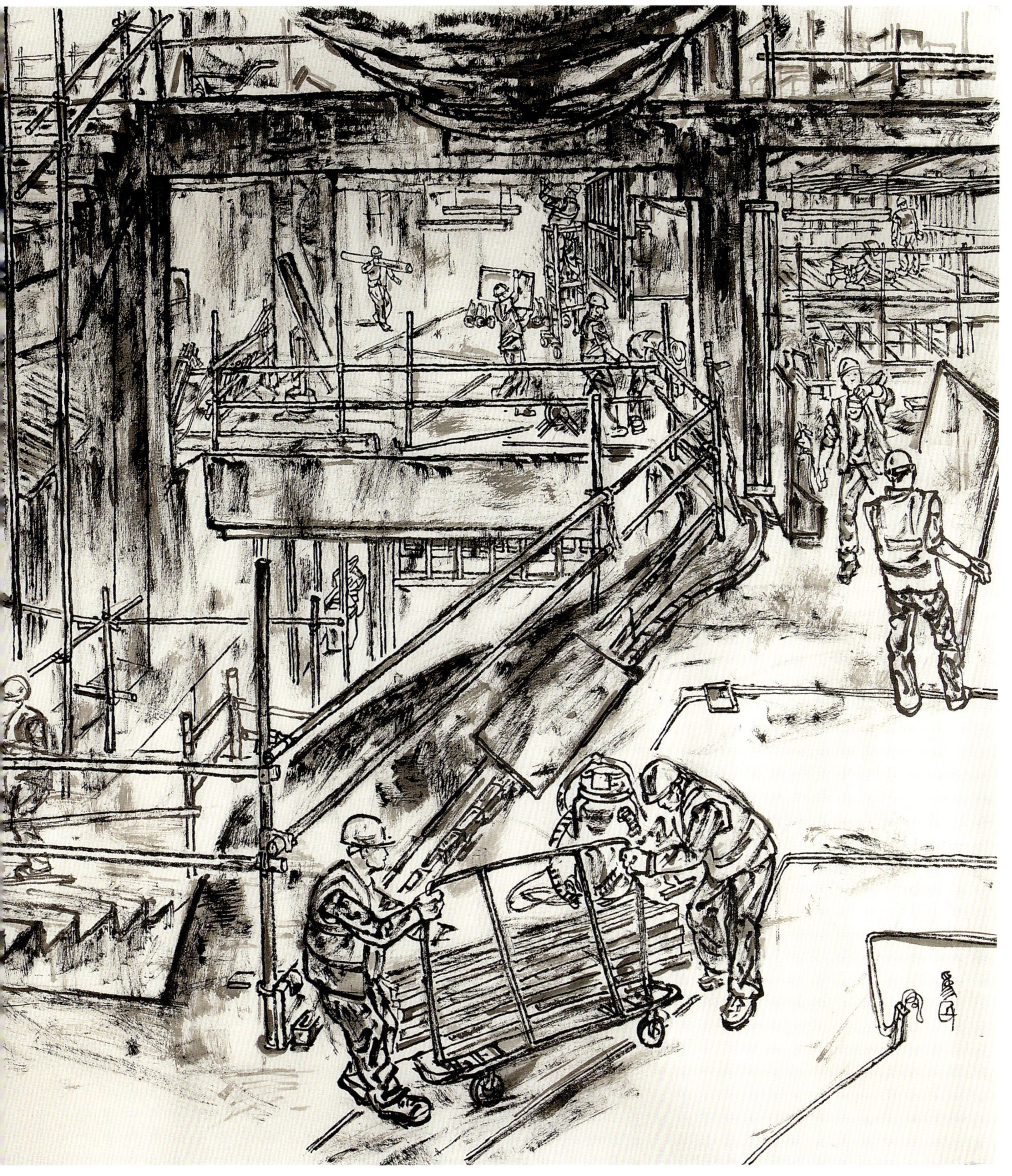

Woodblock Prints

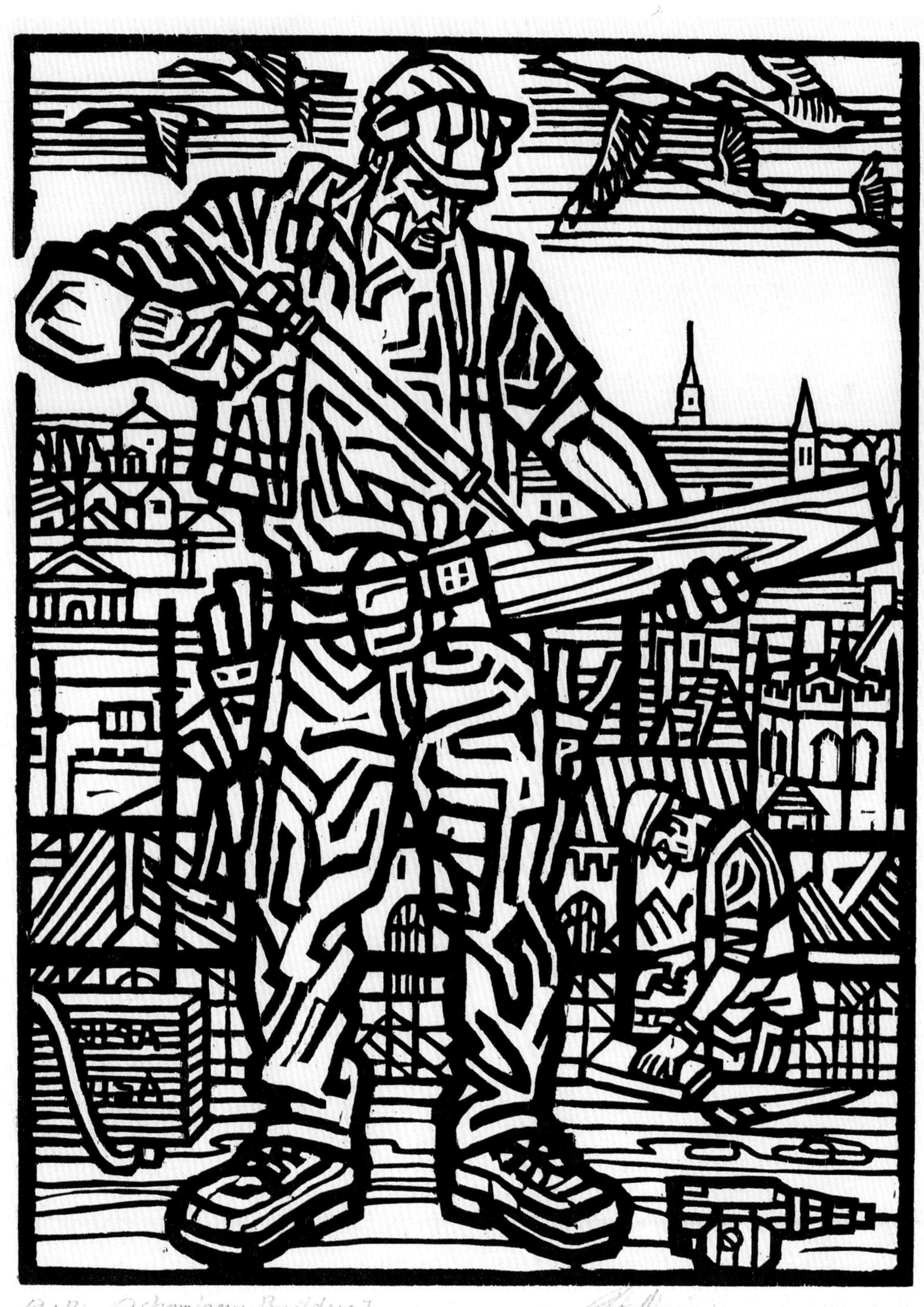

318 Ashmolean builders I
2008. Woodcut printed with oil-based ink. Image size 30.1 × 22.6 cm. Paper size: 46 × 34 cm. Edition: 60

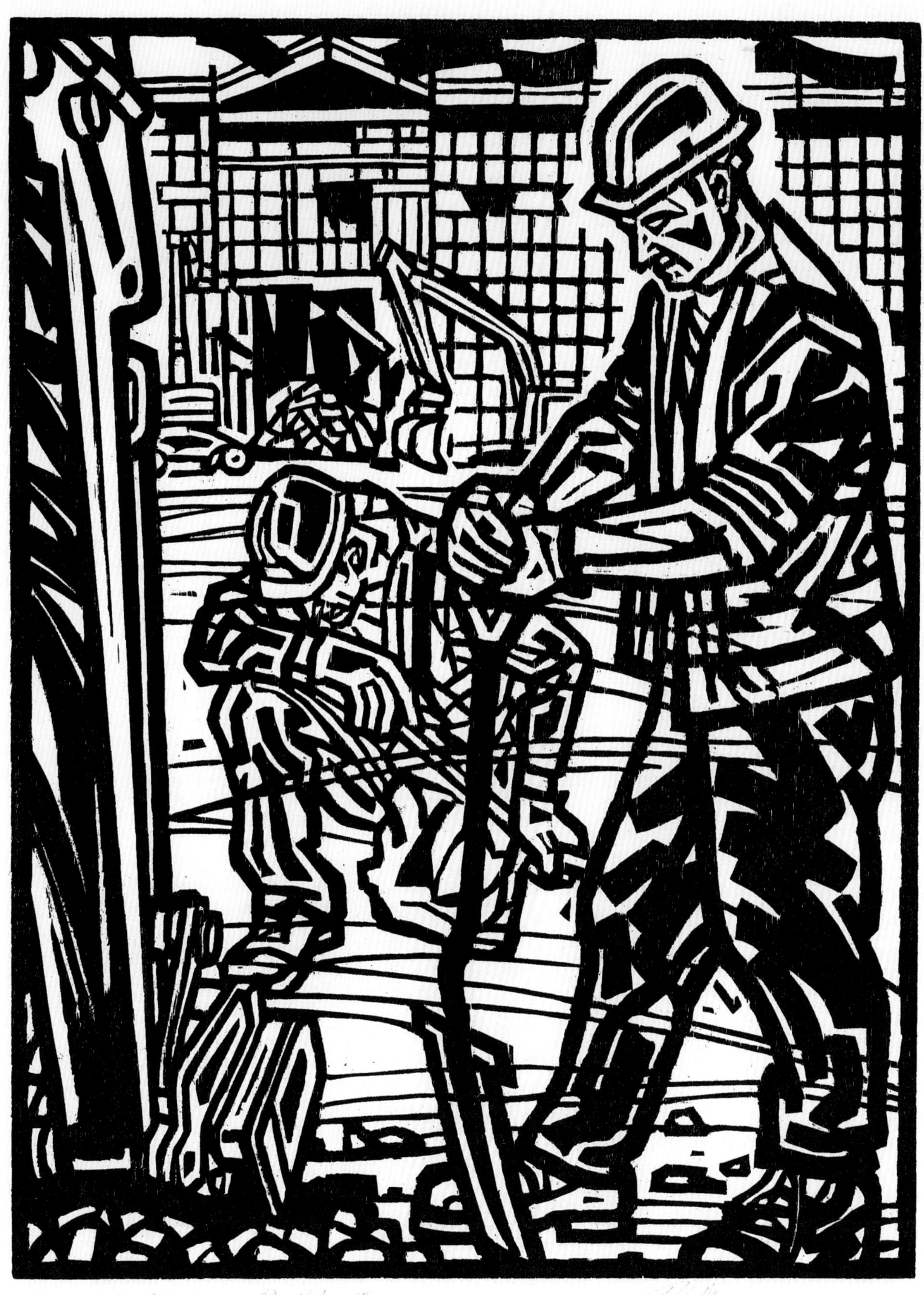

319 **Ashmolean builders II**
2008. Woodcut printed with oil-based ink. Image size 30.1 × 22.6 cm. Paper size: 46 × 34 cm. Edition: 60

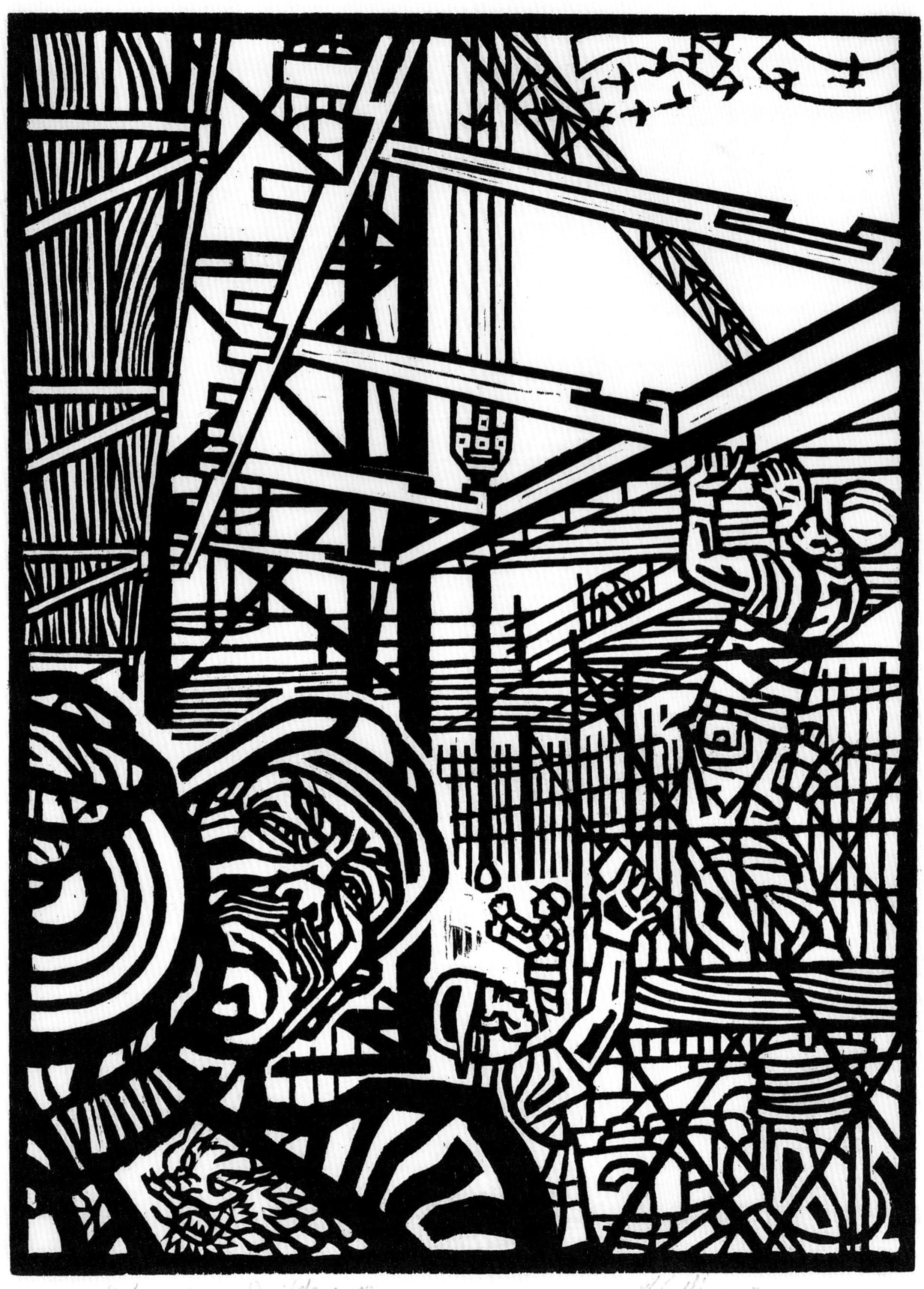

320 Ashmolean builders III

2008. Woodcut printed with oil-based ink. Image size 30.1 × 22.6 cm. Paper size: 46 × 34 cm. Edition: 60

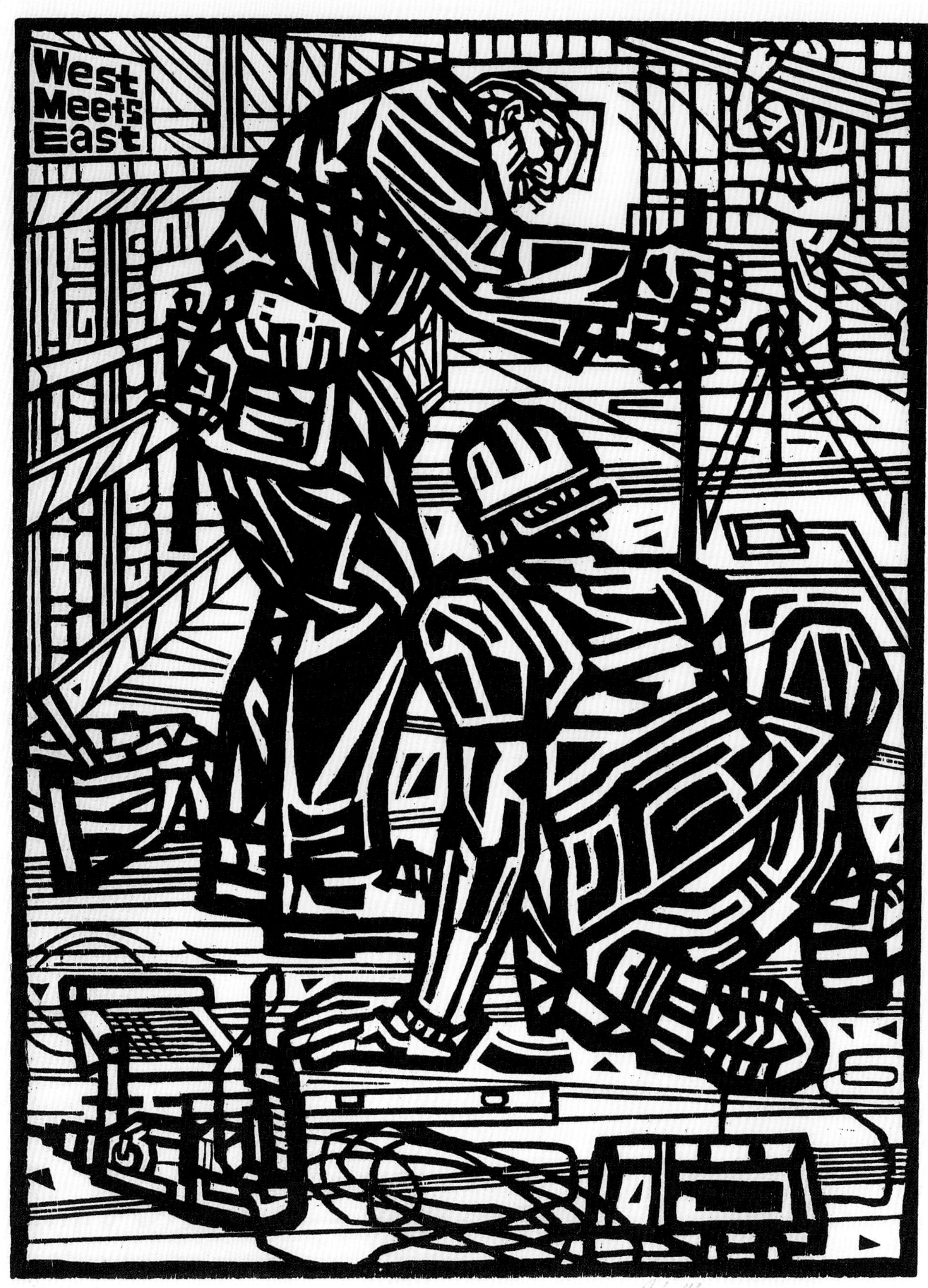

321 Ashmolean builders IV

2009. Woodcut printed with oil-based ink. Image size 30.1 × 22.6 cm. Paper size: 46 × 34 cm. Edition: 60

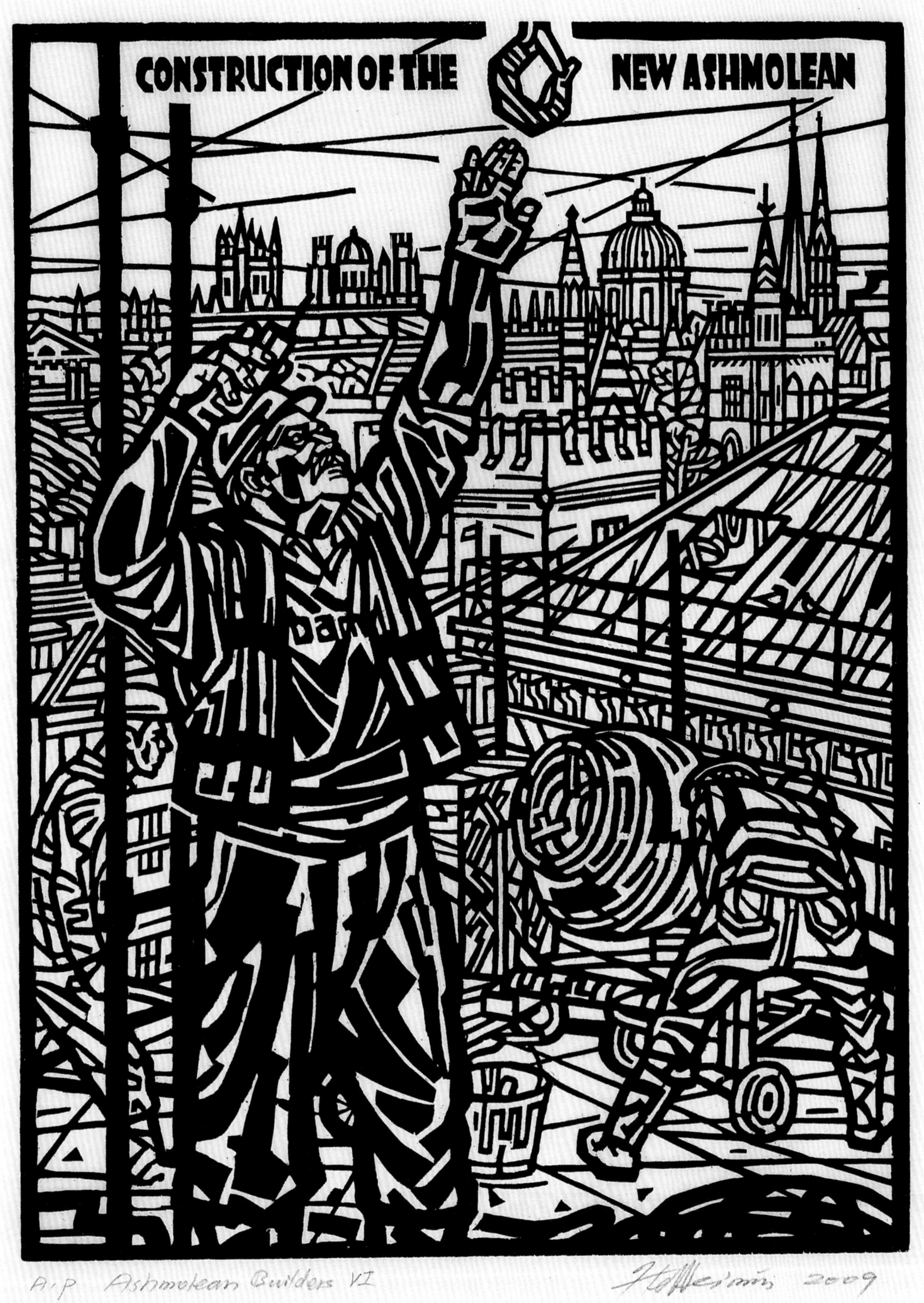

322 Ashmolean builders V
2009. Woodcut printed with oil-based ink. Image size 30.1 × 22.6 cm. Paper size: 46 × 34 cm. Edition: 60

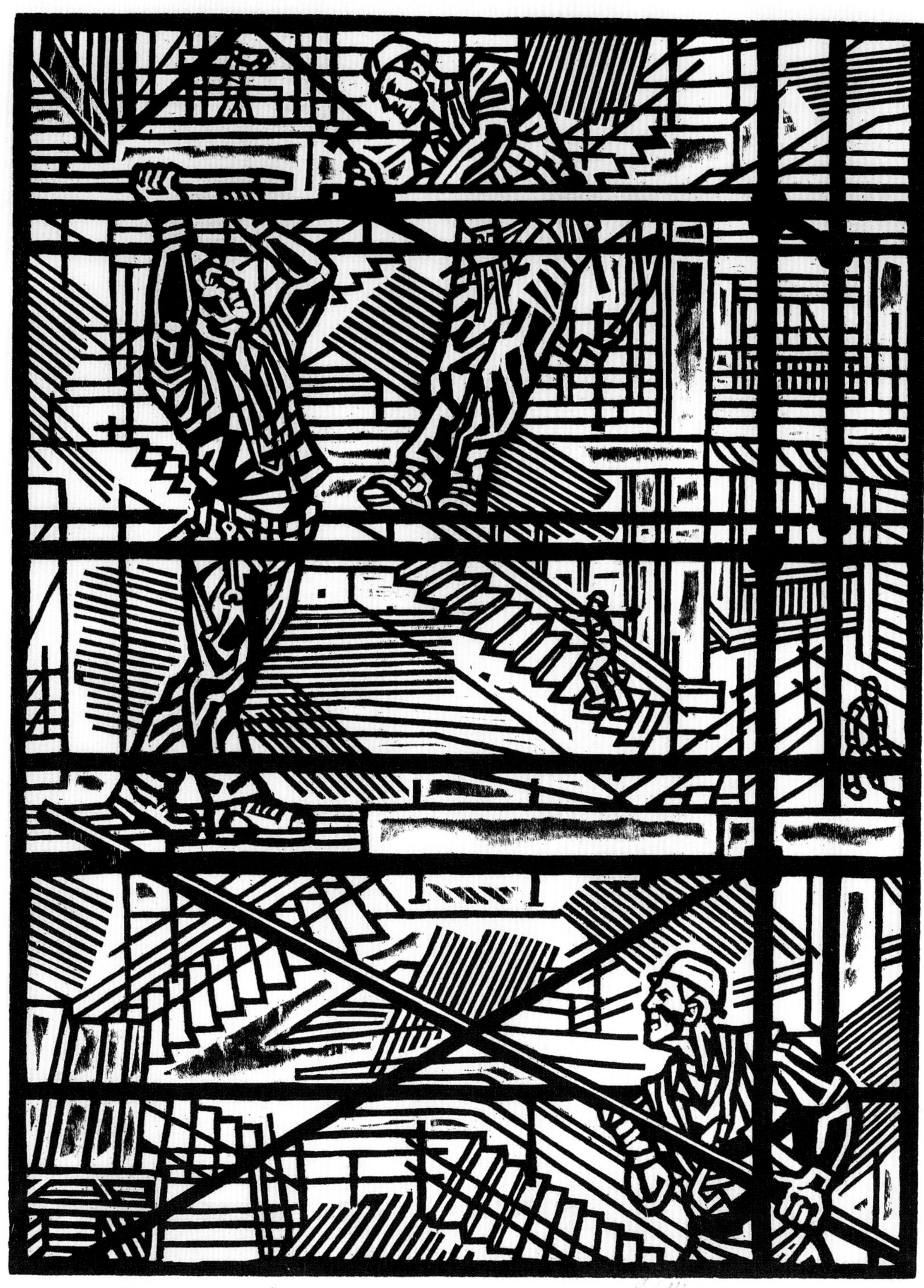

323 Ashmolean builders VI
2009. Woodcut printed with oil-based ink. Image size 30.1 × 22.6 cm. Paper size: 46 × 34 cm. Edition: 60

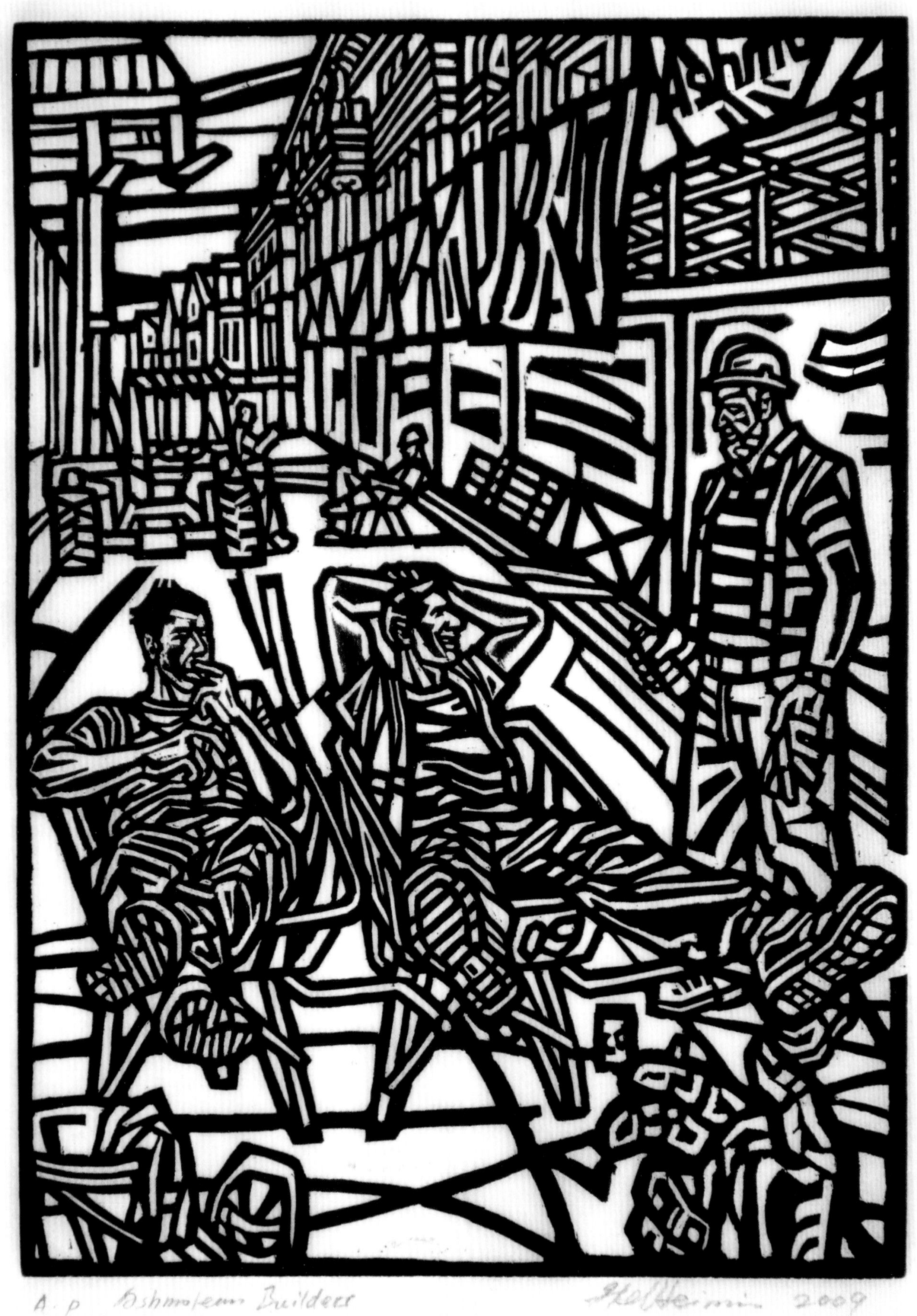

324 Ashmolean builders VII
2009. Woodcut printed with oil-based ink. Image size 30.1 × 22.6 cm. Paper size: 46 × 34 cm. Edition: 60